Thornhill Farm, Fairford, Gloucestershire

An Iron Age and Roman pastoral site in the Upper Thames Valley

by David Jennings, Jeff Muir, Simon Palmer and Alex Smith

with contributions by
Alistair Barclay, Angela Boyle, Greg Campbell, Bethan Charles, L B Jeffcott, Philip de Jersey, Hugo Lamdin-Whymark, Marsha Levine, Donald Mackreth, Mark Robinson, Fiona Roe, Ruth Shaffrey, Jane Timby and K E Whitwell

Illustrations by
Rob Read and Ros Smith

Oxford Archaeology
Thames Valley Landscapes Monograph No 23
2004

The publication of this volume has been generously funded by English Heritage

Published for Oxford Archaeology by Oxford University School of Archaeology
as part of the Thames Valley Landscapes Monograph series

Edited by Chris Hayden

This book is part of a series of monographs about the Thames Valley Landscapes –
which can be bought from all good bookshops and Internet bookshops.
For more information visit www.oxfordarch.co.uk

ISBN 0-947816-72-0

Design by Production Line, Oxford
Printed in Great Britain by Biddles Ltd, Kings Lynn, Norfolk

Contents

Contents

Contents

List of Figures

List of Plates

List of Tables

Summary

Between 1979 and 1989 the Oxford Archaeological Unit (now Oxford Archaeology) undertook extensive excavations of a late prehistoric and Roman cropmark complex at Claydon Pike and Thornhill Farm, Fairford, Gloucestershire. The excavation of the western element of the complex, Thornhill Farm, forms the subject of this report. The excavations were implemented with the co-operation of the Amey Roadstone Corporation (ARC) and formed part of a co-ordinated archaeological response to the threat posed by gravel extraction during the creation of the Cotswold Water Park. The work at Thornhill Farm involved the excavation of numerous evaluation trenches, four open area excavations and extensive salvage operations over a total area of approximately 40.5 ha.

The excavations recovered an unusually complete plan of a highly specialised agricultural unit consisting of a dense palimpsest of paddocks and larger enclosures, which appear to have been designed for the effective control and management of livestock. Environmental evidence confirmed that the immediate landscape was characterised by rough pasture which was grazed by large herbivores including horses and cattle. Ceramic evidence suggests that the earliest enclosures were dug during the middle Iron Age, and that the site continued to develop and be remodelled along similar lines through to the early Roman period.

Evidence for human occupation was recovered in the form of relatively large amounts of domestic waste consisting mainly of pottery, burnt limestone and animal bone. Although a number of roundhouses were revealed, the precise spatial organisation of the settlement proved difficult to discern, largely because of the relatively high degree of truncation and the ephemeral nature of the structural remains.

The site was radically reorganised during the early 2nd century AD when the tightly knit group of paddocks and enclosures which had characterised earlier periods was replaced by a series of newly constructed trackways.

Zusammenfassung

Zwischen 1979 und 1989 unternahm die Oxford Archaeological Unit (nun Oxford Archaeology) ausgedehnte Grabungen eines durch Bewuchsmerkmale gekennzeichneten spätvorgeschichtlichen und römerzeitlichen Komplexes bei Claydon Pike und Thornhill Farm, Fairford, Gloucestershire. Der vorliegende Bericht befasst sich mit der Ausgrabung an der Thornhill Farm, dem westlichen Teil des Gesamtkomplexes. Die in Zusammenarbeit mit der Amey Roadstone Corporation (ARC) durchgeführten Grabungen waren Teil einer koordinierten archäologischen Reaktion auf die Bedrohung der Bodendenkmäler durch die Kiesgewinnung im Rahmen des Aufbaus des Cotswold Water Park. Bei der Thornhill Farm wurden zahlreiche Suchschnitte angelegt und vier Flächengrabungen sowie umfangreiche Rettungsgrabungen in einem Gesamtgebiet von rund 40,5 ha durchgeführt.

Die Grabungen förderten einen ungewöhnlich vollständigen Grundriss einer hochspezialisierten landwirtschaftlichen Anlage zutage, die aus einem dichten Palimpsest aus Koppeln und größeren Einhegungen bestand, die offenbar der effektiven Kontrolle und Verwaltung des Viehbestandes dienten. Umweltfunde bestätigten, dass die unmittelbar angrenzende Landschaft durch Rauweiden gekennzeichnet war, auf denen große Pflanzenfresser grasten, darunter Pferde und Rinder. Aus den Keramikfunden lässt sich schließen, dass die frühesten Einhegungen aus der mittleren Eisenzeit stammen und dass die Stätte bis in die frührömische Zeit hinein am Vorhandenen orientiert weiterentwickelt und umgestaltet wurde.

Die menschliche Besiedlung wurde durch relativ umfangreiche Hausabfälle belegt, die hauptsächlich aus Töpferware, gebranntem Kalk und Tierknochen bestanden. Obwohl etliche Rundhäuser gefunden wurden, war es schwierig, die genaue räumliche Anordnung der Siedlung zu bestimmen, und zwar hauptsächlich wegen des relativ hohen Zerstörungsgrads und der kurzlebigen Natur der baulichen Überreste.

Die Anlage wurde im frühen 2. Jh. n. Chr. radikal umstrukturiert, als die engmaschige Gruppe von Koppeln und Einhegungen aus den davor liegenden Perioden durch eine Reihe neu angelegter Wege ersetzt wurde.

Résumé

Entre 1979 et 1989, l'Oxford Archaeological Unit (maintenant Oxford Archaeology) entrepris les vastes fouilles d'un complexe de traces fossiles d'époque préhistorique tardive et romaine, à Claydon Pike et Thornill Farm, Fairford, Gloucestershire. La fouille de la partie ouest de cet ensemble, Thornhill Farm, fait l'objet de ce rapport. Les fouilles furent réalisées avec la coopération de l'Amey Roadstone Corporation (ARC) et font parties d'une opération archéologique organisée en réponse à la menace posée par l'extraction de graviers durant la création du Cotswold Water Park. Les travaux à Thornhill incluent les fouilles de nombreuses tranchées d'évaluation, quatre aires de fouilles dégagées et des opérations de sauvetage à grande échelle couvrant une superficie totale de 40.5 ha.

Les fouilles mirent au jour le plan, exceptionnellement complet, d'une unité agraire hautement spécialisée, qui se composait d'un palimpseste dense d'enclos et de plus larges enceintes, lesquelles semblent avoir été conçues pour le contrôle et l'exploitation efficace du bétail. Les données environnementales confirmèrent que le paysage environnant se caractérisait par des pâtures où paissaient de larges herbivores y compris chevaux et bovins. Les indices fournis par l'étude céramique suggèrent que les enceintes les plus anciennes furent établies vers le milieu de l'âge du fer et que le site continua de se développer et d'être réorganisé sur un alignement similaire jusqu'au début de l'époque romaine.

Des preuves d'occupation humaine furent découvertes sous la forme de quantités relativement importantes de déchets domestiques consistant essentiellement de poterie, de pierre calcaire brûlée et d'ossements animaux. Bien qu'un certain nombre de maisons circulaires furent découvertes, l'organisation dans l'espace précise du site d'habitation s'avère difficile à décerner, en grande partie parce qu'il fut ultérieurement sévèrement tronqué mais également en raison de la nature éphémère des restes structurels.

Le site fut radicalement réorganisé au cours du début du 2ème siècle après JC lorsque l'ensemble serré d'enclos et d'enceintes qui caractérisait les époques précédentes fut remplacé par une série de sentiers nouvellement construits.

Acknowledgements

The Thornhill Farm project has drawn on the involvement and support of numerous people and organisations who have made contributions large and small over many years. We particularly thank David Miles for his energy and vision in initiating the project and his continued support and encouragement throughout. We are very grateful to the Amey Roadstone Corporation (ARC), now a part of the Hanson Group, for their support of the excavations, and in particular to Steve Cole and Brian Grovesnor for their patience and goodwill. We gratefully acknowledge English Heritage for funding the excavations, post-excavation assessment, analysis and publication, and the support and encouragement of Tony Fleming, Andrew Davison, Helen Keeley and Robert Iles has been particularly appreciated.

Thanks are due to the numerous staff of Oxford Archaeology (OA) and to all others that have worked on the project, both in the excavation and post-excavation stages. Simon Palmer directed the excavations and Alistair Marshall undertook the initial trenching of the site. Gill Hey was co-director of the project during the later seasons of excavation. Particular thanks are due to the many excavation supervisors, who made an invaluable contribution to the project, and also to the large number of excavators who worked at the site over a number of years. The post-excavation phase has taken place over many years, and has been managed by Simon Palmer, David Jennings, Jeff Muir and Alex Smith. A large number of OA staff and external specialists have been involved in the post-excavation process and we gratefully acknowledge all the painstaking work that they have put in. Much of the earlier stratigraphic analysis was undertaken by Greg Campbell, Angela Boyle and Alistair Barclay.

Marsha Levine would like to thank Paul Callow for help with SPSS, Jan Nekovar for help with cattle curves, Gwil Owen for advice about photography, Patsy Whelehan for radiography and John Grandage for help with some abnormal specimens. Also Tony Legge, Patrick Munson, Roel Lauwerier, Keith Dobney, Umberto Albarella, Jean-Hervé Yvinec and Katie Boyle for offprints, references and archaeozoological advice, and Bob Proctor, Matt Buckley, Julie Dawson, Hans Küchelmann, An Lentacker, Anton Ervynck and others for their contributions to the glue question.

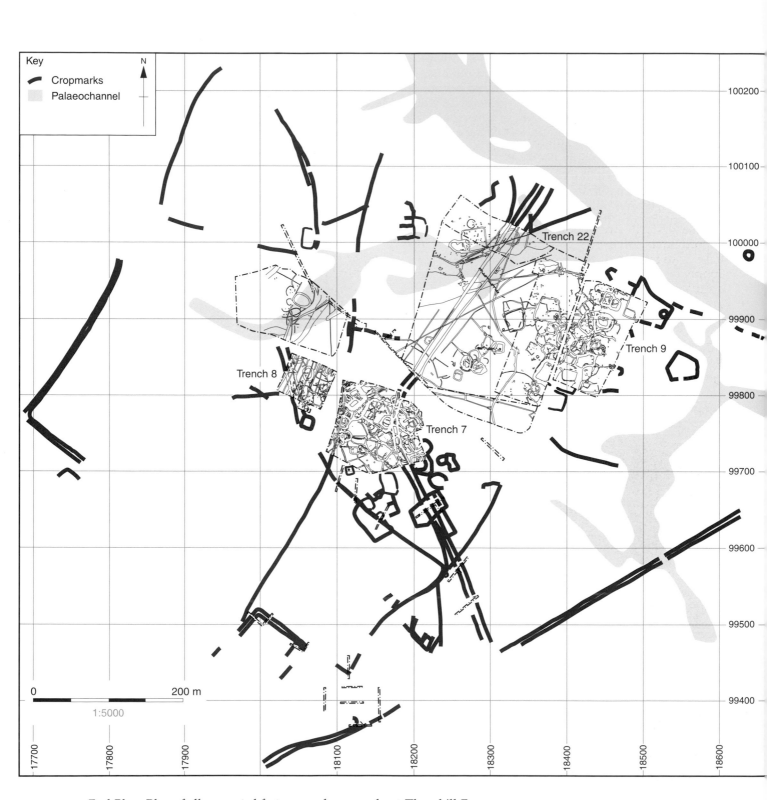

End Plan: Plan of all excavated features and cropmarks at Thornhill Farm

Chapter 1 Introduction

by David Jennings, Jeff Muir and Alex Smith

HISTORY OF ARCHAEOLOGICAL RESEARCH

The Gloucestershire Upper Thames Valley has a long history of piecemeal gravel extraction stretching back over centuries. In the last fifty years a boom in the construction industry caused demand for raw materials to rise to record levels. Increased production meant that for the first time, whole archaeological landscapes became threatened as the industry expanded to meet demand. The Claydon Pike Landscape Research Project was initiated by the Oxford Archaeological Unit (OAU, now Oxford Archaeology) as an emergency response to help mitigate that threat. The result was not simply a series of rescue excavations but a co-ordinated programme of intensive aerial photography combined with targeted evaluation, open area excavation and salvage operations. The results were combined with landscape and geophysical survey in an attempt to evaluate the impact of the Roman conquest on the native population and the developments subsequent to it.

The centrepiece of the project was the extensive excavations at Thornhill Farm and Claydon Pike, Fairford. Here, exceptionally detailed aerial photographs revealed an intensively occupied landscape rich in the remains of what was assumed to be late prehistoric and Roman archaeology (Plates 1.1 and 1.2).

The excavations at Claydon Pike revealed a complex history of occupation from the middle Iron Age through to the late and possibly sub Roman period. The earliest settlement (at Warrens Field) consisted of a series of circular houses and associated paddocks on small gravel islands separated by low-lying wet areas. By the late Iron Age the focus of settlement had shifted (to Longdoles Field) several hundred metres from the location of its middle Iron Age predecessor, demonstrating a degree of discontinuity subsequently noted elsewhere in the Upper Thames region (Lambrick 1992, 83–4).

At some point in the early 2nd century AD, Claydon Pike altered radically. Two large aisled buildings were constructed within a rectangular

Plate 1.1   Aerial photograph of Thornhill Farm Trenches 7 and 8, showing intercutting enclosures.
(© Crown copyright)

Plate 1.2   Aerial photograph showing cropmarks along the lower gravel terrace around Claydon Pike and Thornhill Farm. (Cambridge University Collections: copyright reserved)

enclosure or compound with a gated entrance. A rectangular enclosure lay adjacent on a crossroads and is interpreted as a possible religious precinct. The ceramic and small finds assemblages indicate a highly Romanised status.

The results of the Claydon Pike excavations are part of a forthcoming Oxford Archaeology publication on Iron Age and Roman settlement in the Upper Thames Valley (Miles *et al.* forthcoming). This is due for publication in 2005/6, although detailed interim stratigraphic, finds and environmental reports are currently available on the following website: http://www.oxfordarch.co.uk/cotswoldweb/index.htm.

LOCATION, TOPOGRAPHY AND GEOLOGY

The Thornhill Farm excavations (Fig. 1.1) were located close to the confluence of the rivers Thames and Coln, approximately 3.5 km to the south-east of Fairford and 3 km to the west of Lechlade, Gloucestershire (SU 183997, County Monument 459).

The site straddled the First Gravel Terrace of the Upper Thames Valley approximately 1 km to the north-east of the Coln floodplain at a height of 76 m OD (Fig. 1.2). In prehistory the terrace was dissected by relict water courses and marshy areas, but islands and tongues of gravel provided well drained sites which were dry enough for settlement. To the south of the site, inliers of Oxford Clay and river gravels give way to the alluvium of the valley floor before rising up to the sand and limestones of the Corallian ridge in the direction of Swindon. To the north, the gravel terraces rise to meet the clay and cornbrash of the Cotswold dip slope and limestone uplands.

The topographical variation from floodplain to uplands forms a landscape of considerable ecological diversity, rich in resources which would have been exploited from the time of its first settlement. Evidence for arable production on the higher gravel terraces abounds throughout the Upper Thames Valley and is well documented at later prehistoric sites such as Ashville and Gravelly Guy (Parrington 1978; Lambrick and Allen forthcoming). Evidence for the prehistoric exploitation of grassland on the First Gravel Terrace and floodplain has also become increasingly apparent in the last three decades, and has led to a complete reappraisal of the importance of so-called 'marginal' land prior to the Roman occupation (Lambrick and Robinson 1979; Lambrick 1992).

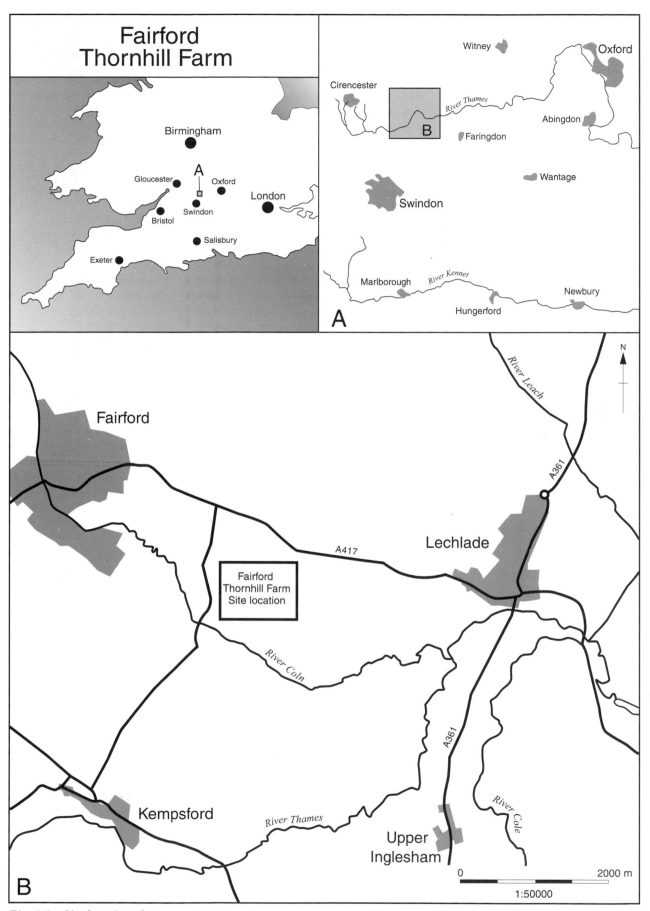

Fig. 1.1   Site location plan

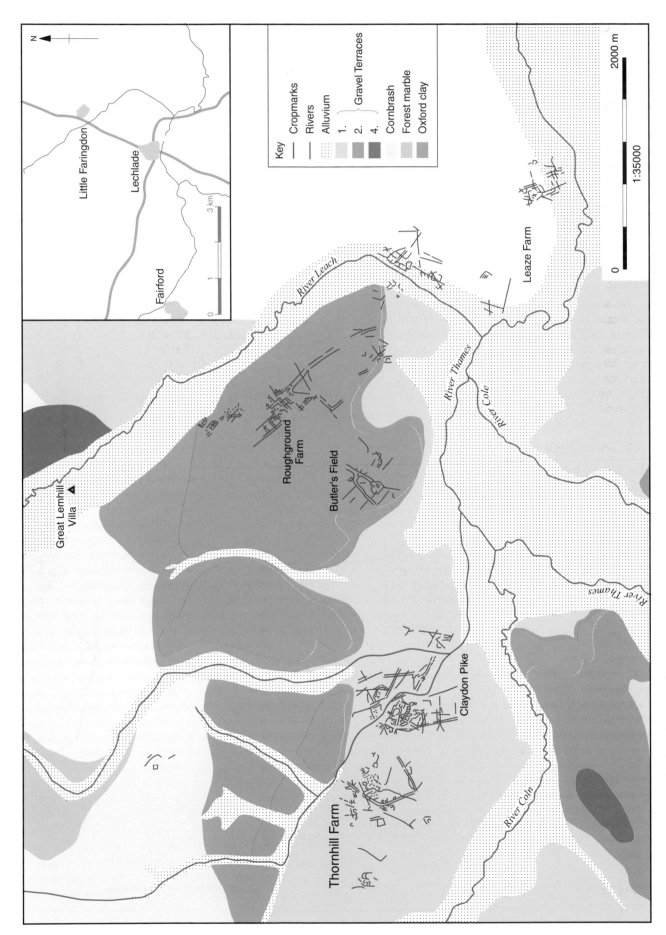

Fig. 1.2 Local geology and selected cropmarks

ARCHAEOLOGICAL BACKGROUND

The archaeological background to the region and to the study area in particular has recently been published in detail with reference to the excavations at Butler's Field, Lechlade (Boyle *et al.* 1998) and the A419/A417 Swindon to Gloucester Road Scheme (Mudd *et al.* 1999). This description draws heavily from both publications, along with the detailed archaeological surveys of the region conducted in the 1970s (RCHME 1976; Leech 1977). It will concentrate largely on the settlement evidence of later prehistory and the Romano-British period, the two periods most pertinent to the site at Thornhill Farm.

Earlier Prehistory

Mesolithic

Since the area's first settlement, the Jurassic Ridge which forms the spine of the Cotswolds has been used as a corridor for trade and communication. The earliest evidence for occupation comes in the form of Mesolithic flint scatters which are mostly concentrated on the higher ground of the limestone uplands, and are known from over 40 sites in Gloucestershire (Mudd *et al.* 1999, 6–7).

Neolithic and Bronze Age

Until fairly recently research into the Neolithic and Bronze Age occupation of the region has tended to concentrate on the monumental classes of evidence such as chambered tombs, barrows and ring ditches (Darvill 1987). Non-monumental sites and find spots are increasingly well-known, but are still relatively rare, particularly away from the limestone uplands. Where they have been located, the majority of such finds have been made by chance as part of investigations aimed at later, more visible settlements. This suggests that the dearth of early prehistoric sites may be more apparent than real. Neolithic settlement evidence in the form of pit clusters has been located at a number of sites in the Lechlade area, including the Loders (Darvill *et al.* 1986), Roughground Farm (Allen *et al.* 1993, 9–15) and Gassons Road in Lechlade itself (King 1998, 269–271).

To the south of Cirencester the remains of an extensive late Bronze Age settlement have been uncovered at Shorncote Quarry, Somerford Keynes (Hearne and Adam 1999). Although only a single settlement, the discovery may go some way to refute the suggestion that the region became more sparsely occupied at the expense of the Middle Thames during this period (Barrett and Bradley 1980).

Later Prehistory

In 1976 the RCHME survey of Iron Age and Romano-British monuments in the Cotswolds described the evidence for Iron Age occupation in the area as lying 'chiefly in earthworks'. As with earlier prehistory, the majority of interest and research has been expended on the more monumental kinds of evidence such as the hillforts. More recently, however, a growing number of excavations have extended our knowledge of Iron Age land use and settlement patterns both on the limestone uplands and on the gravels of the Upper Thames Valley.

Late Bronze Age–early Iron Age

In the immediate area of Thornhill Farm extensive excavations have been carried out on the Second Gravel Terrace close to Lechlade. Evidence of large scale land division dating to the late Bronze Age–early Iron Age has been found at Butler's Field (Boyle *et al.* 1998), Gassons Road (King 1998, 269–271) and Roughground Farm (Allen *et al.* 1993). Despite the relatively large scale of the excavations, evidence for domestic dwellings is sparse with single roundhouses being located at both Butler's Field and Roughground Farm. At Gassons Road a subrectangular posthole arrangement was found but has been interpreted as a fenceline or possible stock enclosure rather than as a house. The apparent scarcity of domestic dwellings does not, however, mean that the surrounding land was not being fully utilised. As Jennings points out 'models of early Bronze Age society in this region envisage an economic system based on pastoralism, and there is little to suggest that a similar regime was not still predominant in the late Bronze Age/early Iron Age' (Jennings in Boyle *et al.* 1998, 34).

Evidence for early Iron Age settlement on the Cotswold uplands remains relatively rare apart from the hillforts, and is mostly known from stray finds (Darvill 1987, 132–133). The apparent scarcity of early settlement has been underlined by the recent excavations along the A417–A419 road scheme which revealed important middle and late Iron Age remains but no settlement dating to the early Iron Age (Mudd *et al.* 1999).

Middle Iron Age

The Upper Thames Valley in east Gloucestershire and west Oxfordshire was densely occupied during the middle Iron Age, a period characterised by increased diversification in settlement type. Excavations at Claydon Pike, Fairford and Shorncote Quarry, Somerford Keynes (Hearne and Adam 1999) have confirmed that many of the cropmarks discovered during the intensive aerial surveys of the 1970s belong to this period, indicating a pattern of dispersed settlement along the gravel terraces. Another rural settlement of this period in the region was excavated prior to gravel extraction between 1984 and 1990 at Cleveland Farm near Ashton Keynes (Coe *et al.* 1991). Further down the Thames Valley in Oxfordshire increasing numbers of middle Iron Age settlements have been discovered, including the temporary encampment of transhumant pastoralists at Farmoor (Lambrick and Robinson 1979), a number of nucleated mixed farming settlements at Abingdon (Allen 1991, 1997) and the enclosed specialist pastoral settlement at Watkins Farm (Allen 1990).

Later Iron Age

Although most excavated middle Iron Age sites in the Upper Thames Valley showed some kind of continuity into the late Iron Age and early Roman period, in many instances the nature and form of occupation altered. At Claydon Pike, the mid to late Iron Age transition (*c* 1st century BC/AD) was particularly striking, as the settlement shifted to another gravel island to the south, and changed from an un-nucleated mixed farmstead to a specialist pastoral settlement with associated stock enclosures. An increase in site specialism, along with other developments such as changes in house types and the abandonment of storage pits, was characteristic of the region during the late Iron Age (Allen 2000, 21). At Roughground Farm, approximately 3 km from Claydon Pike, a similar settlement was established during the early 1st century AD, with individual stock and occupation areas, although this site appears to have been operating a mixed farming economy (Allen *et al.* 1993, 180). Other nearby sites from this period include Cleveland Farm, Ashton Keynes (Coe *et al.* 1991), Stubbs Farm, Kempsford (OAU 1993) and two sites at Somerford Keynes (Neigh Bridge; Miles *et al.* forthcoming, and Shorncote Quarry; Hearne and Adam 1999), and it is clear that occupation along the Upper Thames Valley was quite dense. This settlement was part of an organised agricultural landscape, with the higher terraces being used for arable and the floodplain and part of the first terrace being primarily open pasture (Robinson 1992a, 56).

Further north into the Cotswolds, the late Iron Age extensive dyke complex at Bagendon may have dominated the landscape. It has long been regarded as the tribal seat of the Dobunni despite the fact that its status, function and chronology are far from well-understood.

Roman

The Roman conquest signified no immediate changes to settlement patterns or functions in the region, although a cavalry fort was established at Leaholm near Bagendon in *c* AD 50, and a town at Cirencester (Corinium Dobunnorum), 15 km west of Thornhill Farm, which came to dominate the region during the Roman period. At Claydon Pike, the pastoral settlement continued with relatively little sign of Romanised material culture until the early 2nd century AD, when the layout of the site was altered radically, with the imposition of a series of rectangular enclosures and aisled buildings. It

was originally suggested that the site became an official Roman depot or even military estate (saltus), associated with the cultivation of hay meadows (Miles and Palmer 1990, 23), although any direct official involvement is difficult to substantiate (see Chapter 5). At approximately the same time, a similarly radical reorganisation occurred at Roughground Farm with the construction of a masonry villa complex, and at Somerford Keynes, Neigh Bridge, with the erection of an aisled timber building which may have been a tile depot. Indeed, the settlement pattern across the Upper Thames Valley and beyond appears to have been significantly disrupted during the early 2nd century AD, with many of the sites established in the late Iron Age going out of use, and new sites being established (Henig and Booth 2000, 106).

The Roman period as a whole saw a dense concentration of occupation, estimated at one site per kilometre, in the Upper Thames Valley (Miles 1989). Aerial photographs along the gravel terraces have revealed a dense series of settlements and field boundaries, many of which have proved to be of Roman date, such as that near Leaze Farm, *c* 5 km east of Thornhill Farm (Leach 1977, 17). In general it appears that agricultural patterns of the Iron Age continued into the Roman period, with the floodplain and part of the first terrace being used for the raising of domestic stock, and the higher terraces having settlements operating mixed farming economies. The Roman period did however herald the first introduction of managed grassland, with evidence for hay meadows at Farmoor (Lambrick and Robinson 1979, 83–87) and Claydon Pike (Miles *et al.* forthcoming). Some of these farmsteads on the gravel terraces developed into villas (eg Roughground Farm), although the number of villas in the Upper Thames Valley is much lower than in the Cotswolds further north and to some extent towards the Berkshire Downs to the south. Towns were also very scarce within the Upper Thames Valley, with one of the very few examples being Cricklade which lay along Ermin Street, to the south of Cirencester. Ermin Street was the only major Roman road to pass through this region, and ran south-east from Cirencester (Corinium) through Wanborough and on to Silchester. Nearby was also Akeman Street, which ran *c* 7 km north of Thornhill Farm along the south edge of the Cotswolds in an easterly direction towards Alchester. Recent work has highlighted how much work and effort went into the construction and maintenance of Ermin Street in the 1st and 2nd centuries (Mudd *et al.* 1999, 279), almost certainly involving a military presence at least during the earliest period. Maintenance of the road appears to have declined somewhat in the 3rd and 4th centuries (ibid. 279–280). Aside from the major roads, there appears to have been quite a comprehensive network of minor roads and trackways, which no doubt connected settlements across the Upper Thames Valley. Many examples have been found, such as at Claydon Pike (Miles *et al.* forthcoming), Kempsford Quarry (OAU 1998), Thornhill Farm and Somerford Keynes Cotswold Community (OA 2003).

The Upper Thames Valley in the Roman period would therefore appear to have been a well organised landscape, with numerous farmsteads and a small number of villas operating a variety of agricultural economies, and connected by a system of small roads and trackways.

Evidence for late Roman activity in the region often occurs in the form of finds (specifically coins), although there were also many 3rd and 4th century settlements in the area. The villa at Roughground Farm for example was occupied until the latter half of the 4th century AD, and a modest 4th-century villa and shrine were excavated at Claydon Pike. Activity at the latter site may have continued into the early 5th century. During the later Roman period, the area would have been incorporated into the new province of Britannia Prima, probably centred on the provincial capital at Cirencester. This seems to have been a period of great prosperity in at least part of the region, with a marked increase in villa building and expansion, seen most vividly in the Cotswolds (see Chapter 5).

Anglo-Saxon

When compared to the wealth of evidence for Roman activity in the Gloucestershire Upper Thames Valley, that for Anglo-Saxon occupation is very slight indeed, and, as with much of the country, it is nearly all confined to burials. A cemetery containing at least 180 burials plus an undetermined number of cremations was found at Fairford in the 1850s (Smith 1852), dated to the mid 5th–6th century (Dickinson 1976, 105). Another cemetery was excavated in 1985 at Butler's Field near Lechlade, with over 200 inhumations of men, women and children (Boyle *et al.* 1998). The mass of grave goods confirmed that the cemetery was of mid or late 5th–7th century date. Aerial photographs revealed a possible settlement nearby, with 6th- to 8th-century pottery being recovered from fieldwalking. Anglo-Saxon material has also been found at The Loders in Lechlade (Darvill *et al.* 1986), and at Great Lemhill Farm, about 1 km to the northwest. There is little evidence for continuity of settlement from the late Roman to the Anglo-Saxon period, although the sub-Roman activity at Claydon Pike could be broadly contemporary with the earliest Butler's Field burials, and stone robbing occurred at the Roughground Farm villa at this time.

Medieval

The later medieval settlement pattern in the Gloucestershire Upper Thames valley was similar to that of today. The origins of Lechlade and Fairford can be traced back to the late Saxon period in documentary sources, and they were granted markets in the early 13th century. Prior to this, the earliest record in which Fairford is named is dated AD 850, when two hides of land were transferred to the Abbess of the Church of Gloucester. Domesday Book noted of Fairford that there were 21 hides of land with 56 villeins, 9 bordars with 30 ploughtillages, a priest and three mills.

The towns of Fairford and Lechlade were located too close together for either to develop at great pace, although the position of Lechlade at the highest navigable point of the Thames ensured a significant amount of waterborne trade and traffic (Finberg 1975, 73). By the 15th century the manor of Fairford was held by the earls of Warwick and it was at this time that the town and parish began to flourish, with a new church being financed by the wealthy wool merchant John Thame (Finberg 1955, 73). A medieval roadway called the White Way or Salt Way ran from Droitwich to Lechlade.

ORIGINAL RESEARCH AIMS

The original research questions at Thornhill Farm were formulated against a background of intensive work carried out, largely by the OAU, over the preceding decade. The work culminated in the intensive excavations at Claydon Pike, which began in 1979 and continued to the mid 1980s. Both the evaluation and photographic evidence suggested that Thornhill Farm was of a quite different character. Where Claydon Pike was an intensive, nucleated site which had clearly become highly Romanised, the Thornhill Farm cropmarks sprawled over some 30 to 40 ha with few obvious foci. Fieldwalking, however, suggested that the sites may have been at least partially contemporary.

Thornhill Farm was selected for excavation for a number of reasons:

 The narrow spatial and chronological spread of the Thornhill/Claydon settlements offered the opportunity to study social and economic change in the critical years preceding and following the Roman conquest.
 The area itself lay at the junction of two contrasting settlement patterns (the Cotswolds and the Upper Thames Valley) in both the late prehistoric and Roman periods.
 It was believed that the marginal nature of the land at Thornhill Farm (low-lying gravel terrace prone to flooding) might prove a good indicator of change in society, as such areas are likely to be affected first by expansion or regression of settlement.
 The area's proximity to Cirencester, Roman Corinium, and the disputed late Iron Age tribal centre at Bagendon, offered a rare opportunity to study the effect of major economic and political foci on a rural population. In particular, the documentation of the complex effects of Romanisation on native British culture was seen as a principal aim.

It was against this background that the specific excavation objectives for Thornhill Farm were set. These were threefold, incorporating environmental, structural and relational considerations.

Environmental
The history of land exploitation and adaptation to the low-lying environment of the first gravel terrace

At the inception of the Thornhill Farm excavations, little was known of late prehistoric land use or exploitation of the lower gravel terraces and floodplain of the Upper Thames. An earlier study of the same period at Farmoor, Oxon., suggested that in some areas at least, the utilisation of floodplain grassland had considerable economic and probably also social significance. The specialised nature of the site, implicit in its seasonal and short-lived occupation, raised many questions concerning the organisation of society (Lambrick and Robinson 1979, 134–5). Further research was hampered by the masking qualities of thick alluvial silts, which covered large areas of the Upper Thames floodplain, making sites difficult to locate. Surviving earthworks at Oxford's Port Meadow, however, suggested that Farmoor was not unique.

The excavations at Thornhill Farm offered the chance to shed further light on the nature and scale of organised exploitation of low-lying grasslands, and to draw valuable comparisons with sites along the Oxfordshire stretch of the Thames.

Structural
The economic and social basis of the site

One of the principal aims was to investigate the economic and social basis of the site. Aerial photography had clearly demonstrated that the surviving archaeology was extensive, but it was unclear whether the apparently dispersed nature of the site was genuine or the result of settlement shift over time. Could a chronological sequence be established and if so was it possible to extrapolate identifiable activity zones from the phasing? In particular, was there a domestic focus to the site, and what relationship did it have with the extensive palimpsest of subrectangular enclosures clearly identified from aerial photographs? Enclosure function was likely to prove key in understanding the economic basis of the site and was, therefore, one of the most intensively investigated questions.

Relational
The relationship with surrounding settlement, and in particular the adjacent Claydon Pike complex.

The location of Thornhill Farm, between the contrasting settlement patterns of the Cotswolds and the Upper Thames Valley, meant that the excavations were potentially well placed to investigate the relationship between the two areas.

It was also important to understand what relationship Thornhill Farm had with the more local surrounding settlement, and in particular with the highly Romanised site of Claydon Pike (Figs 1.2 and 1.3). The chronological framework of the site offered an outstanding opportunity to study the impact of the Roman conquest and what effect the subsequent urbanisation at Cirencester had on a native rural settlement.

REVISED RESEARCH AIMS

Following a pre-MAP 1 assessment of the site, the original research aims were fully appraised and revised as appropriate.

Environmental

Environmental and archaeological evidence from Thornhill Farm was used to identify a sequence of changes in land use from the middle Iron Age through to the early medieval period. The sequence includes a changing pattern of pasture, arable, and hay meadow. The revised research aim was to assess the principal factors that influenced these economic shifts.

Structural

The scale of the excavations meant that a coherent plan was produced and different areas of activity were identified, all within a tight chronological framework. The arrangement of enclosures and pens appeared to have been a coherent development and a functional response to a short-lived social and economic situation. It was felt that all of the original research questions were still attainable and could be further enhanced by the careful analysis of artefactual and faunal remains.

Relational

The relationship between Thornhill Farm and Claydon Pike is clearly capable of definition, and changes in emphasis can be documented through time. The relationship is an invaluable key to the late prehistoric economy and settlement pattern of the region, and the impact that the Roman conquest had upon them. It is possible to define real differences between the two landscape areas of the Cotswolds and Upper Thames Valley, but perhaps more importantly to gauge the effects that Roman urbanism at Cirencester had upon its hinterland.

EXCAVATION STRATEGY AND HISTORY

The work at Thornhill Farm investigated an area of approximately 40.5 ha through a combination of trial trenching of cropmarks, planning of large areas of salvage (with selective excavation of features), and area excavation (Figs 1.3 to 1.5). This has provided opportunities to analyse the developments and changes in the use of the landscape from the middle Iron Age through to the late Roman period. Inevitably the area excavations, which covered about 4.5 ha in total, provided the opportunity to develop the most detailed understanding of the site, while the salvage recording (*c* 4 ha) and cropmark trenching provided successively less detailed information. This has had important ramifications in the development of the proposed chronological framework for the site, in that the most complex phasing sequences are seen in the excavation areas, with which, in a number of cases, the cropmarks and salvage evidence can be integrated only at a less certain level of confidence.

However, the logistical and financial constraints of the project would have made it impossible to examine all of the area at a comparable level, and given the dating problems (see below) it was felt that questions regarding the specific phasing of individual features could not have been adequately resolved in every case. In addition, in terms of the project's history, a large number of the cropmarks to the south of Trenches 7 and 8 (End Plan) only became visible in 1990. This was a year after the final season of excavation, when extensive gravel extraction in the immediate vicinity of the site substantially reduced the level of the watertable, further accentuating the differentiation between the ditch fills and the natural gravel.

POST-EXCAVATION METHODOLOGY

Aside from the varying intensity of archaeological investigation, the character of the site required that three strands of evidence be considered in detail to produce a coherent sequence of phasing for the site. These were the stratigraphy, the spatial patterning of the features and the site formation processes, with particular reference to an assessment of the levels of finds redeposition.

While these factors always need to be taken into account during post-excavation analysis, the large-scale, poor to moderately stratified nature of the site means that, as with the majority of rural sites, spatial patterning and site formation processes have an enhanced role to play in understanding the development of the site. This is principally because the 'stratigraphic strings' are limited and tend to separate at relatively early stages, producing matrices with great lateral extension but little depth. For instance in Trench 7, the northern and southern halves of the trench cannot be related stratigraphically beyond the first phase. Therefore while the matrix is the primary core of the post-excavation analysis, it does not provide a sufficiently extensive series of relationships (unlike those on many urban excavations) to establish any coherent phasing for the whole site. This can only be achieved through a detailed consideration of the site's layout and the site formation processes.

While these factors have been apparent to many writers of excavation reports, they have only been addressed in passing or been taken as being implicitly understood. However, the scale of the Thornhill excavations requires a more explicit acknowledgement of the methodologies employed, as the complexity of arguments makes it impossible to present a full discussion of the series of decisions which have influenced the placement of a feature in one phase as opposed to another. There were four main types of argument used to construct the phasing, although because of potential problems with the matrix, the finds data and the spatial patterning were sometimes used to overturn the recorded stratigraphic relationships (see below):

1 - The stratigraphic relationships are accepted and finds dating is used to provide an absolute chronology (when the limits of this mode of argument are reached the reasoning adopted is as in 3)
2 - The stratigraphic relationships are rejected on the basis of the finds evidence and the spatial patterning
3 - Where there is no stratigraphy (or the stratigraphy is rejected) the finds and the spatial patterning are used in isolation
4 - Where there are no finds the stratigraphy and spatial patterning are used in isolation.

The complexity in the argumentation arises from several factors. First, the 'data' being utilised are already relatively high-level abstractions. As a consequence, arguments in terms of 'data'-theory conflicts are less sensitive, as the degrees of confidence in descriptive interpretations and analytical interpretations are less clearly differentiated. This results in frequent stages of assessment where judgements between different interpretations are required on the basis of the balance of probabilities. Secondly, in phasing the site all four types of argument are used in conjunction, with variable levels of confidence. These two factors result in a cat's cradle of multiple options, where the large number of elements can be interchanged to create different phases. Therefore, the ultimate preference of one option over another relies on notions of the best-fit for the totality of the phasing of the site as a whole.

In terms of presentation, it is not possible to present all of the 'blind avenues' which were entered during the analysis of the site. This stated, it is not the intention to present the phasing without justification but to restrict explanation to the key elements of each phase. It is hoped that reference to the matrices will provide adequate reasons for aspects of the phasing. In addition a number of the discarded hypotheses are presented and discussed in note form in the site archive.

The foundations on which the phasing was constructed required that the matrix be compiled and assessments be made of the site formation

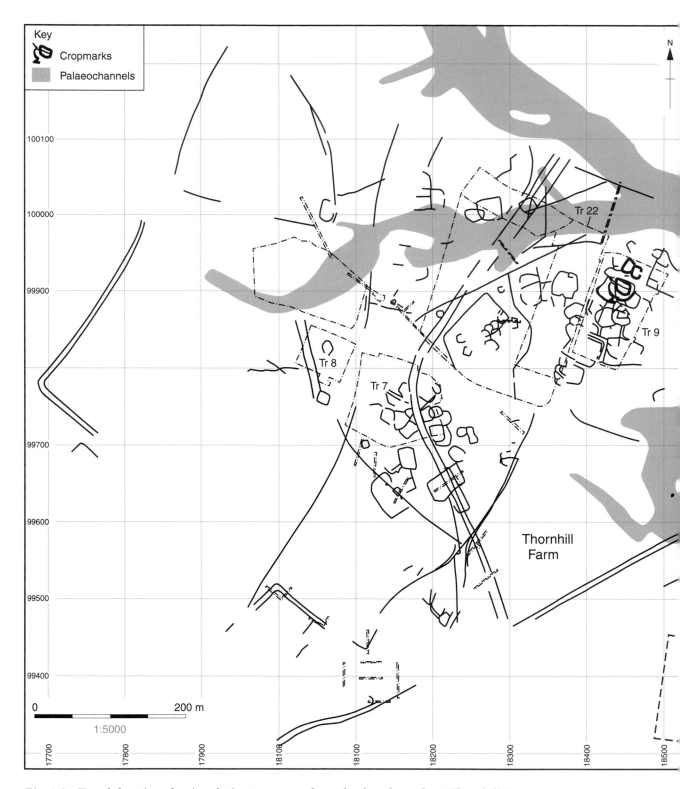

Fig. 1.3   Trench location plan in relation to cropmarks and palaeochannels at Thornhill Farm and Claydon Pike

Trench 22

Trench 9

Salvage Area

Salvage Area

N

100000

99900

99800

18500

18400

18300

18200

18100

18000

1:2500

100 m

0

Fig. 1.4 Northern Area – Trenches 9, 22 and Salvage Area

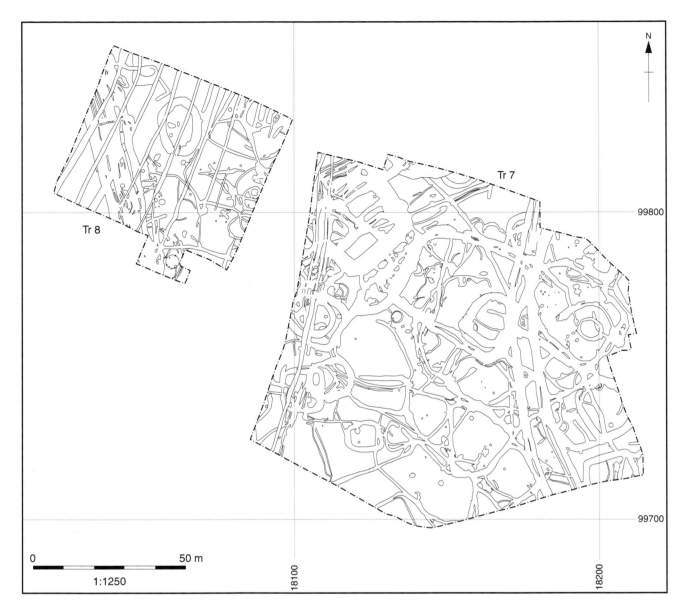

Fig. 1.5   Southern Area – Trenches 7 and 8

processes prior to the evidence being used to phase the site. The obvious consequence of these activities is that assessments are made of the reliability of the 'evidence' (the third strand, spatial analysis, requires little pre-analysis utilising a set of loose concepts founded on the notion that we can recognise structured patterns, using concepts like features respecting each other, enclosing, being parallel to or perpendicular to one another).

In terms of the stratigraphy, assessment is done at a relatively unconscious level, in that stratigraphic 'problems' are resolved in order to form a coherent matrix. In reality this involves recognition that there are errors in the recording of the stratigraphic relationships. This, in turn, draws attention to the potential faults in the matrix. At Thornhill Farm the problems in the stratigraphic record can be ascribed to several factors: the longevity of the excavation programme, the use of

a large number of excavators with differing levels of expertise, and the difficulty of distinguishing the different fills and recuts given that the fills were derived from the same parent soil. An awareness of these factors introduces a degree of latitude in our reliance on the matrix, although this is difficult to quantify in any precise form. In practice it means we permit the other strands of evidence – the finds data and the spatial patterning – to be used to overturn the relationships recorded in the matrix during the process of phasing the site (see arguments 2 and 3 above). Given the essentially unquantifiable character of the uncertainty levels surrounding the matrix, the decision to use the other evidence in preference to the matrix is one obviously founded on an assessment of the reliability of the other evidence (see below), and an assessment of the balance of probabilities based on detailed knowledge of the site. This last factor relies to an extent on the experience, expertise, and ability of the analyst.

A consideration of the site formation processes is most pertinent in relation to the datable artefacts, in that prior to phasing there has to be an evaluation of the reliability of the date provided by them. Therefore, a primary element of this analysis is to consider redeposition, which allows us to judge the potential weaknesses of the dating evidence derived from small pottery assemblages. This stated, the process adopted at Thornhill was to consider the dating evidence, however meagre, but to acknowledge its weakness in the context of the conclusions arrived at concerning the site formation processes.

Given the analytical primacy of the matrix construction and the appraisal of the site formation processes the results of these tasks need to be presented before we can discuss the phasing. The matrix compilation followed the orthodox methodology and the matrices are to be found within the site archive.

STRUCTURE OF THE REPORT

The structure of the report has been partly determined by adherence to traditional methods of presentation and partly by practical considerations peculiar to the nature of Thornhill Farm. No attempt has been made to incorporate all of the detail recovered from the site into the report, as the sheer volume of data would have made a coherent account impossible. That stated all information has been considered in compiling the interpretation and discussion, and the full archive is available for consultation.

LOCATION OF THE ARCHIVE

All of the original site records, including the finds and material generated during post-excavation analysis have been deposited at the Corinium Museum, Cirencester. A copy of the paper archive is also held on microfilm by the National Monuments Record, Swindon. In addition, a digital record of the site plans is held at Oxford Archaeology, Janus House, Osney Mead, Oxford.

Chapter 2   Phasing Summary

INTRODUCTION

The problematical nature of the stratigraphy at Thornhill Farm has been highlighted in the previous chapter, along with the methodology used to establish a phasing sequence. This chapter presents a summary of the phasing established for the site, while a detailed archaeological narrative can be found in Chapter 3. It must be reiterated that features have been assigned to specific phases with varying levels of confidence, with all strands of evidence being combined to produce a 'best fit'. In attempting to phase the site the evidence from cropmarks, the salvage areas and excavation trenches has been considered in an attempt to reconstruct the development of the landscape. As a result, certain features can only be integrated into the phasing at a less certain level, and in some cases it is impossible to be certain to which of several phases particular features belonged. As a consequence, the phasing diagrams presented throughout the volume display two different levels of confidence in the placement of features in specific periods. Those features which can only be phased with a lower level of confidence are shown as a grey tint in the figures, and several features occur on more than one period plan in this form. Nevertheless, the overall phase sequence is clear, and a sound chronological framework has been established for the site, ranging from the middle Iron Age to the later Roman period.

PERIOD A: MIDDLE IRON AGE
c 300–50 BC (Fig. 2.1)

The main features belonging to this period were found in Trench 8 and consisted of a house gully and associated features including pits, an enclosure and ditches. In the salvage areas two more potential house gullies were located, as well as an area of pits. One pit in Trench 22 contained an entire pot and may represent a 'special deposit'. The pottery which dates to this period (Group 1) was found widely distributed across the site predominantly as redeposited material in later contexts. It is argued that the quantity of redeposited material attests to generalised activity in this period. Analysis of the redeposited material in an attempt to identify foci of Period A activity proved inconclusive.

PERIOD B: LATE IRON AGE *c* 50 BC–AD 1

There are few features which can be ascribed to this period, which is defined on the basis of the Group 2 pottery. Indeed the limited quantities of Group 2 material (Table 3.6) would suggest that activity during this period was relatively insubstantial in comparison with subsequent periods, and was probably more similar in character to the Period A occupation than to the activity which followed it. No settlement focus can be defined and there is only minimal evidence for a single structure and none for coherent enclosures. The only features which might belong to this period are relatively isolated from each other, and as a consequence it is difficult to understand their context.

PERIOD C: LATE IRON AGE *c* AD 1–50
(Fig. 2.2)

This period sees a radical change from the dispersed deposits and perhaps ephemeral occupation which characterised Periods A and B. In the northern part of the site (Trenches 9 and 22) large rectilinear enclosures were laid out on the gravel terrace, which were associated with roundhouses and a long linear boundary. To the south-west there was another potential boundary cutting across the terrace and a loosely gridded enclosure system. The period is dated by the Group 3 pottery.

PERIOD D: EARLY ROMAN PERIOD
c AD 50–100 (Fig. 2.3)

Period D was largely dominated by a tightly knit group of enclosures in the Northern Area (Trenches 9 and 22). The enclosures seem to have been arranged around a central enclosure, E58. To the north-west of the enclosures a major droveway suggests that the movement of livestock may have been undertaken on a relatively large scale. The western boundary ditch recorded in Trench 8 was elaborated and recut on numerous occasions.

PERIOD E: EARLY ROMAN PERIOD
c AD 75–120 (Fig. 2.4)

Period E was characterised by two separate groups of enclosures centred within Trench 7 and Trenches 9 and 22. The apparent two-fold concentration of northern and southern enclosures may be more apparent than real, however, as the positioning of open area trenches inevitably distorts the true picture. The southern enclosures (Trench 7) were broadly oriented NW–SE, with a large, subrectangular enclosure (E26) perhaps providing the central point of the group. The northern group of enclosures (Trenches 9 and 22) were dominated by a large double celled enclosure (E62/E75). A number of smaller, subrectangular enclosures quite different in character to E62/E75 were also recorded.

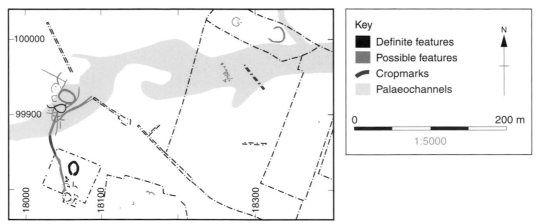

Fig. 2.1

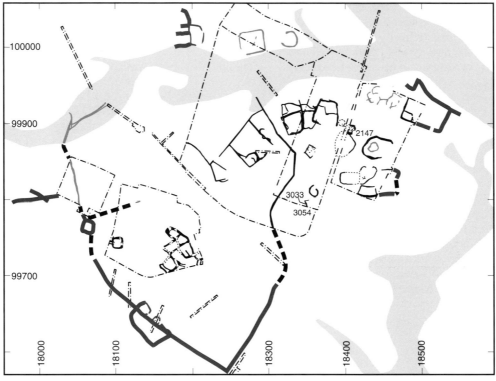

Fig. 2.2

Fig. 2.1 (above): Period A – middle Iron Age, c 300–50 BC
Fig. 2.2 (below)   Period C – late Iron Age, c AD 1–50

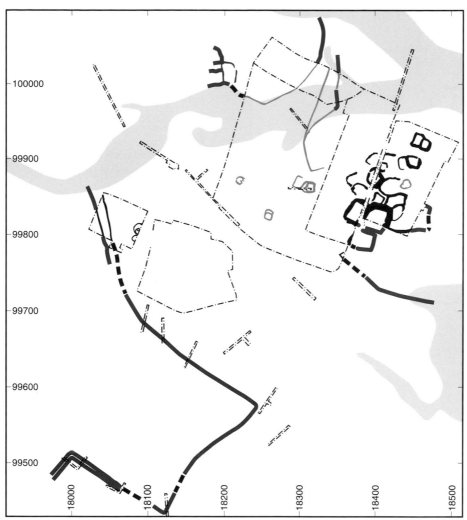

Fig. 2.3

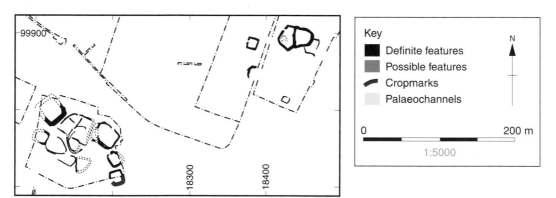

Fig. 2.4

Fig. 2.3 (above)   Period D – early Roman Period, c AD 50–100
Fig. 2.4 (below)   Period E – early Roman Period, c AD 75–120

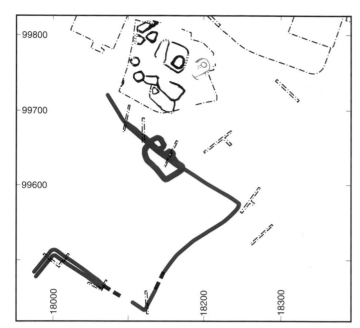

Fig. 2.5

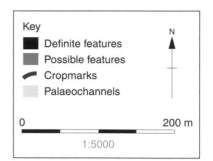

*Fig. 2.5 (above)   Period F – early Roman Period,
c AD 75–120*

*Fig. 2.6 (below)   Period G – early Roman Period,
c 2nd Century AD*

*Fig. 2.7 (opposite) Period H – late Roman Period,
c 3rd–4th Century AD*

Key

■ Definite features
■ Possible features
〰 Cropmarks
░ Palaeochannels

N

0   200 m

1:5000

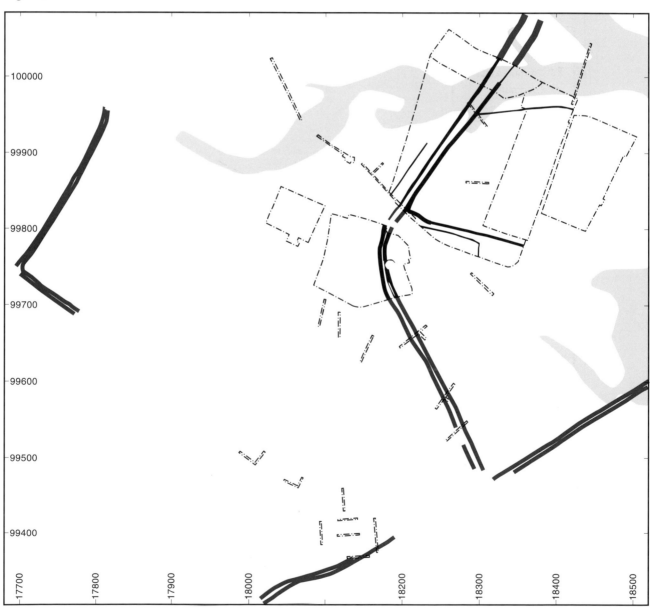

Fig. 2.6

PERIOD F: EARLY ROMAN PERIOD
c AD 75–120 (Fig. 2.5)

This period was characterised by small clusters of enclosures loosely arranged around a large subrectangular enclosure (E29) in Trench 7. The enclosures within individual clusters shared similar characteristics and may have served particular functions as a group. Chronologically, Period F could not be distinguished from Period E.

PERIOD G: EARLY ROMAN PERIOD
2nd CENTURY AD (Fig. 2.6)

Period G saw a radical change in the character of the archaeology at Thornhill Farm. The numerous groups of intensively recut enclosures, which were so typical of earlier periods, appear to have gone out of use, and the landscape was reorganised on a considerable scale. The most significant features were newly constructed trackways, which crossed the site and divided up the landscape, seemingly without any regard for earlier activity. There is no evidence for actual occupation at the site from this period. Instead it seems to have formed part of an outlying field and trackway system. There was thus a shift of emphasis from the movement of animals within the site, to movement through its former area, with it now being tied into a wider landscape of exploitation.

PERIOD H: LATE ROMAN PERIOD
3rd–4th CENTURY AD (Fig. 2.7)

In the late Roman period modifications were made to the landscape which suggest that the major trackway 301 was no longer in use. The period was dominated by a number of linear boundaries, which stretched over the landscape for considerable distances.

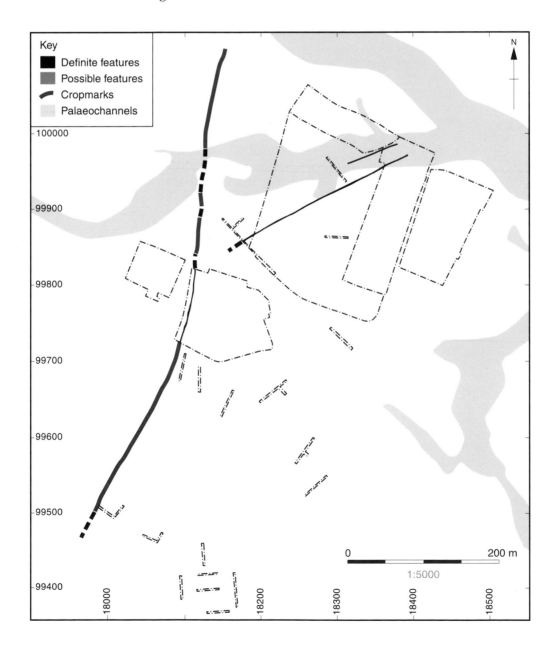

Chapter 3   Archaeological Description

by David Jennings, Jeff Muir and Alex Smith

INTRODUCTION

The discussion of post-excavation methodology (Chapter 1) should make it apparent that the phasing presented is not considered definitive. Rather, it represents the 'best fit' which could be achieved within the time constraints of the analytical phase. The site has been broken down into eight periods, with features phased at a lower level of confidence shown in grey (see Chapter 2 for phasing summary).

PERIOD A: MIDDLE IRON AGE
c 300–50 BC (Fig. 3.1)

Summary

The main features belonging to this period were found in Trench 8 and consisted of a house gully and associated features including pits, an enclosure and ditches. In the salvage areas two more potential house gullies were located, and an area of pits. A pit in Trench 22 contained an entire pot and may represent a 'special deposit'. The pottery which dates to this period (Group 1) was found widely distributed across the site predominantly as redeposited material in later contexts. It is argued that the quantity of redeposited material attests to generalised activity in this period. Analysis of the redeposited material in an attempt to identify foci of Period A activity proved inconclusive.

Distribution of redeposited Group 1 pottery

This period was dated by Group 1 pottery, which was distributed widely across all of the trenches and occurred in 17% of the contexts. In the majority of cases the pottery was clearly redeposited (Table 3.1), being found in conjunction with Group 2–5 pottery, often in the stratigraphically later stages of the site. Except in Trench 8, contexts which contained only Period 1 pottery were rare and their date was extremely difficult to assess. The high incidence of redeposition meant that an isolated feature with a limited Group 1 assemblage in Trenches 7, 9 and 22 could not be placed with a large degree of confidence within this period. The decision to assign some of these features to this period has therefore been made with caution, and the details of the argument are presented below.

Regardless of the lack of features in Trenches 7, 9 and 22 which could be ascribed to this period, the widespread distribution of Group 1 material in later contexts indicated that activity had probably taken place in these areas during Period A. An attempt to map previous foci of Period A activity, on the basis that they might be reflected in higher densities of redeposited Group 1 pottery in later contexts, was undertaken but the results were equivocal.

Trench 7 was selected for mapping on the basis that observations during post-excavation suggested that it might contain a focus of Period A activity, particularly in the south-eastern corner of the trench. Assessment of the number of contexts with Group 1 pottery by trench seemed to support this observation (see percentages of contexts with Group 1 pot, Table 3.1), suggesting that Trench 8 was a clear focus of Period A activity, and that Trench 7 may have been a focus, with progressively less activity being noticeable in Trenches 9 and 22 in the northern half of the site.

A rapid appraisal of the potential for mapping was undertaken by breaking down the core of Trench 7 into a series of eleven 30 x 30 m boxes. The numbers of contexts, sections, pottery sherds, and their weights were calculated for each box and are shown in Table 3.2. While the data does reveal some patterning (Fig. 3.2), the numbers of variables and pottery sample sizes make interpretation difficult.

The excavation strategy of selective sampling (see Chapter 1, 'Excavation methods') in conjunction with the high levels of redeposition means that the percentage of sections with Group 1 pottery provides a more reliable index of variable density than counting pottery by context, as variation in sampling intensity would affect the retrieval of Group 1 pottery from each context. It can be seen in Figure 3.2 that there seems to be a higher incidence of Group 1 pottery in the eastern and south-eastern fringe of Trench 7 on the basis of percentages of sections.

However, several factors mean that this result needs to be treated with extreme caution. First, the pottery assemblages from each box are relatively small, as are the average quantities of material per section (Table 3.2), bringing into question the statistical validity of the results. Indeed the size of the assemblage for the entire trench is so small that it is questionable whether the resulting patterns could be seen as providing a representative sample. For instance, comparisons with the assemblage from Trench 8, a definite focus of Period A activity which produced 34% of the Group 1 pottery from 8% of the contexts, or with assemblages from middle Iron Age farmsteads in the Upper Thames Valley (Table 3.3) demonstrate that the assemblages from Trench 7 (and more particularly Trenches 9 and 22) are relatively insubstantial when the area of excavation is considered.

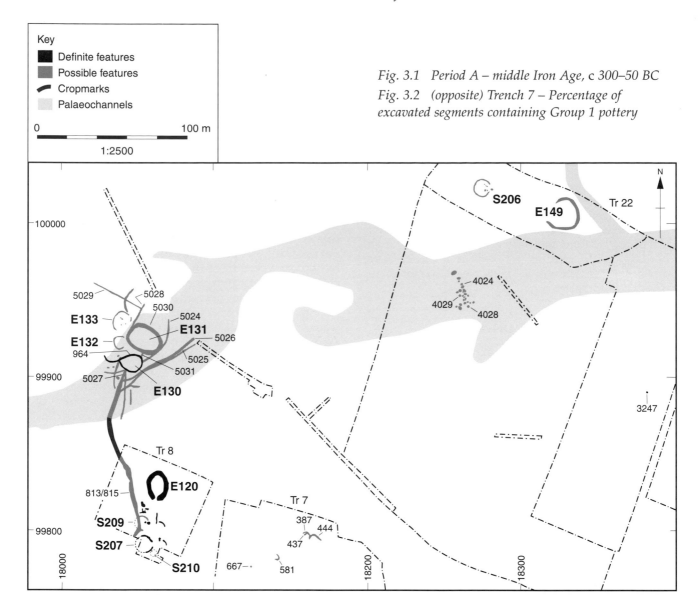

Key
- ■ Definite features
- ▆ Possible features
- ⌐ Cropmarks
- ▢ Palaeochannels

0   100 m

1:2500

Fig. 3.1   Period A – middle Iron Age, c 300–50 BC
Fig. 3.2   (opposite) Trench 7 – Percentage of excavated segments containing Group 1 pottery

Secondly, the incidence of middle Iron Age sherds in later contexts is likely to be affected by the intensity of activity in each area during the late Iron Age/early Roman periods. Several mechanisms may have influenced the dispersal and fragmentation of the pottery: if the sherds were on or near the ground surface they may have been exposed to different degrees of trampling, and the constant recutting of features may have increased the earlier pottery's subsequent dispersal. It might

be countered that the most accurate method of mapping previous foci of Period A activity requires the calculation of the volume of soil from which the sherds were derived, in order to assess the distributions in terms of densities rather than incidences. (The investment of time required to undertake this task would have been unsustainable within the constraints of the project design and funding.) While this point is valid, it is probable, given the relatively limited range of

Table 3.1   Group 1 pottery statistics

Trench	Total no. of contexts	All contexts with Group 1 pot	% of contexts with Group 1 pot	Contexts with only Group 1 pot	% of contexts with Group 1 pot containing only Group 1 pot
7	867	170	20	20	12
8	166	51	31	33	65
9	511	68	13	13	19
22	395	33	8	4	12
Total	1939	322		70	

Table 3.2   Distribution of Group 1 pottery in Trench 7

	Total sections	Total contexts	Sections Group 1	Total sherd no.	Total pot weight (g)	Sherds/ section	Weight/ section	% sections Group 1 pot
Box 1	178	51	13	42	232	3.23	17.84	7.30
Box 2	212	67	25	145	981	5.80	39.24	11.79
Box 3	79	26	9	18	73	2.00	8.11	11.39
Box 4	229	76	34	154	1018	4.52	29.94	14.85
Box 5	200	80	20	69	314	3.45	15.70	10.00
Box 6	225	76	11	21	180	1.90	16.36	4.89
Box 7	121	46	11	21	139	1.90	12.63	9.09
Box 8	349	149	14	32	232	2.28	16.57	4.01
Box 9	333	103	22	46	250	2.09	11.36	6.60
Box 10	232	72	19	64	674	3.37	35.47	8.19
Box 11	163	52	17	27	158	1.60	9.29	10.42

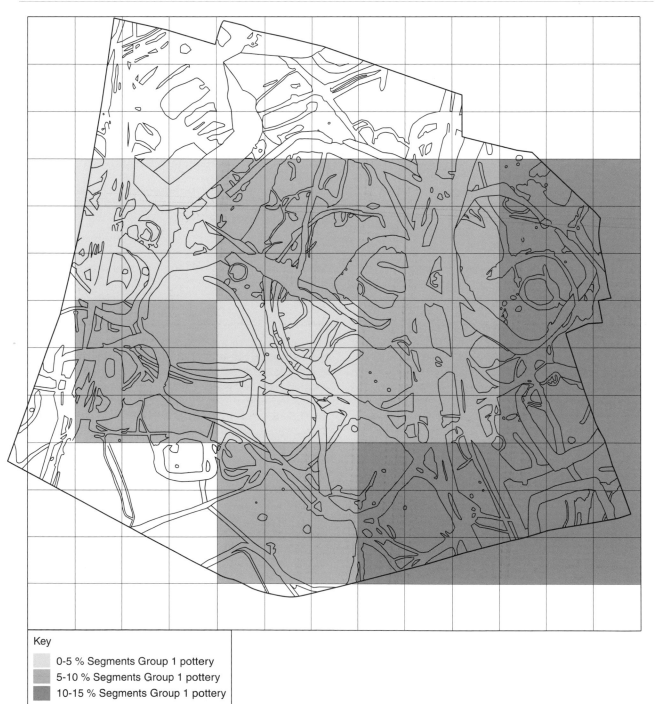

Key

0-5 % Segments Group 1 pottery
5-10 % Segments Group 1 pottery
10-15 % Segments Group 1 pottery

Table 3.3 Group 1 pottery by trench with comparanda

Location	No. of sherds	Weight (g)
Trench 7	786	5448
Trench 8	635	5833
Trench 9	421	3488
Trench 22	271	2486
Subtotal	2113	17255
Watkins Farm	1450	30500
Mingies Ditch	3098	-

Table 3.4 Numbers of sections with Group 1 pottery

Trench	Total no. of sections excavated	No. of sections with Group 1 pottery	% of sections with Group 1 pottery
7	2935	302	10
8	324	55	17
9	1062	105	10
22	745	56	8

dimensions of the features (see burnt limestone distributions below), that the figures derived from using the percentages of sections are coarsely comparable. However, in the context of this qualification, given that the percentages of sections for the eleven boxes have a limited range from 4.01–14.85%, one might question whether the distinctions in zoning are valid, especially when the average percentage for the whole of Trench 7 is 10% (Table 3.4). Finally calculations of the percentages of sections with Group 1 pottery on a trench by trench basis (Table 3.4) show that pottery occurs in 10% of the sections within Trenches 7, 9, and 22, which would suggest that the limited variability seen in Trench 7 is insufficiently enhanced beyond the levels of background noise to be significant.

In the context of these variables the pattern presented in Figure 3.2 is extremely difficult to interpret; if, however, it is taken to reflect a previous focus of activity in the eastern/south-eastern part of Trench 7, then some of the cropmarks defined beyond the adjacent limits of the trench may belong to this period (End Plan).

In general, as stated above, there was an absence of features in Trenches 7, 9 and 22 which contained solely Group 1 pottery (this applies equally to the eastern/south-eastern part of Trench 7), and which could, therefore, be ascribed to Period A. On this basis it must be assumed that either the Period A activity represented by the residual Group 1 pottery did not involve the digging of negative features into the gravel, or that any features dug into the gravel in Period A were sufficiently infrequent to be destroyed by later activity. This would suggest that it is unlikely that there were domestic foci within the other trenches of the type found in Trench 8, as the evidence this would have left behind would probably have been detectable despite the later activity.

It is possible that the Group 1 pottery in Trenches 7, 9 and 22 is rubbish dispersed from the known occupation site in Trench 8 and the potential occupation sites identified in the salvage areas. In which case it might be viewed as background noise to the settlements. This is impossible to substantiate given the lack of any analogous data with which Thornhill might be compared.

Given the opacity of the results for Trench 7, no spatial analysis of the Group 1 pottery was undertaken for the northern trenches, where the quantities of pottery were substantially less (Table 3.3), and where consequently the levels of uncertainty surrounding any resulting pattern would have been even greater.

In summation, the evidence for spatial patterning in the Group 1 pottery is equivocal and difficult to handle; there are a large number of unknowns and the quality of the evidence is poor. There is a pattern in the data from Trench 7, but its interpretation must remain uncertain.

Southern Area and Western Salvage Area

Trench 8: roundhouse and associated features (Figs 3.1 and 3.3)
(S207, S209, S210, E120)

In Trench 8 a focus of Period A activity was found consisting of three potential roundhouses with an associated enclosure (E120), pits and several lengths of ditch or gully.

Structure 207 (Fig. 3.3)

Part of the arc of a gully (861, 862, 921) was found at the southern edge of Trench 8, and the subsequent extension of the trench to the south (Trench 21) located another gully (5013) on the same circumference, defining a roundhouse gully with a diameter of *c* 13 m, and an east-facing entrance 2.8 m wide. The gully was relatively shallow (0.3 m) and was most probably the drip gully, rather than the wall trench of the structure. This is a characteristic of middle Iron Age roundhouses in the Upper Thames Valley (Allen *et al.* 1984, 91–93), although this interpretation cannot be conclusive given our lack of knowledge of the degree of truncation of the Iron Age ground surface. The majority of the gully had been destroyed by the digging of the extensive N–S ditch which ran through the western part of the trench. Only two potential internal features were located: a posthole (865) located inside gully 862, adjacent to its eastern terminal, which might have been associated with a door structure for the building; and a posthole (5014) only defined as a soilmark, located just inside gully 5013 (although see below, 'Structure 210'). The building was dated by

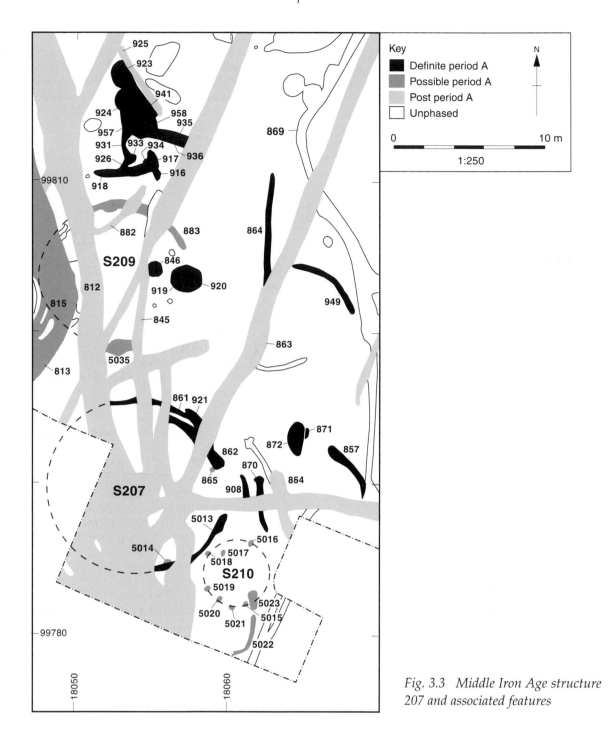

Fig. 3.3 Middle Iron Age structure 207 and associated features

the Group 1 pottery recovered from gullies 861, 862, and 921. One sherd of Group 3 pottery and three sherds of Group 4 pottery were recovered from the outermost gully recut, 921. These are interpreted as being intrusive, being introduced by a medieval furrow (863) which cut through the feature.

Two short gullies 908 and 870 were located *c* 2 m outside of the building's entrance, and may have been functionally related to the structure. Parallels for these features are, however, unknown in the Upper Thames Valley, and their interpretation is unclear. They may have been bedding trenches for windbreaks sheltering the door, although, as the

prevailing winds in the area are south-westerly/westerly (Lambrick and Robinson 1979, 69), the placement of the entrance facing the east would tend to obviate the need for such a feature. Alternately it might be argued that they were unrelated to the building and were associated with the parallel, larger gully, 854, to the east which is dated by a sherd of Group 4 pottery to the second half of the 1st century AD. However, both features contained solely Group 1 pottery which would have to be interpreted as being redeposited if the gullies were to be associated with this later feature. On balance, this interpretation seems less plausible.

Structure 209 (Fig. 3.3)

A second potential structure was defined to the north of structure 207, although the evidence is weak and inconclusive. A ring gully around a building may have been defined by gullies 883 and 5035. There was no dating evidence from either of the two gullies, although gully 883 was cut by the Period B gully 882, and if the two features were related the majority of the gully arc had been destroyed by the linear boundary 812 and its associated recuts. In addition the lack of a satisfactory terminal to the southern arm of the ring gully, which would have been represented by a continuation of gully 5035 to the east of ditch 845, means that the interpretation of these features as a roundhouse remains exceptionally speculative. A further qualification to the interpretation of these two features as elements of a ring-gully is that the arc of the building would probably intercut with the linear boundary 813/815 discussed below (Fig. 3.1). This linear boundary seems to respect structure 207, and so if these gullies are part of a roundhouse it suggests that it must have preceded or succeeded the period during which the boundary was in existence.

Finally, if the roundhouse interpretation is accepted then pits 846, 919 and 920 may have been internal features within the structure. These pits were shallow and had no evidence of intentional backfilling. Pits 846 and 920 contained quantities of pottery, animal bone and burnt limestone, which might be thought to be representative of domestic debris.

Structure 210

A cluster of postholes and several gullies to the south of 209 were not excavated but were planned as soilmarks (Fig. 3.3). As a result no dating evidence was recovered from these features and their attribution to Period A is dependent on their spatial relationship with the roundhouse.

Six of the postholes in this area (5015, 5016, 5018–5021) can be placed on a circle with a diameter of 4.4 m, possibly forming a small building or pen. Circular structures of this size and method of construction are not unknown but they are considerably below the average diameters for roundhouses in the region which seems to be approximately 8–10 m. A potential late Iron Age parallel was found at Barton Court Farm, Oxon., where a structure with a diameter of *c* 5 m was located in a subsidiary enclosure within the main rectilinear enclosure (Structure I; Miles 1986, 4, fig. 6). Structures of similar dimensions have also been located at two other sites in the Upper Thames Valley: at Yarnton, Oxon., two structures, probably of middle Iron Age date, have diameters of 4.5 and 5 m (Hey and Timby forthcoming); while at Gravelly Guy, Stanton Harcourt, Oxon., a middle Iron Age structure (structure AA) with a diameter of 5.5 m was constructed adjacent to a larger round-

house (Lambrick and Allen forthcoming). The location of this last example in relation to the larger roundhouse would seem to replicate that for this putative structure and its relationship with structure 207 to the north. Even if this reconstruction is accepted, the form and function of the structure, and in particular whether it was roofed or not, remains unclear.

However, the irregularity of the spacing of the postholes ought to introduce caution in our acceptance of this reconstruction, and other arrangements of the postholes also require consideration. In particular, the postholes could be taken to form two separate fencelines. One potential fenceline could consist of postholes 5014, 5018 and 5016, which are spaced at intervals of *c* 3 m. The second fenceline comprises 5014, 5019, 5020 and 5021, and might have consisted of posts equidistantly spaced at 1 m intervals, with two postholes between posthole 5014 and the other three posts in the alignment (5019–5021) being removed by the later ditches cutting across the site (Fig. 3.3). In both these cases, the incorporation of posthole 5014 within the post alignments suggests that these postholes may not have been contemporary with the roundhouse, as any structures would have traversed the ring-gully around the building.

Given the limitations of the evidence for this part of the site, it is not possible to decide conclusively between these alternative interpretations and both possibilities should be entertained.

At an equally, if not slightly higher, speculative level, two gully lengths in this area, 5022 and 5023 (Fig. 3.3), may belong to this period, forming some form of subsidiary enclosure attached to the ring gully of roundhouse 207. Enclosures of this kind are known from a large number of Iron Age sites in the Upper Thames Valley, for instance Ashville, Abingdon, Oxon. (Parrington 1978, fig. 12), and Farmoor, Oxon. (Lambrick and Robinson 1979).

Enclosure 120 (Figs 3.1 and 3.4)

Enclosure 120 was located in the northern part of Trench 8 (Fig. 3.1), and while eight sherds were from other Ceramic Groups, the majority of the pottery (92%) consisted of Group 1 fabrics. Consequently the feature has been placed in Period A. In addition, the structured distribution of the pottery, animal bone and burnt limestone around the ditch, with material clustering in the ditch terminals (Fig. 3.4, Table 3.5), suggests that the pottery was contemporary with the period during which the enclosure was in use. The sections of the feature revealed that the substantial ditch defining the enclosure, 803 (*c* 1 m deep and 3 m wide), probably silted gradually, and it is possible that later pottery may have been incorporated in the uppermost fills of the ditch, when it may have appeared as a residual hollow on the ground surface. Alternately, in the instance of the Group 5 sherd (*c* AD 75–120), found in section 803G (Fig.

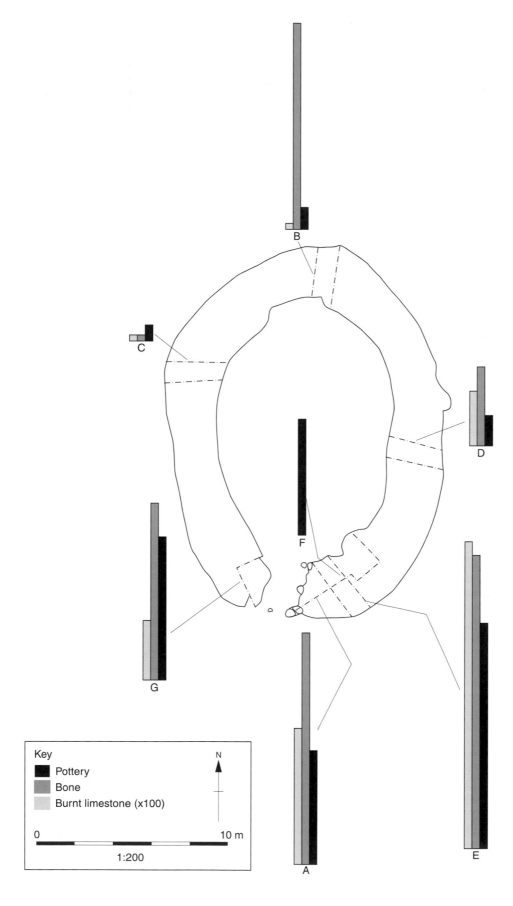

Fig. 3.4   Enclosure 120 – density of finds per m³

Table 3.5 Enclosure 120: density of finds per m³

Section	Quantity (g)				Density (g/m³)		
	Pot	Bone	Stone	Volume (m³)	Pot	Bone	Stone
A	325	550	27250	0.9	361	611	30277
B	25	825	8750	1.05	16	550	5833
C	25	25	6500	1.54	16	16	4220
D	225	325	12500	1.56	144	208	8013
E	1100	1050	80750	1.36	808	772	59375
F	0	0	28500	0.93	0	0	30645
G	225	675	54500	1.45	155	465	37586

3.4), this was probably incorporated in the ditch fill when the ditch was disturbed by a later medieval furrow (907).

The proliferation of postholes around the eastern terminal of the ditch may form part of a gate structure, while any corresponding postholes adjacent to the western ditch terminal would have been destroyed by the later medieval furrow 907.

There is no structural evidence for a building within the enclosure ditch, although this does not preclude the possibility of a building constructed using either mass-wall techniques (ie turf walls) or stake walls, which may have left no trace in the gravel. This must be considered as a possibility given the evidence from the rest of the site, which indicates variable preservation and possibly different construction techniques, although this is difficult to demonstrate definitively given our lack of detailed knowledge of the degrees of truncation of the Iron Age ground surface. For instance structure 200 (Fig. 3.6) was constructed using a post ring, while in the case of structure 207 (Fig. 3.3), only a drip gully remained. The artefactual evidence is equivocal. The concentration and relatively high densities of finds in conjunction with the high average sherd weight (16 g) intimate that there may have been a structure within the enclosure. However, this is insufficiently conclusive, and the presence of a domestic focus in the form of structure 207 to the south may provide a context for the high levels of material in the ditches of this enclosure.

Potential parallels for this enclosure from other sites suggest that, as one might anticipate, there was a diversity of potential functions for this kind of feature. At Claydon Pike, located *c* 850 m to the east, a larger ovoid middle Iron Age enclosure, 24 x 22 m (Island 1, Enclosure 2; Allen *et al.* 1984, 97, fig. 6.6/1), which might be considered broadly comparable, contained a roundhouse within a ring-gully. However, at Farmoor, Oxon., where two enclosures of more comparable form and dimensions were located, evidence for internal structures was not found. In one instance at Farmoor the lack of evidence has the same equivocal status as that for the enclosure at Thornhill Farm (Main enclosure Area II; Lambrick and Robinson 1979, 9–11,

66–68), while in the second case (Area III, enclosure 3; ibid. 25–26, 70–72) the close examination of the stratigraphy suggested that the enclosure could not have been used for domestic occupation, and may have functioned as either an occasional animal pen, or for the storage of materials like timber and/or hay.

Other features in Trench 8 (Figs 3.1 and 3.3)

Other features which can be assigned to Period A within Trench 8 consisted of: a pit cluster to the south of enclosure 120; three pits to the north of structure 207 (846, 919, 920); two pits, one cutting the other, to the east of the building (871 and 872); three gullies (857, 864, 949), and possibly an early phase of the much recut boundary in the western part of the trench (813, 815).

The pit cluster comprised 14 features: eight pits (916, 917, 923, 924, 933, 941, 958, 959), five gullies (918, 926, 931, 935, 936) and a posthole (934) (Fig. 3.3). The features were heavily intercutting suggesting that the location rather than the material derived from the cuts was more significant. These features were predominantly shallow (Pit Class 1; see 'Pits' below), and contained considerable quantities of pottery, animal bone and burnt limestone, which is possibly suggestive of domestic debris. There was no evidence of intentional backfilling, most of the features having only one or two fills. Given the short lengths of the gullies it is possible that they served the same function as the pits. Cremated human bone was recovered from gully 931, although the quantity was so insubstantial that it is probable that the material was redeposited.

The three pits (846, 919, 920) in between the cluster of features just described and structure 207, and the two intercutting pits to the east of the building (871 and 872) were also shallow and had no evidence of intentional backfilling (Fig. 3.3). Pits 846, 871, 872 and 920 contained quantities of pottery, animal bone, and burnt limestone, which again might be considered domestic debris.

The three gullies 857, 864 and 949 (Fig. 3.3) have been placed in this period on the slender basis of the pottery from the fills and limited stratigraphic evidence. In no instance can any convincing interpretation be presented for the form and location of these gullies. Gully 949 might be considered to be part of the arc of a drip gully, although not enough of the feature is preserved to argue this convincingly. Additionally, the limited quantity of finds recovered makes this interpretation less likely, as one might anticipate large amounts of domestic debris from house gullies. A fragment of human bone was recovered from gully 869, to the north of 864, and may belong to period A.

Two of the stratigraphically earliest elements (813 and 815) in the complex sequence of ditches which cut across the western half of the site contained only Group 1 pottery, and these ditches have therefore been assigned to this period (Figs 3.1 and 3.3). The ditches extended beyond the northern limits of the trench and may be related to linear features found in salvage work to the north (see below, 'Western salvage'). The exact alignment and extent of the ditches at the southern end of the trench is difficult to establish with certainty as only limited sampling of the features took place. However it seems most likely that just to the north of structure 207 the alignment of the ditches changed from NNE–SSW to a NE–SW orientation, respecting the roundhouse, and then possibly extended beyond the southern limits of the trench.

Trench 7
(444/385, 581, 667, 387, 437)

In Trench 7 three contexts, 444/385, 581 and 667, were tentatively identified as potential Period A features on the basis of their pottery assemblages and their positions as the stratigraphically earliest features within the matrix (Fig. 3.1). Two of the gullies, 444/385 and 581, were the partial arcs of curvilinear gullies, while feature 667 was a pit. As the gullies 387 and 437 were of similar form and cut gully 444/385, they have also been identified as potential Period A features.

Western Salvage Area, to the north of Trench 8
(Fig. 3.1) (E130, E131, E132, E133, 964, 5024–5031)

A series of soilmarks were planned in this area, *c* 100 x 80 m, after the topsoil had been removed by a boxscraper. The plan revealed a series of curvilinear gullies, linear features and parts of a palaeochannel. Since it is apparent from the plan that some of these features cut others, they must be of several phases, although on spatial grounds the curvilinear elements (E130–E133) could be of a single phase. Only one ditch, 964 (E130), was sampled for dating evidence, as it was noted that it contained large quantities of finds, and Group 1 pottery was recovered. Therefore, with varying degrees of confidence, on the basis of the pottery dating and the spatial layout of the curvilinear enclosures, the curvilinear features planned in this area have been ascribed to Period A.

As stated above, it is apparent that several of the linear features (5024 and 5027) are not contemporary with enclosure 130, given that they have cut or been cut by the enclosure's boundary ditch, 964. However, it is tentatively suggested on spatial grounds that these features may have a Period A date. The basis for this argument is that a short ditch, 5031, seems to respect the boundary ditches of the enclosures 130 and 131 (964, 5030), suggesting that these features were at least partly contemporary. However, ditch 5024, which cuts across or is cut by enclosure 130, seems to respect the boundary ditch, 5030, of enclosure 131, suggesting that ditch 5024 and enclosure 131 were also at least partially contemporary, at a phase either preceding or succeeding enclosure 130. Likewise the ditches 5025 and 5026 partly follow the alignment of ditch 5024, and seem to be associated at their southern end with the north-south ditch 5027. The western side of enclosure 131 also has a linear feature, ditch 5028, which in turn seems to be associated with ditch 5029.

Although it does suggest that enclosure 131 and a large number of the linear features are broadly contemporary during a phase which either precedes or succeeds enclosure 130, this evidence is far from conclusive. Given the supposed partial contemporaneity of enclosures 130 and 131 as well, therefore, it might be suggested that all of the activity in this area is Period A in date. In terms of function, given the quantities of finds from enclosure 130 noted above, the curvilinear form and dimensions (*c* 14 m) of the ditch suggest that it might have been a gully around a structure.

At a more speculative level, it might be suggested that enclosure 131 had a function similar to that of enclosure 120 in Trench 8 (see above). It is broadly comparable in terms of dimensions and plan, while its relationship with the putative roundhouse, enclosure 131, is similar to that of enclosure 120 and structure 207.

The existence of a modern field boundary meant it was not possible to examine the area between Trench 8 and this area of salvage. However, it is possible that the N–S ditch, 813–815, identified in Trench 8, may have continued in this area in the form of ditch 5027. Furthermore, it is notable that several of the features in the trench overlay the palaeochannel, suggesting that by this date at least, the channel was largely filled in.

Northern Area

Pit cluster, Northern Salvage Area (Fig. 3.1)
(4024, 4028, 4029)

A cluster of 30 pits was located and planned in the middle of the old palaeochannel. Three of the pits were sampled (4024, 4028, 4029) and middle Iron Age sherds were recovered from two of them (4024 and 4028). On this basis the cluster of pits has been ascribed to Period A.

Table 3.6   Group 2 pottery statistics

Trench	Total no. sections	Sections with Group 2 pot (%)	Total no. of contexts	No. of contexts with Group 2 pot (%)	No. of contexts with only Group 2 pot	% sections with Group 2 and later pot	No. sherds	Pot weight (g)	Average sherd weight (g)
7	2935	103 (3.5)	867	84 (9.7)	10	90.2	307	2051	6.7
8	324	12 (3.7)	165	9 (5.5)	2	76.9	104	1194	11.4
9	1062	73 (6.9)	511	56 (10.9)	9	87.7	581	2531	4.3
22	745	44 (5.9)	395	32 (8.1)	3	93.2	431	2594	6.0
Salvage	-	-	-	3	-	-	10	61	6.1
Total	5067	233	1939	185	25	-	1434	8433	-

Potential Period A features, Northern Salvage Area (Fig. 3.1) (S206, E149)

Structure 206

In the extreme northern part of the Northern Salvage Area a ring gully was found, planned and the terminals sectioned. Although it was noted in the field records that middle Iron Age sherds were recovered, these have since been lost during processing, and therefore our identification of this house as being of Period A date needs to be treated with considerable caution. However, it is similar in form to other middle Iron Age houses not only on this site (ie structure 207) but also within the region, and on this basis it is postulated that the structure might belong to this period.

Enclosure 149

The placement of this feature on Figure 3.1 as a possible feature of Period A date is extremely speculative. The bases for this argument are that the enclosure is stratigraphically the earliest feature in this area, and the possibility that there is a modular form to the middle Iron Age settlement on the site, consisting of a roundhouse in conjunction with a larger enclosure and possibly a pit cluster (see below). As such this enclosure would replicate the functions of enclosures 120 and 131, to which it is similar in terms of form and size.

Trenches 9 and 22 (Fig. 3.1) (3247, 3133, 3198, 3203)

In Trench 9 it was not felt that any features could be ascribed confidently to Period A as there did not seem to be any focus to the very limited number of features which did contain only Group 1 material, and the quantities of material in each feature were insubstantial.

In Trench 22, by contrast, one pit (3247) contained an almost complete, but broken, Malvernian pottery vessel which had been inverted in the pit. The feature contained no other finds and had only a single fill of silty loam with frequent gravel inclusions. While a Period A date for this feature would seem relatively secure, the vessel could well be earlier than previously thought (see Timby, Chapter 4), and given the seemingly isolated context of the feature it is difficult to interpret the character of the deposit.

The only other features in Trench 22 which solely contained Group 1 pottery, were three pits, 3133, 3198 and 3203. In none of theses instances, however, was the material of sufficient quantity for the possibility that the material was all redeposited to be discounted (3133 = 1 sherd, 3198 = 3 sherds, 3203 = 6 sherds).

PERIOD B: LATE IRON AGE C 50 BC–AD 1

Summary

There are few features which can be ascribed to this period, which is defined on the basis of the Group 2 pottery. Indeed the limited quantities of the Group 2 material (see Appendix 2 Table A2.1), would suggest that activity during this period was relatively insubstantial in comparison with subsequent periods, and was probably more of the character of the Period A occupation than the activity which followed it. No settlement focus can be defined, and there is only minimal evidence for a single structure and none for coherent enclosures. The only potential features which might belong to this period are relatively isolated from other putative Period B features (Table 3.7), and as a consequence it is difficult to understand their context.

Distribution of Group 2 pottery

A rapid appraisal was undertaken of the spatial distribution of the Group 2 pottery in Trench 7 simultaneously with that undertaken for the Group 1 pottery from the same trench (see above 'Distribution of redeposited Group 1 pottery'). However, no pattern was discernible in the material and given the large number of qualifications which applied to the interpretation of the Group 1 material, in conjunction with the more limited occurrence of the Group 2 pottery, it was not considered profitable to pursue this form of analysis further. The plot of the results of this exercise has been deposited in the archive.

The statistics of the Group 2 pottery are presented on a trench by trench basis in Table 3.6.

Table 3.7   Potential Period B features

Context	Type	Trench	Pottery Sherd nos	Weight (g)	Bone (g)	Burnt limestone (g)	Dimensions (m) depth	width
882	gully	8	50 (26)	690 (112)	150	31000	0.30	0.20
925	gully	8	3 (61)	78 (346)	100	8750	-	0.40
2070	pit	9	5	8	0	1750	0.44	0.66
2117	pit	9	9 (1)	5 (2)	0	1250	0.24	0.72
2392	pit	9	11	17	0	0	0.54	0.72
3088	pit	22	2	8	0	6600	0.53	0.40

- = information not recorded

Pottery data in brackets = Group 1 pottery found in features (redeposited)

By comparison with the other Ceramic Groups (see Appendix 2, Table A2.1), it can be seen that Group 2 material occurred in smaller quantities than that of other phases, and that in most instances it was clearly redeposited, occurring in contexts which contained pottery of later Ceramic Groups (Table 3.6: % contexts with Group 2 and later pot). The percentage of contexts in which the Group 2 material occurred is similar for all of the trenches, suggesting that no clear focus of activity can be defined within any of the trenches on the basis of the redeposited material.

Potential Period B Features
(882, 925)

Only 25 contexts were found which solely contained Group 2 material (Table 3.6). In only seven of these instances was a Period B date possible for the feature (Table 3.7), as in the other 18 cases the features were either elements of later enclosures or were stratigraphically later than contexts containing pottery of Groups 3–5.

The seven contexts were so scattered that it is difficult to argue for a Period B date with a large degree of conviction. The best evidence for Period B features is perhaps in Trench 8. In this trench two features were found, one of which, a curvilinear gully 882 (Fig. 3.3), cut by the large linear ditch 812, contained substantial quantities of pottery and burnt limestone and a limited amount of animal bone in its terminal (Table 3.7). This concentration of material in the gully terminal is a feature noted at other house gullies in the Upper Thames Valley (ie Claydon Pike, Allen *et al.* 1984, 90, 94, fig. 6.3; Mingies Ditch, Allen and Robinson 1993, 90). This observation, and its location, in the immediate vicinity of Period A structures (?209 and 207), suggests that gully 882 might be a section of a Period B house gully, representing a direct replacement of the Period A structures, and therefore suggesting continuity of occupation. However, given the lack of a complete arc this identification must be seen as tentative.

A short length of gully, 925, in Trench 8, just to the north of the gully 882 may also have been a Period B feature. It only contained three sherds of Group 2 pottery, and cut the cluster of Period A pits (see above, 'Other features in Trench 8').

PERIOD C: LATE IRON AGE *C* AD 1–50
(Fig. 3.5)

Summary

This period sees a radical change from the dispersed deposits and even ephemeral occupation which characterised Periods A and B. In the northern part of the site (Trenches 9 and 22) large rectilinear enclosures were laid out on the gravel terrace, which were associated with roundhouses and a long linear boundary. To the south-west there was another potential boundary cutting across the terrace, and a loosely gridded enclosure system. The period is dated by Group 3 pottery.

Northern Area

Rectilinear enclosures, structures and associated boundary
(E53, E65, E74, E102, E135, E139, E143, E150, 3077)

In the northern trenches, 9 and 22, and the Northern Salvage Area a series of rectilinear enclosures were uncovered (Fig. 3.5). Although the ceramic dating evidence is limited (Table 3.8), this, in conjunction with the apparently structured layout of these enclosures, suggests that a Period C date is likely.

The sequence of development is complex and can only be partially reconstructed. Enclosure 53 seems to have been one of the earliest elements of the new layout, and up to five phases have been identified within this enclosure. In plan, the enclosure appears to be double-celled with a small pen in the north-western corner of the northern cell. It is unclear, however, during which stages the enclosure existed in this form or whether it was a simple rectilinear feature for most of its existence. Enclosure 102 seems to have been contemporary with either the first or second phase of the enclosure, with its north and south ditches butting E53's eastern ditch (3262).

Enclosure 102 went out of use with the construction of the first phase of E65, which cut the north and south ditches of E102. Whether E65 was a replace-

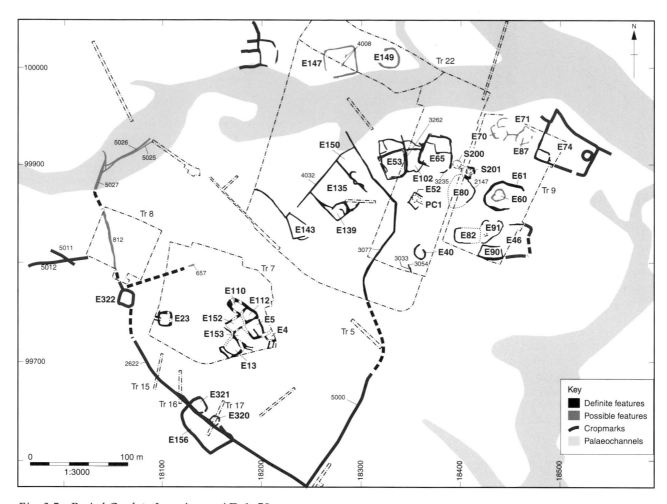

Fig. 3.5   Period C – late Iron Age, c AD 1–50

ment of E53 or whether the later stages of E53 were contemporary with E65 cannot be established.

To the west of these three enclosures, a large rectilinear enclosure, E135, was uncovered in the Northern Salvage Area. The north-western boundary ditch of this enclosure (4032) extended beyond the limits of the enclosure. To the north-east, it defined E150 in conjunction with ditch 3077, while to the south-east it extended towards E143. It is uncertain whether ditch 4032 stopped before E143's western boundary, as shown on the plan, and

therefore demarcated an entrance *c* 9 m wide or whether the southern section of the ditch had been excessively truncated by soil stripping. Enclosure 139 has been tentatively ascribed to this period on the basis of its spatial relationship with E135 and the minimal dating evidence recovered from the single section cut across its ditch.

The placement of the linear boundary 3077 in this period is dependent on its spatial relationship with ditch 4032 of E135, and its relationship with E53, which it seems to respect. In addition, both ditch

Table 3.8   Group 3 enclosures, Trench 22 and Northern Salvage Area

Enclosure	Pottery No. sherds	Weight (g)	Bone (g)	Burnt limestone	No. of sections
53	1 (6)	12 (14)	25	2700	13
65	14 (47)	17 (228)	290	7700	34
74	48	101	10	2750	7
102	14	32	75	800	14
135	29	58	0	0	2
150	-	-	0	0	0
139	2	11	0	0	1
143	117	241	0	0	1
52	4	270	20	2000	7

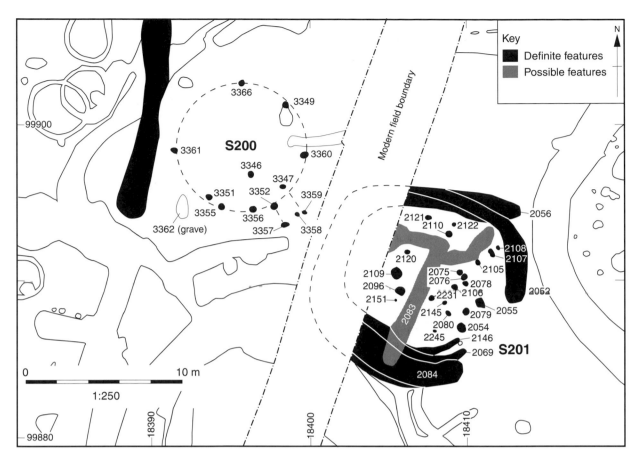

Fig. 3.6   Structures 200 and 201

3077 and E53 are cut by ditch 5006 (Fig. 3.10), demonstrating their stratigraphically equivalent location within the matrix. The dating evidence for ditch 3077 is minimal, consisting of two sherds of pottery: a sherd of Group 2 and a sherd of later, Group 4 pottery. The Group 4 sherd came from a section within pit 3096, which cut the ditch. Therefore, it is conceivable that the sherd was misassigned and was derived from the pit. Alternately, it needs to be borne in mind that the sherd dates the filling rather than the cutting of the feature, suggesting that the ditch may have survived in some form as a feature for a longer period than the Period C enclosures discussed above, but may nevertheless have been contemporary with the enclosures.

Ditch 3077 terminated to the north on the margins of the main east-west palaeochannel, and it was detected in the salvage area to the south of Trench 22. It is possible that it may have continued further to the south in the form of ditch 5000, which was only detected as a cropmark to the south of Trench 5. As no ditch of similar proportions or orientation was detected in Trench 5, it might be thought that the equation of ditch 3077 with the cropmark 5000 requires special pleading. However, given the radical alterations in orientation noted in the exposed length of ditch 3077 it is not inconceivable that the ditch's course could have been beyond the limits of Trench 5. On this basis, a potential link between these ditches has been shown on Figure

3.5. Further support for the interpretation of ditch 5000 as a Period C feature, and therefore a potential continuation of 3077, can be sought in the spatial relationship of ditch 5000 with ditch 2622 (Fig. 3.5).

To the east of E65 there was some of the best evidence for buildings from any of the late Iron Age and early Roman periods at Thornhill Farm. Structure 200 was immediately to the east of E65 (Figs 3.5 and 3.6). It had been constructed using a post-ring which had a diameter of 8.2 m. Three postholes to the south-east possibly demarcated a porch/entrance, with a width of *c* 1 m. It could not be established whether the wall of the building was on the circumference of the post-ring or the putative porch. If the latter possibility is considered, the diameter of the building would be *c* 11.4 m. The dating evidence was extremely sparse, consisting of a single sherd of Group 3 pottery. However, this, in addition to its location with respect to E65, has been taken as a tentative basis for assigning a Period C date to this structure. A grave (3362) containing an inhumation burial (3363) was located just to the south-west of S200, though could not be assigned to any particular period (Fig. 3.6).

Structure 201 (Fig. 3.6) was found immediately to the east of S200 on the western edge of Trench 9. It consisted of a multiply recut penannular gully, within which there was a comparatively dense cluster of pits and postholes. The postholes did not appear to form a coherent building pattern, but it is

33

possible that some postholes had been destroyed by the later feature 2083 which cut across the interior. The gully had a diameter of approximately 9 m, while two postholes, 2054 and 2055, may have held doorposts to a structure, demarcating an entrance *c* 1.4 m wide. The earliest phase of the ring-gully, 2056 and 2146, has been dated to Period C on the basis of the six sherds of Group 3 pottery recovered from 2056. It is not possible to phase any of the internal features in relation to the gullies given the lack of datable material from the postholes.

In the north-eastern corner of Trench 9, approximately 100 m to the east of this complex of rectilinear enclosures and structures, a segment of another large enclosure (E74) was detected, which extended beyond the trench and was visible as a cropmark (Fig. 3.5). Its subsidiary enclosure reflected that found in E53, while a ring-gully was detected as a cropmark in the eastern part of the enclosure. The ring-gully may have belonged to a roundhouse. Its diameter, *c* 8 m, would be commensurate with a roundhouse, although given the lack of investigation this identification must obviously remain speculative.

Other enclosures in the Northern Area
(E40, E46, E52, E60, E61, E80, E82, E90, E91, 3033)

To the south of the rectilinear enclosures a series of isolated enclosures were laid out on the apparently open gravel terrace. They have been ascribed to this period on the basis of the often minimal ceramic dating evidence and the enclosures' stratigraphic relationships with other dated features.

The subrectangular enclosure 52, had a single-phase boundary (3113) which contained four sherds of Group 3 pot weighing 270 g (Fig. 3.7). A cluster of postholes was found inside the boundary ditch, which may have been elements of a roundhouse (Posthole Cluster (PC) 1, Appendix A1.1). Several reconstructions are possible although three are considered as more likely on the basis of the limited evidence (Fig. 3.7). In the cases of rings PC1.1 and PC1.3 it is possible that the postulated structures may have been contemporary with E52, and the break in the enclosure's eastern side would have been commensurate with the recognised trend for south-eastern entrances to roundhouses. As posthole 3114 cut the enclosure ditch 3113, PC1.2 would have been later than the enclosure, and if the structure existed, it may not have belonged to Period C. No dating evidence was recovered from any of the postholes to assist with phasing. As regards size, all of the postulated rings would fall within the normal range for roundhouses in the Upper Thames Valley: PC1.3 has a diameter of 8.5 m, while the diameter of both PC1.1 and PC1.2 is 10 m.

In terms of discriminating between the three possibilities, the other traditional lines of enquiry are of limited assistance: fill descriptions do not radically vary and all of the features have almost vertical sides, suggesting that they would have been

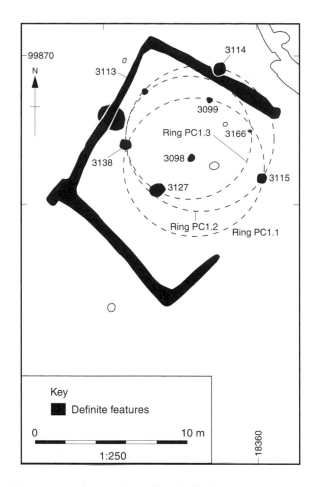

Fig. 3.7 Enclosure 52 and posthole cluster 1

suitable as postholes. However, feature 3127, an element of rings PC1.2 and PC1.3 was exceptionally deep, 0.94 m, and this would tend to suggest that it was a pit or free-standing post rather than an element of a post-ring. In addition, the unnumbered posthole located between 3138 and 3114 in PC1.2 and PC1.3 was not excavated, or numbered during the excavations, only appearing on the site plan. It is, therefore, possible that it was judged as less credible than the other features and hence was not further investigated. Regardless of the weight one gives to these various factors, the evidence is not conclusive, although it does deserve consideration. We would not like to make a definitive claim for any of these post-rings; in all cases the rings are largely incomplete, and, while the cluster is probably related to E52, the postholes could relate to a broad range of other functions.

Approximately 20 m to the east of E52 there was a long and complex sequence of ditches which centred around the later, Period D, E57 (Fig. 3.10). The stratigraphically earliest ditches in this area can be interpreted with a reasonable degree of confidence as forming a large ovoid enclosure, E80 (Fig. 3.5). Consideration of the enclosure's stratigraphic position is the principal reason for placing it within Period C, as only one sherd of pottery was recovered. This belongs to Group 5 and was therefore clearly intrusive. Due to the density of other features and the relative shallowness of E80's ditches, the form of this enclosure can only be partially reconstructed. However, from the everted north-western terminal of ditch 2147 it would seem that the enclosure may have had an entrance facing towards structure 200, while there may also have been an entrance in the south-eastern side of the enclosure. The enclosure's stratigraphic relationship with the penannular gully of structure 201 demonstrates that E80 predated the construction of that building.

Approximately 10 m to the east of E80, two enclosures E60 and E61 had apparently been laid out with respect to each other. Their placement in Period C is open to doubt as a limited number of later pot sherds were recovered (E60: 2 sherds Group 4; E61: 2 sherds Group 4 and 1 sherd Group 5). However, on balance, it would seem more appropriate to consider this pottery intrusive, given the larger quantities of Group 3 pottery (E60: 11 sherds; E61: 17 sherds) and the enclosures' early positions in the stratigraphic sequence. The recovery of a Nauheim Derivative brooch (SF3) from E61, an early type often associated with pre-conquest deposits, may be taken as corroborative evidence, although it could easily be redeposited.

E60 seemed to be associated with a cluster of postholes and pits (Appendix A1.2, PC3), although no coherent building plan can be reconstructed, and the balance of evidence makes a structural interpretation unlikely. Enclosure 61 may initially have had an entrance in its north-western corner which was closed by the later recutting of the boundary.

A number of features at the southern end of Trench 9 may have belonged to this period. However, the precise forms of the enclosures are difficult to define, and the uneven character of the evidence needs to be openly acknowledged.

The most securely dated enclosure within this area is E82, located to the south of E80, which can be disentangled from the large number of recuts which formed the later E45 (Fig. 3.11). Its southern and western boundaries can be seen clearly cutting across the interior of E45, while its northern and eastern sides are less visible. It is probable that ditch 2377 formed its eastern boundary while the northern boundary cannot be discerned from the multiple recuts of E45. The Period C date for this enclosure is relatively secure: it is stratigraphically early and its pottery assemblage is dominated by Group 3 material (64 sherds), while the single sherd of Group 4 pottery can be considered as intrusive.

To the east of E82 accurate reconstruction of the phasing is more difficult. This is in part a consequence of the intensively recut eastern boundary of E45, the limited number of sections and recovered finds, and in some cases the poor quality of the excavation record (Appendix A1.3). In essence, we can understand the activity in relation to the large rectilinear enclosure, E46, which had been subdivided at various points by smaller subenclosures

(Fig. 3.8). On balance it would seem reasonable to suppose that E46 as presented in Figure 3.8 was a Period C feature, although areas of uncertainty remain concerning the full form of all of its boundaries and indeed the status of its subenclosures (Appendix A1.3).

The eastern boundary is only known from aerial photography (Fig. 3.5). The ascription of a Period C origin is therefore dependent on its relationship with the northern and southern boundaries. The continuation of the northern boundary ditch 2288 beyond the limits of the excavation can be detected clearly in the aerial photographs, and it has been argued that this feature had a Period C phase (Fig. 3.8). On this basis, a Period C date is postulated as the eastern boundary clearly forms a right-angled corner with ditch 2288. It is open to debate whether this boundary enclosed all of the eastern side, as the cropmark could only be traced for *c* 10 m from the end of the northern ditch 2288. It is possible that different subsoil conditions affected the visibility of the ditch, which may have continued but did not form a cropmark. Alternately the eastern side may have been partially open.

The most secure element of the (Period C) E46 is the subenclosure E90 and the associated southern boundary, 2374, of the main enclosure. If the western boundary of E46 was formed from elements other than the east side of E82 and the west side of E90, it must remain a matter of conjecture, as it could not be disentangled from the very high number of recuts of the eastern side of E45 given the minimal investigation of that boundary. The phasing of the northern boundary cannot be definitive either. Dating evidence was scarce, excavation was too limited, and, in some cases, it is apparent that the archaeology was misinterpreted on site.

E91 occupied the north-western corner of E46, and its placement in this period is relatively secure, as long as it is accepted that the eastern boundary formed by ditch 2325 was a continuation of the curvilinear ditch 2319. Only a partial reconstruction can be made of this enclosure given the number of later features; in particular, the location of any entrances are unknown. Inside E91 was a group of postholes (PC2) which may have formed a structure. Phasing is uncertain, however, and it is possible that the cluster belonged to either Period C or D (Fig. 3.8; Appendix A1.3).

Standing in relative isolation midway between the linear boundary 3077 and E82 the penannular E40 was assigned to Period C on the basis of a minimal amount of Group 3 pottery (Fig. 3.5). The enclosure had a north-north-east facing entrance, the western terminal of which divided into two. A small quantity of cremated human bone came from the ditch fill. Two shallow postholes (3017 and 3026) were located around the eastern terminal but proved to be stratigraphically earlier.

To the south-west of E40 was a length of slightly curved ditch (3033) which only partially fell

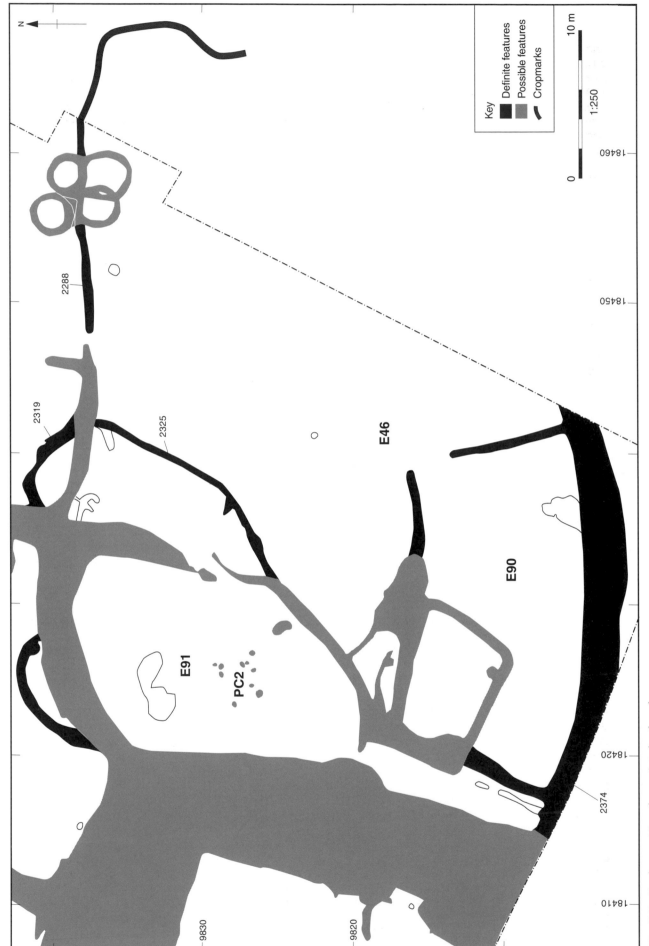

Fig. 3.8 *Enclosure 46 and associated subenclosures*

36

within the excavation area (Fig. 3.5). The ditch contained a single sherd of Group 3 pottery as well as sherds of Groups 1 and 2. Immediately to the north of the ditch was a subcircular posthole (3054) which contained a considerable quantity of Group 3 pot (30 sherds), suggesting a date contemporary with ditch 3033. Although there were other gullies and potential postholes in the area, a lack of dating evidence means they remain unphased (End Plan).

Potential Period C features – Northern Area (E70, E71, E87)

In the northern end of Trench 9, a loose enclosure group of uncertain phase was demarcated by a series of apparently discontinuous ditches (Figs 3.5 and A1.3). Phasing of the enclosures is extremely tentative due to the relatively small quantities of ceramics recovered and the lack of a clear stratigraphic sequence (Appendix A1.4). The enclosure group clearly underwent some remodelling during use, and although it originated in Period C it was still in use in Period D. The most securely dated enclosure in the group was E87. This enclosure was firmly placed in Period C on the basis of both its pottery assemblage, which was dominated by Group 3 sherds, and its stratigraphic relationship with the later, Period D double celled enclosure E72 and E73 (Fig. 3.11).

Enclosure 87 was roughly triangular in shape with a south-west facing entrance *c* 4.5 m wide (Fig. A1.3). A clay-filled circular hollow adjacent to the south-eastern terminal 2518 may have been part of an entrance structure, although there were no other postholes in the vicinity. The north-eastern boundary 2528 was discontinuous, and appears to have been replaced at a later date by ditch 2515. This ditch contained a few droplets of molten copper alloy together with a small quantity of iron slag, suggesting that at some point metalworking had taken place in the vicinity. Attached to the western arm of the enclosure was a small, subrectangular annex (2484) which appears to have been added after the main enclosure was constructed, and has tentatively been dated to Period D by the presence of Group 4 and Group 5 sherds.

An irregularly shaped area adjacent to E87 was demarcated by the curvilinear ditch 2512 to the north-west and by E87 to the south-east (Fig. A1.3). Although no northern boundary was detected, the area has nevertheless been interpreted as an enclosure (E71). Although it is possible that the enclosure was open to the north, its close proximity to the edge of excavation leaves this issue uncertain. The enclosure had a 5 m wide south-west facing entrance flanked by 2512 to the north-west and by the L-shaped ditch 2483 to the south-east. As no pottery was recovered from the enclosure, the phasing of E71 is uncertain. If it is accepted that ditch 2483 formed part of the enclosure, then the truncation of 2483 by the Period D ditch 2484 would

suggest that the enclosure was begun in Period C or earlier. Given the proximity of E87 and the similarity of ditch character, a Period C date would seem to be the most likely.

To the south-west of E71 was a second irregularly shaped enclosure (E70). The north and eastern side of the enclosure was bounded by elements of E71 while the south-eastern edge was demarcated by a series of intercutting gullies which proved impossible to securely reconstruct. It is possible that gully 2460, which forms the majority of E70's south-eastern boundary, is the same as gully 2479 which hooks around towards E71 leaving a 2 m wide north-west facing entrance (Fig. A1.3). It is uncertain if gully 2460 was begun in Period C or D. Although the ceramic assemblage is dominated by Group 3 sherds, a single sherd of Group 5 pottery could be interpreted as evidence for a later date given the large scale redeposition of pottery over the site. On balance, however, it is probably better to consider 2460 and E70 with it as belonging to Period C. As a group, enclosures 70, 71 and 87 seem to work together well. Although a degree of uncertainty must remain as to their exact chronology (Period C or D), the available evidence is such that a definitive reconstruction is not possible.

Further to the north-west, in the salvage area, enclosures E147 and E149 were noted but only very selectively excavated (Fig. 3.5). The enclosures may have belonged to Period C, but in the absence of any dating evidence this is pure speculation. E147 had a probable entrance, *c* 1 m wide, in the south-western corner. Although one of its terminals was excavated, no ceramic evidence was recovered. The interior of the enclosure was dotted with a number of possible postholes and two short lengths of gully (4008). The postholes did not appear to form any coherent structure, however, and it is unclear if they were associated with the enclosure. A number of similar features were recorded to the north. Similarly, gully 4008 contained no dating evidence, and its association with E147 must remain speculative.

To the west of E147 was a cropmark which may define a further series of rectilinear enclosures. The cropmark was not sampled through excavation, however, and in the absence of more direct evidence should merely be noted.

Southern Area

'Co-Axial' enclosure system (E4, E5, E13, E23, E110, E112, E152, E153)

Approximately 200 m to the south-west of the large enclosure complex described above, a small network of loosely gridded enclosures was uncovered in the south-eastern corner of Trench 7. They were often the earliest features in stratigraphic terms and as a result they can only be partially reconstructed due to the density of later features and the frequent recutting of a number of the ditches. Nevertheless, it is obvious that the enclosures in Trench 7 were of a

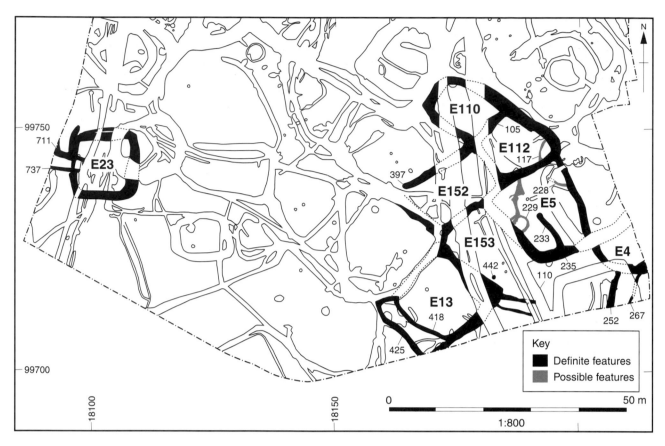

Fig. 3.9   Co-axial enclosure system – Trench 7

quite different character to those in the Northern Area. Although slightly irregular in plan they were generally similarly aligned and had a far more organised appearance (Fig. 3.9).

Before evidence relating to this enclosure system is presented in more detail, it is necessary to mention a number of features which were located underneath the enclosure system. These have been placed in this period on the basis of the minimal pottery evidence, the latest of which belongs to Group 3, and the absence of any convincing evidence of earlier occupation in this part of the site. In general, these features do not form a recognisably structured plan (Fig. 3.9), although some contexts can be given a coherent interpretation. Gully 229, which was cut by E5 (ditch 230), seems to be part of a small annular ditch. On a much more speculative level, two curvilinear gullies, 117 and 228, could be interpreted as components of a roundhouse (Appendix A1.5; Fig A1.4). Although this interpretation cannot be pressed with conviction, the possibility should be considered, given the general difficulty of detecting structures on late Iron Age and early Roman sites in the Upper Thames Valley. If this hypothesis is entertained, the building would have had a diameter of *c* 13 m. However, as evidence against this hypothesis, it should be acknowledged that the putative ring-gully is incomplete, that a west-facing entrance would be atypical for this type of building, and that the low density of

finds does not support a structural interpretation. Given the lack of apparent structure, none of the other pre-enclosure system features merits further consideration.

Although of a more readily identifiable form, the system or group of enclosures which overlay these features was similarly difficult to phase. Despite the difficulties, they have been assigned to Period C on the basis of ceramic and stratigraphic evidence (Appendix A1.6). The group consisted of a network of seven or more subrectangular enclosures (E4, E5, E13, E110, E112, E152 and E153) defined by a series of shared gullies and ditches (Fig. 3.9). The majority of the enclosures were orientated NW–SE, and, although each had a slightly different plan, they were of broadly comparable size.

Enclosure 4 (*c* 7 x 7 m) was partially obscured by the eastern edge of excavation. Although its southern corner had been largely cut away by the later E1, enough survived to suggest the possibility of an entrance at this point which may have been associated with a pair of parallel gullies (252 and 267; Appendix A1.6, 'Enclosure entrances'). To the north-west, enclosure 5 (*c* 16 x 18 m) appeared to be subdivided by the NW–SE ditch 233, which terminated near to the centre of the enclosure. None of the other enclosures within this group had such an internal division, however, and it may be that 233 belonged to an earlier phase. Although there were no obvious entrances to E5, the south-eastern corner was largely cut away by the later E2, and ditch 235 did appear to be narrowing at that point. Similarly, the north-western corner of the enclosure was destroyed by the later Roman trackway 301 (End Plan). An entrance in either corner, therefore, could have been obscured by later activity.

To the north and west of E5 (and sharing its north-western ditch), a pair of slightly smaller enclosures, E110 and E112 (both *c* 10 x 12 m), were separated by the shared NE–SW ditch 105. Neither enclosure appeared to have an entrance, although both had been heavily truncated by the Roman trackway 301 to the south-west.

Enclosure 152, to the south-west of E112, was the only enclosure in the group which had an obvious 2 m wide entrance in its north-west corner (Fig. 3.9). Although the eastern terminal (397) had escaped truncation by later activity, almost all trace of a ditch to the south-west had been cut away by E14 (Fig. 3.15). Enough survived, however, to indicate that E152 did originally have four sides. Slightly more elongated than most, E152 had a ditch in common with E5 and E153 to the south-east and E112 to the north-east.

Enclosure 153 was the only three-sided enclosure within the group. Although it shared a ditch with E152 to the north-west, E13 to the south-west and E5 to the north-east, the south-eastern end appeared to be open. It is possible that pit 442 demarcated a timber structure which closed, or partially closed off the south-eastern end of E153, but the later, Roman trackway 301 (End Plan) would have destroyed any corresponding return, and the possibility must remain speculative.

To the south-west of E153, enclosure 13 had an unusual double ditched arrangement on its south-western side (418 and 425; Fig. 3.9). It is possible that 425 was cut in order to enlarge the original enclosure. A possible entrance in its south-eastern corner appeared to be flanked by parallel gullies, creating an extended gate or 'mini droveway' (Appendix A1.6). Evidence of any ditch to the north-west had been obliterated by the later enclosure 14 (Fig. 3.15).

A sixth enclosure, E23, lay *c* 55 m to the west of the main group. Although physically separated from the others, it was of similar form, if slightly more regular, and of comparable dimensions (11 x 12 m). The enclosure had an obvious west facing entrance flanked by a pair of parallel gullies similar to those detected outside E4 and E13 (Fig. 3.9; Appendix A1.6, 'Enclosure entrances'). It was clear from stratigraphic evidence that E23 was cut by the Period F E22, and on that basis and the evidence of 23 sherds of Group 3 ceramics, E23 was placed in Period C. A single sherd of Group 5 pottery was thought be intrusive from the linear Roman boundary 302 (ditch 715), which cut through the enclosure (End Plan).

The overall impression of the enclosure group is one of organic growth rather than any deliberate planning. Perhaps starting from just one or two enclosures, existing ditches were cleaned out and re-used as new enclosures were added. Since there does not appear to have been any obvious pressure on space, the tightly focused nature of the system is perhaps best explained in terms of function. The corralling and nurture of livestock would be entirely consistent both with the relatively modest size of the enclosures and the piecemeal growth, the number of enclosures necessarily fluctuating along with the size of the herd. Such intensive management of livestock would have been particularly necessary during birthing or through the winter months.

Potential Period C features – Southern Area and Western Salvage
(E320, E321, E322, 812, 2622, 5000, 5011, 5012, 5025, 5026, 5027)

To the west of the co-axial enclosure group described above were a series of linear cropmarks and possible enclosures (Fig. 3.5). The cropmarks were tentatively ascribed to Period C on the basis of their spatial fit with other known Period C features (linear boundary 3077 and the enclosure group described above) and on their spatial coherency relative to each other. It should be noted, however, that a case can be made which would ascribe some of the cropmarks to either Period D or F.

In Trench 8, the complex boundary in the western part of the trench probably originated in Period C. The most easterly recut (812) contained fabric C24 pottery (16 sherds) which has a wide date range from the middle Iron Age through to the beginning of the 1st century AD (see Appendix 3). The ditch also cut Period A and Period B features (S209 and gully 882 respectively; Fig 3.3). Although already described as a potential Period A feature, it is equally possible that ditch 5027, to the north of Trench 8, was a continuation of 812. If this were the case then the Period A date ascribed to 5025 and 5026 would also be called into question. The levels of uncertainty in phasing linear boundaries on purely spatial evidence are clearly considerable. Nevertheless, it is suggested that 812 may also have extended to the south of Trench 8 where it was detected in Trenches 15, 16 and 17, and given the context number 2622 (Fig. 3.5 and End Plan). In Trench 15, 2622 was described as flat-bottomed, with a number of visible recuts. Its dimensions were similar to 812 (2622: *c* 1.9m wide x 0.5 m deep; 812: *c* 1.5–2 m wide and 0.5 m deep), and it would seem reasonable to surmise that 812 and 2622 were the same ditch.

At the southern end of 2622 was the linear ditch 5000 described above. Although the boundary has been ascribed very tentatively to Period C, the phasing is far from certain.

Immediately to the west of Trench 8 was a pair of linear ditches visible only as cropmarks (5011 and 5012; Fig. 3.5). The ditches were not excavated, and could be tentatively ascribed to either Period C or

Period D on the basis of their proximity to, and spatial coherency with, 812 and its later recuts.

To the south-east of 5011, a subrectangular cropmark on the line of 2622 has been interpreted as a small enclosure (E322). The linear boundary does not appear to cut across the enclosure and it is possible that the two were contemporary. No entrances were visible, but if the enclosure was contemporary with 2622, then its location apparently straddling the boundary could mean that the enclosure had access to both east and west. Approximately 100 m to the east of E322, ditch 657 appeared to be aligned on the junction of the enclosure with 2622. Although no dating evidence was recovered from the ditch, its alignment may suggest a possible association with 2622, and thus a Period C date.

To the south of E322, approximately in the centre of 2622, a further series of cropmarks have been interpreted as two subcircular enclosures (E320: 6 x 8 m and E321: 12 x 14 m) apparently set within a larger (c 50 x 30 m), subrectangular enclosure (E156; Fig. 3.5). Little can be said about the enclosures, however, as only one assessment trench was placed in the area and none of the features were excavated. The enclosures could be equally ascribed to Periods C, D or F on the basis of their possible association with 2622.

PERIOD D: EARLY ROMAN PERIOD
c **AD 50–100** (Fig. 3.10)

Summary

Period D was largely dominated by a tightly knit group of enclosures in the Northern Area (Trenches 9 and 22). The enclosures seem to have been arranged around a central enclosure (E58). To the north-west of the enclosures, a major droveway suggests that the movement of livestock may have been undertaken on a relatively large scale. The western boundary ditch recorded in Trench 8 was elaborated and recut on numerous occasions.

Northern Area

Rectilinear enclosures
(E44, E45, E41)

In the Northern Area, a pair of large rectilinear enclosures, E44 and E45, were revealed underlying the division between Trenches 9 and 22 (Fig. 3.11). The enclosures were oriented NE–SW and had been shaped by a bewildering sequence of cuts and recuts of such complexity that a full reconstruction was not possible. On the basis of ceramic evidence and the stratigraphic relationship between E45 and the earlier E82 (Period C), both enclosures were placed in Period D. The presence of Group 5 ceramics suggested that the latest ditches might have remained open into Period E.

The relationship between E44 and E45 was difficult to establish, partly because much of the crucial area was obscured by the boundary between the two trenches, and partly because of insufficient trenching in that area. It seems probable that the two were contemporary for much of their functional lives. Because of the frequent recutting of ditches, the enclosures shifted slightly so that the soil mark demarcating E45 eventually became over 8 m wide. Although recut and even shared ditches were a common feature of the Thornhill Farm enclosures, such extensive remodelling of either a single or a pair of enclosures was quite unusual. It was obvious that E44 and E45 were of a different character to other enclosures in Trenches 9 and 22. Their regularity and lack of curvilinear aspects was striking in comparison to adjacent enclosures thought to be of the same phase (Fig. 3.10: E48, E49, E51, E57 and E58).

Although the enclosures were too complex to wholly unravel, certain aspects can be reconstructed. One of the earlier recuts of E45 incorporated a carefully constructed south-east facing entrance. This consisted of two circular postholes (2379 and 2381) set immediately adjacent to opposing ditch terminals. If the postholes held timber uprights, the entrance gap could have been no wider than 1 m. In the absence of 'antennae' ditches or any other means of channelling animals into the enclosure, it seems unlikely that such a narrow entrance was used as an access for livestock. In the north-west corner of E45, a mass of intercutting features may have obscured a second entrance, but despite extensive trenching, the area was never properly understood on site and remains unresolved. Although the interior of E45 revealed no evidence of a post-built structure, the presumably easy availability of turf would make mass walled construction an economic and therefore potentially attractive option. Since mass walled structures need not leave any negative impression on a site, there is no reason why E45 could not have contained such a structure.

Although similar to E45, enclosure E44 had not been as intensively recut as E45 and was perhaps not as long-lived. Although no definite evidence of an entrance was revealed, a significant narrowing of the enclosure ditch in its south-west corner might have merited further investigation. A group of postholes and two pits were revealed immediately to the south of the enclosure's north-eastern ditch (Fig. 3.11). Ceramic evidence was lacking for the majority of features, but two of the postholes, 3065 and 3066, contained Group 3 and Group 4 pottery respectively. A third posthole, 3078, seemed to be associated, the three postholes forming a triangle in plan. The other postholes, 3082, 3083, 3084 and 3139, were smaller and could be interpreted as a fence-line, although the gap between 3083 and 3193 was over 6 m. The shallow, elongated scoop 3116, adjacent to 3139, is best interpreted as a posthole. The scoop might have been cut deliberately as a means of raising a long post or have been formed accidentally by a levering action, during the removal of a post.

As a group, the postholes do not appear to form a coherent structural plan, but given the possibility of mass walled construction on the site this cannot be precluded. The presence of the two pits, 3007 and 3141, could be interpreted as evidence for domestic activity, but neither pit contained ceramics or any other obvious domestic by-product.

The pits and postholes cannot be phased with any certainty. The conflicting ceramic evidence of postholes 3065 and 3066 might suggest that the group of features were not all of the same phase, although from a purely spatial point of view they do seem to have a certain coherency as a group. As possible internal features of a mass walled struc-

ture, the group would appear to be too close to the enclosure ditch to be of the same phase as E44.

Immediately to the south of E44 a large, multiply recut ditch was revealed in the south-east corner of Trench 22. It would appear that the ditch was the western edge of a subrectangular enclosure (E41), the majority of which lay outside of the area of excavation. The extent of the enclosure was plotted from aerial photographs, and was of comparable size to E44 and E45. No ceramic evidence was obtained from the western ditch, but the enclosure has been ascribed to Period D on the basis of its similarity to E44 and E45.

The south-eastern corner of Trench 9 was subdi-

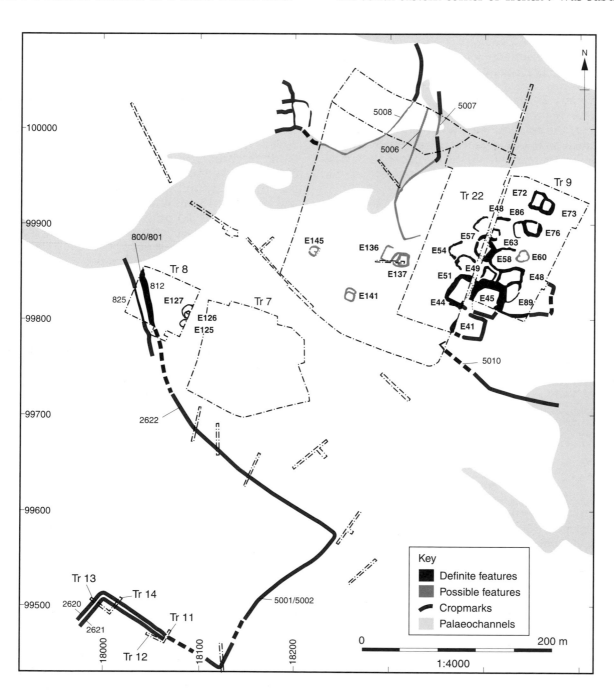

Fig. 3.10   Period D – early Roman Period, c AD 50–100

vided by a complex series of enclosures, which spanned Periods C to E (Appendix A1.3). Overlying the northern and western half of the Period C features (E46, E90 and E91; Fig. 3.8) was E89 (Figs 3.11 and A1.2). Enclosure 89 was bounded to the west by E45 and defined to the north by the hooked ditch 2320. A possible structure (PC2) might also have belonged to this period (Appendix A1.3: Fig. A1.2).

Enclosure group – Trenches 9 and 22
(E48, E49, E51, E54, E57, E58, E60, E63, E72, E73, E76, E86, E98)

Immediately to the north-east of E44 and E45 was a group of smaller enclosures loosely arranged around a central, penannular enclosure E58 (Figs 3.10 and 3.11). Although it is clear from stratigraphic relationships that not all of the enclosures (or recuts of enclosures) could have been contemporary, the group was very coherent in plan, giving the impression of an organised system.

One of the smallest enclosures (E60) has already been attributed to Period C, but the recovery of a number of later pottery sherds introduces the possibility that the later phases may have stretched into Period D.

Enclosures 72 and 73 were isolated to the northeast of the main enclosure group. In plan, the enclosures had a double celled arrangement. Although the stratigraphic relationship shows that E73 was cut or recut later than E72, the likelihood is that the two enclosures were broadly contemporary and functioned as a single unit. There were no obvious signs of an entrance to either enclosure, although the narrowing of the north-western ditch of E72 might indicate that there was a break there at some point. The ceramic assemblage was typical of many at Thornhill with a high percentage of redeposited material, particularly from Group 3. The majority of Group 3 sherds probably came from the stratigraphically earlier enclosure E87 (Fig. 3.6) into which E72 and E73 were cut. Enough Group 4 pottery was recovered to make the Period D phasing relatively secure. The double celled arrangement of the enclosures raises questions of function. The enclosures were relatively small (E72: 8 x 13 m; E73: 8 x 10 m) and may have been used as a form of temporary pen, perhaps during pregnancy or the nurture of recently born animals.

The remaining Period D enclosures were more closely arranged around E58. The subrectangular enclosures 76 and 86 appeared to form a similar double celled arrangement to that of E72 and E73 just to the north. Reconstruction of the two enclosures is problematic, however, and the phasing of E76 is uncertain. On the basis of ceramic evidence the enclosure has been placed in Period D, but its stratigraphic relationship with later features (ditch 2072; Fig. A1.5; Appendix A1.8) suggest that it may be early Period D and may even have originated in Period C. The enclosure had been intensively recut

so that the soil mark which demarcated its ditch had widened to 4 m. A break in ditch 2071, in the north-east corner of the enclosure, marked a 1.75 m wide entrance (Fig. 3.11). The western terminal was flanked internally by a group of three postholes, 2153, 2154 and 2424, and externally by two postholes, 2155 and 2156. A sixth posthole, 2160, lay at the centre of the entrance, midway between the terminals. Although none of the postholes contained any pottery, it is highly likely that the postholes were contemporary with the enclosure, and marked the location of an entrance structure.

The western arm of the enclosure was cut by a shallow gully (2095) which followed the outer edge of the enclosure before turning east and terminating part of the way along its southern boundary. It is unclear whether 2095 formed part of E76 or was a component of enclosure 86.

Enclosure 86 was more securely dated to Period D. The enclosure was clearly cut by the later Period E enclosure 62 (Fig. 3.16). In addition, its ceramic assemblage was dominated by Group 4 pottery, although two Group 5 sherds also present must be seen as intrusive. The enclosure was much slighter than E76, consisting of a single-phase ditch or gully, 2020 (possibly the same as 2095). The enclosure was subrectangular in plan with a south-east facing entrance, c 1.75 m wide between 2095 and the terminal of 2020. A group of pits (2021–2027) and a circular gully (2039) were revealed in the western half of the enclosure (Fig. 3.16). Group 4 pottery was recovered from pit 2021 but it is possible that it was redeposited, and it is not clear if the features were associated with E86 or with the later, Phase E structure 202 (E62) to west.

To the south-west of E86 was the enclosure which is perceived as being spatially central to the enclosure group. Although the precise form of E58 was impossible to reconstruct, we can say that it was penannular in plan with a north-east facing entrance. The enclosure was largely defined by ditches 2016 to the north and 2240 to the south. Although numbered separately for practical reasons during the excavation, sections through each of the ditches were of very similar profile and dimensions, and it seems reasonable to assume that the two were actually one. This would give the enclosure a width of approximately 20 m. The exact positions of the terminals remain uncertain due to heavy truncation by later features and the confusing soil marks left by earlier features.

Immediately to the south of E58 were two irregular rectangular enclosures, E48 and E49 (Fig. 3.11). Their careful layout with respect to E58 suggests that the three enclosures were contemporary and part of a working complex. Enclosure 48, which was roughly orientated north-east by south-west, lay immediately to the south-east of E58. Before excavation it appeared that E48 shared its northern ditch with E58. On further investigation, however, it became apparent that the two enclosures actually lay side by side, separated by a narrow ridge of

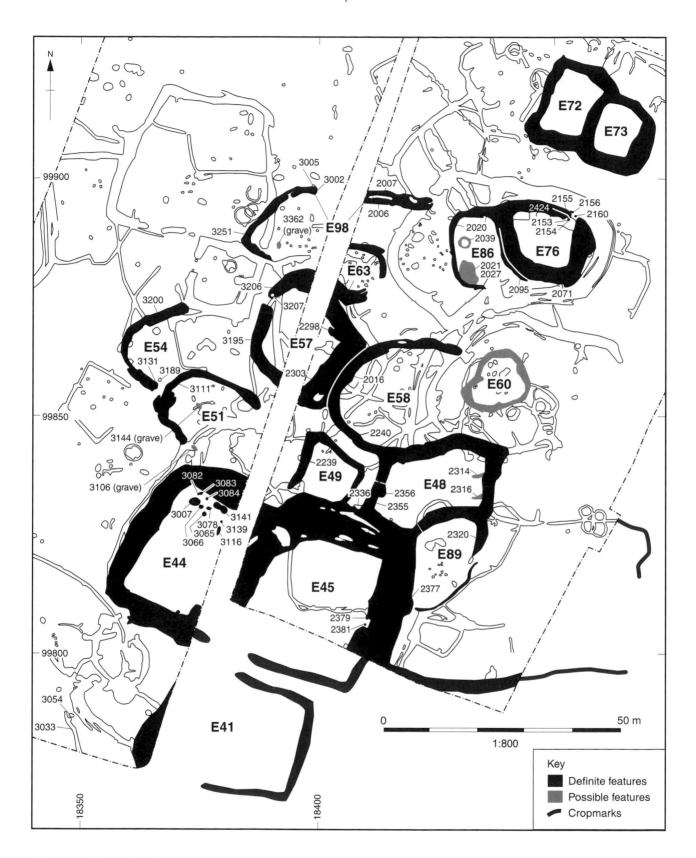

N

99900

3005
3002
2007
2006
3362
(grave)
3251
E98

E63
3206
3207
2298

3200
2303
E57
3195

E54
3131
3189
3111
E51
E58
2016
2240
3144 (grave)
3106 (grave)
2239
3082
3083
3084
3007
3141
3078
3139
3065
3116
3066
E49
2336
2356
2355
E48
2314
2316

99850

E44
E45
E89
2320
2377

E41
2379
2381

99800

3054
3033

E72
E73

2155 2156
2424
2153 2160
2154
2020
2039
E86 E76
2021
2027
2095 2071

E60

0   50 m

1:800

Key
Definite features
Possible features
Cropmarks

18350
18400

Fig. 3.11   Central enclosure group – Trenches 9 and 22

43

gravel. Ceramic evidence suggests that the two enclosures were contemporary. If that is accepted, then the decision to cut a second ditch rather than scour out and share the original (E58) ditch is difficult to explain, given the obvious extra effort required, and particularly since shared ditches were not uncommon elsewhere over the site. The simplest explanation is that the ceramic evidence is misleading and the two enclosures were not contemporary. The ditches follow each other so exactly, however, that it is difficult to believe that the original ditch was not still open when the second was cut. If this was the case then it is probable that the spoil from the second ditch was dumped on the inside edge of E48.

The question of whether the banks were internal or external is potentially crucial to understanding this area. In plan, E49 appears to have been separated from the other two enclosures (E48 and E58) by a 3 m wide gap (Fig. 3.11). This gap could have been illusory, however, if the space was occupied by upcast from the digging of the three enclosure ditches. If the banks were internal to the enclosures, however, the gap may have been used as a droveway or as access between the enclosures. Examination of the relevant sections does not provide definitive evidence either way.

Because of the multiple recutting of E45, it was not always clear of which enclosure a particular ditch or gully was part. If contemporary, the ditch terminals 2336 and 2356 would have formed an entrance *c* 3 m wide in the south-western corner of the enclosure. It is unclear whether E49 existed at this date, so that such an entrance would either have faced a relatively open area or into a narrow gap between the two enclosures. It may be significant that both the entrance and the gap between the enclosures were of approximately the same width (*c* 3 m). Whatever the case, the entrance to E48 was clearly blocked at a later date by the cutting of 2355. The narrow gullies 2314 and 2316 on the eastern side of E48 may have marked the location of a second entrance.

E49 was smaller than E48, and, although the multiple recutting of E45 once again made interpretation difficult, the enclosure appears to have been roughly rectangular in plan. It was believed by the excavators that the western ditch, 2239, terminated in the south-western corner of the enclosure, although this was not verified on site. If this was the case, then an entrance in the south-western corner would seem likely, but is unproven.

The western extent of the enclosure group was defined by two enclosures, E51 and E54 (Fig. 3.11). Enclosure 51, which was subrectangular in plan, was originally defined on three sides by ditch 3111. Although recut on its southern side, 3111 remained largely unaltered throughout the period that the enclosure was in use. The eastern side of E51 appears to have been open, although a barrier such as light wattling or a turf wall might have been archaeologically undetectable.

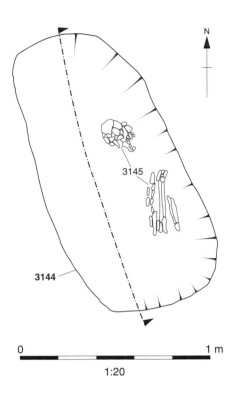

Fig. 3.12   *Grave 3144 containing child skeleton 3145*

A grave (3144) containing the poorly preserved bones of a young human male marked the centre of enclosure 51 (3145; Fig. 3.12; see below, Chapter 4). Although no datable evidence was recovered from the grave, its position, central to the enclosure, suggests that it may have been associated. Another crouched human skeleton (3106) lay within an oval grave just 10 m to the south, and may be contemporary. Based on comparable ceramic evidence and the high degree of spatial coherency displayed between E51 and E54, it is reasonable to suggest that the two enclosures were contemporary. Enclosure 54 was defined on its south-western and north-western sides by the curvilinear ditch 3200, and in the south-east by ditch 3111 (E51). Underlying ditch 3200 was a series of five slightly irregular pits (see below, 'Pits'; Fig. 3.11). The pits appeared to pre-empt the line of 3200 and could either be markers for the excavation of 3200 or an earlier, discontinuous form of enclosure. Only one pit contained any dating evidence (six sherds of Group 1 pottery from 3203), and as a group the pits could not be reliably phased. The north-eastern side of E54 appears to have been open, although as with E51, it is possible that the gap was closed by a light barrier which has left no trace.

The south-western corner of the enclosure was breached by a 1.5 m break in the ditch, which may have served as an entrance. Early silting of 3111 (E51), however, suggests the existence of an external gravel bank (Figs 3.11 and 3.13) which could have plugged the gap and completed the enclosure. Against such a suggestion, the terminal of 3200 was recut on at least two occasions, perhaps lending weight to the entrance theory. That stated, a

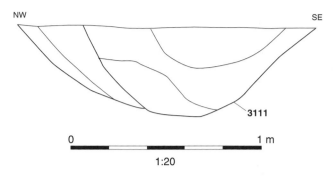

NW   SE

3111

0   1 m

1:20

*Fig. 3.13   Section 1615 showing early silting
of 3111 from the north-west*

terminal dug adjacent to a gravel bank would have needed a higher level of maintenance than other sections of the ditch. Although the matter remains unresolved, on balance, a south-west facing entrance to the enclosure does seem plausible. Postholes 3131 and 3189 may have been part of an entrance structure, but neither contained any dating evidence. It is uncertain if E52 (Period C; Fig. 3.5) was still extant at this time. If not, then the entrance to E54 would have faced an open field probably still bounded by 3077 to the south-west.

Enclosure 57 was located immediately to the west of E58 (Fig. 3.11). It exhibited the characteristic wide soil mark of a long-lived enclosure, its northern and south-eastern sides in particular having been intensively recut. Although the sequence is difficult to reconstruct, a later recut of the south-eastern ditch (2303) clearly cut the upper fills of E58 (2016), suggesting that the two enclosures may not have been exactly contemporary. On the other side of E57 the terminals 3195 and 3206 defined a north-west facing entrance, *c* 1.70 m wide. The existence of a possible gateway structure was indicated by a posthole (3207) set into the northern terminal (3206). No corresponding posthole was found in terminal 3195, however, and it may be that posthole 3207 was unrelated to the enclosure.

Ditch 2298, which appears to be one of the earliest phases of E57, terminated approximately half way along the north-eastern side of the enclosure, and could mark the position of an early entrance. It is possible that E57 was the antecedent of the square enclosure E64 to the west which, although of a later phase (Period E; Fig. 3.15), is similar in many ways. The north-eastern ditch of E57 conjoined with that of another smaller enclosure (E63), although the relationship between them could not be established. E63 was *c* 9 m internally with a 4 m wide entrance facing south-east.

To the north of E57 and E63 the north-western extent of the enclosure group was demarcated by a curvilinear boundary (E98; Fig. 3.11). Although not strictly an enclosure, in the sense that it has only one true side, for the purpose of descriptive convenience the boundary has been given an enclosure number. The boundary was divided into two sections by a gap in the centre which was presum-

ably used as an entrance. Although the exact width of the entrance is unknown (its eastern terminal was obscured by the division between Trenches 9 and 22), it must have been approximately 4–6 m wide. The boundary to the west of the entrance was discontinuous, consisting of two ditches of unequal length, laid end to end (3002 and 3251). Ditch 3251 curved away to the south-west before turning sharply to the east under the corner of the later enclosure 64 (Period E). It is uncertain precisely where 3251 terminated, although it was believed during excavation that it stopped short of 3206 (E57). Ditch 3002 formed the western terminal of the entrance to E98. Immediately adjacent to the terminal, a circular posthole, 3005, may have marked one side of a timber entrance structure. If a corresponding posthole on the other side of the entrance existed, it was obscured by the division between Trenches 9 and 22.

The boundary to the east of the entrance consisted of two parallel ditches, 2006 and 2007 (*c* 14 m in length). Their eastern limit terminated 6 m short of E86 creating a second gap or entrance to the enclosed area, assuming that the ditch and enclosure 86 were contemporary.

An inhumation grave (3362) was positioned within enclosure 98, and although undated, there are parallels with grave 3144 and E51 to the south.

Potential Period D features – Northern Salvage Area (Fig. 3.10)
(5006, 5007, 5008, E136, E137, E141, E145)

Approximately 80 m to the west of the central enclosure group described above, a smaller group of enclosures and other features were recorded under salvage conditions. Perhaps the most significant feature was a funnel shaped track or droveway, which was oriented NE–SW. The droveway consisted of two main ditches 5008 (northern) and 5006 (southern). The south-western end of the droveway splayed out onto what would have been a largely open area during this period. To the east of 5006 was a third ditch 5007. It is unclear what function 5007 would have had but its spatial coherency with 5006 suggests that they were contemporary. Ditch 5010, *c* 120 m to the south-east of 5006, is likely to have been the continuation of the droveway ditch. It had similar characteristics to 5006 and shared its alignment. In addition, both 5006 and 5010 had a small spur-like ditch that protruded towards the enclosure ditch to the east. Although of unknown significance, the two spur ditches provide a certain coherency between the enclosure group and the droveway.

The droveway as a whole has been ascribed to Period D on stratigraphic evidence. The southern ditch 5006 cut across enclosure 149 (Period A or C; Figs 3.1 and 3.5), and at its south-eastern end, boundary ditch 3077 (Period C; Fig. 3.5). The northern ditch 5008 clipped the edge of the subrectangular (Period C) enclosure 147 (Fig. 3.5). It is possible that the droveway was still open and in use during Period E. Certainly, the orientation of the droveway was still important in Period G when trackway 301 was constructed along the same line towards the north-east (Fig. 3.21). The continuity is striking, and provides the only link between the earlier periods, characterised by the mass of organic enclosures, and the new, more formalised landscape of later periods.

To the south of the droveway were a small number of relatively isolated enclosures (E136, E137, E141 and E145 (Fig. 3.10)). Analysis of the plan suggests that enclosures 136 and 137 may have been separate components of a single double-celled structure, not unlike those in the northern end of Trench 9 (E72, E73, E76 and E86). The subrectangular E136 was cut into the south-eastern corner of the (Period C) E135 (Fig. 3.5). A single section was cut through the north-western ditch but no ceramic evidence was recovered. On the basis of soil mark observations, it is suggested that an entrance might have existed in the south-western corner of the enclosure. The enclosure itself appeared to cut E135, which has been assigned to Period C on the evidence of two sherds of Group 3 pottery.

The subrectangular enclosure 137 appears to have consisted of two phases, though no sections were dug to test this inference. An obvious west facing entrance was maintained in both versions of the enclosure. Although the evidence is clearly very weak, enclosures E136 and E137 have been tentatively placed in Period D.

A smaller double celled enclosure was located 50 m to the south-west (E141). Its components consisted of a subrectangular enclosure (*c* 7 x 10 m) with an annex of approximately half the size to the north (Fig. 3.10). Although one section was excavated through the enclosure ditch no ceramics were recovered. The enclosure has been assigned to Period D entirely on the basis of its similarity to E136 and E137, and the fact that it appears in the same local group of enclosures.

Enclosure 145 was isolated, approximately 50 m to the north-west of E141 (Fig. 3.10). The enclosure was smaller than the others (*c* 6 x 7 m), with a clear, north-west facing entrance. The interior was partially divided by a short length of ditch on a NW–SE axis. The south-eastern enclosure ditch was cut by the later Roman trackway 301 (Fig. 3.21).

Southern Area

Curvilinear features and linear boundary
(E125, E126, E127, circular gully 897 and 825)

On the eastern side of Trench 8 were a series of three subcircular enclosures (E125, E126 and E127) and a circular gully (Fig. 3.14). All three of the enclosures fell partly outside the excavation area so that their precise form and dimensions are unknown. They have been tentatively ascribed to Period D on the basis of minimal pottery evidence.

Enclosure 125 was the most southerly of the three. It consisted of a U-shaped gully (877) which enclosed an area approximately 8 m in width. Although there were no apparent breaks in the ditch, it is possible that there was an east facing entrance beyond the area of excavation. No internal features contemporary with the enclosure were recorded. Immediately to the west of the enclosure, three circular postholes were arranged in a triangular pattern (888, 889 and 890). No ceramic evidence was recovered from any of the features, however, and any possible association with E125 is speculative.

Immediately to the north-east of E125 was a small, apparently subcircular feature (E126), which had been cut by E127 and the circular gully 897. Only the western ditch of E126 was visible, and, although the feature is presumed to have been subcircular (its eastern side being obscured by the edge of excavation), it is possible that it consisted of a single arc of curved gully. Although stratigraphically earlier than E127 and 897, two sherds of Group 4 pottery were recovered from E126 suggesting a Period D date. Although it is possible that the pottery was intrusive, the general character of E126 was consistent with the other Period D enclosures in this area.

Enclosure 127 was the largest (*c* 16 m wide) and most regular of the subcircular features revealed. The western ditch (899) was extremely regular in

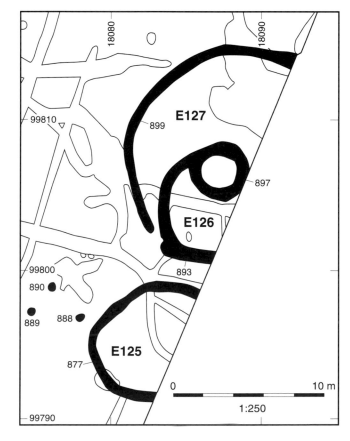

Fig. 3.14   Enclosures 125, 126 and 127 – Trench 8

terms of width and depth but also in the near perfect arc it defined. Its south-western extent terminated 4 m from the edge of excavation, probably defining an entrance. It is uncertain if gully 893 (to the south-east of 899) was a part of E127 or an unassociated feature. Two sherds of Group 2 pottery were recovered from the gully, but its stratigraphic position relative to E126 proves that the pottery must have been redeposited. The gully was wider than 899, and its execution somewhat cruder, raising the possibility that it was a later recut of the terminal. If contemporary with 899, the entrance gap would have been *c* 1 m wide.

The circular gully 897 contained a mixed ceramic assemblage, the latest pottery being a single sherd of Group 4 material. The feature's position within E127 hints that the two may have been contemporary, but the association remains uncertain.

The linear boundary ditch that was revealed in the western half of Trench 8 (812; Period C) appears to have been much elaborated in this period (Fig. 3.10). It consisted of a complex series of linear gullies. Within Trench 8, the resulting soilmark was fourteen metres wide. The majority of the gullies were relatively shallow (0.04–0.30 m), however, so that only the deepest (probably 812) showed as a cropmark to the south-east. The number of times that the boundary was recut suggests that it was quite long-lived. The easternmost ditch, 812, seems to have been one of the earliest cuts (see above, 'Period C'). Although very little ceramic evidence was recovered from any of the gullies, the westernmost gully (825) contained five sherds of Group 4 pottery, suggesting that the boundary was still in use within Period D. Although the precise sequence of gullies and ditches could not be reconstructed, it is possible that the general chronological trend may have been from east to west. From three of the cuts lying in the middle of this sequence (800, 801/A, 801B) was recovered a small amount of cremated human bone (Fig. 3.10). Two of these deposits (801/A, 801/B) were associated with quantities of G4 pottery, suggesting that they belonged to period D (mid–later 1st century AD).

Potential Period D features – Southern Area
(2620/2621, 2622 and 5001/5002)

Although described above as the probable continuation of the Period C ditch 812, it is possible, although perhaps less likely, that linear ditch 2622 (Fig. 3.5) may have been the continuation of one of the later boundary ditches such as 825. At the southern extent of 2622 was a second linear boundary 5001/5002, which could equally have been ascribed to Periods D or F. For the most part, the ditch was only visible as a cropmark, although it was traced but not excavated in Trench 13 (ditch 6) of the Kempsford, Bowmoor evaluation (OAU 1989, 3). At its north-eastern end the ditch appeared to split into two but the relationship was not investigated in the field.

Approximately 250 m to the south-west of Trench 8 was a large double ditched feature (2620 and 2621) which appeared as an L-shaped cropmark on aerial photographs (Fig. 3.10). Only the north-eastern corner of the feature was visible on the photographs, and it remains uncertain if the cropmark was a trackway similar to 301 and 5036, or one corner of a large, subrectangular enclosure. In order to further investigate the nature of the cropmark, and to recover dating evidence, two L-shaped assessment trenches were excavated across the ditches (Trenches 11/12 and 13/14). Despite careful excavation, only one sherd of Group 4 pottery was recovered from ditch 2620. On the basis of that very minimal ceramic evidence, the feature has been tentatively ascribed to Period D. A similar double-ditched enclosure was located during an evaluation at Stubbs Farm, Kempsford, which proved to be of 2nd century AD date (OAU 1993, fig. 3, plate 1).

PERIOD E: EARLY ROMAN PERIOD
c AD 75–120 (Fig. 3.15)

Summary

Period E was characterised by two separate groups of enclosures centred within Trench 7 and Trenches 9 and 22. The apparent two-fold concentration of northern and southern enclosures may have been more apparent than real, however, as the positioning of open area trenches inevitably distorts the true picture. The southern enclosures (Trench 7), were broadly oriented NW–SE, with the large subrectangular enclosure 26 perhaps providing the central point of the group. The northern group of enclosures (Trenches 9 and 22) was dominated by the large double celled enclosure E62/E75. A number of smaller subrectangular enclosures quite different in character to E62/E75 were also recorded.

Northern Area

Enclosures – Trenches 9 and 22
(E50, E62, E64, E75, E77, E81)

In Period E, the Northern Area was dominated by a large pair of enclosures, E62 and E75 (Fig. 3.16). Both enclosures had been intensively recut, so that the original relationship between the two had been obliterated. It is likely, however, given their spatial cohesion and similar ceramic assemblages, that the enclosures were originally contemporary. Site records indicate that at least one of the recuts of E75 cut the fills of E62, but the overall sequence was complex and not fully understood. It is difficult to say, therefore, if the shifting pattern of recuts reflects significant changes in the relative importance of the two enclosures or simply a response to localised conditions. The double-celled arrangement of the enclosures is reflected in the earlier (Period D) pairs of enclosures E72/73 and E76/E86 (Fig. 3.11).

In the north-west corner of E62, an entrance, *c* 1–2 m wide, was defined by multiply recut ditch

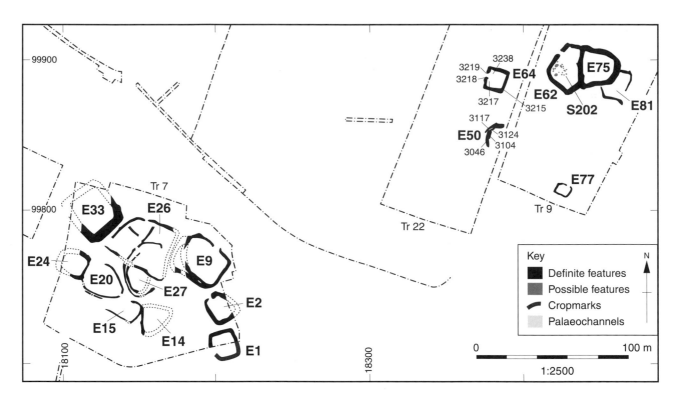

Fig. 3.15 Period E – early Roman Period, c AD 75–120

terminals, 2082 (north) and 2090 (south). To the south of the entrance, in the western corner of E62, was a discrete group of postholes and pits (structure 202; Fig. 3.16). Although immediately to the north-east of structures 200 and 201 (Period C; Figs 3.5 and 3.6), the structure was divided from them by the western edge of E62. Although a coherent circular structure could not be reconstructed, the posthole group had a sufficient degree of symmetry to suggest that some form of structure was present. The triangle formed by postholes 2218, 2219 and 2247, appears to be mirrored by postholes 2223, 2249 and 2250. Whilst this arrangement could be purely coincidental, it might also be interpreted as a symmetrical framework for an entranceway between 2223 and 2247. It is possible that the walls of such a structure were constructed using turf or stakes, neither of which would necessarily have left any trace in the gravel. The group of postholes to the west might have been part of a NE–SW fence-line although they were of widely differing dimensions. Pits 2257 and 2195 may have been inside 202 but could equally have marked the extent of the structure's walls. The structure has been placed in Period E on the basis of its spatial relationship with E62, but it is acknowledged that an equally strong case can be made for a Period C date (Appendix A1.7).

The group of pits to the south-east of 202 (2021–2027 and 2049; Fig. 3.16) is of uncertain phase. Although the ceramic assemblage was no later than Group 4 (Period D), it is possible that the pottery was redeposited allowing for a Period E date and association with structure 202. The circular gully to

the north of the pit group (2039) contained no ceramics and is similarly unphased (Fig. 3.16).

Enclosure 75 was more complex than E62 in that it had been more intensively recut (Fig. 3.16). It was roughly rectangular in plan, although its eastern end was curved. A 1.30 m wide entrance in its north-eastern corner was flanked by terminals 2142 and 2148. Immediately outside the entrance was a group of five undated postholes which may have demarcated an entrance structure (2185–2189). No entrance was visible between E62 and E75. Both E62 and E75 were dated to Period E mainly on the basis of stratigraphic relationships with the earlier enclosures E76 and E86 and with ditch 2072 (Appendix A1.8).

Immediately to the south-east of E75 was the subrectangular enclosure E81 (Fig. 3.16). The northern ditch 2118 apparently cut an early phase of E75 (2141) but could not be traced across the later ditch 2142. This would suggest that E81 was contemporary with the recut of E75 (2142) and was probably used as an annex to the main enclosure. An east facing entrance, c 6 m wide, was clearly visible in the south-eastern corner of the enclosure, suggesting that a portion of E61 (perhaps 2235) had been recut to form the southern edge of E81. Later still, the short ditch 2237 was excavated, although for what purpose is unclear.

Enclosure E64 was located approximately 25 m to the south-west of E62 (Fig. 3.15; Plate 3.1). The enclosure was subrectangular in shape, c 11 x 12 m, with a very clearly defined ditch (3215). The western and southern sides of the enclosure were of a single phase, clearly cutting through the earlier,

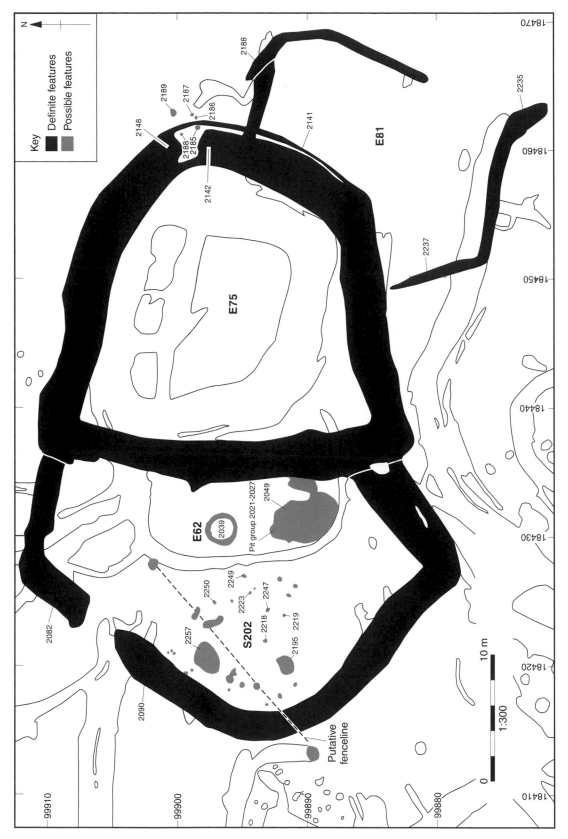

Fig. 3.16 Structure 202 within double celled enclosure E62/75

Plate 3.1 Subrectangular enclosure 64 in Trench 22

Period D E54 (Fig. 3.11). The northern and eastern sides of the enclosure recut the earlier ditches 3235 and 3348 which may have been associated with E65 (Period C; Fig. 3.5). A very clearly defined entrance consisting of two circular postholes (3218 and 3219) adjacent to the opposing ditch terminals, was located close to the centre of the western enclosure ditch. The gap between the postholes was approximately 2 m wide. Two further postholes or small pits were located inside the enclosure, close to the entrance (3217 and 3238). Neither feature contained dating evidence, however, and it is uncertain if they were contemporary with the enclosure. Other features internal to E64 were thought to be earlier in date or were unphased (End Plan).

The ceramic assemblage within the main enclosure ditch of E64 consisted of a mixture of redeposited material which characterised many of the deposits analysed at Thornhill Farm. The majority of the pottery was of Group 2 origin (51 sherds) with Group 3 also being well represented (38 sherds). Three sherds were of Group 4 origin and one of Group 5. The enclosure was placed within Period E partly on the basis of the ceramic evidence, but mainly on stratigraphic grounds. The enclosure ditch 3215 cut every feature it crossed, including the Period D enclosure E54. Furthermore, the enclosure was located immediately in front of the Period D enclosure E57 (Fig. 3.11), further adding to the likelihood of a Period E date.

Approximately 20 m to the south of E64, multiply recut sections of curved gullies constituted E50 (Fig. 3.15). It is uncertain whether the gullies that constituted E50 formed a discrete enclosure or if they were a later addition to the Period D E51 to the west (Fig. 3.11). Although it was not possible to reconstruct the precise stratigraphic sequence which formed the enclosure, the western and southern extent of E50 was largely defined by two relatively shallow ditches, 3117 and 3124. It was unclear if 3117 and 3124 were contemporary or if one was dug to replace the other. Since they never crossed, and ran roughly parallel to each other, it is perhaps more likely that they were contemporary.

At its southern end, 3124 seems to have been replaced by 3046, although no stratigraphic relationship was established. Gully 3046 curved southward and clearly cut the upper fills of Period D E44, providing the main evidence for the Period E date of E50. Immediately adjacent to 3046 to the east was a short length of gully, 3104. Although 3104 contained only a single sherd of (Group 2) pottery, its close association with 3046 suggests that it was broadly contemporary.

The northern ends of 3117 and 3124 were lost in a large soil mark which was never properly understood despite extensive trenching. No obvious eastern side to E50 existed although it is possible that E49 (Period D; Fig. 3.11) survived long enough to provide a suitable barrier. Similarly, there was no obvious northern end to the enclosure, and it may be that that side remained open.

To the east of 3124 were a number of unphased pits and postholes which may have been associated with E50, but the only pottery recovered was six sherds of Group 3 pottery from posthole or pit 3173, perhaps suggesting a Period C date for at least some of the features (End Plan).

Enclosure 77 was located in the south-east corner of Trench 9 (Figs 3.15 and A1.2). The enclosure was subrectangular in form with a probable entrance in its north-eastern corner, between terminals 2376 and 2383. The eastern side of the enclosure (2383) seemed to cut the Period C ditch 2354, although the excavation records were unclear on this point. The western extent of 2383 was apparently cut by the north-south ditch 2382, although again the site records are vague and uncertain. No relationship was recorded between the northern arm of the enclosure and ditch 2334. The enclosure has been tentatively assigned to Period E largely on the basis of the minimal ceramic evidence which consisted of a mixture of Groups 1–3, two sherds of Group 4 material and a single sherd of Group 5.

Rectilinear enclosure group – Trench 7
(E1, E2, E9, E14, E15, E20, E24, E26, E27 and E33)

Covering most of the area of Trench 7 was a group of loosely co-axial, rectilinear enclosures (Fig. 3.17). Although parts of the enclosure group continued into Period F, the majority of the enclosures had their origins in Period E. The group was dominated by two large rectilinear enclosures, 9 and 26, behind which were located a number of smaller enclosures.

Enclosure 1 was located in the south-eastern corner of Trench 7. Although only half of the enclosure fell within the excavated area, aerial photographs are sufficiently clear to show that the enclosure was subrectangular in plan. Site records show that the enclosure ditch (250) had been recut once. As there was no sign of a break in the enclosure ditch, any entrance must have fallen outside of the excavated area to the south.

The enclosure clearly cut the earlier (Period C) E4 and its associated gullies 252 and 267 (Fig. 3.9). The ceramic assemblage contained seven sherds of Group 1 pottery as well as seven sherds of Group 3 and five sherds of Group 4. Although E1 could have had its origins in Period D, it was thought more likely that it belonged to the enclosure group outlined below rather than standing in complete isolation as it would have done in Period D.

A few metres to the north of E1 was a second subrectangular enclosure of similar form and dimensions (E2; Fig. 3.17). The northern end of this enclosure was slightly narrower than the southern end, and was breached by a complex entrance which was not fully understood (Appendix A1.9). The southern end of the enclosure cut through the earlier (Period C) enclosures 4 and 5 (Fig. 3.9). The main enclosure ditch 235, seems to have been recut

on at least one occasion. Most of its eastern extent lay outside the excavation area apart from a small portion at the north-eastern corner of the enclosure. A mandible from a human female was recovered from this ditch, while a pit (320) just to the north contained the cremated remains of another human (Fig. 3.17). This could not be phased either stratigraphically or ceramically.

A substantially larger subrectangular enclosure, E9, lay *c* 4 m to the north-west of E2. Enclosure 9 had two major phases. Its south-western boundary was demarcated by two separate ditches (113 and 116), both of which had been recut on at least one occasion. It was not established stratigraphically which of the ditches was the earlier, and both ditches contained pottery of a similar date. At its north-western end, ditch 116 curved markedly, while ditch 113 continued on a straight line until it reached the edge of E26. Here the ditch was cut by the Roman trackway 301 (End Plan) so that a relationship with E26 was never established. The north-eastern enclosure ditch (101) was breached just to the south-east of its centre by an entrance. Although the south-eastern terminal was clearly defined, the north-western terminal was lost in a soil mark making the width of the entrance difficult to determine precisely. It must, however, have been *c* 2 m wide.

Gullies 100 and 104, which protruded from the south-western corner of E9, may have defined the site of a roundhouse or other structure (Fig. 3.17). If so, no trace of any structure survived, apart from a pair of postholes, 277 and 278. A number of other postholes (261–266, 268 and 269) and a pit (194) were revealed in the north-western corner of the enclosure. None of the postholes contained any dating evidence, and their association with E9 is uncertain. Three of the postholes (261, 262 and 263) formed a tight triangle, an arrangement reminiscent of postholes 3065, 3066 and 3078 located within E44 (Fig. 3.11). Although the remaining postholes did not form a coherent structural plan, the timber uprights might have been supplemented by turf walls, and a structural interpretation cannot be ruled out. In the north-eastern corner of the enclosure, *c* 6 m from the entrance, was a pair of irregular pits, 176 and 188. Although phasing was uncertain, pit 176 contained three sherds of Group 4 pottery, and on that basis, both pits were tentatively ascribed to Period D. A possible four-post structure in the south-west corner of the enclosure (153, 154, 157 and 285) was thought to be of a later phase (Period F) and to be related to E6 (Fig. 3.19).

Approximately 30 m to the south-west of E9, a roughly triangular enclosure, E14, had been badly truncated by the Period F enclosure 154 (Figs 3.17 and 3.19). The northern and south-eastern sides of E14 had been almost totally cut away during the construction of the new enclosure so that only its western ditch, 462/490, had survived. Of a group of pits and postholes in the south-eastern corner of E14 only pit 485, and a single posthole, 484, contained

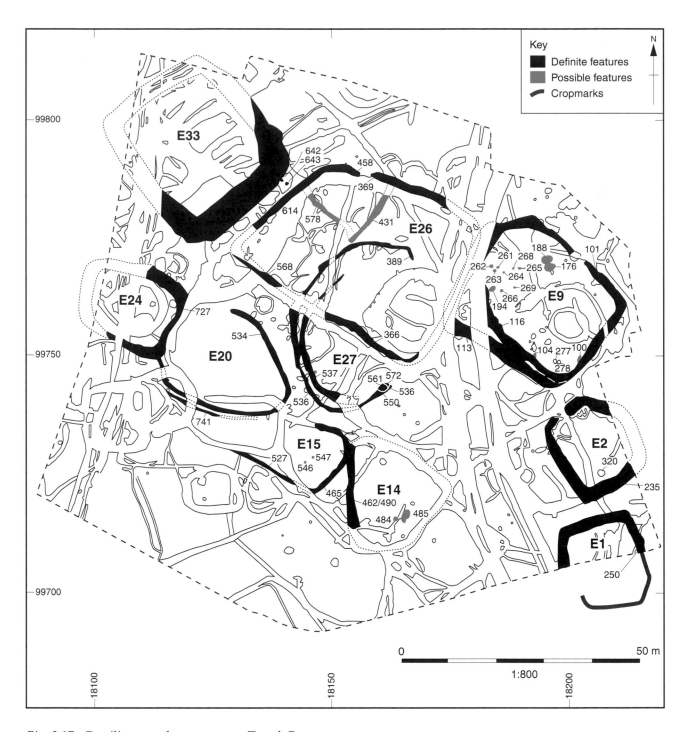

Fig. 3.17   Rectilinear enclosure group – Trench 7

evidence of a possible Period E date (Appendix A1.10; Fig A1.7).

Immediately to the north-west of E14 was a subrectangular enclosure, E15 (Fig. 3.17). The main component of E15 was the enclosure ditch 465 which defined the whole of its south-eastern side and part of its north-eastern side. Half way along the north-eastern boundary the ditch terminated, leaving a 7 m gap between the terminal and E20 to the north-west, which may have been used as an entrance. Enclosure 15's south-western boundary

was demarcated by a linear ditch 527. At its north-western end the ditch was cut by the later, Period F enclosure 16 (Fig. 3.19). A pair of postholes, 546 and 547, were revealed near the centre of the enclosure. The postholes were 1.5 m apart, and contained pottery which was contemporary with E15. No other pits or postholes were found within E15, suggesting that the pair of postholes did not form part of a larger structure. One possible interpretation is that they supported a fodder rack. Their central location within E15 might suggest they were contemporary with the enclosure, but definitive evidence is lacking.

Enclosure 15 was ascribed to Period E because of its stratigraphic relationship with the later, Period F enclosures E154 and E16 (Fig. 3.19), and because of its ceramic assemblage, which contained 36 sherds of Group 5 pottery. It also formed a very coherent spatial group with the contemporary enclosures E20 and E27 (Fig. 3.17).

Enclosure 20 was located 7 m to the north-west of E15. It was U-shaped in plan, with a wide north-west facing entrance. The enclosure was defined by ditch 534 (534=545=744=746), which, although recut once, did not exhibit the high degree of reworking found in many of the other enclosure ditches. The western end of the enclosure was defined by the ditch of E24. Approximately 1 m outside the southern enclosure ditch was a shallow gully, 741. This gully was clearly related to the main ditch, closely following its curved outline for a distance of almost 20 m. It is possible that the gully had originally been longer, but machine truncation caused it to fade out to the east, and its western end was lost in the ditches of the Period F enclosure 22 (Fig. 3.19). The interior of E20 was unusually blank, with no recorded features.

No ceramics were recovered from E20, and its phasing is uncertain. The enclosure was cut to the south by the Period F enclosures E22 and E16 (Fig. 3.19), and to the west by Period E enclosure E24 (Fig. 3.17). The latter relationship is likely to reflect nothing more than a late recut of E24. Nevertheless, it remains possible that E20 was earlier than Period E, although it cannot be any later. Its spatial coherency with surrounding Period E enclosures, however, strongly suggests a contemporary, Period E date.

Enclosure 24 was a subrectangular enclosure to the west of E20. The western enclosure ditch was extremely complex, particularly in the north-west corner, where despite extensive trenching no clear understanding of the area was obtained. The south-western corner of the enclosure lay outside the excavation area and so added nothing to the level of understanding. The eastern half of the enclosure was defined by ditch 727, which was partly cut away in its south-eastern corner by unphased, later activity. The interior of the enclosure had largely been destroyed by the Period F enclosure 155 (Fig. 3.19) and by the later, Period H boundary 302 (Fig. 3.23; Plate 3.3). No entrances were apparent, although the complex nature of parts of the enclosure meant that an entrance might easily have been missed by the excavators or destroyed by later activity.

Enclosure 27, to the east of E24, was a C-shaped, double-ditched enclosure with an open eastern side (Fig. 3.17). The enclosure consisted of an outer ditch (536=574=389) and an inner ditch or gully (537=607=577). The outer ditch was the more extensive, ending in terminals 389 (north) and 536 (south), separated by a gap of 29 m. The eastern side

of the enclosure appeared to be entirely open, although it is possible that a light fence or turf wall might have existed. The southern terminal was intensively recut by a series of small pits or postholes (550, 561 and 572) which may have acted as the terminal point of such a structure.

The inner ditch followed a similar course to the outer, although the two were not exactly parallel. The inner ditch was shorter, terminating 9 and 15 m from the outer southern and northern terminals respectively. Both ditches of the enclosure were cut through by E26 (Period E; Fig. 3.17) and E29 (Period F; Fig. 3.19). The ceramic evidence suggests that E27 began to silt up in Period E. Given its stratigraphic relationship with E26, an early Period E date seems more likely. No contemporary features were revealed within the interior of the enclosure.

Enclosure 26 was a large, subrectangular enclosure, which, although of the same Period, directly overlay E27. The enclosure was complex and of several phases (Periods E and F). For the sake of descriptive ease, it has been separated into three major components: E26 (Period E), E29 and E30 (see below, 'Period F'). Although the stratigraphic sequence was very poorly understood (Appendix A1.11), E26 seems to have been the most extensive phase, defining an area approximately 30 x 40 m (Fig. 3.17). A ditched entrance, *c* 4 m wide was cut into the north-western corner of the enclosure, allowing access to what was presumably open grassland. The entrance was clearly defined by terminal 458 to the west and less certainly by 369 to the east (Appendix A1.11).

From its western terminal the enclosure turned towards the south-west and ran parallel to E33 as ditch 614. It is unclear what happened to 614 at the south-western corner of the enclosure, but presumably it turned towards the south-east, becoming 568 and eventually 366. Defining the eastern enclosure ditch was also problematic. This was largely due to the fact that much of it had been cut away by E30 and the later Roman trackway 301 (Fig. 3.19 and End Plan). It would seem that ditch 366 was cut away by E29 (Fig. 3.19) at its eastern extent, emerging only in the north-east corner of the enclosure where it turned to the north-west before terminating at the entrance as 369.

To the south of the enclosure entrance was an L-shaped ditch 431/578. Although the ceramic and stratigraphic evidence both point to a Period E date for the ditch, the fact that much of it was cut away by E29 makes it uncertain if the ditch was precisely contemporary with E26. If contemporary, the ditch may have formed a holding area, or controlled access to the enclosure.

Immediately to the north-west of E26 was the final enclosure in the group. Enclosure 33 was an extremely complex feature which had been recut on at least four occasions, resulting in a soilmark *c* 6 m wide (Fig. 3.17). The enclosure was subrectangular, but its full extent was difficult to define precisely. The western half of the enclosure had been severely truncated by later gullies and ditches and was never properly understood (Appendix A1.12). The intensively recut nature of the enclosure, together with its size and shape, is very reminiscent of the Period D enclosures E44 and E45 (Fig. 3.11). Enclosure 33 and E26 appear to have been contemporary with each other. The enclosures were parallel, creating a narrow corridor or trackway between the two, *c* 2 m wide. At the northern end of the trackway two oval shaped postholes were revealed (642 and 643), suggesting that access was controlled by a gate. The southern end of the trackway led to an open area in front of the entrance to E20.

Although little can be said about the mass of gullies which obscured a large part of E33, it is clear that both those gullies and E33 itself were cut through by the later Roman boundary 302 (End Plan). The ceramic assemblage, and E33's close spatial relationship with the other enclosures of the group (E26 and E24 in particular), was consistent with a Period E date.

PERIOD F: EARLY ROMAN PERIOD
c AD 75–120 (Fig. 3.18)

Summary

This period was characterised by small clusters of enclosures loosely arranged around the large subrectangular E29 in Trench 7. The enclosures within individual clusters shared similar characteristics and may have served particular functions as groups.

Southern Area

Enclosure group – Trench 7
(E11, E16, E17, E22, E29, E30, E35, E36, E37, E104, E105, E113, E154, E155 and circular gully 630)

The most isolated enclosure, E11, consisted of a recut penannular ditch located to the north-east of E29 (Fig. 3.19). The enclosure only partially lay within the excavated area so that its north-eastern half was obscured by the edge of excavation. The original penannular ditch 220/173 had a west facing entrance *c* 1.25 m wide. At a later date both ditch and entrance were recut, the entrance gap narrowing to 0.50 m. Enclosure 11 was significantly different from the other small enclosures in the vicinity. It was quite regular, had a very obvious entrance, and both the original enclosure ditch and its recut contained significant amounts of burnt limestone and animal bone (Table 3.9).

The diameter of the enclosure was approximately 7 m, which is commensurate with the possibility that E11 was a house enclosure. A similar penannular gully, though of slightly larger diameter, surrounded the post-built structure 201 in Trench 9 (Fig. 3.6). Although no features were found within E11 that might indicate the presence of a roundhouse, construction using a massed wall technique such as turf would not necessarily leave any trace.

Table 3.9   E11 bone and stone weight

Phase	Context	Total bone weight (g)	Total stone weight (g)
A	173	30	7504
A	193	250	8400
A	220	615	8736
B	192	305	11872
B	221	1575	10556

Enclosure 29 was essentially a second phase of the original E26 (Figs 3.17 and 3.19). The enclosure was subrectangular with an entrance in its north-western corner, and an irregularly shaped western annex. Located in its south-eastern corner was a smaller subrectangular enclosure (E30, below). The southern enclosure ditch (346) was approximately half the length of the original ditch of E26. The entrance to E29 was maintained in the same position as it had been for E26 (*c* 3–4 m wide). Its eastern side was defined by the terminal of 334. It is unclear if the western ditch of the main enclosure (454) also terminated at this point (thus allowing access to the western annex), or if it turned to the west and continued as 459 and 601. The annex was roughly wedge shaped, widening gradually towards the south. The southern end appears to have been open, framed between the terminal of 601 to the west and 454 to the east, although all of the previously mentioned difficulties in recognising light or mobile barriers apply once again. Just to the west of 459 lay the vertical-sided circular gully 630, which probably belonged to this phase (Fig. 3.19).

Enclosure 30 (Fig. 3.19) was thought to be of the same phase as E29 (although see Appendix A1.11). Although insufficient sections were cut to obtain a definitive reconstruction, the original enclosure ditch (323) appears to have been recut once (322). All internal features proved to be earlier than the enclosure. A layer of churned up ditch fill (311) on the eastern side of E30 has been interpreted as animal trample (Fig. 3.19). The animal trample contained nine sherds of Group 5 pottery, but must post-date the filling of E30's ditches

Enclosure 30 was unusual in that the outer lip of its western ditch (322) was marked by a series of shallow postholes (352–361; Fig. 3.19). The postholes were evenly spaced in some places and uneven in others, raising the possibility that some may have been missed during excavation. The postholes seem to have been limited to the western ditch only, although any corresponding eastern series would have been cut away by the later Roman trackway 301 (End Plan). It is uncertain if the postholes were associated with the original enclosure ditch (323) or with its recut (322; Appendix A1.11).

The function of the postholes is open to interpretation. One possibility is that they were part of a structure designed to prevent the slippage of an (assumed) gravel bank to the west of E30. If this was

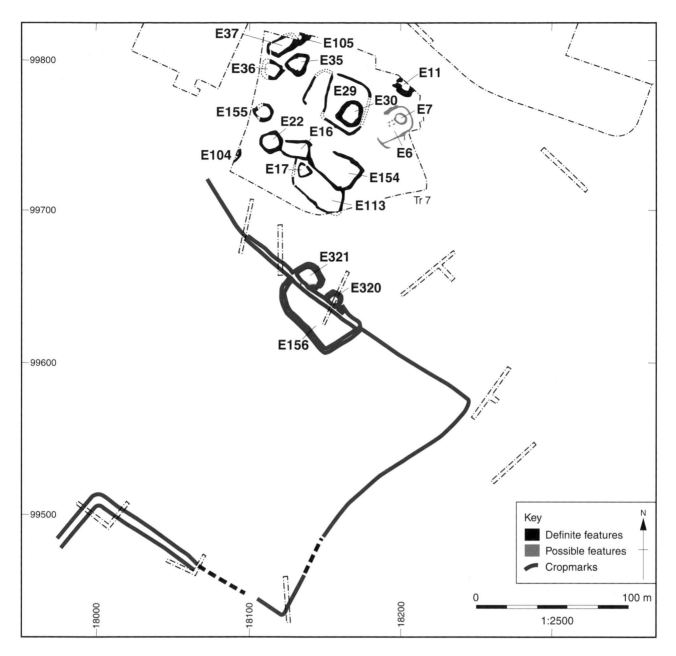

Fig. 3.18   Period F – early Roman Period, c AD 75–120

the case, however, the structure was the only recorded example at Thornhill Farm. The location of the postholes on the western edge of the enclosure suggests a specific relationship with E29, and a perhaps more likely interpretation is that they supported a light fence or screen, perhaps made from wattle panels. The function of such panelling seems to have been to separate or screen the contents of E30 from E29 or *vice versa*. Segregation of livestock would have been desirable during pregnancy or birthing and perhaps to prevent mature calves from reaching their mothers' milk (Lucas 1989). In the latter case it may have been necessary not only to physically separate the calves from their mothers, but also to remove them from their sight in order to prevent distress.

To the south of E30 were three subrectangular enclosures of a more elongated form (E154, E16 and E113; Fig. 3.19). Enclosure 154 directly overlay the Period E enclosure 14 (Fig. 3.17). Its northern and eastern ditches were largely recuts of the earlier enclosure, which presumably must have been still visible when the new enclosure was cut. Enclosure 154 was essentially three-sided, with a broad entrance in the north-western corner (c 15 m wide) defined by terminal 477 to the east and E16 to the west. The centre of the enclosure was traversed by a pair of unphased NE–SW ditches whose relationship with E154 was never understood (End Plan).

Although smaller than E154, enclosure 16 to the west shared many characteristics of the larger enclo-

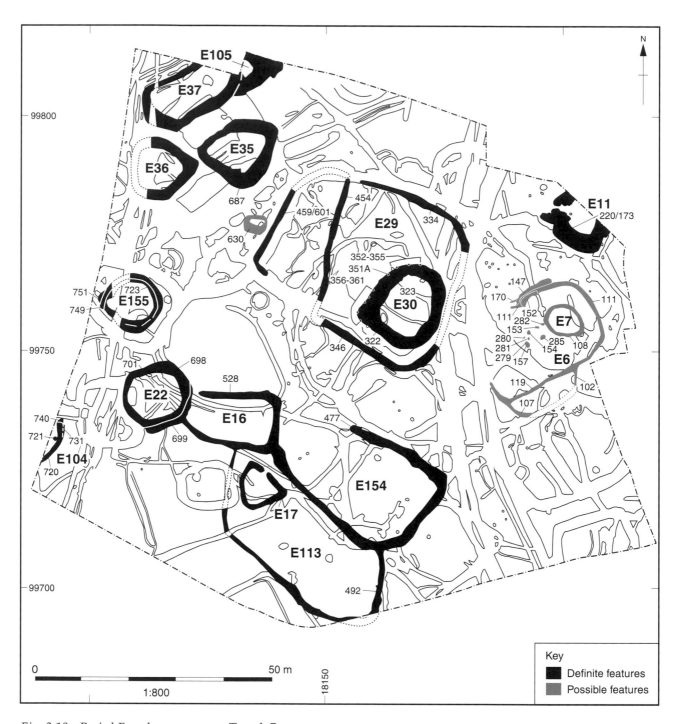

Fig. 3.19   Period F enclosure group – Trench 7

sure. It was elongated in form, on broadly the same axis as E154 and also had an entrance in its north-west corner (*c* 1.10 m wide). The enclosure ditch (528) was of a single phase along its northern and southern length. Its eastern ditch was more complex, however, presumably because it contained an element of E154. No clear stratigraphic relationship was recorded between the two enclosures, and they are presumed to be broadly contemporary. If an access between E154 and E16 ever existed, no evidence of it was found. Neither enclosure had any internal features that were visible in the gravel.

To the south of E154 and E16 was a third elongated enclosure, E113 (Fig. 3.19). The northern extent of the enclosure was defined by components of both E154 and E16. Its south-eastern extent lay partially outside the excavation area, but enough was visible to define its form, which was essentially a parallelogram. The eastern side of the enclosure was defined by ditch 492. Located within the north-western corner of E113 was a small enclosure of roughly triangular shape, E17. The enclosure was well defined, and deeply cut with a narrow (1 m wide), north-east facing entrance. No internal features were identified. Although it is possible that the enclosure contained a modest structure, its relatively small dimensions (*c* 7 m x 7 m) make it unlikely that it ever contained a roundhouse. It has been placed in Period F partly because it was stratigraphically late, but mainly because of its spatial fit within E113.

This same spatial coherency that E113 shared with E154 and E16 strongly suggests that the enclosures were contemporary. Their broadly similar elongated form also points toward a shared function.

To the north and west of this group, a series of enclosures were revealed whose characteristics were quite different (Fig. 3.19). The intensive, intercutting nature of the archaeology and lack of time for a thorough archaeological investigation has meant that this area remains poorly understood (Appendix A1.13). As a result, the majority of the enclosures featured below are described only at the most basic level.

The enclosures were arranged loosely along a north-south axis, and were divided into two subgroups. The southern group consisted of three enclosures, E22, E155 and E104 (Fig. 3.19). Enclosure 22 was a subcircular enclosure defined for the most part by the relatively substantial ditch 698. It appears to have been a recut of an earlier, equally substantial ditch (699), which could only be traced along the south-eastern side of the enclosure. In plan, ditch 699 appeared to terminate in the south-western corner of the enclosure, but this was not verified through excavation. Gully 701, which traversed the centre of E22, was of uncertain phase, but probably did not form part of the enclosure (Appendix A1.14; Fig A1.8). Enclosure 22 has been assigned to Period F on the basis of its stratigraphically later position relative to E23 (Period C; Fig. 3.9) and its similarity in form with other enclosures in the group. The enclosure also seems to have formed the western ditch of E16.

To the north-west of E22 was a second subcircular enclosure, E155. For the most part the enclosure consisted of a continuous ditch (723), which had been recut on one occasion (722). A possible third ditch (749), and an earlier pit (751), of uncertain phase (Appendix A1.14), complicated the western edge. The enclosure was located almost

wholly within the slightly larger E24 (Fig. 3.17) so that consideration of their stratigraphic relationship was limited to the north-western corner of E155. Here, there was clear evidence that E155 was the later of the two enclosures (Fig. 3.20). The interior of the enclosure was largely cut away by the Period H linear boundary 302 (Fig. 3.23).

The third enclosure in the subgroup, E104, was revealed in the south-western corner of Trench 7 (Fig. 3.19). Only its eastern extent fell within the excavation area. This consisted of a slightly curved ditch 720, which ended in a multiply recut terminal (720, 739 and 740). Immediately to the west of the ditch was a circular posthole (721), which is presumed to be of the same phase. E104 has been ascribed to Period F on the basis of a single sherd of Group 5 pottery which was recovered from 740, and because what was revealed of the enclosure was similar to other subcircular enclosures in that area.

The northern subgroup consisted of four enclosures, E35, E36, E37 and E105 (Fig. 3.19), which were also very poorly understood (Appendix A1.15). Enclosure 35 defined a small, irregular area approximately 12 x 12 m. The enclosure consisted of an apparently continuous ditch which had been recut on at least one occasion and possibly twice. The enclosure's south-eastern and north-eastern sides were cut into the upper fills of E33 (Phase E), making a more precise definition difficult. The enclosure's south-western and north-western sides were more clearly defined. Although no definite entrances were revealed, a bulbous shape in the south-eastern corner of the enclosure (687) may have defined a former access (Fig. 3.19).

Enclosure 36 lay *c* 2 m to the west of E35. Its precise dimensions are unknown because its western side was largely cut away by the later, Roman boundary 302 (End Plan). From what remains, however, the enclosure would appear to be slightly smaller than E35, but of similar plan. No entrances were located and all internal features predated the enclosure.

Enclosure 37 lay *c* 2 m to the north-east of E36. Although more elongated than both E35 and E36, the enclosure was of a similar character. The long

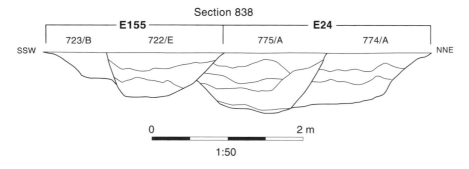

Fig. 3.20 Section 838 showing the relationship between E24 and E155

axis of the enclosure was oriented NE–SW, making the enclosure parallel with E35. Although the enclosure ditch had very few sections cut through it, those recorded show that it had been recut as many as four or five times.

Enclosure 105 lay immediately to the north-east of E37. The majority of the enclosure lay outside the excavation area so that only a very partial reconstruction was possible. The visible portion of the enclosure ditch was oriented NE–SW. At its northern extent it appears to have turned to the north-west where it was lost under the edge of excavation (Fig. 3.19). Though little can be said about the enclosure, its ditch had been recut on several occasions, leaving a soilmark considerably wider than the actual ditch would have been at any one time. The relationship between E105 and E37 was never fully understood. Although both enclosures had a pottery assemblage appropriate to a Period F date, it is possible that E105 was earlier in the stratigraphic sequence than E37.

Potential Period F features – Southern Area

Enclosures, pits and linear features
(E6, E7, E156, E320, E321, 2620/2621, 2622, 5001/5002)

To the east of E29 was a subrectangular enclosure, E6 (Fig. 3.19). The enclosure, which was distinctly regular in plan, was oriented NE–SW, with a possible entrance in the north-west corner. The eastern terminal of the entrance was recut several times (111, 147 and 152) with a posthole at its tip (170), which may have been part of an entrance structure. The western entrance terminal had been cut away by the (Period G) linear boundary 301 (End Plan), so that the actual width of the entrance is uncertain. It must have been approximately 5–10 m, however, if the south-western enclosure ditch carried on to the north-west, closing the rectangle. The main enclosure ditch (111/119) was relatively shallow (*c* 0.20–0.30 m deep), but well defined. A possible annex, immediately to the south of the main enclosure ditch was defined by the gully 107. The gully began at the western end of the enclosure and looped to the south before turning eastward. Although the gully was then lost in a complex of features, its eastern extent may have been defined by 102 which rejoined the main enclosure ditch (111) approximately 10 m from its north-eastern end. Although site records record E6 as cutting 107, the annex contained pottery of the same period as the main enclosure, suggesting that if they were not exactly contemporary then they were at least of a similar phase.

Wholly within E6, at its north-eastern end, was a subcircular enclosure, E7. The enclosure consisted of an annular ditch (108), which defined an area *c* 6 x 7 m across, with no apparent internal features. Although small for the site of a roundhouse, it is possible that E7 marked the location of some kind of storage building or temporary night shelter. Immediately to the south-west was a possible posthole structure (153, 154, 157 and 285) which measured *c* 2.5 x 2.5 m. A number of much smaller postholes (279, 280, 281 and 282) may have been associated with the main structure. Although the structure seems to be quite well defined in plan, two of the main postholes (157 and 285) were thought to be natural features by the excavators. The structure does seem to be coherent, however, and appears to be influenced by the alignment of E6. The level of recording precluded any analysis of the fills, and the validity of the structure as a four-poster must remain open. It should be noted, however, that a second potential posthole structure of similar dimensions was located within Posthole Cluster 2 (see above, 'Period C'; Fig. 3.8).

A group of pits arrayed in a series of three semicircular arcs or pit zones was revealed approximately 30 m to the south-west of E6. The pits appear to have been clustered around apparently blank areas, which may have housed structures or have been used as open working areas (see below, 'Pits'). Ceramics recovered from the pits ranged in date from Period A to Period F, but the majority of the pits could have been contemporary with each other. Several of the pits clearly cut enclosures dated to Period E, and on that basis, the group has been tentatively assigned to Period F.

It is possible that the linear boundary 2622 and its associated enclosures E156, E320 and E321 belonged to this period (Fig. 3.5). Although described above as a possible Period C or D feature, the boundary does appear to be respected by the Period F enclosure group described above. It is possible, therefore, that 2622 was a long lived feature which endured through several periods. If that was the case for 2622, the same could be argued for the other related boundaries 5001/5002 and the enclosure/trackway ditches 2620 and 2621. The degree of uncertainty highlights the difficulty in phasing linear boundaries, many of which were only visible as cropmarks or were subjected to very limited excavation.

PERIOD G: EARLY ROMAN PERIOD
c 2nd CENTURY AD (Fig. 3.21)

Summary

Period G saw a radical change in the character of the archaeology at Thornhill Farm. The numerous groups of intensively recut enclosures which were so typical of earlier periods appear to have gone out of use, and the landscape was reorganised on a considerable scale. The most significant features were newly constructed trackways, which crossed the site, seemingly without any regard for earlier activity. The trackways not only divided up the landscape but, for the first time at Thornhill, give the impression that human (as opposed to animal) traffic had become important.

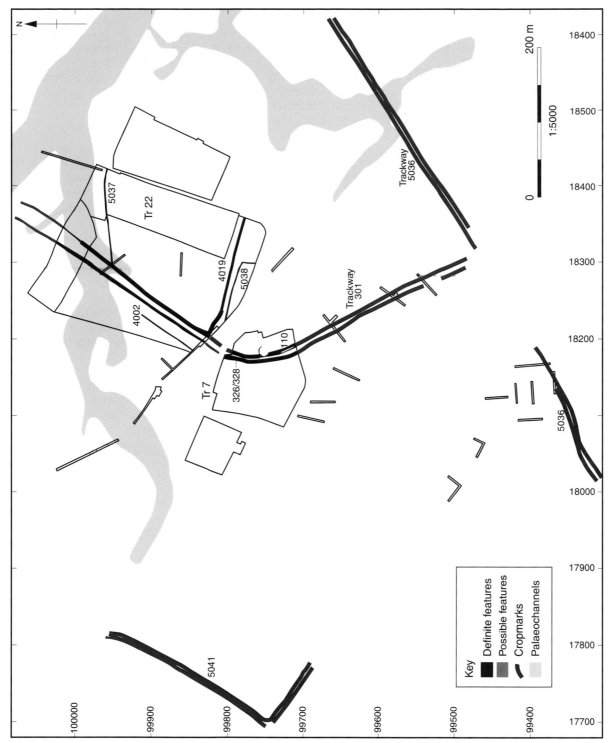

Fig. 3.21 Period G – early Roman Period, 2nd Century AD

Plate 3.2   View looking north from southern end of Trench 7 showing ditches of Roman trackway 301 cutting through earlier enclosures

Southern Area and Northern Salvage Area

Trackways and associated field boundaries
(301, 4019, 4022, 5036, 5037 and 5038)

Linear trackway 301 was traced for almost 600 m across the low gravel terrace and floodplain through a combination of targeted excavation and the plotting of cropmarks from aerial photographs (Plate 3.2). The trackway crossed the Northern Salvage Area on a NE–SW alignment before gradually turning towards the south-east within Trench 7. At its southern end, it almost certainly conjoined with trackway 5036 (see below), although the actual junction was not visible on the aerial photographs. The trackway (301) was most thoroughly understood in Trench 7 where it was defined by two relatively shallow gullies which had been recut on numerous occasions (329/331 and 109/110; Fig. 3.22). In the northern half of the trench the terminal of western gully 326 was revealed slightly to the west of a larger gully 328. No relationship was recovered between the two ditches, and it is possible that 326 was part of an early, possibly discontinuous ditch. The eastern trackway ditch was largely defined by gully 110 which had been multiply recut. Two fragments of adult human skull were recovered from the fill of this ditch.

At both the northern and southern end of Trench 7 the western and eastern trackway ditches visibly divided, giving the appearance of a double ditch on either side of the track. This double ditched arrangement is less obvious in the centre of the trench, however, and it seems probable that the trackway was of more than one phase.

In the salvage area to the north of Trench 7 three linear gullies were revealed projecting from the eastern side of 301 (5037, 4019 and 5038). Gully 5037 was *c* 0.90 m in length, and has been tentatively ascribed to period G on the basis of its apparent spatial coherency with Roman trackway 301 (Fig. 3.21).

Gullies 4019 and 5038 were located *c* 180 m to the south-west of 5037. The gullies were positioned parallel to each other and almost perpendicular to 301, defining a secondary track or droveway which opened to the east. The relationship between 301 and this secondary droveway is uncertain, but given that ditch 4019 appeared to connect with 301, the two may be assumed to be contemporary.

A linear gully (4022) was revealed *c* 15 m to the west of trackway 301. The gully ran parallel to 301, and a Period G date is suggested by its pottery assemblage, which was dominated by Group 5 material.

Trackway 5036 was located at the southern end of 301. Its orientation (NE–SW) suggests that it may have been associated with the reorganised Claydon Pike settlement to the east. The track was largely traced through aerial photographs but was planned and partially excavated during a separate OAU evaluation at Kempsford, Bowmoor (End Plan; OAU 1989, 2–3 and fig. 4), where it was found to be associated with a 2nd century AD Roman settlement. It has been ascribed a Period G date on the

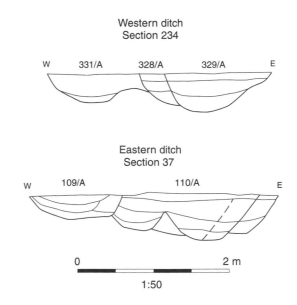

Western ditch
Section 234

W 331/A 328/A 329/A E

Eastern ditch
Section 37

W 109/A 110/A E

0 2 m
1:50

Fig. 3.22 Sections 37 and 234 of trackway 301 – Trench 7

strength of the Bowmoor evidence and because of its presumed association with trackway 301.

Approximately 600 m to the north-west of 5036 was an L-shaped cropmark of similar width and character (5041). Although the cropmark was never sampled through excavation, its orientation and general appearance (probably double-ditched) suggest that it may have been another trackway. Its shorter axis was roughly aligned upon the north-eastern limit of the Kempsford, Bowmoor settlement (Fig. 3.21), and may have redefined an earlier boundary.

PERIOD H: LATE ROMAN PERIOD
3rd–4th CENTURY AD (Fig. 3.23)

Summary

In the late Roman period modifications were made to the landscape, which suggest that the major trackway 301 was no longer in use. The period was dominated by a number of linear boundaries which stretched over the landscape for considerable distances.

Southern Area and Northern Salvage Area

Linear boundaries and possible trackway
(302, 5039 and 5040)

Linear boundary 302 was the most significant feature dated to Period H (Fig. 3.23, Plate 3.3). The ditch was visible on aerial photographs for just over 600 m, snaking gently from the north, through Trench 7 and on towards the south-west. In Trench 2 and parts of Trench 7 the boundary consisted of two individual ditches *c* 2 m apart. The double-ditched arrangement is reminiscent of 301 and 5036 (Period G), and it is likely that the boundary was a trackway, although in places only one ditch was visible.

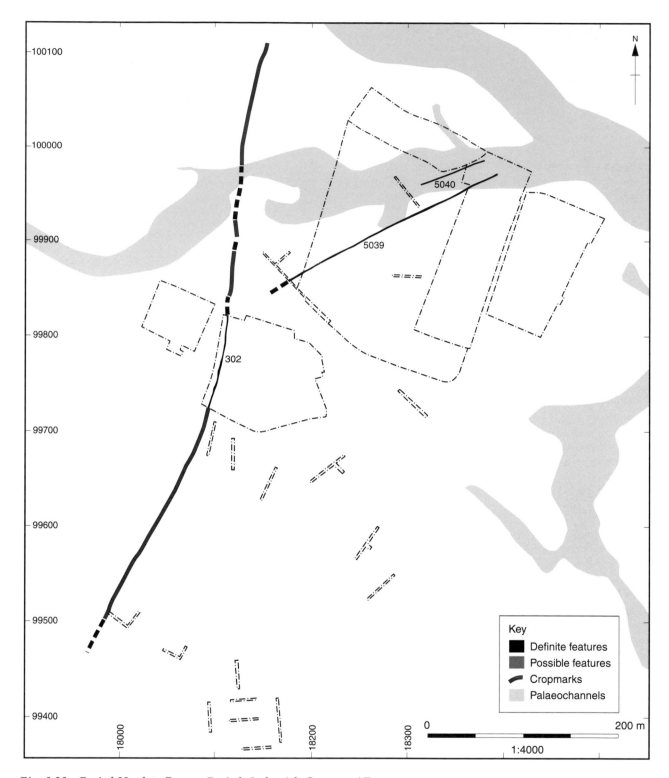

Fig. 3.23   Period H – late Roman Period, 3rd – 4th Century AD

A secondary ditch (5039) which may have been associated with 302 was revealed in the salvage area *c* 50 m to the east. The ditch was linear (250 m in length), with a SW–NE alignment, and was recorded in the north-west corner of Trench 22. If the ditch continued beyond the trench it was not visible on aerial photographs. Towards its south-western end the ditch cut straight across the double-ditched trackway 301 and the parallel ditch 4022,

suggesting that both had been out of use for some time (Fig. 3.21 and End Plan).

A second linear ditch, which ran nearly parallel to 5039, was revealed *c* 35 m to the north (5040). The ditch was considerably shorter than 5039 (*c* 70 m) but shared similar characteristics. Both ditches have been ascribed to Period H on the basis of their spatial coherency with 302 and their unusual alignment relative to features of other periods.

Plate 3.3   View looking south across the western part of Trench 7 showing the late Roman boundary ditch 302 cutting earlier enclosures

Plate 3.4   Clay lined pit 3387 in Trench 22

PITS

Quantity and classification

A total of 465 pits were recorded at Thornhill Farm. The quality of recording was variable across the site, and in many cases either the breadth or depth of the pits was not noted. Pit depth and profile were the most consistently recorded variables and were, therefore, chosen as the basis for a limited statistical analysis. The pit depths were not normally distributed, but could be separated into a shallow group (Class 1, up to 0.28 m in depth) and a deep group (Class 2, those deeper than 0.28 m).

Class 1

Of the 218 Class 1 pits, 65 had no breadth recorded. Where it was recorded, however, it was always greater than the pit depth. Breadth was more than twice the depth for over half (137) of this group. Class 1, therefore, can be described as shallow scoops.

Class 2

There were 247 pits in Class 2, of which 21 had no recorded breadth. The majority of the pits were broader than their depth, while slightly less than half of the group (115) had a breadth more than twice their depth. Broad, shallow profiles, though present, were not as characteristic of this class as they were for Class 1.

Function

The majority of the pits were subcircular with either flattish or more rounded bases, and in most cases exhibited no clear evidence as to their function. The low-lying nature of the site would seem to preclude the presence of grain storage pits, but otherwise function is open to speculation. Some of the deeper pits may have been used as waterholes (eg 3152, Trench 22), but the majority would have been too shallow for this purpose. The pits may have been for rubbish disposal, but if so, relatively little pottery was deposited. Another possibility is that some of the pits were quarried in order to obtain gravel. Environmental evidence suggests that parts of the site were churned up (probably by animal trampling), and were also likely to be wet in the winter months. It is possible, therefore, that gravel was used to infill some of the boggier areas.

Clay lined pits (Table 3.10)

Thirteen of the pits were lined with distinctive, thick yellow clay (Plate 3.4). All but one of the pits were located within Trenches 9 and 22, within which, however, they were widely dispersed. The presumed function of the lined pits was to hold liquid of some kind, probably water. Only one pit contained evidence of burning, and this was probably derived from secondary use. Small, clay lined pits were also revealed at Claydon Pike where they were associated with middle Iron Age circular structures. The lined pits at Thornhill Farm were not obviously associated with structures although the difficulty in locating potential roundhouses has been noted.

Dating and distribution

Although a limited spatial analysis was carried out with reference to pit class, no obvious pattern emerged. Clusters or arrays of pits were noted, however.

Trench 7 (Fig. 3.24)

In the central-southern area of Trench 7, a number of 'blank' areas were defined by curvilinear pit zones (see above 'Potential Period F features'). Stratigraphic and artefactual analysis suggests that the majority of pits could have been contemporary, a conclusion which the unusual shape of the clustering tends to support. Although there is no positive evidence to suggest that the blank areas were ever covered by buildings, the pits did avoid the central areas, and the potential difficulties in identifying structures are discussed in Chapter 5. Excavation of pits around any standing structure would have produced curvilinear pit zones similar to those in Trench 7. Alternatively the pits may have defined open working areas. A reason for digging the pits might have been to obtain gravel in order to raise or repair floor levels within the structures. However, no evidence for floor levels survived.

A series of pits appeared to be arrayed around the edge of the C-shaped enclosure E27 (Period E: Fig. 3.17 and Fig. 3.24). One pit (549) was cut by the enclosure ditch and another (681/682) contained the only dating evidence (two sherds of Group 4 material). Although the evidence is meagre, this would suggest that the pits might be the result of activity before the enclosure was formalised by the digging of its ditch (see E54, Trench 22 below).

Trench 8 (Fig. 3.24)

The majority of the pits in Trench 8 were located in the south-eastern quadrant of the trench in the general vicinity of structures 207 and 209. Pit clusters are relatively unusual at Thornhill Farm, and appear to occur only near to structures. Two examples were noted in Trench 8 (Fig. 3.24: 872/873 and 923/924), which were immediately adjacent to structures 207 and 209 respectively (for a third example see below, Trench 9). Function is difficult to assess. Some of the pits appear to be quite shallow while others are quite deep. It is possible the pits were used for rubbish disposal although why they would need to be redug on or near the same spot is unclear.

Trenches 9 and 22 (Fig. 3.25)

Pits within Trenches 9 and 22 appeared within discrete clusters, the majority of which appeared to

Table 3.10 Clay lined pits

Context	Profile	Plan	Width	Depth	Layer Details	Clay Lining
2032	Round bottom, steep sides	Oval	0.30	0.18	3 layers; 3 is predominantly clay, covering base and part of sides, incorporates organic material	Thick deposit of yellow clay at base, less thick up the sides
2134	Round bottom, sloping sides	Oval	0.54	0.22	3 layers	Thick yellow clay covering base and part of sides
2152	Round bottom, sloping sides	Circular	1.00	0.23	2 layers	Red/orange burnt clay covering base of pit. Lump of burnt clay in upper fill
2167	Flat bottom, sloping sides	Sub-circ.	0.78	0.38	3 layers. Clay layer comprises half of fill	Fairly thick, yellow clay lining over base and up most of sides
2305	Rounded bottom, steep, sloping sides	Sub-circ.	0.72	0.18	2 layers. Clay layer comprises half of fill. Large burnt limestone fragments in upper fill	Thick, yellow clay lining base and sides. Incorporates fired, sandy clay fragments
2384	Flat bottom, steep sides	Sub-circ.	0.92	0.34	2 layers. Frequent med/large burnt limestone frags in upper fill	Thick yellow clay lining covering base only
2440	Flat bottom, one steep, sloping side	Sub-circ.	0.34	0.20	2 layers	Clay lump in base does not appear to have functioned as a lining
2457	Rounded bottom, sloping sides	Oval	0.52	0.13	2 layers	Possibly clay lined but very thick; fills most of pit
2482	Flat bottom, sloping sides	?	0.64	0.22	2 layers	Yellow clay lining covering base and sides
2519	Flat bottomed, steep sloping sides	?	0.70	0.30	2 layers Upper contains slag.	Orange brown clay covers most of bottom and sides
3152	Flat bottom, sloping sides	?	2.10	0.46	7 layers	Dark grey, black sticky clay. Covers bottom but not sides. Probably not a lining, possible waterhole
3263	Round bottom, sloping sides	?	1.06	0.28	2 layers	Med dark green-brown clay covering base and side. Thick if a lining
3387	Flat bottom, steep sides	Circular	0.63	0.25	4 layers	Yellow/grey clay layer covering bottom and sides completely

be associated either with structures or individual enclosures. The pit cluster located within E62, for example, lay immediately adjacent to structure 202 and is likely to have been contemporary (Fig. 3.16). Similar clusters of pits were noted in Trench 8 adjacent to structure 207 and 209 (above). As with the pit clusters in Trench 8, function is uncertain, although the excavators thought that the central pit (2049) was deep enough to be a waterhole.

POSTHOLES

Approximately 246 postholes were recorded across the site, of which some 79 (32 %) formed part of a recognised structure or posthole cluster (Tables 3.11 and 3.12). Three quarters of the postholes were located in Trenches 9 and 22, which also included most of the structures. In most cases the postholes contained little or no dating evidence and where

phasing was possible, it was usually based upon their associations with enclosures.

BURIALS AND OTHER DEPOSITS OF HUMAN REMAINS

Human remains were quite scarce at Thornhill Farm, although they did include three inhumations and four deposits of cremated human bone (Boyle, Chapter 4). The inhumations (3106, 3145, 3363) were all located within Trench 22, and although phasing is far from certain, it is quite probable that all belong to period D, with two of them being surrounded by enclosures (Fig. 3.11). The cremation deposits (320, 800, 801, 3008) were far more dispersed chronologically and spatially, ranging from a possible period E or F pit in Trench 7 (320) to period C enclosure E40 (3008) in Trench 22. Most of the remaining deposits of unburnt human bone could not be phased.

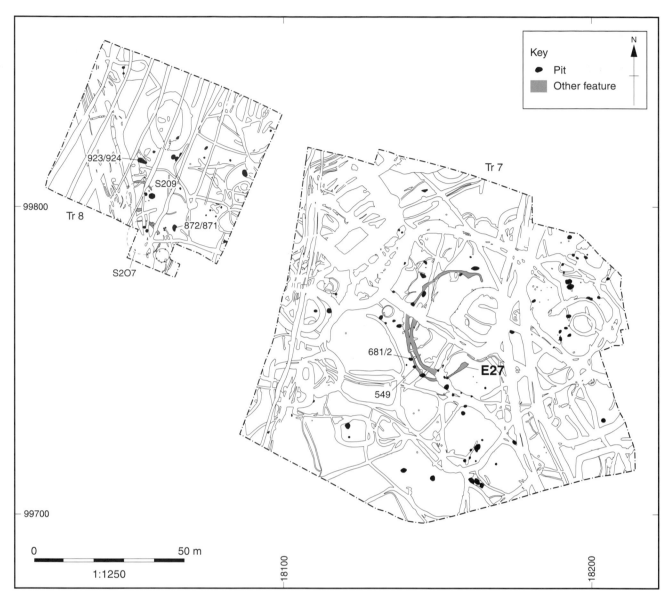

Fig. 3.24   Distribution of pits within Trenches 7 and 8

Table 3.11 Number of postholes by trench

Trench No.	Number of postholes
7	47
8	15
9	104
22	80
Total	246

Table 3.12 Structures containing postholes and posthole clusters

Structure	Number of postholes
PC1	6
PC2	10
PC3	11
Structure 200	13
Structure 201	20
Structure 202	18
Structure 207	1

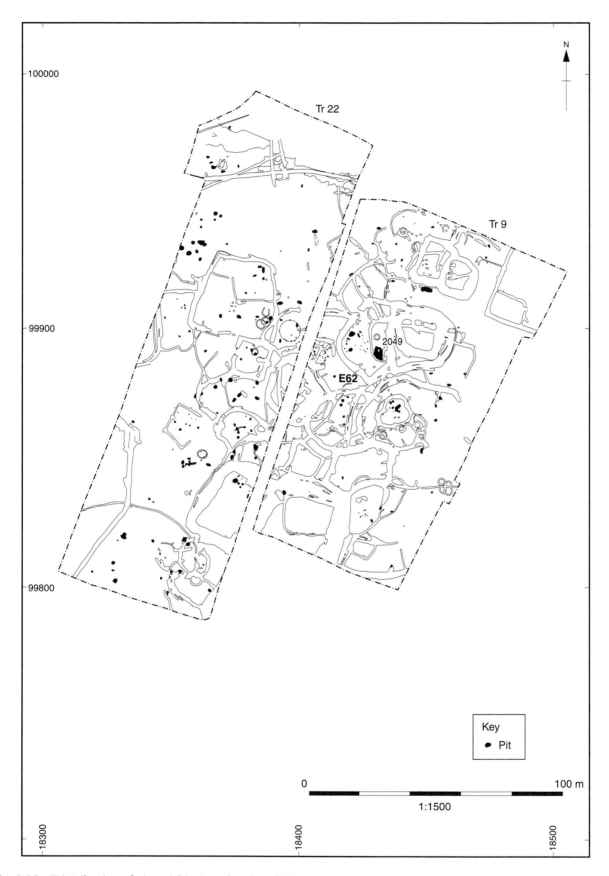

Fig. 3.25   Distribution of pits within trenches 9 and 22

Chapter 4   The Finds and Environmental Evidence

THE FINDS

by Angela Boyle

The quantity of finds from the site is limited, totalling about 262. The bulk of these were metal objects, 88 of iron (including 23 nails) and 50 of copper alloy. A small number of miscellaneous objects were not catalogued. The quantities of catalogued finds by phase are shown in Table 4.1. Of the finds, 61% were either unstratified (U/S) or from unphased contexts, and so it is impossible to carry out a detailed analysis of artefact patterns through time, especially given the high level of redeposition at the site (see Appendix 2). However, the apparently much higher number of finds from Periods D to F (*c* AD 50–120) does suggest that these may have been the period of most intense activity. Appendix 6 relates the context numbers given for the individual finds to their location within the site.

Coins

Iron Age coins

by Philip de Jersey

1   *U/S SF 494* Plated silver, Iron Age, Dobunnic C, Mack 1964, 378a/van Arsdell 1989, 1045–1.
2   *U/S SF 26* Plated silver, Iron Age, Dobunnic H, Mack 1964, 389/van Arsdell 1989, 1110–1 (AD 15–30).

Roman coins

3   *U/S SF 105* Silver Roman republican denarius, 46 BC, MN CORDIVSRVFVS III VIR;
    obverse: jugate heads of Dioscun wearing laureate pilei around RVFVS III VIR
    reverse: Venus stg l, holding scales on right hand, sceptre on left, cupid perched on shoulder, ? CORDIUS
4   *U/S SF 97* Silver Roman republican denarius, 157–156 BC;
    obverse: helmeted head of ROMA, X behind
    reverse: Victory in biga, Roma in exergue

Table 4.1 Quantification of finds by phase

	A	B	C	D	Phase E	F	G	H	Unphased	Total
Coins									6	6
Cu al brooches			2	2	3	3			22	32
Cu al rings, bracelet, pins etc									5	5
Cu al misc.				5					8	13
Silver object									1	1
Iron brooches					1	1			7	9
Iron knives/tools				2	1	1			7	11
Iron fittings	1			1	2				5	9
Iron nails			1	3	4				15	23
Iron misc.	1			3	1	3	1		27	36
Lead weights									2	2
Lead misc.						1			11	12
Stone beads						1			1	2
Shale bracelets				1						1
Quernstones			1		3	4			7	15
Whetstones	1								5	6
Spindlewhorls					1				1	2
Other worked stone				1	2	5			10	18
Briquetage					1				1	2
Loomweights			1	1					7	9
Slingshot						1			2	3
Crucible?									1	1
Tile					1	4			7	12
Bone objects	2		1		1	2			2	8
Worked flint										24
Total	5	0	6	19	21	26	1	0	161	262

Post-Medieval and unknown coins

5   *U/S SF 27* Copper alloy, large, probably Victorian.

6   *U/S SF 29* Irregular round disc, flat with slightly off-centre perforation, max diameter 18 mm, width of perforation 3 mm, max thickness of disc 3 mm. Possible coin.

The Brooches

by Donald Mackreth

All are made from a copper alloy unless otherwise stated.

Late La Tène 1 (Fig. 4.1)

All have or had four-coil springs with internal chords.

7   *402 SF 85* Iron. The surviving part of the bow has a rectangular section, a fairly sharp bend in the profile at the top and two or three mouldings on the front at the top of the straight part.

8   *1088/A SF 251* The bow has a thick rectangular section and tapers to a pointed foot. On the front are two groups of cross-grooves, one near the top and the other in the middle.

9   *2011 SF 330* The bow, with a rectangular section, has an almost straight profile with a high 'kick' at the top. The only decoration consists of two vertical grooves at the very top stopped below by two cross-grooves.

These three brooches betray influences from the group dealt with by Stead in his discussion of the brooches from what he termed the Lexden and Welwyn phases of the Aylesford culture of the late pre-Roman Iron Age (Stead 1976). The chief feature shown on his figures 1–3 is the use of knops or mouldings near the top of the bow. These are conscious derivations from the knop or collar found on La Tène II brooches, and the decoration on the present brooches is also a reflection of this. However, they clearly are not in the mainstream and, typologically, fall between the Stead types and the ordinary ones generally grouped as Nauheim Derivatives.

The only sites which offer a good indication of date are the King Harry Lane cemetery (Stead and Rigby 1989) and the Westhampnett cemetery (Fitzpatrick 1997). The first only has g.270,4 from Phase 1, and g.124,4 from Phase 3, the latter being large and late, and surely an antique. Both have finely fretted catch-plates. The second site produced a very different spectrum of brooches, including many with external chords. Those with La Tène II influences are: g.20132 external chord; g.20169 reminiscent of Brooch 9 here, but with a framed catch-plate; g.20601 no spring but the catch-plate has one shaped bar; g.20622 chord unknown; g.20629 external chord; g.29675 x 2 external chord.

There is a marked difference between the two. The King Harry Lane cemetery is dated AD 1–60, although the initial date is admitted as having been possibly as early as 15 BC (Stead and Rigby 1989, 83–4), while the Westhampnett cemetery brooches are generally dated to 90–50 BC (Fitzpatrick 1997, 203–4). The King Harry Lane cemetery dating is certainly too late: there is only one Colchester Derivative and no real Hod Hills, inconceivable for a site lasting significantly beyond AD 40–45. As for Westhampnett, the evidence for its limited use is good, but the number of external chords may suggest that the dating could be taken 10 to 15 years further back without damaging the rest of the evidence. The presence of only one Nauheim, the rest not belonging to Stead's types, being *Drahtfibeln*, opens another dimension which is not relevant here but may weigh on the dating. In short, the present brooches, assuming all to have had solid catch-plates, should date after *c* 50–25 BC; the difficulty is deciding how late they may have run. Brooch 7 should be safely before the Roman conquest, and may be 1st century BC. Brooch 9 looks as though it ought to be tied to the end of the Nauheim proper, and the profiles of both of these brooches point to a date generally after 25 BC, save that some brooches in the Westhampnett cemetery have the same profile as Brooch 7. The slack profile of Brooch 8 might be before *c* 25 BC but little stress should be placed on this. In short, all three should be earlier than *c* AD 40–45.

10   *2374 SF 333* The bow has a thin rectangular section and tapers to a pointed foot. Down the centre of the broad part is a decorative stamped strip probably made by a narrow bar with notches cut across producing a line of square stamps. The catch-plate is fairly insignificant.

The distribution of brooches using lines of square stamps conforms fairly well with the area once occupied by the Atrebates, but there are examples from further afield; those from Wroxeter in the list below were almost certainly picked up by the Legio XIV Gemina on its way through the home territory.

The dating is: Fishbourne, AD 43–*c* 75, two examples (Cunliffe 1971, 100, fig. 36.6 and 13); Hod Hill, before AD 50 (Brailsford 1962, 7, fig. 7, C25); Wilcote, Claudian (Hands 1993, 31, fig. 24,14); Silchester, not after AD 60 (Boon 1969, 47, fig. 6,3); Wroxeter, after AD 55/60, two examples (Shrewsbury, Rowley's House 48); Harlow temple, before AD 80 (France and Gobel 1985, 75, fig. 39,1); Wilcote, mid 2nd century AD (Hands 1998, 53, fig. 19,42); Verulamium, AD 200–225, AD 350–375 (Frere 1984, 21, fig. 5,15–6); Shakenoak Farm, 4th century plus (Brodribb *et al.* 1972, 72, fig. 30,126).

11   *U/S SF 263* Iron. What is left of the thin rectangular-sectioned bow has a distorted profile.

Nothing of any distinction remains. Iron brooches are generally pre-conquest, but many made then

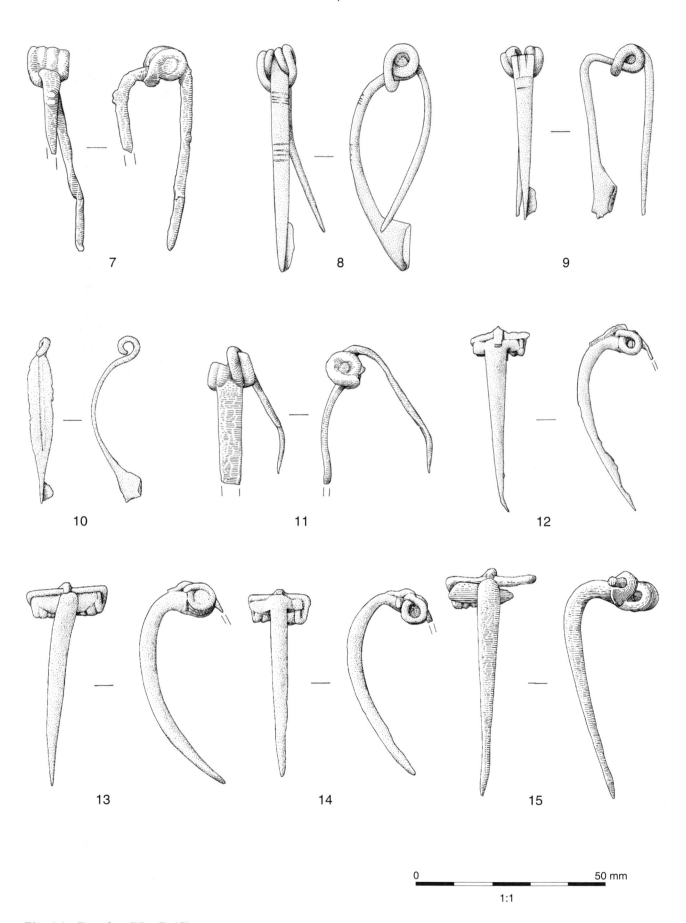

Fig. 4.1 Brooches (Nos 7–15)

survived in use long after. Apart from a simple strip type with a rolled-under head, such brooches should not be expected in the Roman period much after AD 50–60.

Colchesters (Figs 4.1–2)

The bilateral spring is integral with the bow and issues from the lower part immediately behind the head of the bow; from the upper part rises a shorter rod which was fashioned into a forward-facing hook to secure the chord. The condition of these is such that no decoration can be seen.

12 *U/S SF 72* The bow seems to have a rounded front and there are signs of facets on the rear corners. Only the stub of the catch-plate survives.

13 *U/S SF 266* Here the bow has a rounded front and there are facets on the rear corners. No trace of the catch-plate survives.

14 *3253/B SF 523* The bow section is possibly like that of Brooch 12 and the catch-plate is missing.

15 *U/S SF 497* Indeterminate bow section and the catch-plate is completely lost.

16 *313/A SF 63* Possibly has a hexagonal section, the catch-plate may have either had a single opening or, more likely, one divided by a cross bar.

17 *U/S SF 337* There are facets on the back corners, the rest is unclear and only the merest trace of the catch-plate is left.

18 *569 SF 116* Iron. Length cannot be determined due to fragmentary nature of brooch. Eight coils. The catch-plate does not appear to have survived (not illustrated).

19 *3215/B SF 511* Surviving length 39 mm. Six coils. The condition is very poor and all or most of the original surface is missing thus obscuring what the section of the bow had been and also removing traces of any decoration on the wings. The catch-plate is lost.

With so few proven diagnostic features, other than the defining ones which determine that these are Colchesters, there is little to provide a framework for discussion. None is of a great size which is, on the whole, one indicator of an early date. None has the distinctive almost straight profile with a marked bend at the head. None is so small that it could belong to any of the late Colchesters. Only Brooch 16 has enough to suggest that it had a completely faceted section, in this instance hexagonal, the possible rounded fronts of the others are not certain. Again, only Brooch 16 has enough to suggest the style of catch-plate.

Only a very general date range can be proposed: *c* AD 1–60, the latter being the end of the period of survival in use, manufacture having effectively ceased *c* AD 40.

20 *3004/A SF 502* Iron. The spring is lacking, but the form of the head only really suits the Colchester spring arrangement. The wings are damaged. The bow is apparently plain with a rounded section and tapers to what had probably been a pointed foot. The stub of the catch-plate may survive.

Iron brooches may have been more common than we suppose because many have not survived from past excavations and many have been reduced to masses of rust incapable of interpretation. Without the King Harry Lane cemetery (Stead and Rigby 1989), our knowledge of the *floruit* of brooches made in this material would be meagre.

The dating is as follows: King Harry Lane Phase 1, 7 or 8 graves; Skeleton Green, 15–25 (Partridge 1981, 37, fig. 66,5); King Harry Lane Phase 2, 8 graves; Boxford cemetery, pot 9, two examples (Owles and Smedley 1967, 92, fig. 14,c,d); King Harry Lane Phase 3, 5 graves; King Harry Lane Phase ?, 5 graves; Weekley, mid–late 1st century AD (Jackson and Dix 1987, M97, fig. 24,24); Colchester, AD 44–8 (Niblett 1985, 116, fig. 73,6); Longthorpe, AD 44–60 (Frere and St Joseph 1974, 44, fig. 23,3); Bagendon, AD 45–55 (Clifford 1961, fig. 29.6); Thetford, Fison Way, AD 45–61 (Gregory 1992, 120, fig. 112,5); Richborough, late 1st century AD (Bushe-Fox 1932, 77, pl. 9,9); Wall, late 1st century–early 2nd century AD (Jones 1998, 17, fig. 8,1); Alcester, early–mid 4th century (Cracknell and Mahany 1994, 162, fig. 75,1); Skeleton Green, late Roman and later (Partridge 1981, 140–2 f.67,7,8).

The emphasis is on an early date, even if the King Harry Lane cemetery were to be ignored. However, King Harry Lane may reveal a trend in the use of iron for brooches. The totals of graves are: Phase 1, 7 or 8; Phase 2, 8; Phase 3, 3; Phase 4, none. The absence of any graves with iron Colchesters in Phase 4 does not matter as only 14 graves were assigned to it. However, Phase 3 has the greatest number of graves of any phase, 149, and the drop in the incidence of iron Colchesters should mean that they were passing out of use during its life. The dating of the King Harry Lane cemetery is not yet fixed. The absence of any proper Hod Hill and the presence of only one Colchester Derivative should mean that the possible beginning of the cemetery *c* 15 BC (Stead and Rigby 1989, 83) should be invoked, and the phases moved back 15 years as a consequence.

Colchester Derivatives (Fig. 4.2)

Brooches 21 and 22 have or had their springs mounted in the Harlow manner: a plate behind the head of the bow has two holes, the lower one for the axis bar through the coils of the spring and the upper to hold the chord.

21 *569/B SF 10* Each wing has a vertical groove at its end. The plate behind the head of the bow is carried over the top as a ridge which runs down the upper half of the bow possibly to be stopped by two cross grooves. The bow is

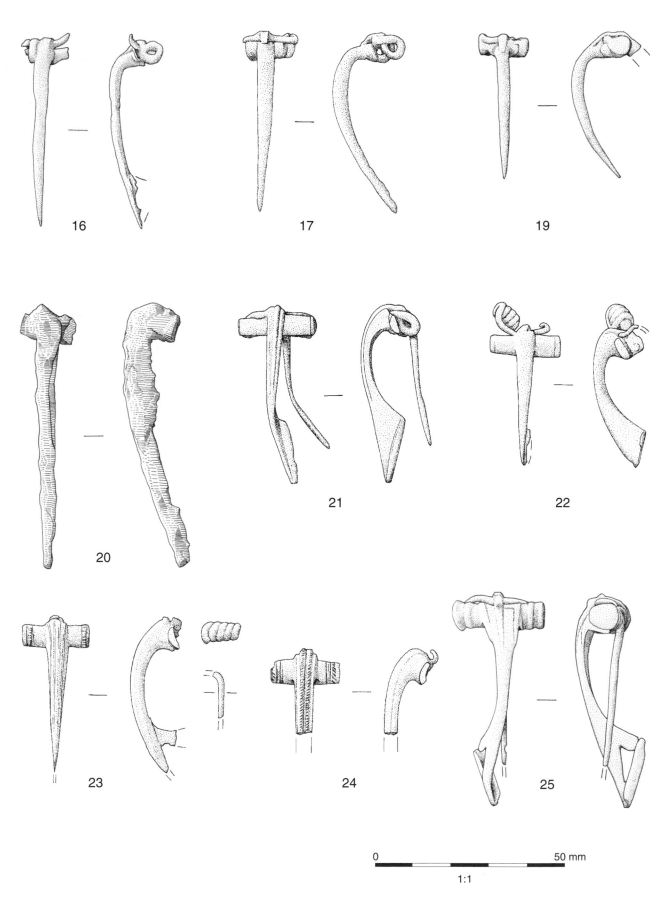

Fig. 4.2 Brooches (Nos 16–17, 19–25)

relatively narrow at the top and tapers to a pointed foot.

This brooch belongs to a distinct group which lies mainly in Wiltshire and southern Gloucestershire, with an extension into Hampshire. The features which mark it out are the overall proportions and the long ridge down the upper part of the bow. The main type often has one or more piercings in the catch-plate, but this variety almost always has a solid one.

The dating is: Kingscote, 1st century BC–AD 140 (Timby 1998, 117, not illustrated); Wilcote, 2nd century plus (Hands 1998, 51, fig. 18,31); Kingscote, late 3rd century ?plus (Timby 1998, 117, not illustrated); Wilcote, 300–360 (Hands 1998, 49, fig. 18,32); Brockworth, late 4th century (Rawes 1981, 65, fig. 8,1). Not a strong representation, the date almost certainly begins in the later 1st century and then runs into the 2nd. British bow brooches ceased to be made by AD 150–175, but many would have lasted in use a little later: effectively only two of the dated examples cover parts of their true *floruit*.

22   *322 SF 31* Like the last, except the bow here is plain and there is a groove at the end of each wing.

Plain brooches are seldom easy to deal with and it is a mark of those with the Harlow spring system that they are not numerous and, as a result, are poorly dated: Quinton, before AD 70–80? (Friendship-Taylor 1974, 49, fig. 18,br6); Verulamium, AD 75–125 (Wheeler and Wheeler 1936, 207, fig. 44,26); Verulamium, 2nd century AD (Stead and Rigby 1989, 17, fig. 10,16); Little Amwell, 2nd century–4th century (Partridge 1989, 133, fig. 76,9); Weldon, before AD 200 (Smith *et al.* 1989, 33, fig. 8,1); Baldock, 3rd century (Stead 1986, 112, fig. 43,68).

Brooches 23 and 24 are not standard, the first being fairly closely related to the Harlow spring system (see above), the second possibly to the Polden Hill system which follows it (see Brooch 25).

23   *620 SF 33* The remains of the spring system show that it had been unilateral, the left hand wing housing the axis bar having behind it a series of ridges simulating a spring. The front of each wing has a pair of vertical mouldings at its end, the inner one being beaded. The bow tapers to a pointed foot and has two grooves down its front. The remains of the catch-plate suggest that there had been at least one piercing.

Very difficult to place, but the indications are that this method of fixing the spring belongs to eastern England. Dating is equally difficult but, like many hybrids, this would have been more at home in the second half of the 1st century than later.

24   *U/S SF 96* The chord of the spring was held by a forward-facing hook tucked in behind the head of the bow which has two cross-cut ridges down it. Each wing has a bead and a reel at its end. The lower bow, with the catch-plate, is missing.

Another hybrid in the sense that it ought to be Polden Hill (see below) but with a forward-facing hook. The alternative version with the hook facing in the other direction is the Rearhook and, like that, the separately-made spring could have been soldered in position behind the left hand wing. The dating of the Rearhook is before AD 60–65 and in the present case, the date may be basically the same but may have run on a little.

25   *U/S SF 264* The spring was held in the Polden Hill manner: an axis bar through the coils is mounted in pierced plates at the ends of the wings; the chord is held by a pierced crest on the head. Each wing has two bold mouldings separated from each other and the bow by deep flutes. The bow has an extra moulding on each side of the head and the pierced crest is run down as a skeuomorph of the hook on a Colchester. The rest of the bow is plain and tapers to a pointed foot. The catch-plate has a large triangular piercing.

The style belongs to the south-west and with a hinged pin would lie further to the south-west than this variety. Large piercings in the catch-plate are frequent and the available dating for brooches such as this, with one or more mouldings added to the bow, is: Camerton, AD 65–85 (Wedlake 1958, 218, fig. 50,7); Broxtowe, before *c* AD 75 (Campion 1938, brooch 9); Verulamium, before late 1st century AD (Lowther 1937, 37, fig. 2,1); Wycomb, late 1st century–early 2nd century AD (Timby 1998, 323, fig. 135,9); Newstead, AD 80–*c* 200 (Curle 1911, 318, pl. 85,4); Verulamium, AD 85–105 (Frere 1972, 114, fig. 29,9); Wilcote, mid 2nd century AD? (Hands 1993, 29, fig. 23,7); Worcester, residual in earliest 3rd century AD dumps (Darlington and Evans 1992, 73, not illustrated). The message is fairly clear: from late Neronian to the earliest 2nd century AD should cover the period of common usage and the period during which survivors in use continued for a while. All later ones should have been residual.

Fragments (Fig. 4.3)

26   *722 SF 114* Only the lower bow with the catch-plate survives. The front of the bow appears to be plain; the catch-plate has in it three circular holes arranged more or less as a vertical line.

27   *U/S SF 495* All that is left is the very bottom of the bow with the catch-plate. The bow has cross grooves on the front above the level of the top of the catch-plate which, itself, is plain.

The holes in the catch-plate in the first might indicate a date before *c* AD 100–125. The second has little to recommend itself and a general date range running from the latter part of the 1st century AD to about AD 150–175 may be suggested.

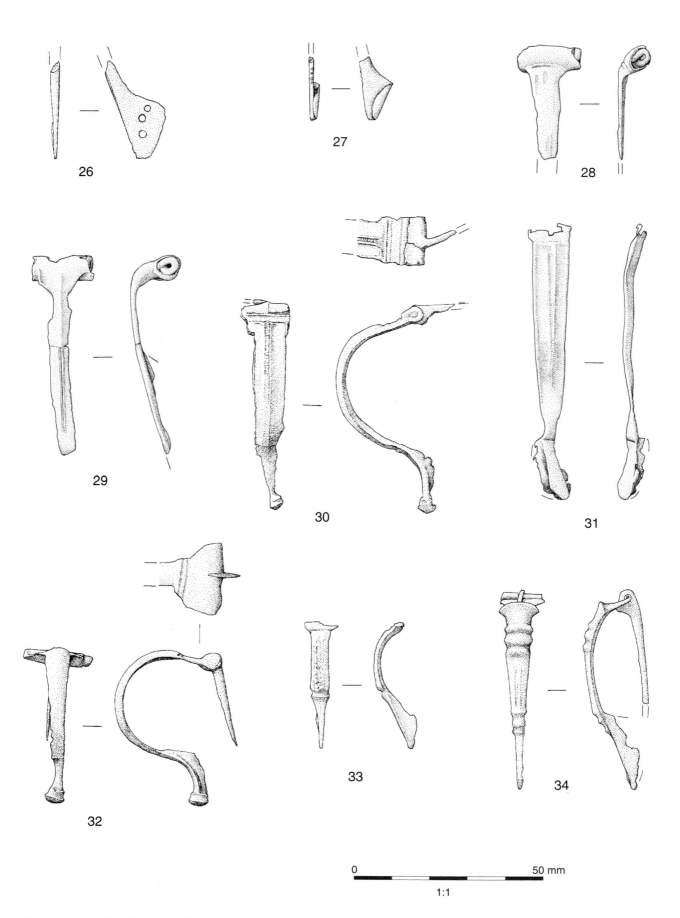

Fig. 4.3   *Brooches (Nos 26–34)*

Late La Tène 2, Langton Downs (Fig. 4.3)

The spring in each of these is separately made and housed in a case on the head of the bow formed by closing two cast flaps round it.

28 *110 SF 28* The eroded remains of the spring-case and the upper bow with the moulding separating the two.

29 *2396 SF 324* There is no sign of the cross-moulding dividing the spring-case from the bow which itself seems not to be the ordinary reeded type, but to have a ridge down the middle.

The condition is so appalling that there is little point in trying to discuss to which variety or what part of the overall floruit these two items belong. There is nothing to suggest that either is early (that is, the last two decades of the 1st century BC into the first or second decade of our era). The latest date at which any Langton Down could be expected to be seen is *c* AD 55–60.

Aucissa–Hod Hills (Fig. 4.3)

All these, where the evidence survives, have or had the axis bars of their hinged pins housed in the rolled-over heads of the bows.

30 *877/C SF 180* The head-plate seems to have a medial flute with what may have been bead-rows on each side. The bow has a bordering ridge on each side and a sunken bead-row down the middle of the swelled front. The foot has the usual cross-mouldings at the top and chamfered sides. The two part foot-knob is soldered or sweated on to a peg at the bottom of the bow.

31 *2042/B SF 301* The same as 30, but distorted and without the rolled over head and foot-knob.

These are Aucissas and in common with the majority are not inscribed with either the name of the most common manufacturer or of any other. No genuine Aucissa from a pre-conquest context has come to the attention of the writer. They arrive at the conquest in some numbers with their progeny, the Hod Hill, having probably ceased being made sometime in the ten years before the conquest. They survive in use for about fifteen years after AD 32, very few indeed occurring north-west of the Fosse Way. The large number from Wroxeter, seemingly not founded before *c* AD 55–60, contrasts with the relatively low number of Hod Hills in the overall collection, and is due to special factors (Webster 2002, 91). The end date for the Aucissa is roughly AD 60–65.

32 *3* Not well preserved, it is the width of the head which suggests that the bow is not particularly eroded on each side and, indeed, has a genuinely rounded front.

Other versions of the main type which gave rise to the Aucissa exist, but are hardly met in Britain. That being the case, when they do occur they can be difficult to place. However, a brooch whose bow resembles this came from the fort at Hod Hill. In which case such brooches are here before AD 50, possibly before the Roman army arrived (Richmond 1968, 39, fig. 31, hut 56; ibid., 117–9). Unfortunately, the head is largely missing so an exact parallelism is denied us.

33 *U/S SF 181* Poorly preserved, with traces of tinning, the upper bow has three vertical ridges which were probably cross-cut, and is separated from the lower bow by a cross-moulding. The lower bow has a flat front face and tapers towards the foot-knob which is now missing.

34 *389 SF 68* The upper bow has, between two sets of three cross-mouldings, the upper set being prominent, two sunken vertical bead-rows. The lower bow is narrow and tapers to the remains of the usual two part foot-knob. There are traces of tinning. The catch-plate has the remains of a circular hole.

Both fit into the Hod Hill category and both in their way show the range of designs to be found. The dating of the first is taken from those which more or less conform with the present example, there always being an element of doubt as to where the exact dividing line between one variety and another should fall: Whitwell, before AD 50 (Todd 1981, 38, fig. 19,2); Colchester, AD 49–61 (Hawkes and Hull 1947, 324, pl. 97,154); Camerton, Claudian-Neronian (Wedlake 1958, 226, fig. 53,32); Exeter, AD 50–80 (Fox 1952, 62, fig. 8,2); Gloucester, before AD 60–65 (Garrod and Heighway 1984, 93, fig. 64,16); Colchester, AD 61–*c* 65 (Hawkes and Hull 1947, 323, pl. 97,140); Broxtowe, before AD 70–5 (Campion 1938, brooches 7, 8); Harlow temple, before AD 80 (France and Gobel 1985, 77, fig. 40,27); Wroxeter, AD 80–120 (Bushe-Fox 1916, 22, pl. 15,3); Baldock, 1st century–3rd century AD (Stead 1986, 120, fig. 47,107); Dorchester, AD 75–120 (Woodward *et al.* 1993, 123, fig. 62,39); Ilchester, before late 2nd century AD (Leach 1982, 245, fig. 116,18); Wilcote, before AD 200? (Hands 1993, 33, fig. 25,25); Leicester, late 2nd–early 3rd century AD (Connor and Buckley 1999, 253, fig. 119,26); Chichester, late 4th century (Down 1981, 257, fig. 10.2,17). The dating begins to break down at about AD 75, thereafter, despite the detail that the dating of archaeological artefacts is no longer so precise as it is before then, there is no real 2nd century presence, and this argues for a relatively sharp cut off as the last survivors in use pass into the archaeological record. The real period of last use should be AD 70–75 as there are so very few found in the lands taken into the province at that time.

As for Brooch 32, in its earlier manifestation (eg Clifford 1961, 182, fig. 35.2) it had iron bars driven through the bow on which were mounted knobs. One of the very few brooches which belonged in any way to the Alesia–Hod Hill sequence from the King Harry Lane cemetery was of the same type (Stead and Rigby 1989, grave 233, Phase 3) where it occurred with one of the very few late Colchesters on the site. Dating for those like the present is really nonexistent. The King Harry Lane brooch had what was effectively a framed catch-plate, a feature which is more frequently found before the conquest than afterwards and the absence of a strong follow up in the rest of the Hod Hills suggests that this brooch is earlier in the sequence than later, say before AD 55–60.

Trumpet (Fig. 4.4)

35 *U/S SF 130* The bilateral spring is mounted on an axis bar which runs through the pierced lug behind the head of the bow. The narrow trumpet head has a median ridge and at the head has an almost triangular shape resting against a semicircle. The knop is made up of a bulbous moulding with a narrow one on each side separated above and below from single ones each of which has a dip in the middle. The lower bow has a central arris and tapers to a two part foot-knob.

The chief characteristics here are the replacement of the petalled knop of the more standard forms with plain mouldings, and the use of small almost lenticular mouldings above and below that. The distribution is not only southern Britain but is specifically the lower Severn Valley with most being concentrated in Gloucestershire and spreading from there into South Wales and Wiltshire. There are occasional outliers. To some extent the picture is biased by the large number from Kingscote (Timby 1998, 134, Nos 102–7), but even without these, there is still the same emphasis. The dating, as ever, when it comes to specific varieties of Trumpet brooches is weak: Tewkesbury, AD 50–140 (Hannan 1993, 66–7, fig. 19,9); Whitton, AD 50–95 (Jarrett and Wrathmell 1981, 175, fig. 70,24); Usk, Flavian-Trajanic (Boon and Savory 1975, 54, fig. 2,9); Chilgrove, Sussex, late 3rd–early 4th century (Down 1979, 147, fig. 48,6); Nettleton, 4th century (Wedlake 1982, 127 fig. 53,53); Whittington Court, Glos., mid 4th century and later (O'Neil 1952, 77, fig. 12,1). As can be seen, the dating falls into two distinct groups and all in the latter were residual; the proper dating is from *c* AD 70 into the earlier 2nd century.

Unclassified (Fig. 4.4)

36 *214/a SF 22* The spring had been mounted in the Colchester manner (see Brooch 7). The wings are rudimentary. The bow has the appearance of a rounded central feature. A cross-moulding separates it from the broad and spatulate foot.

Derived from the *Augenfibel*, this type comes in two forms with the high probability that the second directly derives from the first. The earlier commonly has a bead-row down the middle of the bow and one or two inverted Vs on the end of the spatula-like foot. The second not only lacks these but has a bow which is narrow with a consequently narrow foot. In default of any evidence for decoration, the form alone suggests the first variety. The distribution is mainly in the modern counties of Hertfordshire, Cambridgeshire, Northamptonshire and Rutland, but they also occur in the lower Severn Valley and near the South coast.

The dating is: Rushden, AD 45–60 (Woods and Hastings 1984, 108, fig. 10.1,5); Colchester, AD 49–61 (Hawkes and Hull 1947, 321, pl. 96,120–1); Broxtowe, before AD 70–75 (Campion 1938, fig,4–5); Haddon, late 1st century–early 2nd century AD (French 1994, 133–4, fig. 72,7); Towcester, *c* AD 100 (Lambrick 1980, 60, fig. 12,3); Baldock, AD 180–200 (Stead 1986, 112, fig. 42, 47–8); Orton Hall Farm, AD 225–325 (Mackreth 1996, 95, fig. 61,13); Haddon 4th century (French 1994, 133–4, fig. 72,8). The probability is that all date essentially before AD 75–80 and, if Roman brooches were not generally to be seen in the lands of the Iceni before the suppression of the rebellion, then the virtually complete absence of this variety may be the best indication that it had ceased to be in use by AD 60. One may also note two examples, unpublished, from Kingsholm, Gloucester, which should also be early in date.

Plate (Fig. 4.4)

37 *U/S SF 92* The pin is hinged and mounted between two lugs. The circular plate has traces of annular grooves around the centre which is an equal armed figure defined by four vesicas.

The form is easily recognisable, but this example lacks the common feature of a circular recess in the middle with a central hole for a stud. While the latter is generally to be expected, it is not a prerequisite, the brooch being essentially allied to a family employing different shapes but having that feature in common. The family arrives with the army of conquest and continues to *c* AD 70, but the present form needs to be looked at separately.

The dating is: Colchester, 43–48 (Hawkes and Hull 1947, 326, pl. 98,177); Hod Hill, before AD 50 (Brailsford 1962, 12, fig. 11,F4); Lockleys, Welwyn, Claudian (Ward-Perkins 1938, 352, fig. 2,2); Longthorpe, Claudian-Neronian (Dannell and Wild 1987, 87, fig. 21,11); Waddon Hill, Stoke Abbot, Dorset, *c* AD 50–60 (Webster 1965, 144, fig. 6,5); Wroxeter, Flavian (D Atkinson 1942, 208 fig. 36,H86); Colchester, before AD 150 (Crummy 1983, 17, fig. 14,86). For the small number recorded by the writer a remarkably high proportion is dated and the message seems unequivocal: essentially pre-Flavian. However, an example from near Newcastle (Hattatt 1985, 151, fig. 63, 547) might have derived from a military site which could have been as early as AD 75–80, in which case it could have been a survivor in use.

Penannulars (Fig. 4.4)

38 *3235/F SF 510* The ring has a circular section. Each terminal is folded back along the top of the ring. One has two notches; the other had three. There is a suspicion that there may be a hollow between the main grooves. The pin is straight.

39 *U/S SF 129* The ring has a circular section. Each terminal is folded back along the top of the ring and each bears signs of cross-grooves.

40 *U/S SF 127* The ring has a lozenge section. The surviving terminal is folded back along the top of the ring and has a central cross-flute with a groove on each side. The top arris of the ring is cross-cut.

Penannulars can be divided into those with coiled or folded terminals as here, and those with knobs. As none is well enough preserved for any to be assigned positively to any of the subvarieties, only a general date range is offered here. Although one or two may occur before the conquest, the vast majority are post-conquest and run on to the middle of the 2nd century AD. However, a strand continues and becomes the zoomorphic and pseudozoomorphic varieties of the 4th century, mainly after 350 and later. There is no evidence here to think that any of these three ought to be placed so late.

Unclassified

41 *470/A SF 71* Iron. Head appears to be rolled over. Bow is quite flat and broad with a very rounded back. Brooch is very corroded (not illustrated).

42 *145/C SF 16* Iron. Very fragmented although bow, head and catch-plate are all represented, also spring fragments; small brooch with a heavy solid catch-plate; bow appears to have quite thick cross-section, it tapers towards foot and is quite curved (not illustrated).

43 *113/I SF 17* Iron. Bow and part of head of brooch, in very poor condition and much fragmented, bow tapers in towards its tip, no visible spring (not illustrated).

Fragments (Fig. 4.4)

44 *192/A SF 21* Iron fragments of probable spring, two coils almost discernible (not illustrated).

45 *528/C SF 115* A half spring with the pin and the distorted chord, probably from a Colchester Derivative.

46 *1158 SF 258* Pin with part of a spring; the type of brooch is indeterminate.

47 *537 SF 104* Pin with the typical hole and extension needed to bind on the body of a hinged-pin brooch when the pin is depressed.

The context and distribution of brooches

Of the 43 complete or near complete brooches at Thornhill Farm, 12 (28%) were unstratified, while the remainder were spread throughout the main excavation trenches (7, 8, 9 and 22; see Appendix 6 for relationship of brooch context numbers with trench, feature and phasing information.). The largest number (18) came from trench 7 (Cat nos 7, 8, 16, 18, 21–23, 26, 28, 34, 36, 41–47), mostly from the enclosure ditches of periods E and F, dating *c* AD 75 to 120. One example (cat no. 28) came from period G trackway 301 in this trench (early 2nd century AD). Two (cat nos 9, 10) of the five brooches from trench 9 came from period C enclosure ditches (*c* AD 1–50), with the other three (cat nos 29, 31, 54) being recovered from undated ditch features. Of the four (cat nos 14, 19, 20, 38) brooches from trench 22, two (cat nos 19, 38) came from period D and E enclosures (*c* AD 50–125). Only a single example (cat no. 30) was recovered from trench 8, but as this area produced little evidence for activity beyond the mid 1st century BC (period A), this is perhaps not too surprising. The overall distribution pattern of brooches suggests that they became increasingly common towards the end of the 1st and start of the 2nd century AD, when settlement activity was largely confined to the area of trench 7.

Copper alloy objects

by Angela Boyle

Of the 52 copper alloy objects from the site, 32 were brooches, and have been reported on separately (see above). The remaining 20 artefacts are catalogued below. A selection is illustrated in Figure 4.5.

Pins

48 *U/S SF 8* Round-headed pin, slightly bent at mid-shaft, max length 89.8 mm, max diameter of shaft 1.2 mm. Length of head 4.9 mm, width of head 5.8 mm. The decoration comprises a series of incised lines or grooves which radiate from a central point at the top of the pin head. Two regular ridges circumscribe the neck of the pin.

49 *U/S SF 82* Incomplete round-headed pin, max length 30.3 mm, max diameter of shaft 1.3 mm. Head of pin is circumscribed by an incised line near the neck. Length of head 1.9 mm, width of head 5.2 mm.

Bracelet

50 *U/S SF 12* Fragment of bracelet, ovoid cross-section, appears to be of 'segmented type', pointed extension at one end, hole at the other, it seems that at least two pieces were intended to slot together, max width 9.3 mm. Decoration comprises two incised lines running around the centre with a longitudinal moulding in between, this appears to have a series of 'nicks' or dots either side. Curve of fragment suggests bracelet originally had a circular form.

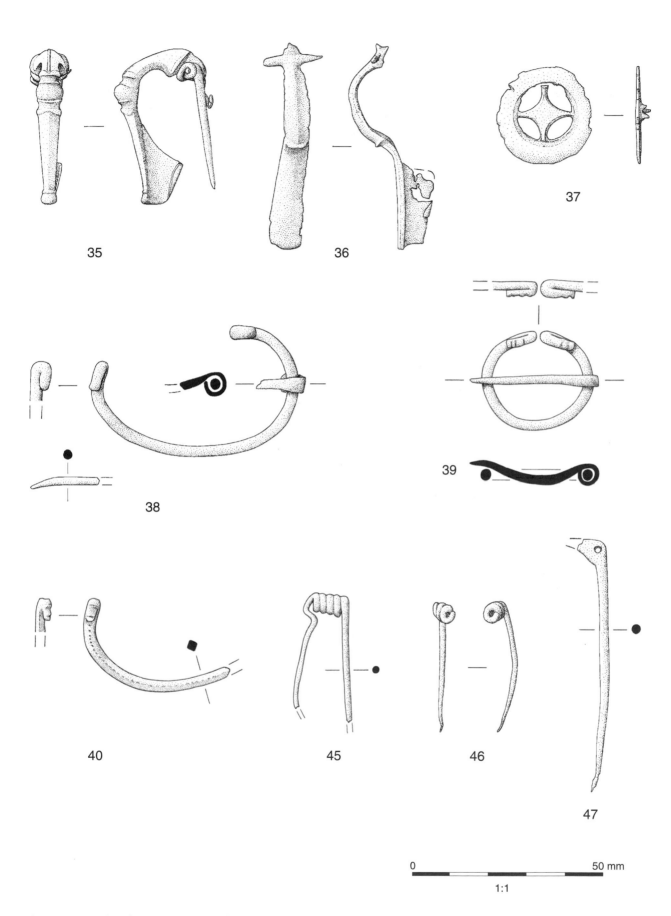

Fig. 4.4 Brooches (Nos 35–40, 45–7)

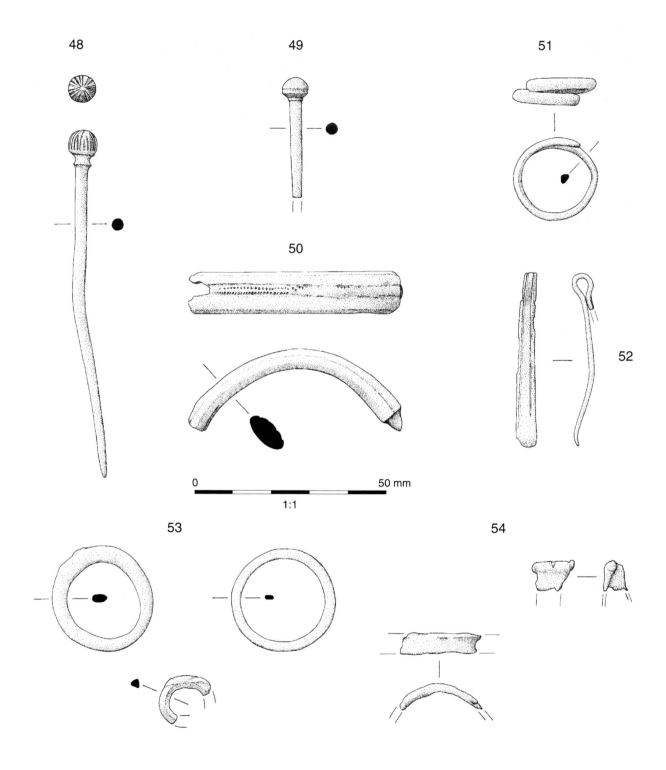

Fig. 4.5 Copper alloy objects (Nos 48–54)

Finger ring

51 *3106 SF 513* Expanding spiral ring, 1/4 turns, max diameter 19.8 mm, ring height 2.2 mm.

Tweezers

52 *U/S SF 271* Incomplete tweezers, rounded loop at head and one half of body survives, this bends outwards at shaft, which widens out towards bottom (ie expanded terminals), flat cross-section. Decoration comprises two longitudinal incised lines either side of body, they run from bottom of body, then up and over loop. Max length 43.6 mm, max diameter of loop 3.3 mm.

A parallel from the cemetery at Skeleton Green (Partridge 1981, 272, no. 14) was found in a grave fill and is probably residual. A further two examples derive from the latest Roman layers at this site (Partridge 1981, 105, nos 10 and 11) and one of them also has expanded terminals and longitudinal grooves which carry on over the hinge loop. Fifteen pairs of tweezers were recovered from the excavations at Baldock (Stead 1986, 130, nos 289–303, fig. 57), some of which had bordering grooves similar to the pair from Thornhill. The excavators remarked on their general absence from early levels (ie pre-Conquest), although rare examples are known from late Iron Age contexts.

Other copper alloy objects

53 *U/S SF 270* Three rings, two complete, one surviving as a fragment, although it was clearly much smaller than the others, and also irregular with one surface rounded and the other flat. Max surviving diameter 13.7 mm, ring thickness 2.2 mm. A second ring is complete and has a maximum diameter of 26 mm, max ring thickness 2.4 mm, though this is variable. The third example, also complete, is the most regular, maximum diameter 25.4 mm, ring thickness 1.4 mm.

54 *2516/A SF 487* A small fitting which may be part of the head of a hinged brooch and a length of curved copper alloy strip which is beaten flat and has a central groove.

55 *2071/B SF 305* Stud? Now in two pieces, max length 17.1 mm, stem of stud has rectangular cross-section, the outer edge of the head appears to have corroded and broken off (not illustrated).

56 *U/S SF 265* Irregular lump, max diameter 15 mm (not illustrated).

57 *U/S SF 267* Irregular lump, originally probably quite flat, *c* 0.5 mm thick, object has been squashed and distorted, *c* 27 mm across, evidence of a possible rim though this is far from clear (not illustrated).

58 *U/S SF 268* A twisted length of copper alloy with rounded cross-section, length 45.9 mm, 3.2 mm thick (not illustrated).

59 *2239/A SF 309* Two fragments (not illustrated).

60 *2284/A SF 314* Irregular fragment, beaten flat (not illustrated).

61 *U/S SF 508* Strip beaten flat, *c* 1 mm thick (not illustrated).

62 *2515/A SF 338* Three 'lumps' and one length of wire bent into a semicircle (not illustrated).

63 *U/S SF 332* Droplet (not illustrated).

64 *2268 SF 334* Droplet (not illustrated).

65 *2515/A SF 498* Three droplets (not illustrated).

Such droplets have been identified as the smooth-surfaced dribbles and blobs from spilt molten metal (Stead 1986), and presumably indicate that a small amount of metalworking was occurring on site.

Silver object (Fig. 4.6)

by Angela Boyle

66 *U/S SF 107* Cylindrical ring or collar, decoration comprises series of incised lines which encircle the body from top to bottom, height 15.2 mm, diameter 10 mm, thickness of metal 1 mm.

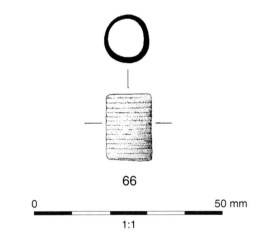

66

0　　　　　　　　　　　　　　50 mm

1:1

Fig. 4.6 Silver object (No. 66)

Iron objects (Fig. 4.7)

by Angela Boyle

67 *801/A SF 207* Incomplete pin, shaft only, much corroded, max length 33.5 mm.

68 *U/S SF 126* Rectangular fitting with two small rivets visible on underside (not illustrated).

69 *840/1 SF 193* Fitting or stud (not illustrated).

70 *937/A SF 190* Small knife, probably complete, little sign of break to blade, tip is very wide and slightly rounded, cutting edge curves upwards towards tip, back of blade is straight and continues into handle, max length 76.2 mm, max width of blade 24.3 mm.

71 *3 SF 1* Incomplete knife blade, in two pieces, nothing remains of cutting edge, back appears to have been straight, larger fragment measures 89.9 mm in length.

72 *2314 SF 336* Complete knife, largest of the assemblage, handle slightly obscured by corrosion (Manning's type 11a?), the back continues the line of the handle and is more or less straight, edge is convex and rises to the tip which is rounded. This example is tanged, max length 131 mm, max width 27.8 mm. Other examples within this general type have rod handles terminating in loops.

73 *761/B SF 246* Possible knife blade, incomplete, seems a little too thick, max length 53.7 mm.

74 *2020 SF 329* Complete knife, max length 92.8 mm, though some distortion caused by marked curve of the knife back, this continues the line of the handle. Blade edge is convex and rises to the tip which is rounded, max width of blade 22.1 mm.

75 *2426/B SF 327* Near complete knife, tip of blade is missing, handle is obscured by dirt and corrosion, cutting edge is straight, back is curved and carries through into handle (Manning type 13), max length 100 mm, width of blade 19.9 mm.

76 *3006/A SF 500* Probable extremely fragmented knife blade, only one substantial piece remains, length 24 mm, max width 11.5 (not illustrated).

77 *2064/D SF 315* Saw, a number of teeth are visible on one side, max length 81.1 mm, max width *c* 15 mm (not illustrated).

78 *2522 SF 491* Incomplete spearhead, little of blade survives, max surviving length 50.3 mm, no central rib. Socket is rounded, short and open, diameter 13.3 mm, undamaged. It tapers slightly towards the blade.

79 *3316/A SF 522* Incomplete reaping hook (Manning type 2), blade is damaged and incomplete, open socket with near rectangular profile, max diameter 27.6 mm.

Manning (1985) states 'as with type 1, type 2 is found on Iron Age sites but is equally common on Roman ones, though Roman examples are more often tanged than socketed and are somewhat better made than their predecessors'.

80 *722/D SF 231* Tang (not illustrated).

81 *3 SF 54* Horseshoe fragment (not illustrated).

82 *146 SF 15* Two very corroded fragments, when joined the two pieces have a hook-like appearance (not illustrated).

83 *3 SF 53* Hook, excellent preservation, complete, single spiked, shaped as a question mark (not illustrated).

84 *537/A SF 75* Flat strip, part of probable rivet hole is visible, max thickness 2.5 mm (not illustrated).

85 *1 SF 179* Spike (not illustrated).

86 *899/B SF 188* Long thin object in fragments, probable rectangular cross-section. Max length 30.1 mm, max width 3 mm (not illustrated).

87 *872/A SF 208* Ring or collar, probably originally rounded although some slight distortion has occurred, 'ring' is not completely enclosed. Max diameter 26.2 mm, max height 20.7 mm, max thickness 6.2 mm. Possible collar ferrule (not illustrated).

88 *802/A SF 235* Rectangular object, one end appears quite rounded, max length 62.1 mm, max width 18.3 mm, max thickness 7.4 mm (not illustrated).

89 *1037/A SF 250* Strip fragment, slight curve, max length 36.9 mm, max width 21.3 mm, max thickness 1.6 mm (not illustrated).

90 *1039/C SF 260* Possible rod or key, in two fragments, max length 98.8 mm (not illustrated).

91 *1046/E SF 262* Incomplete hook-like object, rounded end and flattened cross section (not illustrated).

92 *2020 SF 329* Strip which tapers inwards slightly at one end, both ends are damaged, also at both ends the incomplete outline of a probable rivet hole is visible, max length 105.3 mm, max width 31.2 mm, max thickness 4.1 mm (not illustrated).

93 *2325 SF 331* Object, two conjoining fragments, one has possible rivet hole, max length 110.1 mm (not illustrated).

94 *2515/A SF 489* Three flat fragments (not illustrated).

95 *3004/4A SF 501* Fitting, possibly decorative (not illustrated).

96 *U/S SF 506* Thin rectangular object, one end has a regular v-shaped point, the opposing end is broken, max length 55.3 mm, max width 15.2 mm, max thickness 5.2 mm (not illustrated).

97 *U/S SF 507* Hook like object (not illustrated).

98 *3286/B SF 525* Bar, rectangular, broken at one end, max length 55.2 mm, max width 19.1 mm, max thickness 5.7 mm (not illustrated).

99 *101/G SF 48* Two fragments with flattened cross-section, lengths 18 and 20 mm. Rivet traces on at least one of these (not illustrated).

100 *176/A/1 SF 47* One fragment with flattened cross-section, length 29 mm. Probable rivet at one end (not illustrated).

101 *235/C/3 SF 39* Strip fragment, length 45 mm (not illustrated).

102 *110/G SF 24* Extremely corroded cylindrical object which appears to be solid. Max diameter 19 mm, max length 34 mm (not illustrated).

103 *803/A/3 SF 172* Two conjoining fragments, possible knife blade. Combined length 54 mm (not illustrated).

104 *913/J SF 195* Two conjoining fragments, possible knife haft (not illustrated).

105 *192/B/1 SF 49* One fragment, 29 x 20 x 6 mm (not illustrated).

106 *913/J SF 196* Fragment, length 40 mm (not illustrated).

107 *2284/A SF 312* Fragment, shapeless lump with max diameter of 31 mm (waste?) (not illustrated).

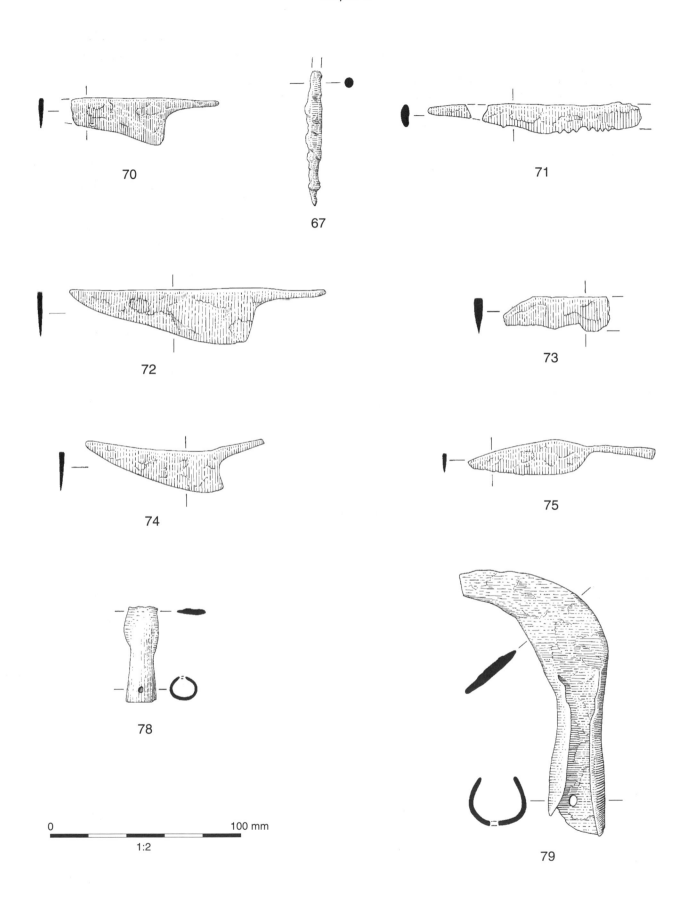

Fig. 4.7   Iron objects (Nos 67, 70–5, 78–9)

Iron nails (not illustrated)

108 *116/G SF 13* Nail, stem only, flattened cross-section, length 39.8 mm.

109 *176/A SF 18* Nail, possible stem, bent at right angle and much corroded, length 17.8 mm.

110 *179/A 19* Nail, fragmented nail stem only, probable rounded cross-section, length 34 mm.

111 *U/S SF 25* Nail, fragmentary stem only, possible square cross-section, length 32.4 mm.

112 *U/S SF 34* Nail? Possible stem only, bent at an angle of 45°, probable rectangular cross-section, max surviving length 45.4 mm.

113 *146/E SF 41* Nail, possible tack with wide disc shaped head, stem much obscured by corrosion, length 34.5 mm; iron fragments of a second unidentified object also present.

114 *166/A SF 46* Nail, stem only with circular cross-section, length 47.8 mm.

115 *3 SF 51* Nail, probable rectangular head, length 20.3 mm.

116 *311 SF 59* Nail, stem only, rounded cross-section, length 36.3 mm.

117 *323 SF 79* Nail, stem only, rectangular cross-section, length 48.3 mm.

118 *431/B SF 87* Nail, head is flat and rounded, stem much obscured by corrosion, length 38 mm.

119 *462/C SF 90* Nail, stem only, flattish cross-section, length 44.6 mm.

120 *431/A SF 159* Nail, very fragmented and much corroded, head circular and probably flat, length 57.1 mm.

121 *1 SF 177* Nail, stem only, probable rectangular cross-section, max surviving length 30.6 mm.

122 *1 SF 178* Short nail, stem probably incomplete, domed head, length 13.7 mm, Manning type 8?

123 *855/D SF 185* Two fragments, not clearly nails, lengths 13.1 and 17.5 mm.

124 *776/B SF 243* Nail, slightly bent stem only, length 50.6 mm. A second thinner fragment measures 13.9 mm in length and does not seem to be associated with nail.

125 *1073/D SF 256* Nail, stem bent at right-angle. length 37.7 mm.

126 *2052/A SF 302* Nail, incomplete stem only, length 27.6 mm.

127 *2214 SF 307* Nail, near complete, head appears rectangular, stem has rectangular cross-section, max length 41.9 mm.

128 *2292/A SF 316* Nail, stem only, length 31 mm.

129 *2295/A SF 317* Nail, stem only, length 51.5 mm.

130 *2371 SF 490* Nail, stem only, flat rectangular cross-section, length 32.8 mm.

131 *U/S SF 505* Nail, rounded head, stem has rectangular cross-section, length 17.4 mm.

132 *U/S SF 512* Nail, incomplete stem only, probable circular cross-section, length 26.2 mm.

133 *3195/A SF 520* Nail stem, length 38.5 mm.

Miscellaneous iron objects (not illustrated)

134 *U/S SF 30* Irregular fragment, length *c* 29.6 mm.

135 *U/S SF 35* Irregular fragment, length *c* 28.6 mm.

136 *U/S SF 36* Irregular fragment, length *c* 20.3 mm.

137 *U/S SF 37* Flat fragment, length *c* 23.8 mm.

138 *U/S SF 38* Irregular fragment, length *c* 14.2 mm.

139 *U/S SF 73* Irregular disc-shaped weight, diameter 21.7 mm, thickness 3.2 mm, width of perforation 5.3 mm.

140 *323 SF 86* Squashed object, originally probable circular collar or fitting, max diameter 22.3 mm, length 17.4 mm.

141 *U/S SF 106* Irregular fragment, *c* 10.4 mm across.

142 *U/S SF 108* Irregular fragment, *c* 15.7 mm across.

143 *U/S SF 113* Circular weight with dome-shaped profile, central perforation, max diameter 20.5 mm, thickness 7.5 mm, width of perforation 3.7 mm.

144 *U/S SF 274* Misc. fragments.

145 *U/S SF 335* Two fragments, lengths 30 and 27 mm.

Lead (not illustrated)

146 *U/S SF 73* Weight.

147 *U/S SF 113* Weight.

148 *323 SF 86* Sheet.

149 *U/S SF 29* Unidentified object.

150 *U/S SF 335* Strip, rolled.

151–159 Nine miscellaneous fragments.

Worked stone (Figs 4.8–4.9)

by Ruth Shaffrey (except where specified)

Beads

by Angela Boyle

160 *1051 SF 248* Fragment of melon bead, appears to be made of stone or other calcareous material, very worn although up to five segments can be distinguished. Max height 17.9 mm, grey in colour with traces of pale blue.

161 *U/S SF 64* Stone or coral, incomplete cylinder with slightly curved sides, off-white, diameter 5 mm, height 7 mm (not illustrated).

Shale bracelet

by Angela Boyle

162 *2016 SF 300* Fragment of shale bracelet, no visible decoration, max thickness 7.9 mm, height 12.5 mm. Curve of fragment suggests that bracelet originally had a circular form.

Quern fragments (not illustrated)

163 *458/F/2 SF 118* Fragment of saddle quern. Worked on opposite faces. Slightly burnt quartz sandstone.

164 *468/D/3 SF 88* Large fragment of lower stone of rotary quern. Very irregular shape. Base may have been reused as slightly dipped. Quartz Conglomerate of the Upper Old Red Sandstone.

165 *489/C/2 SF 89* Small fragment of upper stone of rotary quern. Pebbly Upper Old Red Sandstone.

166 *526/B/2 SF 95* Fragment of upper stone of rotary quern with approximate diameter of 450 mm. Extremely worn suggesting possible reuse in a floor. Quartz Conglomerate of the Upper Old Red Sandstone, Forest of Dean.

167 *528/F/- SF 94* Fragment of possible quern. One flat smooth surface and a few grooves suggesting use as a whetstone. Upper Old Red Sandstone.

168 *536/I/- SF 117* Large disc which may have been a saddle quern. One obviously worked face. Grey coarse grained variety of the Old Red Sandstone. Measures 110 x 120 x 20 mm.

169 *643/A/1 SF 122* Fragment of probable saddle quern. Two worked surfaces. Burnt Greensand.

170 *689/D/- SF 197* Fragment of saddle quern worked on two faces, both very smooth and dipped. Measures 95 x 95 x 45 mm. Grey slightly glauconitic sandstone, probably Greensand.

171 *1123/A/1 SF 254* Possible rotary quern fragment with two worked surfaces. May Hill Sandstone. 55 mm thick.

172 *2085/A/1 SF 356* Possible rotary quern or rubber fragment with two convex surfaces, one of which is slightly polished. Sarsen.

173 *2274/A/- SF 311* Probable quern fragment. Quartz Conglomerate of the Old Red Sandstone.

174 *2471/A/- SF 339* Very small rotary quern fragment with one worked surface. May Hill Sandstone.

175 *3375/A/5 SF 524* Probable rotary quern fragment. Diameter 300 mm or less x 60 mm thick. Slightly curved upper surface and natural edges with smooth grinding surface. May Hill Sandstone.

176 *U/S SF 100* Fragment of upper stone of probable rotary quern, possibly a 'Beehive-style' quern. Pebbly Upper Old Red Sandstone, Forest of Dean.

177 *2352/A/- SF 319* Fragment of upper stone of rotary quern. Worn concave grinding surface. The very smooth upper surface has also been utilised. Curved thick edges. Approximately 300 mm diameter x 85 mm thick. Very coarse shelly limestone, possibly Forest Marble.

178 *U/S SF 1200* Probable rotary quern fragment although not perfectly round. Upper Old Red Sandstone.

179 *2396/A/- SF 328* Three fragments. Possible rotary quern with two worked faces: a smooth grinding surface and a slightly pecked upper surface. Orange/pink, fine grained slightly micaceous sandstone.

180 *221/I/- SF 44* Possible rubber. Roughly shaped rectilinear object, with two possible worn surfaces. Quartzite.

Mortars (not illustrated)

181 *465/-/- SF 128* Fragment of possible mortar or saddle quern. One surface very dipped and smoothed. Measures 270 x 170 x 50–90 mm thick. Very coarse shelly, light coloured limestone.

182 *U/S SF 101* Probable grinding stone. Broken cobble with one dipped surface and one very smoothed surface. Grey sandstone, possibly sarsen.

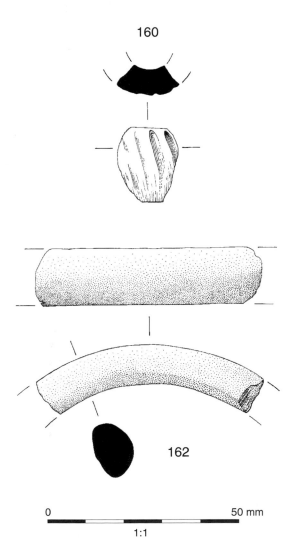

160

162

0   50 mm

1:1

Fig. 4.8 Worked stone personal ornamentation (Nos 160, 162)

Whetstones (not illustrated)

183 *121/-/- SF 11* Very worn fragment of rectilinear whetstone. Very fine grained calcareous, quartzitic grey limestone.

184 *653/A/3 SF 123* Fragment of possible whetstone. Very fine grained quartzitic micaceous stone.

185 *670/A/3 SF 125* Long thin whetstone fragment, well-used along one side. Very fine grained micaceous pale grey sandstone.

186 *795/A/- or 942 SF 242* Possible whetstone. Small rectilinear slab showing signs of some use along one edge. Very fine grained, calcareous, slightly micaceous limestone.

187 *803/E/1 SF 173* Rectilinear whetstone fragment with smoothed sides. Very fine grained calcareous slightly micaceous limestone.

188 *3004/A/- SF 503* Possible whetstone with two dipped surfaces. Very fine grained micaceous grey sandstone.

Polishers (not illustrated)

189 *344/A/- SF 69* Polisher. Almost complete pebble with distinct traces of polish on one face, quartzite. Measures 90 x 70 x 30 mm.

190 *459/H/2 SF 217* Fragment of large pebble used as a polisher. One highly polished surface. Measures 80 x 60 x 50 mm. Burnt sarsen.

191 *3253/B/1 SF 530* Burnt polisher. Half large pebble with clear evidence for polishing on one side and slight on other sides. Measures 110 x 70 x 60 mm.

Pierced items (Fig. 4.9)

192 *176/A/- SF 20* Small fragment of flat spindle whorl measuring 34 mm diameter x 9 mm thick. Very fine grained calcareous quartzitic grey limestone (not illustrated).

193 *2708/A/- SF 325* Complete spindle whorl with round cylindrical hole. One face and all edges very smooth. 53 mm diameter.

194 *322/C/4 SF 81* Pierced irregular oval shaped object. Possibly a loomweight. One face slightly polished, possibly from rotating against another similar item if suspended. Coarse shelly oolitic limestone. Measures 110 x 85 x 30 mm.

195 *221/E/- SF 42* Irregular flat chunk pierced in the two top corners. Possible roof stone. Measures 140 x 80 x 15 mm. Shelly limestone.

Discs (Fig. 4.9)

196 *524/A/4 SF 93* Large flat disc. Possible counter or base or lid. Roughly shaped with one surface more worked than the other. Now blackened, light coloured slightly oolitic limestone. 125 x 120 x 20 mm.

197 *2284/A/- SF 313* Small flat, roughly circular disc, possible counter or base. Smoothed on one face. Very fine grained pale grey limestone. 64 x 70 x 10 mm (not illustrated).

Miscellaneous stone (not illustrated)

198 *2090/A/- SF 355* Probable paving stone. Measures 75 x 55 x 27 mm. Burnt. Probably pennant sandstone.

199 *3213/E/2 SF 527* Probable roofing stone. Burnt, very fine grained calcareous micaceous grey sandstone.

200 *3197/A/- SF 518* Possibly utilised fragment with one uneven dipped surface.

201 *311/-/- SF 67* Probably utilised large chunk with dipped surfaces. White fine grained limestone.

202 *1080/E/- SF 261* Possibly used chunk of stone. Measures 85 x 35 x 35 mm. Grey fine-grained micaceous sandstone.

Discussion

Of the eighteen quern fragments, eleven are from rotary querns, five are from saddle querns, one is from a rubber and one is of unknown form. The querns were largely from undated contexts but those which were phased were all from early Roman contexts. The presence of Old Red Sandstone is unsurprising as it was an almost ubiquitous material on Roman sites in Gloucestershire (Saunders 1998) and was present at the nearby sites of Claydon Pike (Roe forthcoming; Saunders 1998) and Roughground Farm (Saunders 1998). With the exception of Old Red Sandstone, however, the quern materials used here differ from those at Claydon Pike, where Millstone Grit dominates and where lava was also found. Neither sarsen nor Greensand, which occur here, have been identified among the quern materials at Claydon Pike, and the differing use of materials must reflect the different status or connections of the two sites.

The presence of two spindle whorls (SFs 20 and 325; Fig. 4.9, 193) and a probable loom weight (SF 81; Fig. 4.9, 194) is a clear indication that domestic activities such as spinning were taking place on the site, while other discs have a less obvious function. Small finds 93 (Fig. 4.9, 196) and 313 may have been large counters of some sort, but one of these (SF 93) was very blackened. The size and thickness suggests it may have been used as a base to place other, perhaps hot, items on, and the burning that it may have been used as a lid to a pan or oven. Similar objects found at Danebury were interpreted in this way and it was suggested that wear was present on only one face because the item lay flat on one side (Brown 1984, 419), although the item would have to have been in a static position to produce this wear pattern.

Other stone objects are useful indicators of activity taking place on site. Three large pebbles show distinct signs of polish on one or more surfaces, and would have been utilised as polishers,

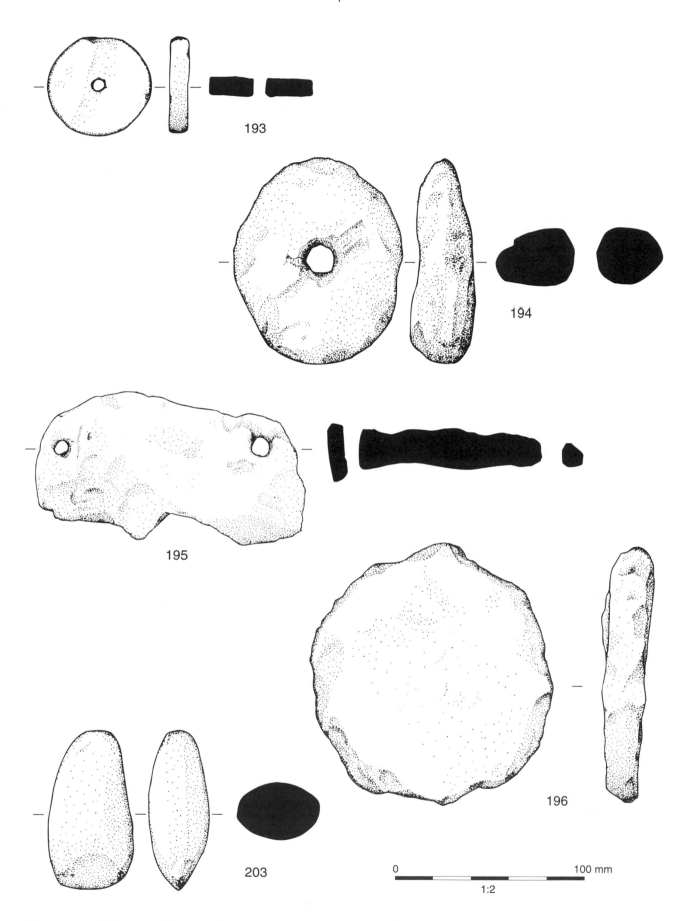

Fig. 4.9   Worked stone objects (Nos 193–6, 203)

although it is difficult to determine as part of what process. It seems unlikely that they were used as pot burnishers such as those found at Cowley (Atkinson 1941, 15), as there is no evidence for pottery production on the site. They were probably utilised in another industrial process such as metal working, which did take place nearby.

Polished Axe (Fig. 4.9)

by Fiona Roe

203 *847/C/1 SF 186* The axe is asymmetrical in length and on the small side, measuring 88 mm in length, 47 mm maximum breadth and 34 mm maximum depth. The rock shows traces of banding. Thin sectioning has demonstrated that the axe is made of greenstone, with a probable provenance in south-west England. Such greenstones were used quite extensively for stone axes in Oxfordshire and Gloucestershire. In these two counties, axes both of undifferentiated and Group I greenstone, when added together, come second in popularity, though by a small margin only, to the Group VI Langdale axes from Cumbria. The find from Thornhill Farm thus helps to demonstrate the importance of materials brought into the area from the south-west during the Neolithic period.

Fired clay

by Jane Timby

Approximately 28.5 kgs of fired clay were recovered from the site. This was examined for any distinguishing features and quantified by broad fabric type (see below). Most of the pieces were very fragmentary, abraded amorphous-shaped fragments of no discernible form or purpose, with an average weight of only 8 g. Some of these could tentatively be identified as pieces from poorly fired clay loomweights of a triangular type (contexts 17, 1046, 1081, 2084, 2506 and 3352). A few fragments are probably associated with metal working, either from moulds or crucibles. A number of pieces exhibited a flat upper surface and irregular underside suggesting linings or surfaces. Two fragments from 2372 and 2351 appeared to be formed around a circular opening, and possibly represent pit linings or something similar. A rounded lip fragment from 1039 may also be from a lining. One piece from 1155 shows an incomplete paw print, probably from a dog.

Fabrics (Table 4.2)

F1: A brownish-red, moderately hard clay with a smooth soapy feel and a generally laminated fracture. The clay contains rounded limestone fragments up to 3–4 mm. Surfaces when present often show organic impressions.

F2: A very sandy textured clay, soft with a scatter of rounded limestone. Easily abraded.

F3: A soft, very fine, dark orange, slightly micaceous clay with red iron and possible clay pellets.

F4: A sandy textured clay with abundant fine to coarse limestone and fossiliferous fragments.

F5: As F2 but with no discernible limestone component.

F6: Fine, soft clay with organic tempering.

Briquetage

204 *897/C SF 676* Fragment of Droitwich briquetage.

205 *113/D/3* Possible fragment of Droitwich briquetage.

Amongst the fired clay was at least one fragment of Droitwich briquetage (no. 204; identification by Dr E Morris). Another less certain fragment was no. 205. Droitwich briquetage is generally associated with Iron Age contexts, and was widely distributed across the West Midlands. Thornhill Farm appears at present to be on the extreme limit of its distribution.

Loomweights

206 *397/C/4 SF 84* Fragment of fired clay triangular loomweight, Fabric F1.

207 *612/A/2 SF 119* Fragment of fired clay triangular loomweight, Fabric F1.

208 *630//B/3 SF 120* Fragment of fired clay triangular loomweight, Fabric F1.

209 *776/B SF 233* Fragment of fired clay triangular loomweight, Fabric F1.

210 *927/C/1 SF 191* Fragment of fired clay triangular loomweight, Fabric F2.

211 *3173 SF 515* Large fragment of fired clay triangular loomweight, Fabric F2.

212 *3173* Fragment of fired clay triangular loomweight, with at least one extant perforation, Fabric F2.

213 *3200/A SF 519* Fragment of fired clay triangular loomweight, Fabric F2.

214 *2379/A SF 321* Fragment of fired clay triangular loomweight, Fabric F4

Table 4.2 Quantities of each fired clay fabric

Fabric	1	2	3	4	5	6
No.	334	747	357	135	1612	47
Weight (g)	3086	5569	2637	1005	15445	181

Sling shot

215 *1091/D SF 259* Oval slingshot, complete, fine sandy clay, 36 mm x 20 mm.

216 *2396/A SF 323* Oval slingshot, complete, fine sandy clay, 40 mm x 22 mm.

217 *3253 SF 526* Incomplete slingshot, with limestone tempering (making a heavier missile).

Crucible?

218 *1021/A* Handmade base, possibly of a crucible. Very fine, soft, slightly micaceous greyware. The fabric contains rare grog, oolitic limestone, shell and quartz. Unphased.

Tile

219–230 *Tile fragments* (see below)

Twelve fragments of Roman tile were recovered (1753 g). The majority of these appear to derive from the north-eastern area of Trench 7. Many of the pieces are fragments of flat tile with thicknesses ranging between 34 and 40 mm (contexts 214, 322, 334, 365, 372, 431 and 859). Fragments of thinner flat tile were recovered from contexts 192 and 197. A possible imbrex fragment came from 200. Post-Roman brick and tile was noted in contexts 3 and 8.

Bone objects

231 *456/C SF 149* An immature animal long bone, probably sheep metapodial, length 91.4 mm. A hole has been drilled through the centre of the shaft, max diameter of hole 1.7 mm.

232 *322/C/3 SF 78* Fragment of probable metapodial which has a hole drilled through the surviving articular surface; only a small part of the shaft survives.

Parallels are known from Gravelly Guy, Bagendon and Maiden Castle and are thought to be used in weaving (Clifford 1961) or as bobbins (Laws 1991). An example from Skeleton Green pit F.9, described as a sheep metacarpal, with a hole drilled through its centre, was possibly used as a toggle (Partridge 1981, 72, no. 15 and fig. 33).

233 *3046/C/1 SF 504* Burnt animal long bone shaft.

234 *3077/J/3 SF 514* Bone fragment, slight signs of polishing.

235 *322/C/1 SF 131* Animal bone with possible drilled hole.

236 *803/D/1 SF 170* Three long bone shaft fragments with polished broken edges.

237 *133 SF 43* Polished animal rib bone.

238 *803/D/1 SF 171* Animal bone fragment with polished surface.

Worked flint

by Hugo Lamdin-Whymark

A total of 24 worked flints were recovered from excavations during 1987 and 1988, comprising a mixed assemblage dating from the Mesolithic to the Bronze Age (Table 4.3). The assemblage would appear to be residual and represents general background activity throughout these periods rather than specific activity areas.

The raw material used was a variable quality gravel flint, available locally from the river gravels. The condition of the flintwork was variable, with the majority of pieces exhibiting a light white cortication. A few pieces were uncorticated, whilst a blade and flake bore a heavy white cortication (SFs 103 and 70). Two further blades were iron stained an orange brown colour (SFs 189 and 206).

The assemblage contains a mixture of core reduction techniques. Both broad hard hammer flakes and fine soft hammer blades were present. Three of the blades (the two iron stained pieces and heavily corticated SF 103) were the product of a blade based industry, exhibiting both platform abrasion and dorsal blade scars. One of the blades was struck from an opposed platform blade core. In addition, a fragment of an opposed platform core was recovered from context 2016/C/1 (enclosure 58 ditch). These pieces appear to be Mesolithic in date, although without a larger assemblage dating cannot be more precise.

The remaining part of the assemblage dates broadly to the Neolithic or Bronze Age; a date in the latter period is more probable given the generally low standard of technology employed on many of the pieces. Context 2016/C/1 contained seven flints, representing the largest concentration on site, and, with the exception of the fragment of opposed platform blade core, these pieces are all of a probable Bronze Age date.

The retouched pieces consist of two scrapers and a retouched flake. The side and end scraper (SF 150) is small and crudely retouched, whereas the end scraper (SF 80) was manufactured on a long blade-like flake with abrupt distal retouch, forming a fine edge although having numerous step fractures.

Table 4.3 The flint assemblage

Category type	Total
Flake	14
Blade	4
Bipolar (opposed platform) blade core	1
Tested nodule/bashed lump	1
Multiplatform flake core	1
End scraper	1
End and side scraper	1
Retouched flake	1
Total	24

THE POTTERY

by Jane Timby

The excavations at Thornhill Farm yielded in the region of 111 kg of pottery, approximately 11,450 sherds. Most of this appears to belong to one uninterrupted period of occupation dating from the middle Iron Age through to the early Roman period. Following comments on the methodology employed and the general condition of the material, this report first discusses the pottery in the context of the site and second considers the assemblage as a whole in its local and regional context. A brief description of the fabrics and associated forms can be found in Appendix 3.

Condition

Soil conditions on the site were not conducive to the preservation of pottery. Heavy clay conditions meant that whilst relatively large sherds were present *in situ*, and substantial parts of individual vessels appeared to be present, their removal upon excavation caused many of the sherds to fragment, creating new fractures and thus hampering an accurate sherd number count. This fragmentation was also aided by the nature of the material itself, which for the most part consisted of poorly fired handmade or slow wheelmade wares. The average sherd size is thus quite low at 9.7 g. A comparison of this figure with other contemporary assemblages shows this to be lower than most and that possibly other mechanisms need to be sought for explaining the higher fragmentation rate. This is explored in more detail in Appendix 2 which looks at site formation processes and redeposition. Many of the sherd surfaces were also poorly preserved. There were a few exceptions, with the preservation of some very sizeable pieces, particularly from storage vessels which tend to be physically more robust. Some of the storage vessels may also have been sunk into the ground as has been documented elsewhere (eg Frocester, Glos; Price 2000), which might have aided their preservation. The pre- and post-excavation fragmentation of sherds and subsequent crumbling and abrasion made it difficult to reconstruct vessel profiles.

Methodology

Preliminary recording work commenced in 1992 when the pottery was sorted into fabrics using a pre-existing recording system established for the OAU. Discrimination between fabrics is based on the relative size, density and type of inclusions macroscopically observable in the paste along with other distinctions such as firing colour and surface finish. Each fabric was recorded by weight, sherd number and estimated vessel equivalent (EVE) for every excavated context, and the data entered into a computer database. Following a hiatus, work resumed on the pottery report in 1998 when the original data was converted to Excel (archive). This formed the basis of the following report. A representative selection of forms, along with decorated or unusual sherds, have been illustrated (Figs 4.10–13). The vessels are arranged as they occurred on site as Period groups rather than as a chronological progression.

In total 752 contexts yielded pottery. Of these less than 2% produced more than 100 sherds, and only 12% produced in excess of 30 sherds. Work by De Roche on Iron Age assemblages from the Thames Valley considered 30 sherds to be the minimum viable size with which to ascribe a date to a context with any degree of confidence, and this figure was adopted here as a rule of thumb (De Roche 1977). Consequently the sample of well dated contexts from Thornhill is low.

As a result of the complexities of the site in terms of ascribing individual contexts to particular periods or phases of activity from the stratigraphic record, the pottery was divided into five broad Ceramic Groups. It was hoped that this might assist in deciphering the chronological development of the site (see Chapter 1 for discussion of post-excavation methodology). The five Ceramic Groups comprised several fabrics, but analytical work focused on just those highlighted in bold as these were perhaps the most diagnostic and more frequently occurring:

Group 1. (3rd–1st century BC): fabrics C15, **C24**, C29, R00, E63
Group 2. (1st century BC–AD): fabrics C21, **C22**, C23, C26, C32, E72
Group 3. (early 1st century AD onwards): fabrics E11, E62, **E83–85**, E92, R23, R24, R48, O41, O43, O47, O49
Group 4. (mid 1st century AD onwards): fabrics **E81–82**, E86, E88, **R33**, R26, R49
Group 5a. (later 1st century–early 2nd century): fabrics E87, E91, **R11–13**, R14, R22, R27, R34, R36, **R44, R46,** R47, O30, **O31**, O32–33, O35, O40, O46
Group 5b. Roman wares (late 1st–early 2nd century): fabrics **S, M11, A11, B10, W22, W24**

The groups cannot be totally prescriptive as certain fabrics have a longer lifespan than others (eg Malvernian wares span the mid–later Iron Age into the 2nd century AD). The starting points are thus more accurate than the finishing dates. Group 5 is subdivided into 5a and b to distinguish between local/indigenous wares and those imported to the site.

Discussion of fabrics and forms

The middle Iron Age through to the early 2nd century AD saw a number of changes and innovations in pottery technology and style resulting in a particularly diverse range of fabrics. As a result some 80 fabrics have been described, the details of which can be found in Appendix 3. Table 4.4 presents a summary quantification. The pre-Roman

Table 4.4 Quantities of individual pottery fabrics

Group	Fabric	Description	No.	%	Wt (g)	%	EVE	%
I CALCAREOUS	C14	wm sparse shell	74	+	740	+	134	1.5
	C15	coarse hm shell	34	+	316	+	0	0
	C20	general limestone	186	1.5	1202	1	0	0
	C21	Palaeozoic limestone	194	1.5	1393	1	32	+
	C22	Malvernian limestone	909	8	4637	4	636	8
	C23	Palaeozoic lime + grog	12	+	47	+	4	+
	C24	oolitic limestone+ shell	1840	16	14999	13.5	779	10
	C25	wm black with red core	84	+	540	+	90	1
	C26	Jurassic limestone + shell	139	1	1315	1	81	1
	C27	sparse oolitic limestone	39	+	258	+	42	+
	C28	sandy with sparse limest	5	+	38	+	6	+
	C29	coarse tempered	31	+	225	+	6	+
II CALCITE	C31	sparse calcite greyware	4	+	15	+	0	0
	C32	calcite-tempered	175	1.5	1021	1	50	+
III GROG	E80	general grog-tempered	147	1	1522	1.5	144	2
	E83	native grog-tempered	192	1.5	2287	2	91	1
	E84	native grog-tempered	298	2.6	3013	2.5	53	+
	E85	grog/organic/flint	1569	13.5	12416	11	1068	13.5
	E88	grog and fine sand	77	+	3157	3	43	+
	E89	grog and flint-tempered	3	+	17	+	0	0
	E90	grog and sand-tempered	1	+	20	+	0	0
IV ROCK	E71	coarse Malvernian rock	170	1.5	1591	1.5	0	0
	E72	Malvernian rock	5	+	20	+	0	0
V ORGANIC	E10	organic-tempered	13	+	59	+	15	+
	E11	fine organic	1	+	5	+	0	0
VI FLINT	E60	general flint	8	+	76	+	7	+
	E62	calcined flint	6	+	81	+	5	+
	E63	calcined flint	3	+	41	+	0	0
VII SANDY	R00	fine black hm sandy	98	+	703	+	32	+
VIII IMPORTS	A11	Dressel 20	9	+	308	+	21	+
	A30	coarse unassigned	9	+	296	+	0	0
	A35	Dressel 2-4	1	+	37	+	0	0
	M11	N Gaulish mortaria	1	+	25	+	7	+
	S	samian	14	+	94	+	31	+
IX REGIONAL	B10	Dorset black-burnished	9	+	128	+	55	+
X LOCAL	E81	hm Savernake ware	594	5	19458	17.5	480	6
Wiltshire	E82	sandy Savernake type	448	4	6722	6	407	5
	E86	Savernake variant	159	1	5020	4.5	134	1.5
	E87	Savernake variant	57	+	433	+	64	+
	E91	Savernake ware	431	3.5	4281	4	387	5
	R13	Wilts fine grey sandy	302	2.5	1763	1.5	330	4
	R44	Wilts medium sandy	94	+	687	+	117	1.5
	O30	Wilts oxidised	24	+	117	+	59	+
	O31	fine sandy ? Purton	15	+	87	+	1	+
	O32	fine sandy with iron	83	+	376	+	32	+
Wilts/Oxon?	R12	greyware with red core	220	2	1299	1	218	3
	R33	black burnished wm ware	225	2	766	+	95	1
	R34	black sandy with red core	53	+	363	+	65	+
	R36	hard fine greyware	9	+	98	+	32	+
	R46	sandy with flint/grog	141	1	2192	2	101	1.5
	R47	sandy with black iron	23	+	256	+	28	+
	O33	sparse coarse sand	31	+	298	+	8	+
	O35	red-brown sandy	2	+	15	+	0	0
Oxon	R11	Oxon fine greyware	299	2.5	1957	1.5	367	4.5
	W22	Oxon sandy whiteware	4	+	64	+	0	0
Severn Valley ware	R48	charcoal-tempered SVW	64	+	535	+	30	+
	R49	reduced SVW	6	+	69	+	11	+
	O40	early SVW variant	6	+	77	+	0	0

Table 4.4   Quantities of individual pottery fabrics (continued)

Group	Fabric	Description	No.	%	Wt (g)	%	EVE	%
	O41	organic-tempered oxidised	77	+	806	+	107	1.5
	O42	hm SVW storage jar	1	+	20	+	0	0
	O43	Severn Valley ware	1153	10	5712	5	843	11
	O47	early SVW variant	144	1	761	+	64	+
	O49	grogged early SVW	37	+	188	+	7	+
XI UNKNOWN	R10	misc fine grey sandy	24	+	114	+	6	+
	R20	misc medium grey sandy	14	+	48	+	10	+
	R22	sparse medium sand	25	+	178	+	46	+
	R23	medium sandy + quartzite	6	+	60	+	11	+
	R24	medium sandy with iron	48	+	345	+	33	+
	R26	medium black sandy	93	+	1558	1.5	110	1.5
	R27	sand with grog	61	+	560	+	17	+
	O10	misc fine orange sandy	2	+	7	+	0	0
	O12	fine micaceous sandy	20	+	163	+	0	0
	O20	misc medium sandy	4	+	27	+	0	0
	O28	ill-sorted sand and iron	2	+	49	+	0	0
	O44	fine sandy	1	+	4	+	0	0
	O45	fine with organic	3	+	41	+	0	0
	O46	sandy with calcareous	25	+	135	+	78	1
	O83	coarse sandy	13	+	55	+	0	0
	W20	misc sandy whiteware	2	+	9	+	0	0
	W24	misc sandy whiteware	12	+	175	+	0	0
XII UNCLASS	OO		33	+	471	+	24	+
TOTAL			11450	100	111061	100	7754	100

+ = Less than 1%

wares or native wares can be broadly divided into seven classes on the basis of the main tempering agents used: I calcareous; II calcite; III grog; IV rock; V organic; VI flint and VII sand. The Roman wares are divided into foreign imports, local wares (up to 40–50 km), regional wares (beyond 50 km) and source unknown.

The middle Iron Age (Group 1) assemblage is essentially characterised by calcareous wares, in particular coarse fossil shell (C15) and oolitic limestone and fossil shell tempered wares (C24). The sandy wares (fabric R00) may also date back to this period. Other sherds potentially dating to this period – for example, a calcined flint-tempered fabric (E60, E62, E63) – are too rare to date closely. Fabric C24 very much dominates the group, accounting for 13.5% by weight of the total site assemblage.

The vessels mainly comprise slack-sided jars with simple undifferentiated or curved rims (eg Fig. 4.10: 2–4, 9, 15–16; Fig. 4.13: 79, 88), ovoid or barrel-bodied jars with slightly beaded rims (Fig. 4.10: 7, 10; Fig. 4.13: 83), slightly everted rim jars (Fig 4.10: 8, 17; Fig. 4.13: 75) or globular bodied bowls or jars with beaded rims (Fig. 4.10: 13, 24; Fig. 4.12: 59, 60, 65; Fig. 4.13: 82). Less common forms include a small carinated cup with incised diagonal lines around the rim (Fig. 4.10: 6). Other Group 1 decorated vessels in the assemblage include a jar (C24) from enclosure 77 with diagonal incised lines (Fig. 4.11: 50), a small jar (C24) with parallel incised

horizontal grooves on the upper body (Fig 4.10: 23), a sherd with a complex burnished line design (Fig. 4.11: 37) in fabric C28, and a sherd of fabric C26 decorated with an incised lattice (Fig. 4.10: 14). Other stratified wares in Group 1 include an ovoid-bodied, simple rim jar in a coarse limestone-tempered fabric (C29; Fig. 4.10: 5). Many of the vessels in fabric C24 show evidence of use in the form of sooted exterior or internal burnt residue.

During the 1st century BC the pottery assemblage becomes much more diverse with numerous new fabrics and the introduction of new forms. The rapid changes which manifested themselves during this period across Britain are not yet fully understood in the west. In the south-east, at sites like Silchester, grog-tempered wares appear in the later half of the 1st century BC, and wheelmade wares around the turn of the century BC/AD (Timby 2000b). In the west, evidence to date suggests that grog-tempered wares only perhaps became common from the early 1st century AD, preceded by the widespread occurrence of Malvernian limestone-tempered wares (fabric C22) which continue through into the 1st century AD. The frequent appearance of Malvernian wares is, therefore, taken to signify a date from the later Iron Age (Group 2) along with more diverse local limestone-tempered fabrics and a calcite-tempered ware (C32). This does not preclude the possibility of the presence of some middle Iron Age Malvernian limestone-tempered sherds such as the jar with a slightly thickened rim (Fig. 4.10: 1) from enclosure 120 (Period A). There are, however, no duck-stamped vessels characteristic of middle Iron Age Malvernian rock-tempered wares which tend to be concentrated nearer to the source area (Peacock 1968, figs 2–3).

Malvernian limestone-tempered ware most commonly occurs as cooking pots with short thickened rims, often with a burnished finish (Fig. 4.11: 26). Necked bowls such as Fig. 4.10: 22 are less common. Also present from Thornhill is a counter-sunk handle from a jar (Fig. 4.13: 86), and a sherd decorated with incised lines and oval stabs (Fig. 4.10: 21). Fabric C21, also of Malvernian origin, occurs almost exclusively as large diameter hammer-rim bowls (Fig. 4.11: 49). Other featured sherds include two bodysherds of calcite-tempered ware, both from 366 with curvilinear decoration. One sherd (Fig. 4.11: 43) is decorated with a raised applied ridge; the other (Fig. 4.11: 44) with a depressed dimple above which are incised curvilinear lines. The style is reminiscent of the Glastonbury style bowls (cf Cunliffe 1991, A:21) of which at least two others have been found in Gloucestershire, one in a gabbroic-tempered ware from Abbeydale (Timby unpubl. a), the other in a similar calcite-tempered ware from Frocester (Timby 2000a).

Other vessels which may have originally derived from pre-conquest levels include an everted rim Malvernian rock-tempered jar with incised chevron(?) decoration (Fig. 4.12: 66) and a beaded rim jar or bowl in a black sandy ware (R00; Fig. 4.13: 89).

The calcareous wares tend to decline in deference to grog-tempered fabrics in the early 1st century AD with the appearance of a mixture of handmade and wheelmade wares. This juxtaposition of technologies continues to feature up to the end of the 1st century AD. The appearance of the grog-tempered tradition is used to define ceramic Group 3 along with several mixed grog/organic/clay pellet type fabrics in forms linked with the early Severn Valley ware repertoire (Timby 1990).

The earliest grog-tempered vessels are the handmade jars (fabric E83–4) which occur in similar styles to the Malvernian limestone-tempered wares, even including elsewhere the large hammer-rim bowls. The vessels frequently have burnished line decoration. The most common form is again the cooking pot with a short everted or beaded rim (Fig. 4.13: 72). A less common form is a globular bowl with a slightly beaded rim (Fig. 4.12: 57). Other forms appearing towards the end of this group include necked bowls and jars, sometimes cordoned around the neck (Fig. 4.10: 12, 18, 25; Fig. 4.11: 27–8, 32–5; Fig. 4.12: 56, 63; Fig. 4.13: 69), other jars (Fig. 4.11: 30–1, 36, 45), and carinated bowls or cups, plain or cordoned (Fig. 4.10: 19; Fig. 4.13: 87).

Ceramic Group 4 is characterised by the appearance of products of the Savernake-Oare industry and a black-burnished wheelmade sandy ware

(R33). Savernake ware occurs almost exclusively as large handmade storage jars with beaded (Fig. 4.11: 41; Fig. 4.12: 54), thickened finger-depressed (Fig. 4.12: 58) or everted rims (Fig. 4.11: 46; Fig. 4.13: 84), wheelmade jars (Fig. 4.11: 42) and rarely as lids (Fig. 4.12: 64). Traditionally, Savernake ware is thought to have been in production from the second half of the 1st century AD; its subsequent expansion and distribution being attributed to military movements (Swan 1975). It appears to occur on a large number of sites established in the pre-Roman period throughout Gloucestershire such as Frocester (Timby 2000a); below the Kingsholm fort (Timby 1999); at Bagendon (Clifford 1961, figs. 68–70) and The Ditches, North Cerney (Trow 1988, fabric 11). Although none of these sites can provide unequivocal dating for the pottery, its widespread circulation might suggest production was already underway prior to any Roman intervention. A date sometime in the mid 1st century may be appropriate on present evidence for its first appearance in the ceramic record. Vessels continue to be made well into the 2nd century AD.

Fabric R33 is also quite widespread and vessels are found on many 1st-century sites in Gloucestershire including both Cirencester (Rigby 1982, 153 fabric 5) and Gloucester (Ireland 1983, fabric 201). Evidence from Cirencester suggests it first appears in quantity from the Neronian period continuing to feature into the early–mid 2nd century.

The final ceramic phase, Group 5, is marked by the occurrence of more Romanised vessels, wheelmade more standardised forms including products of the early Oxfordshire and North Wiltshire industries and Severn Valley ware proper. Jars again dominate the repertoire, mainly in various grey sandy fabrics (eg Fig. 4.11: 51; Fig. 4.12: 52, 55, 62; Fig. 4.13: 67–8, 74, 80), lids (Fig. 4.13: 77), a small number of non-Severn Valley ware tankards (Fig. 4.13: 85) and beakers (Fig. 4.11: 47; Fig. 4.12: 53). Oxidised wares include dishes (Fig. 4.11: 48), jars (Fig. 4.13: 76) and, amongst the Severn Valley ware range, tankards (Fig. 4.13: 73, 78), small necked bowls (Fig. 4.11: 38; Fig. 4.13: 71, 81), jars (Fig. 4.13: 70) and carinated cups (Fig. 4.12: 39; Fig. 4.12: 61).

A small quantity of regional and foreign imports also appear in Group 5, including Dorset black burnished ware, samian, mortaria and amphorae. Many rural sites in the Thames Valley only seem to acquire such Roman fabrics along with an increased range of forms including mortaria and flagons towards the end of the 1st century AD into the early 2nd century AD.

Looking at the assemblage as a whole (Table 4.5), the three dominant groups are Roman local wares at 41% by count, 49% by weight, followed by the calcareous group at 31% (count) 23% weight and the pre-Roman grog-tempered wares at 20% (count and weight). Each group is effectively the dominant ware at different points in the site history. A lower percentage weight for the earliest group, namely the

Table 4.5   Proportions of different ware groups

Group	Ware	No.	%	Wt (g)	%	EVE	%
I	Calcareous	3547	31	25710	23	1810	23
II	Calcite	179	1.5	1036	1	50	+
III	Grog	2287	20	22432	20	1399	18
IV	Rock	175	1.5	1611	1.5	0	0
V	Organic	14	+	64	+	15	+
VI	Flint	17	+	198	+	12	+
VII	Sandy	98	+	703	+	32	+
VIII	Roman imports	34	+	760	+	59	+
IX	Roman regional	9	+	128	+	55	+
X	Roman local	4702	41	54420	49	3987	51.5
XI	Source unknown	388	3	3999	3.5	335	4
Total		11450	100	111061	100	7754	100

+ = Less than 1%

calcareous group, against the sherd number, is a reflection of the longer period of time the sherds have been in the soil, and of the increased likelihood of redeposition. The proportions are reversed for the Roman wares which are amongst the latest wares on the site.

Site discussion

The site has been divided into eight periods (Periods A–H), commencing in the middle Iron Age, with a further U category for contexts assigned to enclosures but whose position in the sequence is uncertain. Table 4.6 summarises the total amount of material from the defined chronological periods whilst Table 4.7 provides detailed information of the fabrics from each of the defined chronological periods only. Full details of the ceramic record can be found in the site archive.

Ceramic research subsequent to the initial pottery analysis has suggested that one feature (pit 3247) could well predate the rest of the site, although at present it is subsumed into Period A (see below).

Table 4.6   Quantity of sherds from each period

Period	No.	Wt (g)	EVE
A	699	7009	168
B	168	1266	27
C	1424	9736	729
C/D	39	190	1
C/E	4	37	0
D	1021	9419	750
E	1370	14153	1170
F	2124	21838	1769
G	264	1526	204
H	18	441	32
U	499	6695	273
Other	3820	38751	2631
Total	11450	111061	7754

Periods A–H account for 62% by count (59% by weight) of the total pottery assemblage. The remaining 38% is essentially unphased. Considerable use has been made of the pottery data to elucidate the site history which is discussed above (see Chapter 3). The following briefly summarises the pottery from the main defined structures and enclosures allocated to each period in terms of its composition.

Period A (middle Iron Age)

Period A is very much dominated by fabric C24, an oolitic limestone and fossil shell-tempered ware typical of the middle Iron Age in this region. Coarse shell-tempered wares (C15) more characteristic of the early Iron Age are extremely rare. There are relatively few featured sherds, and most come from slack-sided jars with no distinguishing characteristics.

An unusual and surprising element of the assemblage is the presence of approximately 166 sherds from a coarse Malvernian rock-tempered vessel (E71) all from one pit (3247) in Trench 22. The sherds are in very poor condition, many reduced to just crumbs. The vessel appears to be an urn with a flat base, a plain vertical rim and walls. The sherds have a red-brown exterior and brown core and interior surface. The vessel is poorly fired and the coarsely tempered fabric is particularly friable. This is a curious presence not only as the site is on the limits of the distribution of this ware, but also because its coarse nature suggests it may belong to an early facet of the Malvernian industry about which little is known. Recent identification of coarse Malvernian wares in mid–later Bronze Age deposits at Sandy Lane, Cheltenham (Timby 2001), Tewkesbury (Timby in prep.) and Much Marcle, Heref. (Darvill pers. comm.) demonstrates not only the exploitation of the Malvernian deposits earlier than perhaps has been hitherto acknowledged, but also the transportation of vessels away from the immediate source region. The date of the Thornhill

Farm vessel is unclear but may be earlier than previously thought, especially as the pit appears to be an isolated feature, and this ware was not recorded elsewhere on the site.

Other significant groups of pottery from Period A came from the roundhouse (structure 207) and associated enclosure (S120) in Trench 8. The roundhouse gully yielded 46 sherds of oolitic limestone and shell-tempered ware (C24) along with four later intrusive sherds. The assemblage from the enclosure ditch (803) is similarly dominated by fabric C24 with a small number of other wares including calcareous fabrics C14, C15 and C29 along with three sherds of Malvernian limestone-tempered ware (C22) and two very small sherds of Malvernian rock-tempered ware (E72). If these are not intrusive sherds they suggest relatively early links with the west.

The remaining pottery from Period A features comprises small groups from various pits and gullies. Nearly all these contained only fabric C24, the only exceptions being pits 916 and 924, and gully 917 which also contained handmade black sandy wares (fabric R00).

Period A illustrated sherds (Fig. 4.10)

1   Handmade bowl with thickened rim. Black in colour, originally with a burnished finish, since worn. Fabric C22. 803/E/4. Enclosure 120.
2   Handmade barrel-bodied jar. Fabric C24. Marked with a zone of sooting around the upper body. 803/G/3. Enclosure 120.
3   Handmade globular or barrel-bodied jar. Fabric C24. 803/C/2. Enclosure 120.
4   Handmade rim fragment from a jar or bowl. Fabric C24. 803/E/2. Enclosure 120.
5   Simple ovoid-bodied, simple rim jar. Grey exterior with a grey–brown interior and core. Fabric C29. 803/A/4. Enclosure 120.
6   Small carinated handmade cup. Decorated with lightly incised lines around the rim. Fabric C24. Pit 667/A/1.
7   Handmade, beaded rim wide-mouthed jar or bowl decorated with a single groove below the rim. Fabric C24. Pit 846/A/1.
8   Slack-shoulder handmade jar with finger depressions below the rim made in forming the vessel. Fabric C24. Pit 962/A.
9   Simple rim, handmade slack-sided jar. Fabric C24. Pit 962/A.

Period B (late Iron Age c 50 BC–AD 1)

Only a small number of features could be allocated to this period on the basis of the pottery. Although Malvernian limestone tempered ware was selected as a ceramic marker for this period in the absence of other easily identifiable types, only two Period B features yielded examples: pit 2392 and posthole 2117. Fabric C26, another Jurassic source ware,

appears in the ceramic record at this point with 50 sherds coming from gully 882 and a further three from gully 925 alongside 56 sherds of sandy ware (R00).

Period B illustrated sherds (Fig. 4.10)

10   Handmade barrel-bodied jar. Dark grey with a red-brown interior. Fabric C24. Gully 925/A/1.
11   Handmade jar with a thickened rim. Red-brown to grey exterior with a lighter grey-brown interior and grey inner core. Fabric C26. Gully 925/A/1.

Period C (late Iron Age c AD 1–50)

Period C is distinguished principally on the basis of the widespread occurrence of grog-tempered wares (fabrics E83–5) in the ceramic record, accompanied, towards the end of the period, by proto-Severn Valley wares in the form of handmade and wheelmade carinated grog-tempered cups and necked bowls (fabrics E85, O41, O43) and handmade storage jars of Savernake ware (fabrics E81–2). An increased amount of pottery from this Period (Table 4.7) suggests renewed or more intensive activity in the early 1st century AD. It is unfortunate that the nature of the site does not permit a more refined ceramic sequence to be established from the stratigraphic record.

Of the buildings allocated to Period C, structure 200 produced relatively little pottery, sherds being confined to pits 3349 and 3353. Amongst these were several sherds from a Malvernian limestone cooking pot and a number of pieces of grog-tempered fabric E85, including a necked, cordoned jar and a storage jar. A much larger group of pottery, some 245 sherds, was recovered from features associated with structure 201. At least 11% (by count) are redeposited sherds of fabric C24, and 49% grog-tempered wares, fabrics E83–5. A single Savernake sherd (E91) came from gully 2084.

Grog-tempered fabrics E83–85 feature in many of the defined enclosures, and form the dominant wares in enclosures E5, E46, E48, E52, E61, E70, E74, E82, E90 and E112. In addition to the storage jars and necked cordoned jar noted above, forms include carinated cups, necked bowls, everted rim jars and carinated bowls.

Period C illustrated sherds (Fig. 4.10)

12   Wheelmade necked bowl with thickened rim. Fabric C14. Gully 120/F/3. Enclosure 5.
13   Handmade beaded rim bowl. Fabric C29. 230/A/1. Enclosure 5.
14   Handmade bodysherd with incised lattice decoration. Fabric C26. 724/A. Enclosure 23.
15   Handmade simple rim bowl. Fabric C24. 725/A. Enclosure 23.

Table 4.7 *Quantities of individual fabrics from each period*

Ceramic Group	Fabric	A No.	A Wt (g)	B No.	B Wt (g)	C No.	C Wt (g)	D No.	D Wt (g)	E No.	E Wt (g)	F No.	F Wt (g)	G No.	G Wt (g)	H No.	H Wt (g)
0	E71	166	1427	0	0	0	0	0	0	0	0	0	0	0	0	0	0
1	C24	506	4944	32	194	233	1725	89	668	146	831	138	1162	29	167	2	29
1	C15	2	134	0	0	3	3	7	33	3	30	0	0	5	15	0	0
1	C29	7	81	0	0	9	43	1	10	0	0	13	85	0	0	0	0
1	E60	0	0	0	0	0	0	0	0	0	0	2	23	0	0	0	0
1	R00	5	50	56	266	1	10	0	0	2	13	2	1	0	0	0	0
2	C21	0	0	7	16	7	37	51	227	36	439	1	16	0	0	0	0
2	C22	3	88	20	22	116	455	286	1396	87	362	46	157	0	0	0	0
2	C23	0	0	0	0	1	4	3	12	0	0	5	10	0	0	0	0
2	C26	0	0	53	768	11	53	7	65	1	4	4	57	0	0	0	0
2	C32	0	0	0	0	95	427	6	19	43	136	1	38	0	0	0	0
2	E72	2	1	0	0	0	0	0	0	0	0	0	0	0	0	0	0
3	C14	1	7	0	0	29	139	25	266	9	277	0	0	1	4	0	0
3	C20	0	0	0	0	1	1	0	0	0	0	1	3	0	0	0	0
3	C25	0	0	0	0	1	5	6	23	7	36	5	70	1	9	0	0
3	C27	0	0	0	0	5	19	8	30	5	26	12	139	0	0	0	0
3	C31	0	0	0	0	3	12	0	0	0	0	0	0	0	0	0	0
3	C00	0	0	0	0	1	3	0	0	1	4	0	0	0	0	0	0
3	E11	0	0	0	0	0	0	0	0	0	0	1	5	0	0	0	0
3	E62	0	0	0	0	0	0	0	0	1	6	4	40	0	0	0	0
3	E83	0	0	0	0	39	295	24	2039	38	270	23	366	1	9	1	36
3	E84	0	0	0	0	33	500	17	975	6	129	225	558	2	31	0	0
3	E85	1	6	0	0	469	3481	298	2122	163	1501	86	612	24	100	0	0
3	O41	0	0	0	0	2	27	8	40	15	148	26	326	1	7	0	0
3	O43	0	0	0	0	243	643	78	317	102	469	217	1579	23	76	2	19
3	O47	0	0	0	0	2	26	0	0	24	104	35	218	5	25	0	0
3	O49	0	0	0	0	9	37	1	10	5	29	7	50	3	3	0	0
3	R23	0	0	0	0	0	0	2	33	0	0	1	10	0	0	0	0
3	R24	0	0	0	0	21	59	2	62	8	34	2	64	4	6	0	0
3	R48	0	0	0	0	15	35	1	24	20	142	12	166	5	41	0	0
4	E81	1	15	0	0	14	270	49	1692	101	3758	150	4419	25	375	3	241
4	E82	1	28	0	0	12	236	34	242	119	1821	114	1329	0	0	1	20
4	E86	3	156	0	0	10	60	10	386	9	561	44	1407	0	0	0	0
4	E88	1	72	0	0	8	823	5	224	8	232	6	228	0	0	0	0
4	R26	0	0	0	0	0	0	4	26	22	48	36	471	0	0	0	0
4	R33	0	0	0	0	0	0	5	16	33	165	63	220	4	16	0	0
4	R49	0	0	0	0	1	24	0	0	1	17	4	28	0	0	0	0
2/4	C20	0	0	0	0	1	1	0	0	0	0	1	3	0	0	0	0

Group	Code																
2/4	C28	0	0	0	0	0	0	30	4	0	0	0	0	0	0	0	0
2/4	G10	0	0	0	0	158	16	46	3	250	14	0	0	0	0	0	0
2/4	E89	0	0	0	0	0	0	17	3	0	0	0	0	0	0	0	0
2/4	E90	0	0	0	0	13	1	0	0	6	0	0	0	0	0	0	0
2/4	G31	0	0	0	0	0	0	0	0	0	1	0	0	0	0	0	0
2/4	O28	0	0	0	0	45	1	4	1	0	0	0	0	0	0	0	0
2/4	O45	0	0	0	0	37	2	4	1	0	0	0	0	0	0	0	0
4/5	O12	0	0	0	0	98	12	0	0	0	0	0	0	0	0	0	0
4/5	O20	0	0	0	0	3	1	0	0	0	0	0	0	0	0	0	0
4/5	O44	0	0	0	0	4	1	0	0	0	0	0	0	0	0	0	0
4/5	O83	0	0	0	0	52	12	3	1	27	1	0	0	0	0	0	0
4/5	R10	0	0	0	1	27	3	57	19	4	1	13	1	0	0	0	0
4/5	R22	0	0	2	0	101	16	8	3	0	0	0	0	0	0	0	0
4/5	R27	0	0	0	2	495	44	14	1	17	3	0	4	0	0	0	0
4/5	R34	0	0	7	0	80	14	25	5	0	0	8	5	0	0	0	0
5	E87	0	0	0	9	146	11	108	23	175	10	38	11	0	0	0	0
5	E91	7	2	65	0	2031	192	545	43	0	0	156	0	0	0	0	0
5	O30	2	1	0	3	11	4	83	15	0	0	0	0	0	0	0	0
5	O31	0	0	8	0	45	7	2	1	0	0	0	0	0	0	0	0
5	O32	0	0	0	0	84	17	88	15	0	0	0	0	0	0	0	0
5	O33	0	0	0	0	206	9	49	15	0	0	0	0	0	0	0	0
5	O35	0	0	0	0	15	2	0	0	0	0	17	2	0	0	0	0
5	O40	0	0	0	0	60	4	0	0	0	2	0	0	0	0	0	0
5	O46	0	0	0	6	97	11	0	0	0	0	2	1	0	0	0	0
5	R11	67	2	17	80	934	141	149	52	10	2	0	0	0	0	0	0
5	R12	0	2	264	6	231	37	186	19	6	2	6	2	0	0	0	0
5	R13	13	2	47	7	696	107	396	61	0	0	0	0	0	0	0	0
5	R14	0	0	74	1	139	18	84	15	2	1	0	0	0	0	0	0
5	R36	0	0	14	2	39	3	6	1	0	0	0	0	0	0	0	0
5	R44	7	2	9	6	271	34	47	5	17	1	6	2	0	0	0	0
5	R46	0	0	72	1	1210	87	187	9	11	1	0	0	0	0	0	0
5	R47	0	0	31	0	150	7	20	7	0	0	0	0	0	0	0	0
5	A11	0	0	0	1	244	4	18	1	0	0	0	0	0	0	0	0
5	A30	0	0	3	0	0	0	0	0	0	0	0	0	0	0	0	0
5	A35	0	0	0	3	0	0	0	0	0	0	37	1	0	0	0	0
5	B10	0	0	13	0	34	3	81	3	0	0	0	0	0	0	0	0
5	M11	0	0	0	1	0	0	25	1	0	0	0	0	0	0	0	0
5	S	0	0	1	0	79	6	1	1	0	0	0	0	0	0	0	0
5	W20	0	0	0	1	1	1	0	0	0	0	0	0	0	0	0	0
5	W22	0	0	13	0	0	0	2	1	0	0	0	0	0	0	0	0
5	W24	0	0	0	1	0	0	175	12	0	0	0	0	0	0	0	0
	Unclass.	0	0	2	1	142	9	101	14	0	0	0	0	0	0	0	0
	Total	441	18	1526	264	21838	2124	14153	1370	9646	1064	9736	1424	1266	168	7009	699

16   Slack-sided handmade jar. Blackened rim with exterior sooting, a light brown body and a grey interior. Fabric C24. 725/A. Enclosure 23.

17   Handmade everted rim jar. Fabric C24. 725/A. Enclosure 23.

18   Wheelmade necked, cordoned bowl. Black with a dark grey-brown interior. Fabric C14.

Ditch 2353/A. Enclosure 90.

19   Handmade, wheel finished cordoned tankard. Black exterior, brown interior. Fabric E85. Ditch 2354/A. Enclosure 90.

20   Handmade thickened rim globular-bodied bowl. Fabric C24. Ditch 118/E/1. Enclosure 112.

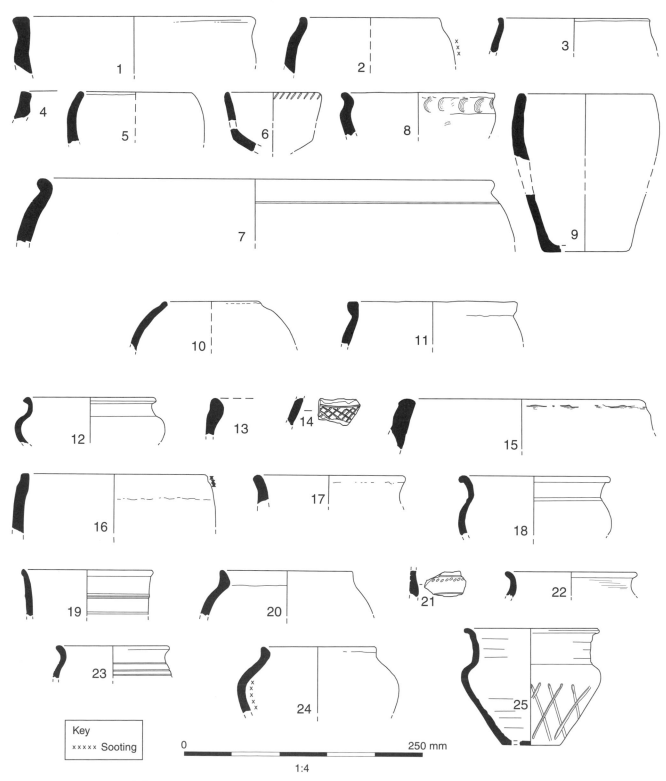

Key
xxxxx Sooting

0   250 mm
1:4

Fig. 4.10   Pottery periods A to C (Nos 1–25)

21 Bodysherd decorated with incised horizontal lines and a line of small oval impressions. Fabric C22. Ditch 118/C/2. Enclosure 112.

22 Possibly wheel-turned necked bowl. Fabric C22. Black burnished exterior and fabric. Ditch 118/C/2. Enclosure 112.

23 Possibly wheel-turned necked bowl decorated with spaced incised horizontal lines on the upper body. Fabric C24. Gully 118/E/2. Structure 112.

24. Globular bowl with short thickened rim. Fabric C24. Burnt residue in the interior surface. 118/E/3. Enclosure 112.

25 Wheelmade necked bowl decorated with slightly irregular burnished line lattice decoration on the body. The base has at least one perforation. Fabric E85. Ditch 412/D/2.

Period D (early Roman period c AD 50–100)

The Period D assemblage is very much dominated by two fabrics: Malvernian limestone-tempered ware (C22) and grog-tempered ware E85. Fabric C22 occurs almost exclusively as ovoid bodied jars or cooking pots with short everted rims, an everted necked example from ditch 44 being more unusual. Fabric E85 mainly features as necked cordoned bowls and jars. Several quite large assemblages were recovered from the fills of the enclosure ditches associated with this period of use, in particular enclosures 44, 45, 48, 49, 51, 54, 57, 58, 72 and 76 (Table 4.8). In every case sherds of middle Iron Age date were present, mixed in with the later material. A number of Roman wares start to appear alongside the native wares, notably various products of the Savernake industry in both handmade and wheelmade forms, and fine grey wares from the North Wiltshire and to a lesser extent the Oxfordshire industries. Various products akin to the Severn Valley industry also occur. Forms of note aside from the usual cooking and storage jars and necked bowls include carinated cups or bowls, straight-sided bowls (fabric R23) and two grey sandy ware beakers (fabrics R14 and R34).

Period D illustrated sherds (Fig. 4.11)

26 Handmade jar with a worn vertical exterior burnish. Black in colour. Fabric C22. Ditch 2284/A. Enclosure 48.

27 Wheelmade necked bowl. Fabric E85. Ditch 2317/A. Enclosure 48.

28 Wheelmade, necked, cordoned bowl. Black exterior with a mid brown interior and grey inner core. Fabric E85. Ditch 2317/E. Enclosure 48.

29 Handmade simple rim bowl. Black in colour with a brown interior and grey core. Fabric R23. Ditch 2317/F. Enclosure 48.

30 Beaded rim jar, dark grey in colour with a red–brown core. Fabric C25. Ditch 2317/F. Enclosure 48.

31 Beaded rim globular-bodied jar or bowl. Brownish-orange with a dark grey core. Fabric R24. Ditch 2317/F. Enclosure 48.

32 Wheelmade everted rim bowl. Fabric E85. Ditch 2355/A. Enclosure 48.

33 Handmade, wheel finished necked bowl. Black with a dark grey interior. Fabric E85. Ditch 2357/B. Enclosure 45.

34 Wheelmade, small, necked globular bowl with a burnished exterior. Post-fracture sooting on the interior and exterior surfaces and break. Fabric E85. 2071/F. Enclosure 76.

35 Wheelmade necked jar. Fabric E91. 877/C/1. Enclosure 125.

36 Handmade or wheel-turned jar. Fabric C26. Sooted on the exterior below the rim. Ditch 899/H. Enclosure 127.

37 Small bodysherd from a handmade bowl with incised decoration. Fabric C28. 899/B. Enclosure 127.

Periods E–F (early Roman period c AD 75–120+)

The large quantities of pottery recovered from Periods E and F, amounting to some 36 kg, suggest this was a particularly intensive phase of occupation, both in terms of the redistribution and redeposition of wares, and from the marked appearance of several new wares in the ceramic record. Tables 4.9–10 summarise the pottery from the main enclosures where the groups exceed 50 sherds. Taking the two periods together, at least 8% of the assemblage by sherd count comprises middle Iron Age fabric C24. Imported wares such as samian, amphorae and mortaria feature for the first time, albeit in very small amounts. The dominant fabrics continue to be the grog-tempered wares, in particular local E85 and Savernake wares (E81–2, E91) accompanied by a significantly greater number of Severn Valley type wares (O43). Other new products include six sherds of Dorset black-burnished ware (B10) including a straight-sided dish and jars, and a number of whitewares, some of which at least derive from the Oxfordshire industries. Jars continue to dominate the group along with bowls. New forms include a single mortaria, a small number of flagons, including ring-necked versions (fabrics O32, O46, O47), smaller flask types (O33, O47), plain walled tankards (O43, R48), platters (R26) and lids (R26, R34, R46). Further beakers occur in fabrics R11, R13 and R14, including a local example of a butt beaker in fabric R33 from ditch 30. Dishes include both straight-sided and curved wall forms (R11, C22, G15), along with a single squat-flanged bowl (R11). The only recorded rim fragment from one of the large hammer-rim bowls or jars in Malvernian limestone-tempered ware (C21) was recovered from ditch 33 (Period E).

Table 4.8 Period D enclosures

Enclos. Fabric	Codes	44 No.	44 Wt (g)	45 No.	45 Wt (g)	48 No.	48 Wt (g)	49 No.	49 Wt (g)	51 No.	51 Wt (g)	54 No.	54 Wt (g)	57 No.	57 Wt (g)	58 No.	58 Wt (g)	72 No.	72 Wt (g)	76 No.	76 Wt (g)	127 No.	127 Wt (g)
MIA calcar	C24	9	85	3	107	18	44	3	25	4	27	9	87	11	53	7	48	4	11	8	78	2	20
Palaeozoic lime	C21-23	35	246	7	12	88	477	7	44	20	96	46	187	11	72	36	113	10	49	29	111	28	152
Other calcar	C14-5, 25-7, 29	4	12	0	0	3	62	3	8	1	10	6	30	4	12	30	243	0	0	0	0	3	50
Calcite	C32	0	0	0	0	3	6	0	0	0	0	0	0	0	0	0	0	0	0	1	5	0	0
Native grog	E80, 83-5, 88-9	36	429	14	128	79	370	22	244	12	135	26	676	26	220	27	229	30	236	33	621	9	26
Local, Wilts	E81-2, 86,91, O30	3	116	4	197	12	224	0	0	6	323	5	155	3	128	1	15	16	429	44	3	2	18
Local ?Wilts	R12,33,34, 44, O33	3	17	1	8	1	5	4	8	0	0	0	0	0	0	1	17	0	0	0	0	0	0
Oxon	R11, R44, W22	0	0	0	0	0	0	0	0	0	0	0	0	0	0	0	0	2	10	0	0	0	0
Severn Valley	R46,48,O41, 43	0	0	1	11	19	50	6	35	2	4	0	0	0	0	9	43	34	155	1	24	0	0
Source unknown	R10, 23-4, 26	0	0	0	0	3	51	5	43	0	0	0	0	0	0	3	47	0	0	0	0	0	0
Total		81	820	27	356	208	1245	47	382	41	568	83	1048	44	432	107	707	92	879	68	804	44	266

Table 4.9 Period E enclosures

Fabric	Enclos. Codes	2 No.	2 Wt(g)	9 No.	9 Wt(g)	15 No.	15 Wt(g)	24 No.	24 Wt(g)	26 No.	26 Wt(g)	27 No.	27 Wt(g)	33 No.	33 Wt(g)	50 No.	50 Wt(g)	64 No.	64 Wt(g)	75 No.	75 Wt(g)
MIA calcar	C24	1	7	56	347	5	14	5	32	7	83	11	51	6	33	11	18	3	24	3	15
Palaeozoic lime	C21-23	2	22	13	56	0	0	1	20	1	7	0	0	8	110	24	97	51	211	10	34
Other calcar	C14-5, 25-7, 29	1	1	3	10	0	0	0	0	1	4	2	12	2	19	0	0	4	30	8	268
Calcite	C32	0	0	25	69	0	0	0	0	9	36	4	15	0	0	0	0	0	0	0	0
Native grog	E80, 83-5,88-9	4	55	43	240	0	0	34	175	0	0	2	10	9	161	11	86	31	378	20	164
Flint -tempered	E62	1	6	0	0	0	0	0	0	0	0	0	0	0	0	0	0	0	0	0	0
IA sandy	R00	0	0	0	0	0	0	0	0	0	0	0	0	0	0	1	4	0	0	0	0
Roman imports	M11	0	0	0	0	0	0	0	0	1	25	0	0	0	0	0	0	0	0	0	0
Roman regional	B10	0	0	1	28	0	0	0	0	0	0	0	0	2	53	0	0	0	0	0	0
Local, Wilts	E81-2, 86,91, O30	8	252	70	2459	29	356	0	0	0	0	40	770	20	411	1	18	3	193	11	199
Local ?Wilts	R12,33,34,44, O33	1	4	24	255	22	138	4	19	8	30	37	256	3	25	0	0	0	0	1	4
Oxon	R11, R44, W22	2	10	37	79	1	11	0	0	1	90	6	24	5	15	0	0	0	0	0	0
Severn Valley	R46,48,O41, 43	13	90	69	348	6	81	6	39	7	53	15	88	26	55	0	0	0	0	6	35
Source unknown	R10, 23-4,26	0	0	11	36	4	64	20	66	1	3	4	33	4	18	1	6	4	19	0	0
Total		33	447	352	3927	67	664	70	351	36	331	121	1259	85	900	49	229	96	855	59	719

Table 4.10 Period F enclosures

Fabric	Enclos. Codes	6 No.	6 Wt (g)	11 No.	11 Wt (g)	16 No.	16 Wt (g)	22 No.	22 Wt (g)	29 No.	29 Wt (g)	30 No.	30 Wt (g)	36 No.	36 Wt (g)	37 No.	37 Wt (g)	154 No.	154 Wt (g)	155 No.	155 Wt (g)
MIA calcar	C24	14	80	4	23	8	71	8	52	20	147	21	343	18	104	5	86	29	167	2	33
Palaeozoic lime	C21-23	0	0	0	0	2	4	2	5	9	30	2	2	32	120	3	2	0	0	0	0
Other calcar	C14-5, 25-7, 29	0	0	3	7	4	55	1	3	2	10	1	31	2	38	5	113	9	30	5	53
Calcite	C32	0	0	0	0	0	0	0	0	0	0	0	0	1	38	0	0	0	0	0	0
Native grog	E80, 83-5,88-9	58	414	12	47	2	32	8	139	5	213	6	38	9	233	5	43	19	382	31	502
Organic	E11	1	5	0	0	0	0	0	0	0	0	0	0	0	0	0	0	0	0	0	0
Flint-tempered	E60, E62	0	0	1	6	0	0	0	0	0	0	0	0	1	18	1	5	3	17	0	0
IA sandy	R00	0	0	0	0	0	0	0	0	0	0	0	0	0	0	0	0	2	1	0	0
Roman imports	A11, A30	0	0	1	4	0	0	0	0	0	0	1	2	0	0	1	3	0	0	0	0
Roman imports	S	0	0	0	0	1	2	0	0	0	0	2	13	0	0	3	64	0	0	0	0
Roman regional	B10	0	0	0	0	0	0	0	0	0	0	0	0	3	34	0	0	0	0	0	0
Local, Wilts	E81-2,86,91, O30	52	617	109	1859	84	769	55	664	11	758	42	1136	51	810	86	1577	54	598	41	844
Local ?Wilts	R12,33,34,44, O33	24	60	17	227	59	803	8	67	9	78	27	96	2	7	23	290	40	356	16	1
Oxon	R11, R44, W22	16	42	15	100	8	60	8	65	1	10	5	16	1	13	37	253	0	0	1	3
Severn Valley	R46,48,O41,43	20	123	40	213	34	268	13	90	16	160	34	293	36	384	59	404	18	99	17	180
Source unknown	R10,23-24,26	18	140	27	170	37	464	7	86	13	111	4	17	5	75	6	136	13	100	6	57
Total		203	1481	229	2656	239	2528	110	1171	86	1517	145	1987	161	1874	234	2976	187	1750	119	1803

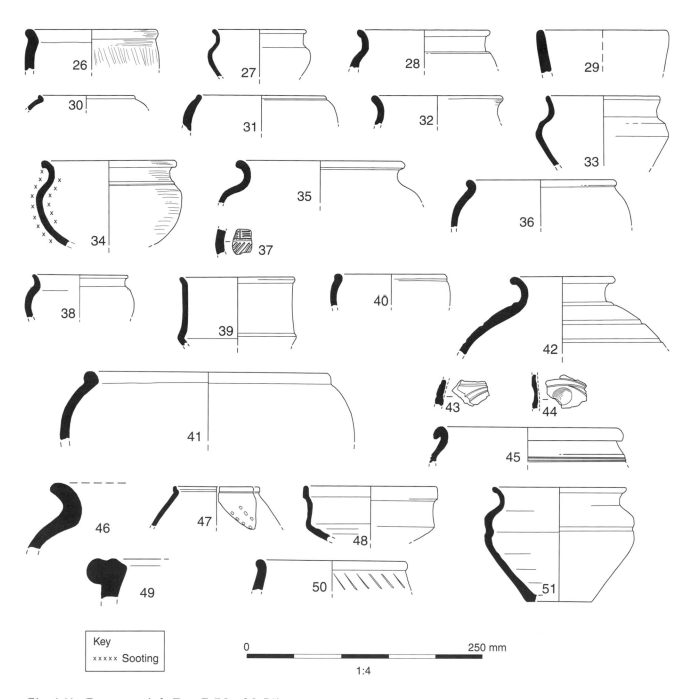

Fig. 4.11   Pottery periods D to E (Nos 26–51)

Period E illustrated sherds (Fig. 4.11)

38   Small wheel-made, necked bowl. Fabric O43. 250/C/3. Enclosure 1.

39   Wheelmade carinated bowl or cup. Fabric O43. Ditch 101/4. Enclosure 9.

40   Handmade, black, calcite-tempered beaded rim bowl. Fabric C32. 113/D/2. Enclosure 9.

41   Large, handmade beaded rim bowl. Fabric E81. 101/H/2. Enclosure 9.

42   Wheelmade narrow-necked jar decorated with horizontal spaced grooves. Fabric E91. 461/G/1. Enclosure 14.

43   Bodysherd decorated with a band of raised curvilinear decoration. Fabric C32. Ditch 366/H/1. Enclosure 26.

44   Bodysherd decorated with a depressed circular dimple and incised curvilinear lines. Fabric C32. Ditch 366/H/1. Enclosure 26.

45   Wheel-turned wide-mouthed jar. Fabric E88. 381/F. Enclosure 27.

46   Handmade everted rim storage jar. Fabric E81. 389/C/2. Enclosure 27.

47   Wheel-made, globular beaker with barbotine dot decoration. Fabric R17 with worn surfaces. 537/J/1. Enclosure 27.

48 Wheel-made carinated bowl. Patchy orange, brown and grey in colour. Fabric O30. 577/B. Enclosure 27.

49 Very large diameter, handmade bowl with a heavy finger-grooved rim. Diameter *c* 640 mm. Fabric C21. 695/A/3. Enclosure 33.

50 Handmade beaded rim jar decorated with incised diagonal lines. Fabric C24. 2338/A. Enclosure 77.

51 Wheel-made necked bowl with a girth constriction. Black in colour with a grey core and interior. Fabric E85. 578/J. Probably Period E.

Period F illustrated sherds (Fig. 4.12)

52 Everted rim necked bowl. Fabric R11. Dark grey exterior, lighter interior. Ditch 108/C/2. Enclosure 7.

53 Everted rim beaker. Fabric R13. Gully 111/F/1. Structure 6.

54 Handmade beaded rim jar with a wheel-finished rim. Horizontal smoothing lines on the interior. Fabric E81. Ditch 172/A/2. Enclosure 11.

55 Wheelmade, angular shouldered jar. Grey with traces of white slip on the exterior. Lightly incised decoration both on the upper shoulder as three-line chevrons and a single wavy line on the upper body. Fabric R26. 528/H. Enclosure 16.

56 Wheelmade, small necked bowl. Fabric E91. 698/E. Enclosure 22.

57 Handmade small globular bowl. Blackened residue on the exterior. Fabric E83. 698/E. Enclosure 22.

58 Large, handmade storage jar with finger-pressed decoration on the rim edge. Fabric E81. 601/A/2. Enclosure 29.

59 Handmade/wheel-turned beaded rim bowl. Grey-black exterior, brown-grey interior. Fabric C24. 454/N/2. Enclosure 29.

60 Handmade, beaded rim jar. Fabric C24. 322/C/3. Enclosure 30.

61 Wheelmade, carinated cup. Fabric O43. Ditch 1080/B/2. Enclosure 37.

62 Wheelmade globular jar with short everted rim. Black fabric R26. 740/A. Enclosure 104.

63 Handmade/wheel-turned necked jar. Black exterior with a light brown interior. Fabric E85. 722/F. Enclosure 155.

Period G (early Roman period c 2nd century AD)

The ceramic record suggests a much reduced level of occupation on the site by the early–mid 2nd century either as a result of a shift in the focus of activity, or of alternative methods of rubbish disposal. Only 264 sherds (1526 g) sherds are attributable to Period G, and most of these came from ditch 301. The assemblage contains a higher proportion of Roman grey sandy wares than earlier phases, but the continued presence of middle Iron Age fabrics (C24) demonstrates the continued high level of redeposition. Other 2nd-century products include further sherds of Dorset black burnished ware and Oxfordshire whiteware (W22).

Period H (late Roman period)

This period is not well represented in the ceramic record, with only 18 sherds, all from linear gully 302. Most of the sherds appear to be redeposited.

Catalogue of illustrated sherds from unphased contexts (Fig. 4.12–13)

64 Small lid. Fabric E86. 2043/A. Enclosure 68.

65 Beaded-rim jar. Mid grey with brown patches. Fabric C24. 2241/B. Enclosure 97.

66 Wheel-turned everted rim necked jar. Dark brown–black with a burnished finish. The upper body is decorated with an incised chevron-style decoration. Malvernian rock-tempered fabric, E72. 623/A/1. Enclosure 34.

67 Wheelmade thickened rim jar. Dark grey surfaces with light grey core with red–brown margins. Fabric R34. 6/A/3.

68 Wheelmade necked cordoned jar with a moulded rim. Black exterior with a light grey core and interior surface. Fabric R46. 6/A/2.

69 Necked bowl with a brownish-black exterior, orange–brown interior and grey core. Fabric E85. 18/A/2.

70 Wheelmade everted rim jar or bowl. Fabric O43. Ditch 103/B/6.

71 Wheelmade necked bowl. Fabric O43. Ditch 124/C/2.

72 Crude, handmade slack-sided jar with a beaded rim. Blackened around the rim, with a light brown body. Fabric E83. Gully 160/B/1.

73 Handled tankard. The handle has been pegged in through the wall to the body. The base fracture, which shows score marks for keying, suggests that the base, now lost, was added separately. Fabric O43. Pit 219/A.

74 Wheelmade, sharply everted rim jar. Fabric R47. 321.

75 Handmade necked bowl. Fabric C24. Pit 388/A.

76 Wheelmade necked cordoned jar. The vessel has warped slightly in firing. Fabric O2. Pit 446/A/2.

77 Conical flat-topped lid. Fabric E91. Sooted around the interior rim area. Pit 485/A/4.

78 Wheelmade tankard. Fabric O43. Pit 541/A.

79 Handmade barrel-bodied jar. Fabric C24. Pit 884/A/2.

80 Wheelmade, beaded rim jar. Black in colour with slightly irregular horizontal burnishing or smoothing marks giving a slightly facetted finish. A hole has been drilled through the centre of the base. Fabric R26. Ditch 895/D.

81 Wheelmade, necked bowl with girth grooves.

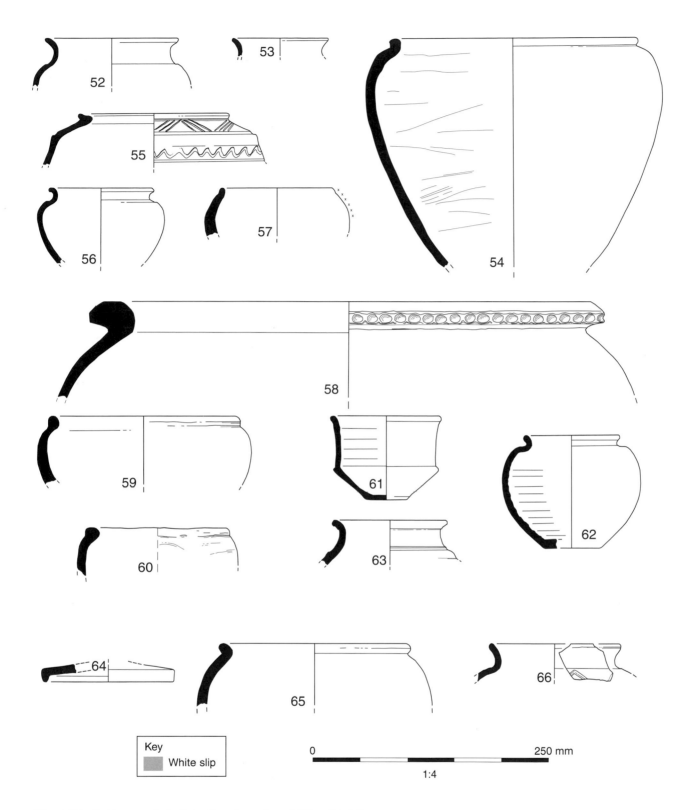

Key
White slip

0   250 mm

1:4

Fig. 4.12   Pottery periods F to G and unphased (Nos 52–66)

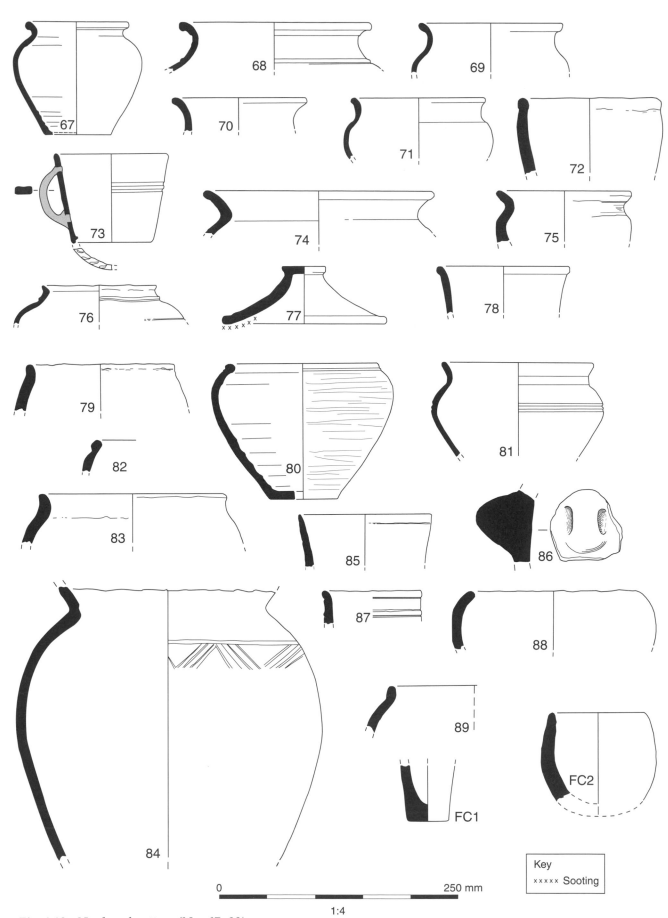

Fig. 4.13   Unphased pottery (Nos 67–89)

Fabric O43. Pit/ditch 1054/A.

82   Wheel-turned beaded rim bowl with a worn interior surface. Grey in colour. Fabric C24. Ditch 2295/A.

83   Handmade simple rim jar. Fabric C24. Pit 2450/A.

84   Handmade, everted rim storage jar. Upper rim edge worn. Decorated with a band of burnished line decoration on the shoulder above which the body is burnished. Fabric E86. Pit 3060/A/10.

85   Wheelmade tankard. Light grey sandy fabric, R44. Gully 3122/A/1.

86   Countersunk handle from a jar. Oxidised. Fabric C22. Ditch 3253/B/4.

87   Handmade cordoned tankard. Patchy dark brown/orange/grey in colour. Fabric O40. Layer 3259/C.

88   Crudely handmade simple curved rim jar. Dark grey to buff exterior with a dark grey interior. Fabric C24. Pit 3286B.

89   Beaded rim jar. Black, very friable fabric. Fabric R00. Pit 4023/A/1.

General discussion

The assemblage from Thornhill Farm presents a group of wares that are becoming increasingly familiar within a general region extending from the Upper Thames Valley across the Cotswolds and into the Severn Valley. Notable sites include Lechlade (Allen *et al.* 1993) and Claydon Pike in the Upper Thames Valley, settlements such as Bagendon (Clifford 1961) and The Ditches, North Cerney (Trow 1988) on the Cotswold ridge, and lowland rural settlement sites such as Frocester (Price 2000), Abbeydale (Timby unpubl. a), Kingsholm (pre-military levels; Timby unpubl. b) and Saintbridge (Timby unpubl. c) on the Severn Plain.

Early–middle Iron Age Jurassic fossiliferous shelly limestone wares (fabric C24) appear at present, superficially at least, to be fairly ubiquitous. Wares of apparently identical type occur either side of the Cotswolds although this may be a reflection of a similar tradition rather than the sharing of one or more sources. Published sites of middle Iron age date west of the Cotswold ridge are rare, and the absence of this type of ware on a number of other sites is likely to be a reflection of chronology. For example, the ware does not appear to feature in any significant quantity at Bagendon or The Ditches, North Cerney. It is similarly absent from the earliest excavated levels in both Cirencester and Gloucester and is only represented by small quantities from the Gloucester suburb sites such as Kingsholm. A slightly greater amount is present from Frocester indicating a middle Iron Age component to this multiperiod site. It does, however, dominate the assemblages from most of the upland early Iron Age hillfort sites such as Winson (unpubl. material Corinium Museum), Crickley Hill (Elsdon 1994), Shenberrow (Fell 1961a) and Uley Bury

(Saville and Ellison 1983) and the middle Iron Age upland settlements at Huntsman Quarry, Naunton (Timby forthcoming) and Guiting Power (Saville 1979). Two new middle Iron Age sites, recently investigated as part of the Birdlip–Latton road improvement scheme, at Preston and Cowley have similarly produced several such wares (Timby 1999, 325, 339–65). By the same token, most of the early-middle Iron Age sites in the Upper Thames Valley feature similar wares, as, for example, at Farmoor (Lambrick and Robinson 1979), Watkins Farm (Allen 1990) and Gravelly Guy (Lambrick and Allen forthcoming). Its almost complete absence on sites like Old Shifford (Hey 1996), first occupied from the later Iron Age, is again chronological.

From the later part of the middle Iron Age Palaeozoic limestone-tempered wares from the Malvern region start to appear in some quantity across the region, continuing to occur well into the 1st century AD. These wares, first highlighted by Peacock (1968), have been taken to indicate semi-specialist production. Around this time briquetage (salt containers) from Droitwich begin to appear in assemblages, indicating the existence of exchange networks, the two commodities presumably using the same routes. Less common are the Malvernian rock-tempered wares which rarely penetrate this far east. Thornhill is at present one of the most easterly findspots for Droitwich briquetage.

Only three reasonably large groups of pottery dating to the later Iron Age and early Roman periods have been published from Gloucestershire: Salmonsbury (Dunning 1976), Bagendon (Fell 1961b) and The Ditches (Trow 1988). Several smaller groups have been noted, for example, Rough-ground Farm, Lechlade (Green and Booth 1993), Duntisbourne Abbots (Fell 1964), Wycomb (Timby 1998), Frocester Court (Timby 2000a) and Saint-bridge on the outskirts of Gloucester (Parry 1998). Unpublished material can be added from Abbey-dale (Timby unpubl. a), Coppice Corner, Kings-holm, Gloucester (Timby unpubl. b) and Claydon Pike (Booth forthcoming).

Palaeozoic limestone-tempered wares form a significant component of the later Iron Age assemblages from Highgate House, Cowley (Timby 1999, 327–9), Birdlip (Parry 1998, Period 2), The Ditches, North Cerney (Trow 1988, fabric 1), Coppice Corner, Kingsholm and Frocester. The large hammer-rim vessels have a much more limited distribution, but are well represented at Kingsholm (the pre-military levels), Frocester and less well at The Ditches (Trow 1988, fig 38.133). The Thornhill example is, like the briquetage, at the limit of the distribution.

In the early 1st century AD the limestone class of wares begin to be supplanted by grog-tempered wares, initially handmade and then in wheelmade forms. The transition can be seen at sites within the Bagendon complex including The Ditches and satellite sites at the Duntisbournes (Timby 1999, 329–35) as well as Kingsholm, Uley (Leach 1993) and Salmonsbury. By the second half of the 1st century AD handmade Savernake ware storage jars (fabrics E81–2) feature prominently in the ceramic record.

A comparison of the individual fabric components of assemblages spanning the later 1st century BC to later 1st century AD in Gloucestershire is beginning to show some localised regional differences, either in the presence or absence of certain fabrics, or the relative quantities of particular fabric types. For example, the products of the Savernake-Oare and related industries of North Wiltshire show a concomitant increase in presence on sites to the south-east of the Cotswolds compared to those sites on the north-west side. Savernake ware proper (fabric E81) at Thornhill Farm accounted for 18% by weight of the total assemblage compared to 5% at Frocester. A lower incidence of large storage jars in Savernake ware on sites north-west of the Cotswolds appears to be compensated by large jars in other fabrics, such as Severn Valley wares, which are only present in very minor amounts south-east of the Cotswolds. Other differences can be perceived between the east and west side of the Cotswolds. For example, the large hammer rim bowls in limestone or grog-tempered fabrics are very rare in the Upper Thames Valley, but are becoming quite familiar in the Gloucester area. At Kingsholm (non-military) they accounted for 31% by weight; at Frocester (1st–4th century) 8%.

The grog-tempered ware (fabric E85), which accounts for 11% of the Thornhill Farm material, does not seem to appear on sites west of the Cotswolds, suggesting a source within the Upper Thames Valley area. However, grog-tempered fabric E83, along with some of the earlier grog-tempered variants of the Severn Valley industry, does occur on both sides, with perhaps a higher incidence on the north-western side.

A comparison between Thornhill Farm and the adjacent site at Claydon Pike shows that the only overlap involves the area designated Trench 13 at Claydon Pike, dated to the late Iron Age-early Roman period (Phase 2), although Thornhill Farm does not share the more Romanised wares associated with the other site (Booth forthcoming). Thornhill Farm does not appear to have had any access to the luxury end of the market in terms of finer tablewares, platters, cups, flagons and mortaria. Samian, although present, is minimal and can only belong to the very last phases of occupation; only one sherd of mortaria was recovered and very little amphora. An absence of fineware table forms is also reflected in an absence of comparable forms in coarsewares; there are, for example, very few platters and negligible beakers, although the forms are known to exist within the fabrics present. Fabric R33, a wheelmade black-burnished ware which appears in post-conquest deposits across the region, frequently features as platters and dishes imitating imported moulded forms. Although the fabric is present at Thornhill, the platter forms are not. This also puts the site in direct contrast to Bagendon which, even putting aside the fact that a number of fineware imports were reaching the site certainly by the Claudian period, has a significant number of Roman forms amongst its coarseware component (Fell 1961b, figs 48–9). This might suggest first, that Thornhill was of a lower economic status, and second, that the occupants or users of the site were throughout indigenous natives, either not familiar with, or not prepared to adopt, new vessels or products such as oil and wine reflective of Roman cooking, eating and drinking habits. Although Thornhill was not receiving merchandise from abroad it does seems to have some quite strong regional trading links, particularly to the north-west which may have been connected with the movement of stock. As with many sites, just as the new Roman wares begin to manifest themselves, occupation ceases and the sites become abandoned or the focus shifts, reflecting, perhaps, a new generation with different ways of life and the wider adoption of Roman customs and products.

HUMAN REMAINS
by Angela Boyle

The assemblage comprised three inhumations (3106, 3145, 3363) which are summarised below, as well as four deposits of cremated bone (320/A, 800/A, 801/A, 3008/A) and five fragmentary unburnt deposits (110/L/2, 235/C/4, 324/B/2, 869/B, 935/A) which are summarised in Table 4.11. One deposit (3081/E) which was believed to be human consisted entirely of animal bone. Bone preservation was uniformly bad. All bones were fragmentary and surfaces extremely degraded. Estimation of sex was based on skull morphology (Workshop 1980). Estimation of adult age was based on dental attrition (Brothwell 1981, 72) and subadult age on dental root development and closure (van Beek 1983, 126). The dental notation used was as follows:

/ = post mortem loss
X = ante mortem loss
np = not present
c = caries
- = tooth and socket missing

Catalogue of inhumations
Skeleton 3106

18375.65 99851.45 0.80 x 0.50 x 0.30–0.34 m
Within grave which cuts 3080, associated with one sherd of Group 1 and one sherd of Group 4. An oval shaped grave with sharply sloping sides. Skeleton crouched with skull facing north-east.
Preservation poor; skeleton comprised skull, mandible, cervical vertebrae 1 and 2, left(?) and right(?) ulnae, radius, femora and fibulae, carpals, metapodials and phalanges.

Table 4.11   Human cremations and disarticulated deposits

Context	Sample no.	Weight	Colour	Other inclusions	Fragment size	Comments
110/L/2 Romano-British ditch, Group 1-5 pottery			unburnt			2 fragments of adult human skull
235/C/4 part of enclosure 2, G1-5 pottery associated, second half of 1st century AD			unburnt			mandible, possibly female, no surviving dentition
320/B possible pit	65	37 g	white, blue-grey	pottery, charcoal	1-3 cm;1 fragment measures 4.2 cm	long bone shaft fragments
324/B/2 part of enclosure 30, G3-5 pottery associated, second half of 1st century AD	8	< 1 g	unburnt	wood	c 2 cm	
800/A, within boundary ditch, 1 sherd G5 associated	61	< 1 g	white	pottery, charcoal, clinker	< 0.5 0.5-1 cm	
801/A within boundary ditch, 19 sherds G4 associated	62	4 g	white	pottery, charcoal	0.5-2 cm	
801/B within boundary ditch, 19 sherds G4 associated	66	< 1 g	white	pottery, charcoal	0.5-1 cm	skull vault fragment
869/B ditch, possibly late Iron Age	90	c 12 g	unburnt	pottery, charcoal	2-4 cm	possible femur
935/A ditch, post Middle Iron Age	84	< 1 g	unburnt	pottery, charcoal	1.5 cm	
3008/A part of enclosure 40, ?Group 4 pottery, second half of 1st century AD	167	< 1 g	white	pottery, charcoal, shell	1 cm	

Adult male (33–45 years). Marked wear affecting all teeth is possibly indicative of an edge-to-edge bite. Interstitial caries present between 1st and 2nd right mandibular incisors.

Dentition

```
- -  6  5  4  -  2  1  1  -  -  4  5  -  -  -
np7  6  5  4  3  2  1  /  /  3  4  X  X  7  np
        c     c
```

Skeleton 3145 (Fig. 3.12)

18377 99860.60 1.04 x 0.87 x 0.26 m
Within grave 3144 which cuts 3080. Grave has a flat bottom and near vertical sides. Skeleton crouched and orientated NW–SE. Associated spiral finger ring (cat. no. 51).
Preservation poor; skull, femora and tibiae.
Probable adult. Three very badly degraded teeth are present; two premolars and a canine, probably maxillary. Canine wear is marked, other crowns destroyed.

Skeleton 3363

99895.85 18394.35 1.10 x 0.70 x 0.28 m
Within grave 3362 which is located outside S 200. An oval grave with irregular sides and bottom. Skeleton crouched and orientated NNE–SSW. Preservation poor; skull, right arm and both legs. Subadult 10–15 years.

Dentition

```
7  6  5  4  3  2  1  1  -  -  4  5  6  7
-  -  -  -  -  -  1  -  -  -  -  -  -  -
```

THE FAUNAL REMAINS
by Marsha Levine

A total of 24,853 fragments of bone was recovered by hand from Thornhill Farm. There was no sieving programme, which may have resulted in some loss of information, particularly in the loss of small anatomical elements (Payne 1972). The complete osteological record is with the site archives. This report is a summary of the data contained in the archive.

Quantification

The animal bone recovered from the site was divided into two categories: postcranial and cranial elements. Animal bone was quantified using Number of Identified Specimens (NISP), based upon a simple specimen frequency determination. For example, a piece of mandible with three teeth in it will count as four elements. In order to distinguish articulated from disarticulated anatomical elements, the coding system used here includes a variable for 'Group'. Postcranial and cranial elements identified as belonging to a single animal (for example, articulated bones or teeth from a single jaw) are referred to as belonging to an

Anatomical Element Group. Each such group is given a unique number. The group number for elements not belonging to a group is '0'. The identification of cranial and postcranial element groups is not always certain. Whether a group identification is certain is recorded in the database variable, 'Certainty'.

In order to account for associated and articulated material the 'Element Units' (ELUs) were calculated. An ungrouped bone equals 1 ELU, as does a group of bones or teeth belonging to one individual (a group). That is, 1 individual bone + 1 whole skeleton (group) = 2 ELU.

In general the MNI was not calculated at Thornhill Farm as a small proportion of the deposits was excavated and the sample was biased through the recovery methods used. However, it was calculated for horses, as indicated below.

The anatomical element representation for cattle and sheep was compared with Brain's data from Makapansgat in South Africa and the Kuiseb River in Namibia (Brain 1967, 1969, 1976, 1981). The equids are compared with the French cave site, Jaurens (radiocarbon date *c* 29, 300–32, 630 BP), in which a natural catastrophe concentrated a large assemblage of mammals (Debard 1979, 380; Guerin *et al.* 1979, 381). For Jaurens the anatomical element counts were used and the MNI as determined by C. Mourer-Chauviré (1980).

Methodology

Taphonomy

A variety of analytical methods were used to explore the assemblage formation processes and history. These include comparisons of bone surface condition, gnawing, bone part representation, anatomical element representation, butchery marks and evidence for tool manufacture. The surface condition of each bone recovered from the site was recorded and grades as:

'Slightly eroded' – some wear to the surface of the bone, but mainly confined to sharp edges, such as on spines and processes. Accurate measurements can be taken and butchery marks would be visible.
'Eroded' – a larger proportion of the surfaces have been damaged, but accurate measurements are still usually possible and some butchery marks will be visible.
'Very eroded' – almost the whole surface of the bone has been damaged. Any measurements taken will be minimum and most butchery marks will be obscured or destroyed.

Identification

Animal bone was identified using the reference collection at the Faunal Remains Unit at the University of Cambridge. Sheep and goat were distinguished using the criteria described in Boessneck (1969), Kratochvil (1969) and Payne (1969

and 1985). Where it was not possible to distinguish between the two species, fragments were classified under a single heading of sheep/goat. Since, however, no goat bones or teeth were found at the site, all *Ovis/Capra* (sheep/goat) elements were pooled with *Ovis aries* (domestic sheep). Rib and vertebral fragments, except the atlas and axis, were only assigned to size categories as either 'cattle-size' or 'sheep-size'.

Ageing

The ageing of the animals relies solely on tooth-wear analysis and crown height measurement as it was felt that this would provide a more accurate result than using bone fusion data. For cattle, Grant (1982), Ewbank *et al.* (1964), Legge (1992) and the author's coding methods were used for the eruption and wear. For sheep, the mandibular teeth were assigned to age stages according to the eruption-wear method formulated by Payne (1973) and Legge (1992), and modified by the author. The maxillary and mandibular pig teeth were aged according to Bull and Payne (1982), with further details from Sisson and Grossman (1953), Matschke (1967) and Wenham and Fowler (1973). It is assumed that the age system developed for horses is valid for all large equids (horse/mule size rather than mule/ass/hinnie size). The large equid teeth (that is, excluding mule/ass/hinnie) were aged according to Levine (1982, 1983) and from data on root development (see archive).

Each tooth and jaw was aged as closely as possible. Loose teeth were included. Tooth fragments (that is, where less than half the tooth is present), canines and incisors were excluded. To compensate for the under-representation of immature individuals, due to recovery, preservation and element abundance biases, hypothetical adjustment factors are used in calculating the mortality curves for each of the main taxa.

Cattle crown height measurements were not used as an independent source of ageing data as there is no standard reference collection available. Crown height was plotted against age as determined by tooth eruption and wear, and can be found in the archives. This demonstrates that the crown heights of mature teeth decrease with age.

Table 4.12   Surface condition of postcranial elements for all taxa

Condition	No.	%
Uneroded	18	1
Slightly eroded	381	1.8
Eroded	2464	12.1
Very eroded	17341	85.4
Other damage	83	0.4
Total	20287	
(including 6 human bone fragments)		

Table 4.13   Surface condition of cranial bone and teeth for all taxa

Surface Condition		Material		Total
		Bone	Tooth	
Indeterminate	No.		3	3
	% within material		0.2	0.1
Uneroded	No.		40	40
	% within material		2.3	0.9
Slightly Eroded	No.	131	368	499
	% within material	4.7	20.9	10.9
Eroded	No.	1541	868	2409
	% within material	54.7	49.3	52.6
Very eroded	No.	1138	478	1616
	% within material	40.5	27.2	35.3
other damage	No.	3	2	5
	% within material	0.1	0.1	0.1
Total	No.	2813	1759	4572

Measurements

Measurements are based upon von den Driesch (1976) for most taxa, and upon the methods of Prat for horses (see the archive). Relatively few anatomical elements could be accurately measured. The frequency (N), mean, minimum, maximum, standard deviation, skewness and kurtosis were calculated for those elements, and all measurements are included in the archive.

Sexing

Horses were sexed using the characteristics of the pelvis outlined in Sisson and Getty (1975) due to the low number of other indicative elements. Sexing was attempted for other species using morphological criteria but was not successful.

Results

Species represented

Bones from cattle, horse, sheep and pig were the main elements, in order of prevalence, recovered from the site, and represent the main domestic species that would have been present at the site. It is likely that sheep and pig are underrepresented due to the poor condition of many of the bones (see below). The pig teeth from Thornhill Farm are likely to be from domestic animals, but this cannot be determined with any certainty from the assemblage available for study (Payne and Bull 1988). It should, however, be noted that wild boar did not become extinct in England until the 13th century AD (Rackham 1980). Other species identified were ass, dog and a single heron carpo-metacarpus. The heron bone was found in the fill of gully 118 (Group 112). Most of the equids from Thornhill Farm were probably horses (*E. caballus*). There is good evidence for ass (*E. asinus*), and it seems likely that some of the large equids were, in fact, mules.

Taphonomy

The bone surface preservation is very poor. The cranial and postcranial data demonstrate that almost all bone surfaces have sustained some damage and many are very damaged.

Table 4.12 indicates that over 85.5% of the postcranial elements (including fragments unidentifiable to taxon) are 'very eroded'. Even if bone unidentifiable to taxon is excluded, the proportion of 'very eroded' elements remains high at around 41–54%, except in the case of dog.

Table 4.13 demonstrates the poor condition of the cranial material. The surface condition of the teeth is, unsurprisingly, better than that of the cranial bone: 20.9% of the teeth are slightly eroded and 27.2% very eroded, as against respectively 4.7% and 40.5% for the cranial bone.

It is clear from this short analysis of surface condition that the bones and teeth from Thornhill Farm, with the notable exception of a dog skeleton (Context 716; Plate 4.1), are very eroded. For most bones little, if any of the original bone surface remains. As a result, many bones are unmeasurable, butchery marks would have abraded off and gnawing evidence is subsumed into the overall poor preservation state of the material. There are many possible causes for the surface erosion referred to here, such as trampling, exposure to the elements before burial and soil chemistry. No one agent can be assigned.

Gnawing

Because of the high level of bone surface damage, the proportion of gnawed bone at Thornhill Farm is certain to be underestimated. Gnawing is only detectable on 261 out of a total of 20,281 postcranial elements (1.3%). However, when only identifiable bones are considered, the proportion increases to 12.9% (Table 4.14).

It is noteworthy that the taxon with the smallest

Plate 4.1   Dog skeleton within pit 716 on the western edge of Trench 7

percentage of gnawed bone is sheep. Payne and Munson (1985) have shown that sheep bones gnawed by dogs could be entirely consumed. We know that there were dogs at this site, although humans, pigs and wild carnivores could also have chewed the bones from the Iron Age and Roman deposits. That such a relatively high proportion of pig bones show traces of gnawing is hard to explain, since their bones are usually even more vulnerable than those of sheep. The pig sample is, on the other hand, very small. Interestingly, the proportion of equid bones with gnawing marks is almost as great at that of cattle. This suggests that both equid and bos bones were not buried soon after death but were left exposed on or near the surface of the ground, where they would have been accessible to carnivores. The use of cattle for food will lead to their disarticulation and disposal as rubbish, and the high proportion of horse gnawing could be indicative of a similar fate for the horse bones.

Bone part representation

Fragmentation

Using the simplified quantification system, 89% of all elements recovered were fragments, while only 1.3% were whole or almost whole. While 'proximal', 'distal' and 'shaft', mainly refer to long bones, 'incomplete' is used for such elements as vertebrae, carpals, tarsals, sesamoids and so on. Aside from

fragments, at 4%, shafts are the parts best represented. The poor preservation of faunal material is thus confirmed by part representation.

If unidentifiable and unimportant taxa (eg heron bones) are excluded from the calculations, the proportion of 'fragments' greatly decreases: shafts are best represented, proximal and distal similarly represented (Table 4.15).

If part representation is broken down by taxon, dog has the highest proportion of whole bones (28.8%), followed at some distance by horse and cow (15.8% and 13.7% respectively), and with sheep and pig trailing a long way behind (6.9% and 8.4% respectively). It is also perhaps noteworthy that equid and cattle are represented by higher percentages of proximal and distal ends and lower percent-

Table 4.15   Part representation: equid, cattle, sheep, pig, dog only

	No.	%
Fragment	171	9.4
Whole	260	14.3
Proximal	361	19.8
Distal	338	18.5
Shaft	440	24.1
Incomplete	254	13.9
Total	1824	100

Table 4.14   Incidence of gnawing in postcranial bone from identifiable taxa

| | | Gnawing | | Total |
		Present	Undetectable	
Equid	No.	43	261	304
	% within Taxon	14.1	85.9	100
Bos taurus	No.	172	855	1027
	% within Taxon	16.7	83.3	100
Ovis aries	No.	11	236	247
	% within Taxon	4.5	95.5	100
Sus scrofa	No.	10	73	83
	% within Taxon	12	88	100
Canis familiaris	No.	0	163	163
	% within Taxon	0	100	100
Ardea cinerea	No.	0	1	1
	% within Taxon	-	100	100
Homo sapiens	No.	0	6	6
	% within Taxon	0	100	100
Total	No.	296	1595	1831
	% within Taxon	12.9	87.1	100

ages of shaft pieces than sheep and pig. The dog is a special case: 148 out of a total of 163 dog postcranial elements came from a dog burial (Context 716; Plate 4.1) in which the preservation state was, by comparison with the rest of the assemblage, extraordinarily good, as has already been noted.

Because the breakage patterns of the different anatomical elements are not necessarily comparable – for example, carpals and long bones break differently and often have very different taphonomic histories – it is useful to compare the part representation solely of the long bones of the various taxa (excluding dog). Table 4.16 shows the part representation for humerus, radius, ulna, femur, tibia, and central metapodials. In this case, horse has by far the highest proportion of whole bones. Sheep and pig still have the lowest. The

representation of shafts is much higher for sheep and pig than for cattle and equids. Moreover, the proportion of shafts is certainly under-represented for sheep and pig, since there are additionally 122 more shafts only identifiable as medium ungulate, while only 55 additional shafts are identifiable as large ungulate. It is difficult to explain this pattern except as further evidence of the poor preservation state of sheep and pig.

The general poor preservation of the whole assemblage, together with the great variety of potential agents involved in the destruction of the bones, means that it is not possible to say whether bones had been fragmented due to breakage – for example, for marrow, bone grease, gelatine – or due to being trampled, weathered, eroded, ploughed over and so on.

Table 4.16   Part representation by taxon: long bones only

| | | Taxon | | | | Total |
		Equid	Bos taurus	Ovis aries	Sus scrofa	
Fragment	No.	15	54	2	1	72
	% within taxon	8.9	8.4	1.1	2.3	6.9
Whole	No.	21	34	5	1	61
	% within taxon	12.4	5.3	2.7	2.3	5.8
Proximal	No.	46	214	38	7	305
	% within taxon	27.2	33.2	20.5	15.9	29.2
Distal	No.	46	166	28	10	250
	% within taxon	27.2	25.7	15.1	22.7	24
Shaft	No.	37	173	111	24	345
	% within taxon	21.9	26.8	60	54.5	33.1
Incomplete	No.	4	4	1	1	10
	% within taxon	2.4	0.6	0.5	2.3	1
Total	No.	169	645	185	44	1043

Table 4.17   Representation of taxon with loose teeth and teeth in bone

		Material		Total
		Loose teeth	Teeth in bone	
Equid	No.	198	10	208
	% within taxon	95.2	4.8	100
	% within material	15.2	3.5	13.1
Bos taurus	No.	624	133	757
	% within taxon	82.4	17.6	100
	% within material	47.9	46.3	47.6
Ovis aries	No.	414	74	488
	% within taxon	84.8	15.2	100
	% within material	31.8	25.8	30.7
Sus scrofa	No.	60	56	116
	% within taxon	51.7	48.3	100
	% within material	4.6	19.5	7.3
Canis familiaris	No.	7	14	21
	% within taxon	33.3	66.7	100
	% within material	0.5	4.9	1.3
Total	No.	1303	287	1590
	% within taxon	81.9	18.1	100
	% within material	100	100	100

Anatomical element groups

For cranial material it is obvious that many of the loose teeth derive from toothrows. 54.3% of the teeth (2481 elements), including loose ones, from all taxa could be identified (with varying but usually high degrees of certainty) as belonging together in Groups – for example, based upon the shape of the contact facets between adjacent teeth and their stratigraphic context (see the archive). At the same time, the proportion of teeth in bone for all taxa is only 18.1% with a total of 287 teeth (Table 4.17).

Only 4.7% of the total number of postcranial elements, identifiable and unidentifiable (that is, 957 elements, of which 148 were from one dog) can be assigned to Groups.

Species representation: postcranial material

The faunal assemblage from Thornhill Farm comprises a total of 20,281 postcranial anatomical elements out of which only 9.1% are identifiable to genus (Table 4.18). Almost 90% of all the phased postcranial material recovered came from contexts assigned to the late Iron Age–early Roman period.

Exclusion of uncertain identifications reduced the total percentage of taxa identifiable to the genus level to 8.9%. Considering the low species variability at this site, most uncertain identifications are probably correct at least to the genus level. Most other bones were from medium (sheep/pig size) or large (horse/cow size) taxa. A large proportion, if not the majority, of the postcranial elements were probably from cattle and horse.

Excluding taxa which cannot be identified to the genus level, the postcranial assemblage breaks

Table 4.19   Identifiable taxa

	No.	%
Equid	304	16.6
Cattle	1027	56.1
Sheep	247	13.5
Pig	83	4.5
Dog	163	8.9
Heron	1	0.1
Total	1825	100

down as in Table 4.19. Only 1825 postcranial elements are identifiable. 56.1% belong to cattle, the best represented taxon. The equids (mainly horse) are the next most numerous at 16.6%.

Most of the dog postcranial elements (148 out of 163) from Thornhill Farm belonged to one skeleton. The dog skeleton, which was at least partially articulated, was buried in a shallow round pit (context 716) on the western edge of trench 7 (Plate 4.1). The feature could not be phased. However, it was cut by the late Roman trackway 301 (context 715) and situated in the middle of two successive subrectangular enclosures: E24 from Period E and E155 from Period F. It is unsure whether the burial was contemporary with any of those features.

Species representation: cranial material

Cranial elements (skull bones and teeth; Table 4.20) were requantified separately, and almost 96% of the phased cranial material was assigned to the late Iron Age–early Roman period. Only a small amount of material was identified to species from

Table 4.18   Taxon frequencies including uncertain identifications

Taxon		Middle Iron Age	Late Iron Age-early Roman	Late Roman	Medieval	Unphased	Total
Horse	No.	14	146	7	1	112	280
	%	1.8	1.3	1.4	7.6	1.4	1.3
Ass	No.	0	2	0	0	0	2
	%	0	0.01	0	0	0	0.01
Equid	No.	4	8	0	0	9	21
	%	0.5	0.1	0	0	0.1	0.1
Cattle	No.	41	540	11	0	433	1025
	%	5.3	4.8	2.3	0	5.4	5
Sheep	No.	1	16	0	0	15	32
	%	0.1	0.1	0	0	0.18	0.1
Sheep/goat	No.	8	125	2	0	80	215
	%	1	1.1	0.4	0	1	1
Pig	No.	4	41	0	0	37	82
	%	0.5	0.3	0	0	0.4	0.4
Dog	No.	1	5	0	0	157	163
	%	0.1	0.04	0	0	2	0.8
Heron	No.	0	1	0	0	0	1
	%	0	0.01	0	0	0	0.004
Medium animal	No.	38	296	8	0	215	557
	%	4.9	2.6	1.7	0	2.7	2.7
Large animal	No.	133	2057	99	2	1504	3795
	%	17.2	18.5	21	15.3	19	18.7
Medium/large animal	No.	525	7870	337	10	5205	13947
	%	68.2	70.8	72	77	65.7	68.7
Small animal	No.	0	1	0	0	0	1
	%	0	0.01	0	0	0	0.004
Total	No.	769	11108	464	13	7767	20121
	%	100	99.9	99	100	98	99.2
Indeterminate	No.	0	5	4	0	151	160
	%	0	0.04	0.8	0	2	0.7
Total	No.	769	11113	468	13	7918	20281

the other phases of occupation, limiting the interpretation of the animal bone assemblage from these phases.

This category of data is rather heterogeneous, including several kinds of material – cranial bone with teeth, cranial bone without teeth, loose teeth and teeth in bone – necessitating descriptive terms quite different than those used for postcranial material. As mentioned above, a large proportion of the teeth from Thornhill Farm are loose: that is, not embedded in bone. Table 4.21 shows that 11.5% of the loose teeth and 52.2% of the cranial bone were unidentifiable to genus. This is because of their very fragmentary state. That 55.8% of the cattle (*Bos*) elements are categorised as cranial bone, while the figure for *Equus* is only 36%, is probably down to the relatively greater ease with which cattle skull fragments – notably horncore – can be identified. That cranial bone identifiability drops even further with sheep and pig is most probably a direct reflection of their relative fragility. The under-representation of sheep and pig elements will be an ongoing refrain in this report.

The comparison of loose teeth with teeth in bone shows that of all the taxa, horse has the fewest teeth in bone 4.8% (Table 4.17). Cattle and sheep are almost equal at 17.6% and 15.2% respectively. Pig and dog have a higher proportion of teeth in bone than the rest, 48.3% and 66.7% respectively, but they are also represented by far fewer specimens. It is also possible that loose dog and pig teeth were simply under-collected by the inexperienced excavators, because many of them are relatively small. Perhaps the best explanation for the high representation of loose horse teeth is simply that they are larger and easier to see than those of the other taxa and thus more likely to be collected.

The Element Unit (ELU)

From the above, it is apparent that 163 postcranial and 71 cranial elements were identifiable as *Canis familiaris*. However, of those, 148 postcranial and 5 cranial elements, in fact, came from a single dog (ie a single group). Table 4.22 shows the number of post-cranial element groups. Overall there were

Table 4.20   Cranial material

Taxon		Middle Iron Age	Late Iron Age -early Roman	Late Roman	Medieval	Unphased	Total
Horse	No.	10	71	2	0	105	188
	%	10.5	2.5	10	0	6.2	0.16
Ass	No.	1	5	0	0	0	6
	%	1	0.1	0	0	0	0.13
Horse/mule	No.	0	12	0	0	3	15
	%	0	0.4	0	0	0.1	0.3
Mule/ass	No.	0	7	0	0	0	7
	%	0	0.2	0	0	0	0.1
Equid-small	No.	0	2	0	0	2	4
	%	0	.0	0	0	0.1	0.1
Equid	No.	1	55	0	0	52	108
	%	1	2	0	0	3	2.3
Cattle	No.	33	1266	8	3	503	1813
	%	34.7	45.7	40	100	29.8	39.6
Sheep	No.	7	22	0	0	29	58
	%	7.3	0.7		0	1.7	1.2
Sheep/goat	No.	9	279	3	0	267	558
	%	9.4	10	15	0	15.8	12.2
Pig	No.	10	87	1	0	61	159
	%	10.5	3.2	5	0	3.6	3.4
Dog	No.	0	55	0	0	17	72
	%	0	2	0	0	1	1.5
Medium animal	No.	0	25	0	0	11	36
	%	0	1	0	0	0.6	0.7
Medium/large animal	No.	9	240	0	0	360	609
	%	9.4	8.6	0	0	21.3	13.3
Large animal	No.	15	570	6	0	277	868
	%	15.7	20.5	30	0	16.4	19
Total	No.	95	2696	20	3	1687	4501
	%	100	97.4	100	100	100	98.4
Indeterminate	No.	0	71	0	0	0	71
	%	0	2.6	0	0	0	1.5
Total		95	2767	20	3	1687	4572

very few, and of all the taxa considered here, the equids are represented proportionally by more postcranial bone groups than the others. This suggests that their bones were less disarticulated and dispersed than those of other animals.

Table 4.23 demonstrates that a higher proportion of cranial elements are in groups. That is unsurprising, as many are simply teeth in jaws. Additionally, equids, cattle and sheep have rather similar proportions of loose teeth (77.8–80.7%). As mentioned previously, this probably relates to variation in recovery patterns.

Table 4.24 aggregates the cranial and postcranial data in order to obtain a better idea of the ratios of the main taxa to one another. It is first of all worth noting that, except for dog, the cranial representation of the smaller taxa (sheep and pig) is considerably greater than that for the larger taxa (horse and cattle; Figure 4.14). This disparity is likely to have taphonomic origins. Teeth are denser than bone and

thus more likely to be preserved. It is worth remembering that the figures for dog are greatly influenced by the fact that most elements (5 cranial and 148 postcranial) came from one individual.

Given our admittedly inadequate data, the best estimate of the ratios of the main taxa to one another are in the last row of Table 4.24 and in the cranial + postcranial columns of Figure 4.14.

Anatomical element representation

Sheep bone survivorship

The sample of sheep is small, and of 197 anatomical elements only 114 were postcranial. Nevertheless, of the three taxa from Thornhill Farm for which the Brain (1981) method has been used, sheep best fit the expected pattern.

We can see in Table 4.25 and Figure 4.15 that while the percentage survival of teeth from Thornhill Farm is almost as high as that of the

Table 4.21   Representation of material by taxon (simplified)

		Loose Teeth	Teeth in bone	Material Bone with teeth	Cranial bone	Total
Indeterminate	No.	169			1416	1585
	% within Taxon	10.7			89.3	100
	% within Material	11.5			52.2	34.7
Equid	No.	198	10	2	118	328
	% within Taxon	60.4	3	0.6	36	100
	% within Material	13.5	3.5	2	4.3	7.2
Cattle	No.	624	133	44	1012	1813
	% within Taxon	34.4	7.3	2.4	55.8	100
	% within Material	42.4	46.3	44	37.3	39.7
Sheep	No.	414	74	28	100	616
	% within Taxon	67.2	12	4.5	16.2	100
	% within Material	28.1	25.8	28	3.7	13.5
Pig	No.	60	56	23	20	157
	% within Taxon	37.7	35.2	14.5	12.6	100
	% within Material	4.1	19.5	23	0.7	3.5
Dog	No.	7	14	3	47	71
	% within Taxon	9.9	19.7	4.2	66.2	100
	% within Material	0.5	4.9	3	1.7	1.6
Total	No.	1472	287	100	2713	4572
	% within Taxon	32.2	6.3	2.2	59.3	100
	% within Material	100	100	100	100	100

Table 4.22   Quantification of grouped and ungrouped postcranial material

	Equid	Cattle	Sheep	Pig	Dog
Frequency: ungrouped elements	206	849	230	83	15
Frequency: groups	32	57	7	0	1
ELUs: ungrouped elements + groups	238	906	237	83	16
% ungrouped elements	86.6	93.7	97.0	100.0	93.8
% taxon ELUs	16.1	61.2	16.0	5.6	1.1

Table 4.23   Quantification of grouped and ungrouped cranial material

	Equid	Cattle	Sheep	Pig	Dog
Frequency: ungrouped elements	99	624	318	57	4
Frequency: groups	28	149	91	32	9
Total: ungrouped elements + groups	127	773	409	89	13
% ungrouped elements	78.0	80.7	77.8	64.0	30.8
% taxon ELUs	9.0	54.8	29.0	6.3	0.9

Table 4.24   Quantification of grouped and ungrouped cranial and postcranial material

	Equid	Cattle	Sheep	Pig	Dog	Total
Total cranial (loose + groups)	127	773	409	89	13	1411
Total postcranial (loose + groups)	238	906	237	83	16	1480
Total cranial + postcranial	365	1679	646	172	28	2890
% cranial elements	34.8	46.0	63.3	51.7	44.8	48.8
% taxon ELUs (cranial + postcranial)	12.6	58.1	22.4	6.0	1.0	

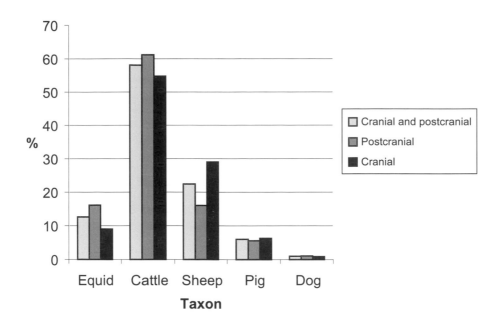

Fig. 4.14   Taxon element units

Table 4.25   *Comparison of differential element representation: Kuiseb Bushman goats and Thornhill Farm sheep*

Anatomical element	Kuiseb goats (MNI = 64)			Thornhill Farm sheep (MNI = 47)		
	Number found	Original number	% survival	Number found	Original number	% survival
Half-mandibles[1]	117	128	91.4	83	94	88.3
Humerus, distal	82	128	64.0	8	94	8.5
Tibia, distal	72	128	56.3	9	94	9.6
Radius and ulna, proximal	65	128	50.8	9	94	9.6
Metatarsal, proximal	39	128	30.4	12	94	12.8
Scapula	35	128	27.4	7	94	7.4
Pelvis, half	34	128	26.6	6	94	6.4
Metacarpal, proximal	32	128	25.0	8	94	8.5
Axis vertebrae	14	64	21.9	4	47	8.5
Atlas vertebrae	12	64	18.8	0	47	0.0
Metacarpal, distal	23	128	18.0	2	94	2.1
Radius and ulna, distal	22	128	17.2	3	94	3.2
Metatarsal, distal	20	128	15.6	3	94	3.2
Femur, proximal	18	128	14.1	6	94	6.4
Astragalus	16	128	12.5	3	94	3.2
Calcaneus	14	128	10.9	3	94	3.2
Tibia, proximal	13	128	10.1	4	94	4.3
Lumbar vertebrae	31	384	8.1	5	282	1.8
Femur, distal	9	128	7.0	3	94	3.2
Cervical 3-7 vertebrae	12	320	3.8	5	235	2.1
Thoracic vertebrae	21	832	2.5	5	611	0.8
Sacrum	1	64	1.6	0	47	0.0
Phalanges	21	1536	1.4	9	1128	0.8
Humerus, proximal	0	128	0.0	0	94	0.0

[1] There is no way to estimate with any pretence to accuracy how many half mandibles were originally present at Thornhill Farm. I have, therefore, decided to use the minimum number of animals represented by the teeth instead (36 left, 47 right). Ribs are excluded since they cannot be reliably identified at Thornhill Farm.

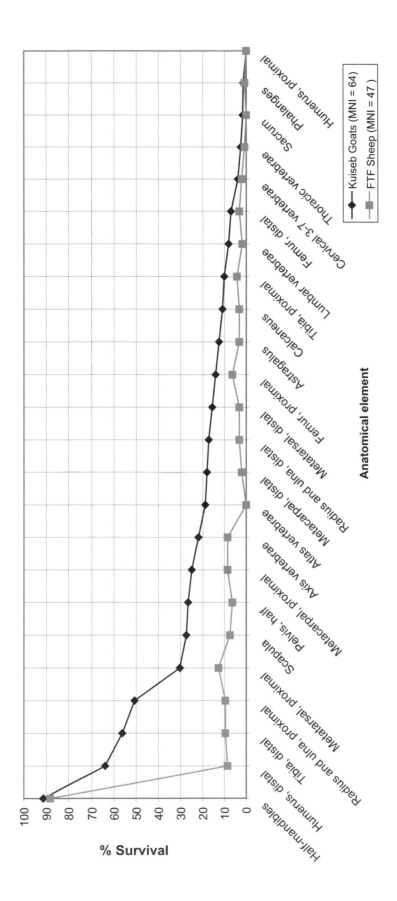

Fig. 4.15   Percentage survival of caprines from Thornhill Farm and Kuiseb

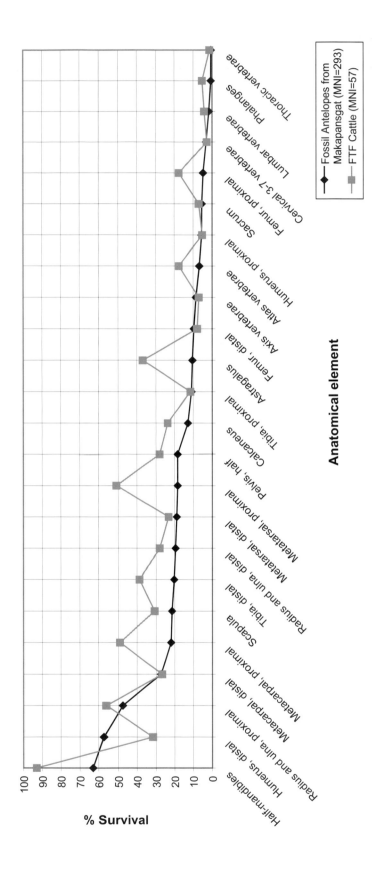

Fig. 4.16 Thornhill cattle survival compared with Makapansgat

Kuiseb jaws, the preservation state of all the other anatomical elements is consistently worse. However, the trend of the two samples is generally similar, suggesting that the Thornhill Farm material might well have had a taphonomic history not very different from that of the African material. On the one hand, the two taxa, sheep and goats, are anatomically very similar and, on the other hand, the evidence suggests that, as with the Kuiseb material, the Thornhill Farm sample came from animals which were butchered for human consumption, exposed to gnawing by dogs, and were probably trampled by both people and livestock. That the Thornhill Farm sheep were preserved at all is probably due to their eventual burial. The much greater age and poor preservation conditions would be enough to explain the much worse state of the material from Thornhill Farm.

Groups
Only relatively few sheep bones were found in groups. Some were reconstructed broken bones, but four probable groups apparently comprised butchery units: Group 25, a metapodial and two first phalanges of newborn or fetal lamb; Group 92, two thoracic vertebrae; Group 93, the axis and cervical vertebrae, and Group 94, the axis and two cervical vertebrae.

Butchery
It is worth keeping in mind the poor surface condition of the postcranial material from Thornhill Farm when discussing butchery marks. Many of the marks present at the time of their disposal would have been lost due to the poor preservational conditions.

Only six postcranial and one cranial sheep elements show any evidence of butchery marks. Knife cuts to the femur, metacarpal, metatarsal and astragalus are probably all associated with disarticulation. Two cervical vertebrae (3–7), which probably belonged in a group (94) with an axis, were both chopped across the transverse plane. Only one was chopped through. A third cervical vertebra was chopped through diagonally. The chop mark on the horncore could relate to the removal of the horn for working or access to the brain.

Cattle bone survivorship
As with sheep, the sample size for cattle is relatively small. By comparison with Brain's (1981) data (Fig. 4.16), certain anatomical elements are under-represented (for example, distal humerus, distal metacarpal and proximal tibia), while others are over-represented (perhaps proximal metatarsal, proximal femur and astragalus). There could be a number of noncultural explanations for these discrepancies: the palimpsest of activities which resulted in the Thornhill Farm assemblage (eg tool making), the heterogeneity of the comparative assemblage, or the differences in age structure of the two assemblages. For the latter, the young age of the Thornhill Farm cattle assemblage may have an effect (63% of the cattle were 2–3 years of age or less at their death). For a younger population, the later fusing bones may preserve less well and be under-represented.

These explanations do not account for all the differences in the pattern of element representation between the two assemblages, as, for example, there is a relative under-representation of the distal humerus.

In addition to the Brain method, it is useful to compare the ratios of various anatomical elements to one another, to see if any informative patterns manifest themselves (Table 4.26). As predicted by Brain, with one exception, there is a clear relationship between the proximal:distal frequency ratio and the age of epiphyseal fusion of the proximal and distal epiphyses. If the proximal fusion age is greater than the distal fusion age the ratio is less than 1.0, and if the proximal fusion age is smaller, the ratio is greater than 1.0, except for the femur. The proximal and distal fusion ages are about the same for the femur, but the ratio is 2.22, with the proximal end much better represented than the distal end. It is possible that the cattle proximal end of the femur, especially the head, is significantly denser than the distal end in spite of its late fusion date. There is some reason to believe that this is true for bison (Lyman 1994, 245).

By adding the humerus to the radius, and the femur to the tibia, we can see that the representation of proximal and distal ends for fore and hind limbs is not very different (Table 4.27). This table also

Table 4.26   Comparison of the proportions of proximal to distal ends of cattle long bones

Anatomical element	Proximal end	Distal end	Prox/dist ratio	Age of proximal fusion	Age of distal fusion
Humerus	6	36	0.17	3.5-4y	12-20m
Radius	64	32	2.00	12-18m	3.5-4y
Metacarpal	56	16 (30.5)	1.84	fetal	2-2.5y
Femur	20	9	2.22	3.5-4y	3.5-4y
Tibia	13	44	0.30	3.5-4y	2-2.5y
Metatarsal	58	12 (26.5)	2.19	fetal	2-2.5y

Fusion ages from Grigson 1982

indicates that the anterior limb is rather better represented than the posterior, a matter which might, however, be explained with reference to the relatively late fusion dates of the posterior limb bone epiphyses.

Table 4.27 Comparison of upper anterior and posterior cattle long bones

Upper limb bones	Proximal end	Distal end	Total prox + dist
Humerus + radius	70	68	138
Femur + tibia	33	53	86
Total	103	121	

There is no clear distribution pattern in the metapodials either. The proximal (early fusing) metacarpal and metatarsal are both well and almost equally represented (56:58). The distal ends (later fusing) are not so well represented (16:12), partly because fragmented distal ends may only be identifiable as metapodials. When the 29 distal metapodials are equally distributed between anterior and posterior limbs the ratio raises to 30.5:26.5.

There is no straightforward explanation for the small differences between Brain's distribution of antelope and the Thornhill Farm cattle. The data suggest that all anatomical elements were originally present and that all stages of carcass processing, consumption and disposal took place at the site. This

Table 4.28 Differential element representation: Jaurens horses and Thornhill Farm equids

Part[3]	Fossil horses from Jaurens (MNI=46)[1]			Thornhill Farm equids (MNI=18)[2]		
	No. found	Original no.	% survival	No. found	Original no.	% survival
3rd Metacarpal - proximal	39	92	42.4	13	36	36.1
3rd Metatarsal – distal	37	92	40.2	12	36	33.3
3rd Metacarpal – distal	36	92	39.1	12	36	33.3
Tibia – Distal	34	92	37.0	18	36	50.0
3rd Metatarsal – proximal	34	92	37.0	18	36	50.0
Phalanges	200	552	36.2	14	216	6.5
Astragalus	33	92	35.9	7	36	19.4
Calcaneum – proximal	33	92	35.9	5	36	13.9
Calcaneum – distal	33	92	35.9	7	36	19.4
Accessory metapodials	122	368	33.2	9	144	6.3
Radius – distal	27	92	29.3	6	36	16.7
Atlas	13	46	28.3	0	18	0.0
Axis	13	46	28.3	1	18	5.6
Tarsals[4]	97	368	26.4	13	144	9.0
Innominate[5]	23	92	25.0	26	36	72.2
Patella	23	92	25.0	0	36	0.0
Carpals	160	644	24.8	5	252	2.0
Radius – proximal	22	92	23.9	10	36	27.8
Humerus – distal	21	92	22.8	9	36	25.0
Sesamoids	113	552	20.5	0	216	0.0
Scapula – distal	18	92	19.6	7	36	19.4
Cervical vertebra[6]	45	230	19.6	2	90	2.2
Lumbar vertebra	39	276	14.1	1	108	0.9
Tibia – proximal	12	92	13.0	8	36	22.2
Ulna – proximal	11	92	12.0	9	36	25.0
Humerus – proximal	8	92	8.7	2	36	5.6
Femur – proximal	7	92	7.6	6	36	16.7
Thoracic vertebra	57	828	6.9	0	324	0.0
Femur – distal	6	92	6.5	7	36	19.4
Coccygeal vertebra	33	828	4.0	0	324	0.0
Sacrum	1	46	2.2	3	18	16.7
Fibula	1	92	1.1	0	36	0.0

[1] Jaurens data and MNI from Mourer-Chauviré 1980

[2] Includes mule/ass

[3] Excludes shafts except more or less complete unfused diaphyses. Teeth and mandibles (upon which the MNIs are based) are not included because the number of teeth per individual varies by age and the population structures of the two sites are very different

[4] Except astragalus and calcaneum which are recorded separately

[5] Including at least part of the acetabulum

[6] Except the atlas and axis, which are included separately

Table 4.29   Comparison of the proportions of proximal and distal ends of equid long bones

Anatomical element	Proximal end	Distal end	Prox/dist ratio	Age of proximal fusion[1]	Age of distal fusion
Humerus	2	9	0.22	3.5y	15-18m
Radius	10	6	1.67	15-18m	3.5y
Metacarpal	13	12	1.08	fetal	10-15m
Femur	6	7	0.86	3-3.5y	3.5y
Tibia	8	18	0.44	3.5y	2y
Metatarsal	18	12	1.50	fetal	10-15m

[1]Ages from Sisson and Getty 1975

is to be expected at a site where animal husbandry was a subsistence (rather than commercial) activity.

Groups

Only a relatively few cattle bones were found in groups (see archive). The vast majority comprised either broken bones, which could be reconstructed, or fused radii and ulnae. Only two groups included separate anatomical elements, which clearly belonged to a single individual. Both groups, consisting of lower limb bones, are likely to have been connected with the earliest stages of butchery or skinning (Halstead *et al.* 1978).

Butchery evidence

Only 47 cattle postcranial and 11 cranial elements have butchery marks, probably due to the poor surface condition of the bone.

The poor representation of the axis (4 bones) by comparison with the atlas (10 bones) could have a cultural explanation. If chopping through the axis were the way cattle were customarily decapitated, the resulting damage might have weakened the whole bone sufficiently to prejudice its preservation. In fact, no butchery marks are visible on any of the cattle axes. However two atlases do bear marks: one had been chopped through the median plane, cranio-caudally, as if for cutting into sides, rather than through the transverse plane for decapitation. The knife cuts on the ventral surface of the second atlas could have been related to the disarticulation of the skull.

Other butchery marks on postcranial cattle bone are, for the most part, the result of disarticulation, defleshing and skinning. Cut and chop marks on the horncores probably relate to the removal of the horncores, probably to utilise the horn. Cut marks on the mandibles mainly seem to result from skinning, but some may be connected to the disarticulation of the mandible from the maxilla or removal of the cheek flesh for consumption.

Equid bone survivorship

Comparison of Thornhill Farm with Jaurens suggests that the preservation conditions at the two sites were very different (Table 4.28 and Figure 4.17). These differences appear to be much greater than those found between sheep, cattle and their respective comparative populations described by Brain (1967, 1969, 1981). As noted for cattle, the different age structures of the two equid populations might be partly responsible, but other factors almost certainly play a more significant role.

The Thornhill Farm equid long bones (proximal radius, central metapodials, tibia, humerus, ulna and femur) have a similar representation to the Jaurens long bones, with the exception of the distal radius. The scapula are present in expected quantities, but the pelvis is very over-represented. It is difficult to account for this except perhaps to point out that there is a difference in the degree of fragmentation between the two sites, with the possibility that some Thornhill Farm elements are over-represented on account of their higher level of fragmentation. The low representation of vertebrae, accessory metapodials, patellae and fibulae at Thornhill Farm is not unexpected in an assemblage where the preservation state is so poor. There is also a low representation of relatively small, but very dense bones: phalanges (especially the first phalange), carpals and tarsals (especially the astragalus) and sesamoids. The phalange ratio – first : second : third – at 7 : 5 : 2 correlates with their relative sizes; that is, the first is largest and the third is smallest. This seems to indicate that some kind of taphonomic agent could be relevant.

As with cattle, there is a clear relationship between the proximal:distal frequency ratio and the age of epiphyseal fusion of the proximal and distal epiphyses (Table 4.29). If the proximal fusion age is greater than the distal fusion age, the ratio is less than 1.0, and if the proximal fusion age is smaller, the ratio is greater than 1.0. Except for the distal tibia (which will be discussed below), the best represented anatomical elements – the metapodials – are also the earliest fusing. This pattern is best explained by natural taphonomic agents, and cannot therefore be attributed to cultural activities.

Comparison of the anterior and posterior upper limb bones shows that the back leg posterior (39 elements) is better represented than the front (27 elements; Table 4.30). Further scrutiny shows that this is because of the high numbers of distal tibiae. For the lower leg the ratio of early fusing fore and hind metapodials is close to 1:1. This suggests that bone density was the most important determinant of bone preservation. The sample sizes involved

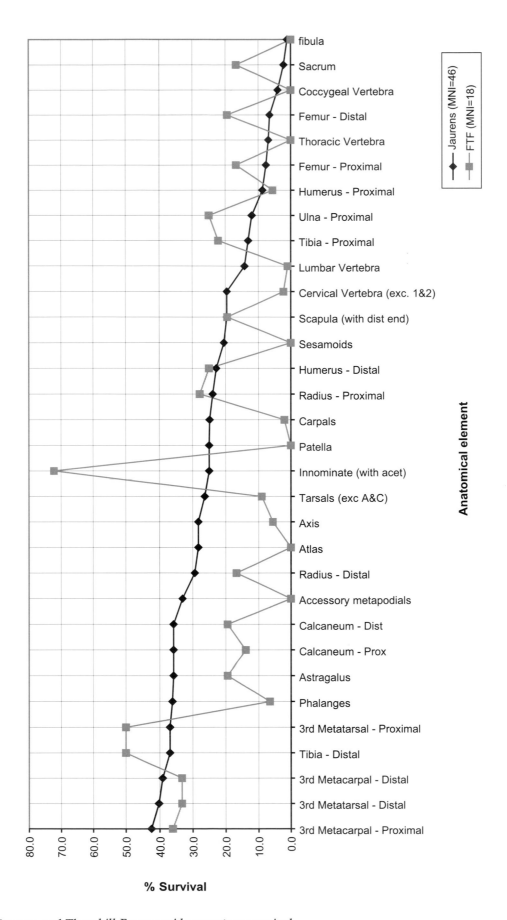

Fig. 4.17 Jaurens and Thornhill Farm equid percentage survival

Table 4.30   Comparison of anterior and posterior equid long bones

	Proximal end	Distal end	Total prox + dist
Humerus + radius	12	15	27
Femur + tibia	14	25	39
Total	26	40	-

here are not very large, but one could speculate that the over-representation of tibia could be connected with some sort of cultural behaviour. As we shall see later, tibiae were, in fact, worked at Thornhill Farm.

Groups

Few Thornhill Farm equid bones were found in articulation. Grouped elements were largely limited to metapodials, accessory metapodials and the radius and ulna. There were, however, four other more interesting groups which suggest that at least some of the equid skeletons could have been at least partially disarticulated before they were discarded. The lower limb bone groups could be associated with the initial stages of butchery for meat or with skinning (Halstead *et al.* 1978). The tibia groups could have more complex explanations, especially considering the fact that a relatively large proportion of them have evidence of butchery bone working.

Worked and butchered equid bones

Only a very small proportion (2%) of the equid bones have butchery marks. Of the six butchered equid bones, three tibiae showed chop, saw or drill marks. A fourth tibia had cut marks, as did an astragalus (which articulates with the distal tibia). It is possible that the fourth tibia had originally been destined for working, but was discarded instead. The cut marks on this bone could also relate to skinning, but meat preparation seems less likely. The only other equid elements with butchery marks were a first phalange and a partial pelvis. The first phalange, a non-meat bearing bone, seems to have been cut in the course of skinning. It is difficult, however, to think of any other explanation for the cut marks on the pelvis aside from butchery for meat.

Discussion of equid taphonomy

The Thornhill Farm equid bones are relatively less fragmented and more are complete than those of the cattle, and the vast majority of the bones show no evidence of having been worked or butchered. This suggests a lower utilisation of horse meat compared to cattle meat, for whatever purpose. We have no definite evidence that any of the horses were consumed by humans, although that cannot be ruled out. Nor is there any reason to believe that any horses were buried intact as they were in some Roman military sites in the Netherlands (Lauwerier and Robeerst 2001) and at Icklingham (late Roman,

Suffolk; unpubl.), as no complete or partially articulated skeletons were recovered.

Some of the horses were partially butchered after death, almost certainly for hides and possibly for meat. Some of their bones were exposed to carnivore gnawing, and others used for tool fabrication. The long bones, in particular, were then disposed of more or less in the same way as the bones of other taxa. There is no evidence that horses received any special treatment after death at Thornhill Farm. The standard processing of horse carcasses after death for both the hides and meat appears consistent with Iron Age and early Roman sites such as Farmoor, Oxon. (Wilson 1979), Ashville Trading Estate (Wilson 1978) and Danebury (Grant 1991).

Pig bone survivorship

The pig assemblage at Thornhill Farm is very small with only 159 cranial elements (an ELU of 89) and 83 postcranial elements (an ELU also of 83), of which 32 are shaft pieces. No postcranial elements are in groups and none are worked. One scapula shows evidence of butchery, probably connected with disarticulation.

Population structure

One of the best ways of understanding past human-animal relationships is to study the population structure – that is, the age and sex structure – of the economically important animals in archaeological assemblages.

The ageing data for each of the main taxa are presented in the form of mortality distributions.

Large equids

The crown height measurements reveal that the Thornhill Farm material is similar in size to the New Forest and Pleistocene material; they are slighter larger than the Forest Pony teeth and rather smaller than the late Pleistocene teeth. The mule/ass teeth are excluded from this analysis because too little is known about their eruption/wear and crown-heights to age them with any degree of reliability.

Figure 4.18 shows the age structure of the teeth from Thornhill Farm when each tooth is plotted individually, while Figure 4.19 shows the age structure when the teeth are plotted as ELUs – that is, tooth rows are plotted as a unit rather than as individual teeth. The first method would suffice if we believed that every tooth from the site had an equal chance of being preserved and collected, which is not the case. Plotting teeth from jaws together has the advantage of more accurate ageing, and it is likely that jaws are more likely to be recovered than loose teeth. The number of tooth rows (or ELU) frequencies in any individual age class are very small, ranging from only 1 to 9.7 ELUs. Such a small sample size would certainly be an important factor in the jaggedness of the distribution.

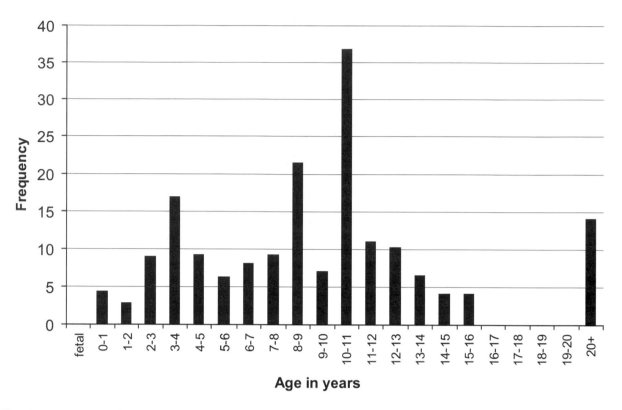

Fig. 4.18 Large equid mortality distribution (counting each tooth individually)

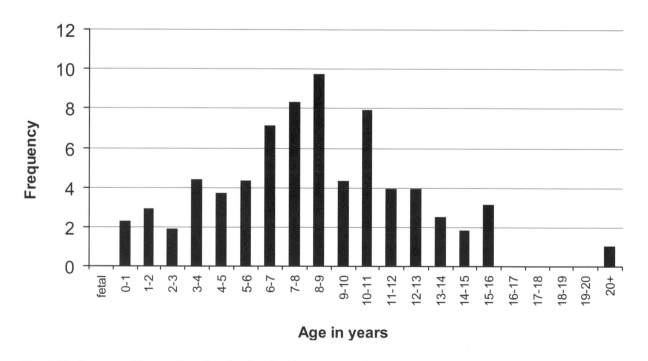

Fig. 4.19 Large equid mortality distribution (teeth aggregated by group)

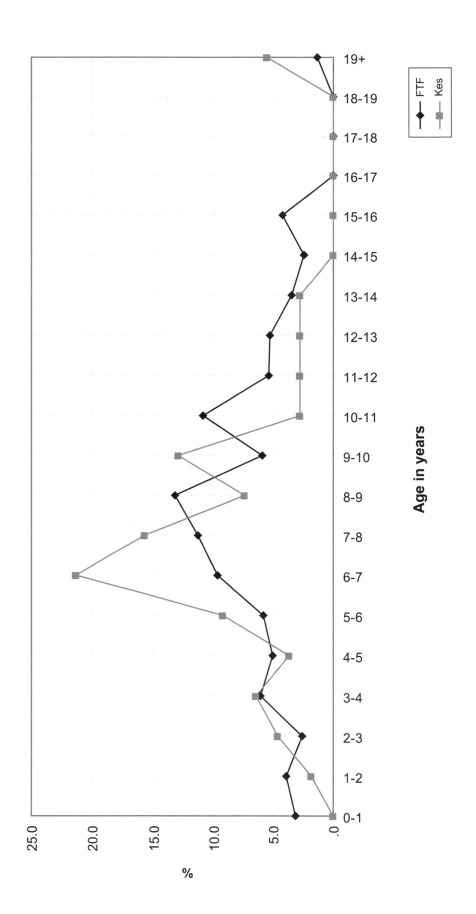

Fig. 4.20 Equid mortality distributions

The majority of the large equids (73.4%) died at an age expected for work animals, 6–7 years of age or older. If we compare age distribution to the available mortality models for equids (Figure 4.21; Levine 1983; 1999b), the Thornhill Farm data best fits the attritional model. In this the mortality is low for mature adults and high for juveniles and senescents (Caughley 1966). This kind of pattern is characteristic of natural attrition, scavenging, coursing on foot and livestock husbandry, where meat production is of secondary importance.

Due to the high number of horse bones in addition to the recovery of elements from immature animals there has been some speculation in the past that Thornhill Farm might have been a stud farm (Miles and Palmer 1990). There is, in fact, no evidence for this and much evidence against it. Had Thornhill Farm been used as a stud farm, the sex and age structure should have been quite different. There should be more evidence of infant and juvenile (0–2 years of age) mortality – even taking into account the poor preservation conditions – and the mortality rate for animals between the ages of 5 and 15 years should be very low indeed (Levine 1999a and b). This was not the case at Thornhill Farm. The sex ratio was calculated from the small number of sexable pelves, and suggested a male:female ratio of 3:4. Ethnographic evidence suggests that if horses are kept to provide meat and milk, the ratio of stallions to mares is around 1:50, thus Thornhill Farm has none of the characteristics of a stud farm.

Ann Hyland, in *Equus, the horse in the Roman world*, argues that Roman equids commonly sustained injuries that would have been caused by poor living conditions and gross overwork (1990, 59). She estimates that a horse was only expected to last about 3 years in active military service and on average 4 years as a post horse (*op cit.* 86, 88). Moreover, the breeding period was also comparatively abbreviated, with mares being considered past their prime at 10 years of age, though some did breed until 15 (*op cit.* 238). The relatively high incidence of pathology (see Appendix 4), as well as the population structure, seem to confirm this pattern both at Thornhill Farm and the Kesteren cemetery in the Netherlands (Fig. 4.20; Lauwerier and Hessing 1992).

In conclusion, the population structure at Thornhill Farm suggests that the large equids were used primarily as work animals. The taphonomic evidence suggests that after death some equid bone, hides and possibly meat were also used, but these uses were of secondary, and possibly, minor importance. There is no reason to believe that the site was ever used as a stud farm.

Equid identification

Equus caballus (the true horse) and *Equus asinus* (the ass) are both present at Thornhill Farm. Mules (male asses crossed with female horses) and/or hinnies (female asses crossed with male horses) might also be present. Positive identifications of the hybrids are exceedingly difficult to make at the best of times, since the differences between them and their progenitors are relatively subtle and overlap at both ends of their ranges of variation (for example, see Eisenmann and Beckouche 1986; Zeder 1986; Eisenmann and Baylac 2000). Very little research has been done on this problem and very few specimens are available for study.

The difficulties at Thornhill Farm are magnified by the small sample size and poor preservation of the material. In some cases *E. caballus* identifications can be made with considerable certainty, particularly in the case of cheekteeth. Tables 4.31 and 4.32 show the frequencies of records for cranial and postcranial material as assigned to taxon. Each anatomical element is counted separately whether or not it belongs to a group. A more detailed breakdown suggests that there is considerably more uncertainty with cranial than postcranial elements, but that is not entirely true: even the 'Certainty' variable is only relative.

The tables (4.31 and 4.32) suggest that *E. caballus* is likely to be by far the most important taxon, but we really do not know enough about the hybrids to judge the use and importance of mules and hinnies.

At the extreme ends of the range of variation it seems clear that both ass and horse were present. However, where sufficient data are available, the size range clines almost without interruption from one extreme to the other (taking into account the small sample sizes available). A series of photographs were taken to compare the Thornhill Farm equid bones (tibiae, metacarpals and metatarsals) with one another, and with an *Equus asinus* from the Department of Archaeology collections (specimen number 123, from Greece) and with two New Forest ponies (all data can be found in the archives).

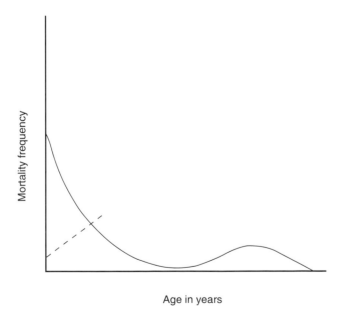

Fig. 4.21 Attritional model of age structure

Table 4.31   Breakdown of equid cranial elements

	No.	%
E. caballus	188	57.3
E. asinus	6	1.8
Horse/mule	15	4.6
Mule/ass	7	2.1
Equid-small	4	1.2
Equid	108	32.9
Total	328	100

Table 4.32   Breakdown of equid postcranial elements

	No.	%
E. caballus	281	92.4
E. asinus	2	0.7
Equid	21	6.9
Total	304	100

Like the long bones, the teeth of the various equids are very difficult to distinguish from one another. Attempts to do so have been described in considerable detail elsewhere, always with the caveat that the various species and their hybrids overlap in form (Eisenmann and Beckouche 1986; Zeder 1986; Eisenmann and Baylac 2000). It is significant that, as cheekteeth age, the pattern of enamel folds upon which the distinctions are based becomes progressively more simplified and less diagnostic. The teeth illustrated in the archive all seem to have at lease some noncaballine characteristics. Most significantly, while the caballine linguaflexid is usually U-shaped, some Thornhill

Farm specimens are V-shaped like asses (Eisenmann 1986). The Thornhill Farm size range might indicate that some of those animals were hybrids.

Cattle

The cattle mortality distributions (Fig. 4.22) have been plotted using only mandibular ELUs. The ELU frequency at 210 is considerably greater than that for large equids. The category for fetal–0 does not, in fact, include any definitely fetal teeth, but only those which could be fetal (for example, fetal to one month old). As with equids, there is little doubt that immature individuals are under-represented at Thornhill Farm.

Figure 4.23 shows the adjusted and unadjusted mortality distributions (percentages) for the cattle at Thornhill Farm (see Appendix 5). It is interesting to compare this age distribution with mortality data derived from Dahl and Hjort's 'baseline herd model' (Fig. 4.24) where the population of a herd is stable and the age structure static. The examples they used in the development of the model are largely from African nomadic pastoralists, raising cattle primarily for milk and blood and secondarily for meat (Dahl and Hjort 1976). There is no discussion of their use as work animals, although the use of bullocks as pack animals is mentioned.

Both the Dahl and Hjort model and the Thornhill Farm distribution best fit an attritional mortality model (Figure 4.21; see Large equids). They differ from one another, however, in that the Thornhill Farm distribution suggests that a much higher proportion of animals were slaughtered before 4 years of age and a much lower proportion after 8 years of age. The low proportion of animals greater than 8–9 years of age suggests that meat production

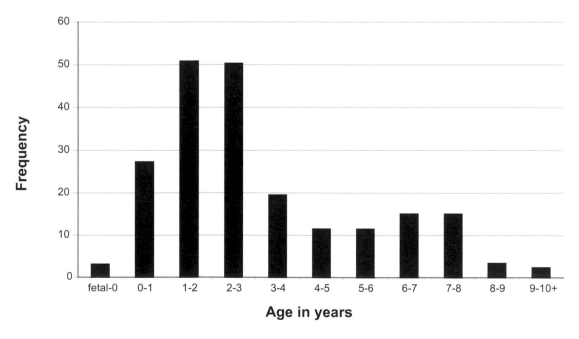

Fig. 4.22   Cattle mortality distribution – ELU frequencies

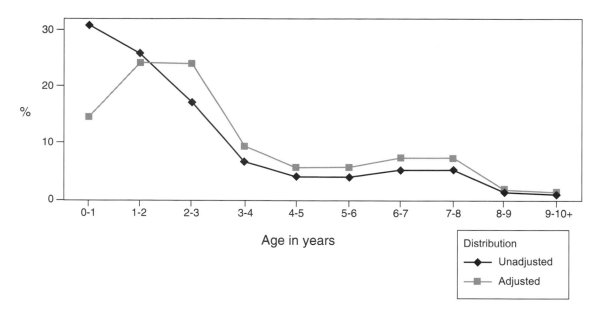

Fig. 4.23   Age structure of cattle from Thornhill Farm – unadjusted and adjusted for under-representation of immature animals

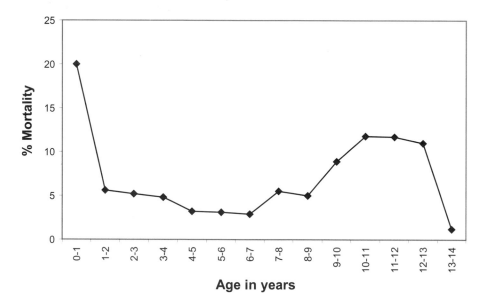

Fig. 4.24   Cattle mortality based upon Dahl and Hjort's 'base line herd model'

is of primary importance. Dahl and Hjort suggest that bullocks, raised for meat, would normally be slaughtered at around the age of 4–5 years, since they would, by that time, be fully grown (Dahl and Hjort 1976, 157).

According to Dahl and Hjort's baseline herd model, productive female cattle are rarely slaughtered. However, especially where herd growth is not desired, female as well as male young surplus to the maintenance requirements of the herd could be butchered. In the case of a fixed settlement, like Thornhill Farm, available grazing might not have been sufficient to allow a herd to grow at its maximum rate. The preservation state of the bones

was such that no attempt was made to calculate the male:female ratio.

The presence of teeth from individuals 1–3 months of age, suggests that some cattle were bred on-site, although their remains are probably under-represented due to poor preservation. It is possible that some calves were brought to Thornhill Farm. The animals were fattened and butchered between the ages of 1–2 and 3–4 years, or a smaller number might have been kept on to be used for traction and were butchered mainly between the ages of 6–7 and 8–9 years. The cows would have been kept on until a decline in fertility, perhaps from the ages of 10 to 12 years or even earlier, depending upon their nutri-

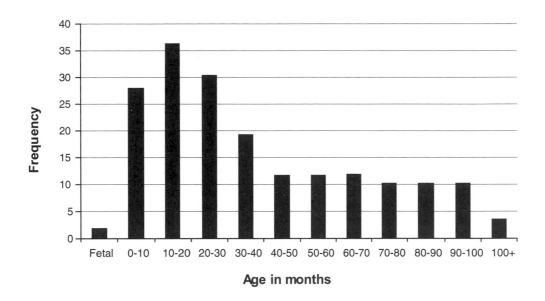

Fig. 4.25   Sheep mortality distribution: ELU frequencies

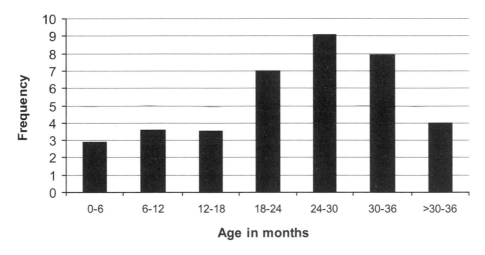

Fig. 4.26   Pig mortality distribution: ELU frequencies

tional status, and were then probably butchered for meat (Dahl and Hjort 1976). Draught cattle, which might have comprised cows, bulls and/or oxen could have been worked, as suggested by Stokes, till around the age of 6 to 8 and then butchered for meat.

That such a high proportion of cattle died, presumably slaughtered, between the ages of 1–2 and 3–4 years might suggest that relatively little surplus meat would have been available to sell. Unfortunately we do not have the means to investigate this question further.

Sheep

The sheep mortality distribution is shown in Figure 4.25. The mandibular ELU frequency is 185, less than the cattle but more than horse. The fetal category does not include any definitely fetal teeth, but only those which could be fetal (for example, fetal to 10 months of age). These teeth are grouped with teeth 0–10 months old.

As with the equids and cattle, there is little doubt that immature sheep are under-represented at Thornhill Farm. The age structure for Thornhill Farm best fits Payne's model for a mortality distribution in which meat production is the primary objective (Payne 1973), with the majority of animals dying between 10 and 40 months (about one to three years).

Pig

The pig ELU distribution has been plotted using the same method as for the other taxa (Fig. 4.26). With an ELU of 38, the maxillary and mandibular pig sample is very small indeed. The pigs at Thornhill Farm are relatively short-lived, as is usual for this species which is raised primarily for meat (Dobney *et al.* 1996). As with the other Thornhill Farm taxa, immature pigs are under-represented at this site, although the vast majority died by the age of 3 years. This seems to be a normal pattern for British Iron Age/Roman domesticated pig populations (Halstead 1985; Levine 1986; Levine 1995; Maltby 1996). Because they are usually used primarily for meat and hides, and because of their high fecundity by comparison with the rest of our taxa, there is usually no advantage in keeping pigs past their third year, and sometimes considerable advantage in butchering them earlier.

Discussion

by Bethan Charles

At Thornhill Farm, in order of importance, the animal bones consist of cattle (58%), sheep (22%), equids (13%), pig (6%) and dog (1%). After separating the identified material by phase the majority was assigned to the late Iron Age–early Roman period of occupation. As we have already seen, the preservation of the bones is generally very poor. It is likely that the small taxa are certainly disproportionately affected by all the taphonomic agents involved in the destruction of animal bone at this site: poor soil conditions, secondary or even tertiary redeposition in ditches and other recut features with pottery from mixed periods, and the presence of dogs at the site. The absence of sieving and the nonsystematic nature of the bone collection will also have led to the serious under-representation of small species, and small or immature bones of both large and small taxa (Payne 1972; Brain 1981; Payne and Munson 1985; Munson 2000). Therefore the ratio of horse/cow to sheep/pig should not be taken at face value.

Studies of the species proportions in late Iron Age–early Roman samples from the Upper Thames Valley by Ellen Hambleton (Hambleton 1999, 59) have demonstrated that there is a general increase in the number of cattle, possibly as a result of Romanisation. It is not possible to compare variations in animal husbandry techniques at this site during separate periods of occupation due to the predominance of material from one phase. However, other similar late Iron Age and early Roman sites in the region such as Ashville Trading Estate, Abingdon (Wilson 1978), Farmoor (Wilson 1979) and Bicester Fields Farm (Charles, in Cromarty *et al.* 1999) have shown an increase in the proportion of cattle being kept at sites during the late Iron Age and early Roman periods in comparison with earlier periods of occupation.

The location of Thornhill Farm close to the Upper Thames Valley floodplain indicates that whilst the settlement itself was on a well-drained gravel island, at least some of the land around the site may have been wet and marshy. This may not have provided ideal conditions for sheep, which are better suited to dryer conditions and are prone to suffer from foot rot on wet sites. The presence of the snail *Lymnea truncatula* which is the immediate host of sheep fluke in early Roman deposits (see below) may also have discouraged the large scale farming of sheep.

Horses and cattle are less susceptible to these diseases. Both require a good supply of water and do not like to feed on short turf, which implies that they would have been suited to the lower, wetter pastureland surrounding the settlement area. Additional environmental evidence indicating that much of the site was pastureland can be drawn from the remains of the coleoptera identified from the site. Scarabaeoid dung beetles which feed on the dung of large herbivores under pastureland conditions were found to be the most numerous identified from the site (see below).

The cattle age structure data from Thornhill Farm confirm the impression left by the taphonomic study that the site had, for the most part, a subsistence level of economy. Meat and possibly milk products surplus to the settlement's requirements could have been taken to market, but we have no evidence for this on-site. The cattle appear to have been bred on site, with a proportion being butchered between the ages of 1 and 4 years, and the remaining animals probably being kept for breeding or for work as draught cattle before being slaughtered at the end of their useful lives.

Oxen were the most important animals for ploughing and haulage (Langdon 1986). The Romanian draught oxen studied by Bartosiewicz and Van Neer (1997, 18) ranged in age from 6 to 19 years, with a mean age at death of 10.5 years. The training of oxen in Estonia and Lithuania usually started at 3 years of age, and in Finland by 1.5–2 years (*op cit.*, 120). At the end of their working lives draught oxen were often fattened up and slaughtered for meat: 'traditions of exploitation at the beginning of the last century ... dictated that Hungarian Grey oxen be regularly slaughtered before 10 years of age when the beef they provided was still of reasonably good quality' (*op cit.*, 121).

The equids at the site appear to have been primarily used as work animals, although no associated horse trappings were found. According to Langdon (1986), until well after the collapse of the Western Roman Empire, for practical purposes, equid traction was limited to asses and mules. However, at Thornhill Farm the evidence is inconclusive. Evidence of partial disarticulation of the bones indicates that at least some of the horses may have been slaughtered for their meat and hides, although the ages of the horses, with few young animals recovered, does not indicate that the animals were being bred on the site.

It is probable that the sheep kept at the site were kept primarily for their secondary products (wool, milk and dung). However, the evidence available was not conclusive. The pigs at the site were clearly kept primarily for their meat.

It is evident that there were dogs kept at the site, even though the majority of the bones came from one animal. It is possible that the dog burial found at the site represents a ritual deposition, although there were no finds associated with the skeleton, and it was not clearly related to any surrounding features. As previously mentioned, the presence of dogs at the site will have affected the distribution and survival of many of the animal bones discarded across the site. It is likely that the dogs were working animals, kept for hunting, herding and to guard.

No wild mammals were identified from within the assemblage although this is not conclusive evidence that wild animals were not being eaten. Wild species have not been found in particularly high quantities at other late Iron Age and Early Roman sites in the region such as Gravelly Guy (Mulville and Levitan forthcoming), Farmoor (Wilson 1979), and Ashville, Abingdon (Wilson 1978). The lack of bird and fish remains is almost certainly a result of the poor bone preservation. It is possible that the single heron bone recovered from the site does not relate to human activity and may be the result of a natural fatality. However, heron bones have been found at a number of other Iron Age sites, including Gravelly Guy (Mulville and Levitan forthcoming), Danebury (Serjeantson 1991) and Gussage All Saints (Harcourt 1979).

The site appears to have been based around subsistence farming, although the relatively high number of horse bones recovered may indicate that the site was of some higher status, since the animals would have been expensive to keep, with little in return in terms of secondary products.

THE PLANT AND INVERTEBRATE REMAINS

by Mark Robinson

The Iron Age to early Roman settlement at Thornhill Farm was situated on the first gravel terrace of the Thames, above the confluence of the Rivers Thames and Coln and about 0.75 km upstream from a contemporaneous settlement at Claydon Pike. Although the settlement showed many similarities with Claydon Pike, the environs of Thornhill Farm were less low-lying. Whereas the late Iron Age settlement at Claydon Pike was on an island of first gravel terrace surrounded by broad late Glacial floodplain hollows, the area of uninterrupted gravel terrace at Thornhill Farm was more extensive. This late Glacial system of channels extended as far as Thornhill Farm, some channels containing humified peat, but its hollows of floodplain had become relatively narrow (Plate 4.2). As was the case at Claydon Pike, these channels had ceased to flow or even hold water long before the Iron Age.

Plate 4.2   Section through palaeochannel in Trench 22 showing layer of humified peat

The water table of the site was about 1.2 m below the surface of the gravel and many of the deeper Iron Age and Roman features contained moderately preserved organic remains. Extensive sampling took place throughout the duration of the excavation for waterlogged and carbonised plant and insect remains.

The samples

A total of 57 samples from phased contexts were floated for carbonised plant remains. Ten litres of each sample was floated onto a 0.5 mm mesh and the flots were dried. The flots were spread out, scanned under a binocular microscope and, if necessary, sorted in detail. The flots were also scanned for mollusc remains.

Subsamples of the 32 potentially waterlogged samples were investigated, and eight of the samples were found to contain reasonably well-preserved organic remains. 250 g of each sample was water-sieved down to 0.2 mm and sorted for noncarbonised macroscopic biological remains. In view of the abundance of *Juncus* seeds, which are very small, only a tenth subsample of the fraction between 0.5 mm and 0.2 mm was sorted for seeds and their number was then multiplied by ten for inclusion in the table of results. Insect remains were most abundant and best preserved in Sample 706/A. A further 2.75 kg of this sample was washed over a 0.2 mm sieve and then subjected to paraffin flotation. After washing with hot water and detergent, the flot was sorted for insect remains. Sorted waterlogged plant remains and insects were stored in 70% ethanol. Mollusc shells were dried to await identification. Specimens were identified with reference to the various collections housed in the University Museum, Oxford.

Details of those contexts for which sample results are individually listed are given in Table 4.33.

Results

The identifications from the samples have been listed in Tables 4.34–40.

Carbonised plant remains

The identifications of carbonised plant remains (excluding charcoal) for the six samples in which ten or more items were identified have been listed separately in Table 4.34. The results for all the remaining samples have been summed by period in Table 4.35. Nomenclature follows Clapham *et al.* (1987).

Waterlogged macroscopic plant remains

The results for the identification of waterlogged seeds are given in Table 4.36 and the identifications of other waterlogged plant remains are given in Table 4.37. Wood was absent from the samples. Nomenclature follows Clapham *et al.* (1987). All samples were of 250 g.

Coleoptera

Table 4.38 gives the minimum number of individuals represented by the fragments in Sample 706/A and the total number of individuals represented by the minimum number of individuals from Samples 101/D/4, 324/B/2, 473/A/4, 803/D, 2287/B and 2530/A. Nomenclature follows Kloet and Hincks (1977).

Table 4.33   Samples analysed for plant and invertebrate remains with results presented individually

Context	Trench	Feature type	Enclosure/structure	Period	
101/D/4	7	ditch	E9	E	Early Roman
101/Q/3	7	ditch	E9	E	Early Roman
108/C/3	7	ditch	E7	F*	Early Roman
110/H/8	7	roadside ditch	301	G	Early Roman
111/E/1	7	gully	E6	F*	Early Roman
189/1	7	hearth	-	C/D*	Late Iron Age-early Roman
206/B/3	7	pit/gulley	E8	?	Late Iron Age
324/B/2	7	ditch	E30	F	Early Roman
473/A/4	7	pit	-	A-B*	Middle-late Iron Age
706/A	7	pit	E23	C	Late Iron Age
803/D	8	ditch	E120	A	Middle Iron Age
2084/B	9	ditch	S201	C	Late Iron Age
2239/F	9	ditch	E49	D	Early Roman
2287/B	9	ditch	E48	D	Early Roman
2530/A	9	pit	-	C*	Late Iron Age
2620/A/11	south of 8	trackway ditch	trackway	D-F	Early Roman

*Phase uncertain

Table 4.34 Carbonised plant remains for samples in which ten or more items were identified (excluding charcoal)

Period		Late Iron Age			Early Roman		
		C	?	C/D	D	E	F
Context		2084/B	206/B/3	189/1	2239/F	101/Q/3	111/E/1
Sample Volume (litres)		10	10	10	10	10	10
CEREAL GRAIN							
Triticum spelta L.	Spelt Wheat	1	-	-	-	-	-
Triticum sp.	Wheat	1	-	-	-	-	1
cf. *Avena* sp.	Oats	-	-	-	-	-	1
cereal indet.		9	-	-	1	-	3
Total Cereal Grain		11.0	0.0	0.0	1.0	0.0	5.0
CHAFF							
Triticum spelta L. - glume base	Spelt Wheat	2	-	-	-	1	-
T. dicoccum Schübl. or							
spelta L. - glume base	Emmer or Spelt Wheat	2	1	-	3	2	1
Avena sp. - awn	Oats	-	-	-	-	-	1
Total Cereal Chaff (excluding awns)		4.0	1.0	0.0	3.0	3.0	1.0
WEED SEEDS							
cf. *Ranunculus* sp.	Buttercup	-	-	1	-	-	-
Barbarea vulgaris R. Br.	Yellow Rocket	2	-	-	-	-	-
Atriplex sp.	Orache	-	1	-	-	4	-
Medicago lupulina L.	Black Medick	-	-	-	1	-	-
Vicia or *Lathyrus* sp.	Vetch, Tare etc	1	-	-	-	-	-
Potentilla sp.	Cinquefoil	-	-	-	-	2	-
Polygonum aviculare agg.	Knotgrass	1	-	-	-	-	-
Fallopia convolvulus (L.) Löve	Black Bindweed	-	-	-	-	1	-
Rumex sp.	Dock	2	-	25	-	1	2
Sherardia arvensis L.	Field Madder	-	-	-	-	1	-
Galium aparine L.	Goosegrass	1	-	1	2	-	2
Centaurea sp.	Knapweed	-	-	-	1	-	-
Juncus effusus gp.	Tussock Rush	-	-	-	-	13	-
Eleocharis S. *Palustres* sp.	Spike-rush	1	1	-	-	-	-
Carex spp.	Sedge	41	8	5	-	52	-
Gramineae indet.	Grass	-	1	-	3	1	-
Weed Seed indet.		3	1	3	1	1	-
Total Weed Seeds		52.0	12.0	35.0	8.0	76.0	4.0
OTHER REMAINS							
Juncus inflexus L. - stem fragments	Hard Rush	-	-	-	-	+	-
No. of Items/Litre		6.7	1.3	3.5	1.2	7.9	1.0
(excluding awns and *Juncus* stems)							

+ present

Other insects

Table 4.39 gives the results for the identification of other insects following the arrangement used for Table 4.38.

Mollusca

The only waterlogged sample to contain a significant quantity of molluscan remains was Sample 324/B/2. The minimum numbers of individuals from this sample (of 250 g) are given in Table 4.40. Mollusc shells were abundant in some of the flots for carbonised plant remains, particularly the early Roman ditches of Trench 7. The presence of shells in a range of flots has also been given in Table 4.40.

Nomenclature follows Kerney (1976) for freshwater molluscs and Waldén (1976) for land snails.

The origin of the assemblages

The survival of organic remains in the deeper features suggests that they would have held stagnant water when they were open. The seeds show that some of the ditches had developed an aquatic flora. Seeds of the water plant *Ranunculus S. Batrachium* (water crowfoot), *Nasturtium officinale* (watercress), *Apium nodiflorum* (fool's watercress) and *Glyceria* sp. (flote grass) were abundant in Sample 324/B/2 (Table 4.36). This sample contained a slum aquatic molluscan fauna (Table 4.40). Many

Table 4.35   Carbonised plant remains for samples in which less than ten items were identified (excluding charcoal)

Period		Iron Age				Early Roman			
		Middle	Mid/Late	Late	Late				
		A	A/B	C	?	C/D, E	C/E, E	F	EG, G
Total Number of Samples		1	1	8	1	13	12	16	5
Number of Samples with Items		1	1	3	1	8	3	9	2
Total Sample Volume (litres)		10	10	80	10	130	120	160	50
CEREAL GRAIN									
Triticum spelta L.	Spelt Wheat	-	-	1	-	-	-	-	-
Triticum sp.	Wheat	-	-	1	-	1	-	1	-
Hordeum sp.	Barley	-	-	-	-	1	-	1	-
cf. Avena sp.	Oats	-	-	-	-	2	-	1	-
cereal indet.		-	-	15	-	2	1	7	1
Total Cereal Grain		0	0	17	0	6	1	10	1
CHAFF									
Triticum spelta L. - glume base	Spelt Wheat	-	-	2	-	3	1	1	-
T. dicoccum Schübl. or spelta L. - glume base	Emmer or Spelt Wheat	-	-	2	1	-	2	-	-
Avena sp. - awn	Oats	-	-	-	-	-	-	1	-
Avena sp.	Oats	-	-	-	-	1	-	-	-
cereal indet. rachis fragment		-	-	-	-	1	-	-	-
Total Cereal Chaff (excluding awns)		0	0	4	1	5	3	1	0
WEED SEEDS									
cf. Ranunculus sp.	Buttercup	-	-	-	-	1	-	-	-
Barbarea vulgaris R. Br.	Yellow Rocket	-	-	2	-	-	-	-	-
Atriplex sp.	Orache	-	-	-	1	-	4	-	-
Chenopodiaceae gen. et sp. indet.		1	-	-	-	-	-	-	-
Medicago lupulina L.	Black Medick	-	-	-	-	1	-	-	-
Vicia or Lathyrus sp.	Vetch, Tare etc	-	-	1	-	-	-	-	-
Potentilla sp.	Cinquefoil	-	-	-	-	-	2	-	-
Polygonum aviculare agg.	Knotgrass	1	-	1	-	-	-	-	-
Fallopia convolvulus (L.) Löve	Black Bindweed	-	-	-	-	1	1	-	-
Rumex sp.	Dock	1	-	3	-	25	1	4	-
Hyoscyamus niger L.	Henbane	-	-	-	-	1	-	-	-
Glechoma hederacea L.	Ground-ivy	-	-	-	-	-	1	-	-
Sherardia arvensis L.	Field Madder	-	-	1	-	-	-	-	-
Galium aparine L.	Goosegrass	-	-	1	-	3	1	2	1
Carduus or Cirsium sp.	Thistle	-	-	-	-	-	-	1	-
Centaurea sp.	Knapweed	-	-	-	-	1	-	-	-
Juncus effusus gp.	Tussock Rush	-	-	-	-	-	13	-	-
Eleocharis S. Palustres sp.	Spike-rush	-	-	1	1	-	-	1	-
Carex spp.	Sedge	-	2	41	8	5	52	1	-
Gramineae indet.	Grass	-	-	-	1	3	1	3	-
Weed Seed indet.		1	-	3	1	4	1	4	-
Total Weed Seeds		4	2	54	12	45	77	16	1
OTHER REMAINS									
Juncus inflexus L. - stem fragments	Hard Rush	-	-	-	-	-	+	-	-
No. of Items/Litre (excluding awns and Juncus stems)		0.40	0.20	0.94	1.30	0.43	0.68	0.17	0.04

+ present

Table 4.36   Waterlogged seeds

Period		No. of Seeds							
		Iron Age				Early Roman			
		Middle	Mid/Late	Late	Late				
		A	A/B	C	C	D	E	F	D/F
Context		803/D	473/A/4	706/A	2530/A	2287/B	101/D/4	324/B/2	2620/A/11
Ranunculus cf. *acris* L.	Meadow Buttercup	2	-	-	-	1	-	-	1
R. cf. *repens* L	Creeping Buttercup	1	-	5	2	-	-	4	-
R. parviflorus L.	Small-flowered Buttercup	-	-	-	-	1	-	-	-
R. flammula L.	Lesser Spearwort	-	-	-	2	-	-	1	-
Ranunculus S. *Batrachium* sp.	Water Crowfoot	14	-	-	-	-	-	31	1
Papaver rhoeas L., *dubium* L., *lecoqii* Lam. or *hybridum* L.	Poppy	-	-	-	-	-	-	-	1
P. argemone L.	Poppy	-	-	3	1	-	1	1	-
Brassica rapa L. ssp. *sylvestris* (L.) Jan.	Wild Turnip	-	-	1	-	-	1	-	-
Coronopus squamatus (Forstr.) Asch.	Swine Cress	-	-	-	-	-	-	4	-
Thlaspi arvense L.	Field Penny-cress	-	-	1	-	-	-	-	-
Nasturtium officinale R. Br.	Water Cress	-	-	-	-	-	-	10	-
Viola S. *Viola* sp.	Violet	1	-	-	-	-	-	-	-
Hypericum sp.	St John's Wort	10	-	-	1	-	-	-	-
Cerastium cf. *fontanum* Baug.	Mouse-ear Chickweed	-	-	-	-	1	-	2	-
Stellaria media gp.	Chickweed	4	1	7	1	3	1	7	-
Sagina sp.	Pearlwort	-	-	10	10	-	-	-	-
Arenaria sp.	Sandwort	-	10	-	30	-	-	-	-
Montia fontana L. ssp. *chondrosperma* (Fenz.) Walt.	Blinks	-	-	-	-	-	-	1	-
Chenopodium polyspermum L.	All-seed	4	-	-	-	-	-	-	-
C. album L.	Fat Hen	-	1	1	-	1	-	1	-
C. cf. *rubrum* L.	Red Goosefoot	-	-	-	-	3	3	64	-
Atriplex sp.	Orache	-	1	1	-	3	1	2	4
Chenopodiaceae gen. et sp. indet.		-	-	-	-	1	-	-	1
Linum catharticum L.	Dwarf Flax	14	-	1	-	1	-	-	1
Medicago lupulina L.	Black Medick	-	-	2	-	-	-	-	-
Filipendula ulmaria (L.) Maxim.	Meadowsweet	-	-	-	-	-	-	-	2
Rubus fruticosus agg.	Blackberry	-	-	-	1	2	-	-	-
Potentilla anserina L.	Silverweed	1	-	11	-	-	1	2	-
P. cf. *reptans* L.	Creeping Cinquefoil	7	-	1	14	8	-	2	-
Potentilla sp.	Cinquefoil	-	-	-	-	-	-	-	1
Aphanes arvensis L.	Parsley-piert	-	-	-	-	1	-	-	-
Callitriche sp.	Starwort	-	-	-	-	-	-	1	-
Hydrocotyle vulgaris L.	Pennywort	-	-	-	-	3	-	-	-
Anthriscus caucalis Bieb.	Bur Chervil	-	-	1	-	1	3	9	-
Conium maculatum L.	Hemlock	-	-	-	-	-	-	1	-
Apium nodiflorum (L.) Lag.	Fool's Parsley	-	1	-	-	-	-	30	-
Polygonum aviculare agg.	Knotgrass	-	3	3	1	-	-	2	-
P. persicaria L.	Red Shank	-	-	-	-	1	-	5	-
Rumex conglomeratus Mur.	Sharp Dock	-	-	-	1	2	1	10	-
Rumex spp. (not *maritimus*)	Dock	1	1	-	1	6	-	8	1
Urtica urens L.	Small Nettle	4	11	2	3	12	2	1	1
U. dioica L.	Stinging Nettle	25	23	11	20	14	12	49	4
Anagallis sp.	Pimpernel	-	-	-	-	-	1	-	-
Hyoscyamus niger L.	Henbane	-	9	-	-	3	1	1	-
Solanum sp.	Nightshade	-	-	-	-	1	-	-	-
Rhinanthus sp.	Yellow Rattle	-	-	-	-	-	-	-	1
Odontites verna (Bell.) Dum.	Red Bartsia	1	-	1	-	-	-	-	-
Mentha cf. *aquatica* L.	Water Mint	2	-	1	-	1	-	-	-
Lycopus europaeus L.	Gipsywort	5	-	-	-	2	-	-	1
Prunella vulgaris L.	Selfheal	4	-	-	14	-	-	1	7

Table 4.36   Waterlogged seeds (continued)

		No. of Seeds							
		Iron Age				Early Roman			
Period		Middle	Mid/Late	Late	Late				
		A	A/B	C	C	D	E	F	D/F
Context		803/D	473/A/4	706/A	2530/A	2287/B	101/D/4	324/B/2	2620/A/11
Ballota nigra L.	Black horehound	2	-	-	-	-	-	2	-
Glechoma hederacea L.	Ground-ivy	-	-	-	-	-	-	1	-
Plantago major L.	Great Plantain	1	2	19	2	1	2	6	-
Galium aparine L.	Goosegrass	-	-	1	-	-	-	-	-
Valerianella dentata (L.) Pol.	Cornsalad	-	-	-	-	1	-	-	-
Tripleurospermum inodorum (L.) Sch.	Scentless Mayweed	-	-	-	-	2	-	-	-
Leucanthemum vulgare Lam.	Ox-eye Daisy	-	-	-	-	-	-	-	1
Carduus sp.	Thistle	4	-	3	1	-	1	1	1
cf. *Cirsium* sp.	Thistle	-	-	4	1	2	-	1	-
Onopordum acanthium L.	Cotton Thistle	-	1	-	-	-	-	-	-
Centaurea cf. *nigra* L.	Knapweed	-	-	-	-	-	-	-	4
Leontodon sp.	Hawkbit	-	-	-	2	1	-	1	-
Picris hieracioides L.	Hawkweed Ox-tongue	-	-	1	-	-	-	-	-
Sonchus asper L.	Sow-thistle	-	-	4	1	-	-	14	-
Potamogeton sp.	Pondweed	-	-	-	-	-	-	-	11
Juncus effusus gp.	Tussock Rush	30	200	60	570	80	40	150	20
J. bufonius gp.	Toad rush	30	-	20	20	30	-	20	30
J. articulatus gp.	Rush	20	30	10	40	40	70	-	50
Juncus spp.	Rush	10	40	10	60	10	20	-	10
Eleocharis S. *Palustres* sp.	Spike-rush	-	1	-	4	4	-	-	-
Isolepis setacea (L.) R. Br.	Bristle-rush	-	-	-	-	-	1	-	-
Carex spp.	Sedge	14	4	2	10	5	3	5	6
Glyceria sp.	Reed-grass	-	-	-	-	-	-	88	-
Gramineae gen. et sp. indet.	Grass	1	-	12	1	3	-	7	-
Totals		212	339	209	814	251	165	546	160

4.37   Other waterlogged items

			Presence or Number of Items							
			Iron Age				Early Roman			
Period			Middle	Mid/Late	Late	Late				
			A	A/B	C	C	D	E	F	D/F
Context			803/D	473/A/4	706/A	2530/A	2287/B	101/D/4	324/B/2	620/A/11
Bryophyta	(Moss)	leaves	-	-	+	+	-	+	+	-
Chara sp.	(Stonewort)	oospore	-	-	-	-	-	-	-	1
Pteridium aquilinum (L.) Kuhn	(Bracken)	frond fragment	-	-	1	-	-	-	-	-
Rumex sp.	(Dock)	stem with peduncles	-	-	-	-	-	-	5	-
Salix sp.	(Willow)	bud	-	-	-	-	1	-	-	-
Trifolium sp.	(Clover)	calyx and flower	-	-	-	-	-	-	-	1
Triticum spelta L.	(Spelt Wheat)	glume	-	-	2	-	-	-	-	-
T. dicoccum Schübl. or *spelta* L.	(Wheat)	glume base	-	-	4	-	-	-	-	-

+ present

Table 4.38 Coleoptera

Period	Minimum No. of Individuals		
	Late Iron Age C	Late Iron Age to Early Roman	
Context	706/A	Remaining Samples	Species Group
Sample Weight (kg)	3.0	1.5	
Trechus obtusus Er. or quadristriatus (Schr.)	3	2	
Bembidion properans Step.	-	1	
Pterostichus cf. gracilis (Dej.)	1	-	
P. melanarius (Ill.)	1	1	
P. cupreus (L.) or versicolor (Sturm)	-	1	
Calathus fuscipes (Gz.)	2	1	
C. melanocephalus (L.)	2	1	
Agonum muelleri (Hbst.)	1	-	
Amara aulica (Pz.)	-	1	
Amara sp.	1	-	
Harpalus rufipes (Deg.)	1	1	6a
Harpalus S. Ophonus sp.	-	2	
H. affinis (Schr.)	1	-	
Hydroporus sp.	1	1	1
Agabus bipustulatus (L.)	1	-	1
Helophorus grandis Ill.	1	1	1
H. aquaticus (L.) or grandis Ill.	-	1	1
H. nubilus F.	-	1	
H. rufipes (Bosc.)	1	-	
Helophorus sp. (brevipalpis size)	5	2	1
Sphaeridium bipustulatum F.	1	-	
S. lunatum F. or scarabaeoides (L.)	1	-	
Cercyon haemorrhoidalis (F.)	1	-	7
C. melanocephalus (L.)	1	-	7
Cercyon sp.	-	1	7
Megasternum obscurum (Marsh.)	5	3	7
Anacaena bipustulata (Marsh.) or limbata (F.)	-	1	1
Laccobius sp.	-	1	1
Histerinae gen. et sp. indet.	1	-	
Ochthebius bicolon Germ.	1	-	1
O. minimus (F.)	1	-	1
Ochthebius spp.	-	3	1
Hydraena testacea Curt.	-	1	1
Hydraena sp. (not testacea)	-	1	1
Ptenidium sp.	1	-	
Silpha atrata L.	-	1	
Lesteva longoelytrata (Gz.)	3	-	
Omalium sp.	1	-	
Bledius cf. gallicus (Grav.)	1	-	
Platystethus cornutus gp.	1	1	
P. nitens (Sahl.)	-	2	
Anotylus nitidulus (Grav.)	1	-	
A. rugosus (F.)	1	-	7
A. sculpturatus (Grav.)	4	-	7

Table 4.38 Coleoptera (continued)

Period	Minimum No. of Individuals		
	Late Iron Age C	Late Iron Age to Early Roman	
Context	706/A	Remaining Samples	Species Group
Sample Weight (kg)	3.0	1.5	
Stenus spp.	2	1	
Lathrobium sp. (not longulum)	-	1	
Rugilus sp.	1	-	
Gyrohypnus angustatus Step.	-	1	
G. cf. angustatus Step.	1	-	
Xantholinus linearis (Ol.)	1	-	
Philonthus spp.	3	1	
Gabrius sp.	-	2	
Tachyporus sp.	-	1	
Aleocharinae gen. et sp. indet.	3	2	
Geotrupes sp.	1	1	2
Aphodius contaminatus (Hbst.)	7	-	2
A. foetidus (Hbst.)	2	3	2
A. granarius	7	3	2
A. rufipes (L.)	1	-	2
A. cf. Sphacelatus (Pz.)	2	2	2
Aphodius spp.	1	2	2
Oxyomus sylvestris (Scop.)	2	2	
Onthophagus sp. (not ovatus)	1	1	2
Phyllopertha horticola (L.)	1	-	11
Agrypnus murinus (L.)	1	1	11
Agriotes lineatus (L.)	1	1	11
A. obscurus (L.)	1	-	11
A. sputator (L.)	1	-	11
Agriotes sp.	-	1	11
Cantharis sp.	1	-	
Anobium punctatum (Deg.)	5	-	10
Brachypterus urticae (F.)	2	-	
Atomaria sp.	1	-	
Orthoperus sp.	1	2	
Propylea quattuordecimpunctata (L.)	1	-	
Lathridius minutus gp.	-	1	8
Enicmus transversus (Ol.)	-	1	8
Corticariinae gen. et sp. indet.	3	-	8
Gastrophysa polygoni (L.)	-	1	
G. viridula (Deg.)	1	1	
Phyllotreta vittula Redt.	1	-	
Longitarsus spp.	1	1	
Psylliodes sp.	1	1	
Apion aeneum (F.)	1	1	
A. urticarium (Hbst.)	1	1	
Apion sp. (not above)	2	-	3
Phyllobius cf. roboretanus Gred.	-	1	
Sitona hispidulus (F.)	2	-	3
Sitona sp.	-	2	3
Ceutorhynchus erysimi (F.)	1	-	
Total	112	71	

Table 4.39   *Other waterlogged insects*

Period	Late Iron Age C	Late Iron Age to Early Roman
Context	706/A	Remaining Samples
Sample Weight (kg)	3.0	1.5
Forficula auricularia L.	10	1
Heterogaster urticae (F.)	1	1
Aphrodes cf. *Fuscofasciatus* (Gz.)	1	-
Aphrodes sp.	1	1
Aphidoidea gen. et sp. indet.	2	-
Myrmica scabrinodis gp. worker	-	1
Lasius flavus gp. worker	1	-
L. niger gp. worker	2	-
Lasius sp.male	1	-
Hymenoptera gen. et sp. indet.	8	2
Chironomid larval head capsule	+	+
Bibionidae gen. et sp. indet.	1	-
Diptera adults (not Bibionidae)	6	-
Diptera puparia	2	1

+ present

of the flots from the nonwaterlogged ditches also included shells of some aquatic molluscs which probably lived in temporary bodies of water in these contexts (Table 4.40).

The majority of the waterlogged plant and insect remains had their origins in the terrestrial landscape beyond the features in which they were found, and they mostly seem to have entered them via natural agencies. The seeds and land snails are mostly likely to have had very local origins, whereas the insects would have been derived from a larger catchment. However, Sample 706/A, from a pit, contained significant quantities of imported plant material (Table 4.37). Some of the shells in Context 110, a Roman trackway ditch, might have been transported by flowing water (Table 4.40). The carbonised plant remains represented various categories of cultivated and collected material (Tables 4.34–5).

Middle Iron Age (Period A)

Environment and site activities

Only limited evidence was available for the middle Iron Age. A sample from 803/D, a ditch in Trench 8, contained seeds of *Ranunculus S. Batrachium* sp. (water crowfoot) likely to be from aquatic vegetation growing in the bottom of the ditch (Table 4.36). The majority of the seeds, however, were from terrestrial plants growing in or near the settlement. There was a strong element of seeds from plants of nutrient-rich waste or disturbed ground, such as *Urtica dioica* (stinging nettle), *Hyoscyamus niger* (henbane) and *Ballota nigra* (black horehound).

Table 4.40   *Mollusca*

Period	Late Iron Age C	?	E	Early Roman F	F	F	G
Context	2084/B	206/B/3	101/Q/3	324/B/2	108/C/3	111/E/1	110/H/8
Bithynia tentaculata (L.)	-	-	-	-	-	-	+
Aplexa hypnorum (L.)	-	-	-	9	-	-	+
Lymnaea truncatula (Müll.)	+	+	+	2	+	+	+
L. palustris (Müll.)	-	-	-	2	-	-	+
L. peregra (Müll.)	-	-	-	-	-	-	+
Planorbis planorbis (L.)	-	-	-	-	-	-	+
Anisus leucostoma (Müll.)	+	-	-	16	+	-	+
Bathyomphalus contortus (L.)	-	-	-	-	-	-	+
Gyraulus albus (Müll.)	-	-	-	-	-	-	+
Succinea or *Oxyloma* sp.	+	-	-	-	+	-	-
Cochlicopa sp.	-	-	-	-	+	-	-
Vertigo pygmaea (Drap.)	-	-	-	1	-	-	-
Pupilla muscorum (L.)	-	+	-	-	-	+	+
Vallonia costata (Müll.)	-	+	-	-	-	-	+
V. pulchella (Müll.)	-	+	-	1	-	-	-
V. excentrica Sterki	-	-	-	-	-	+	+
Vallonia sp.	-	+	-	-	-	+	+
Helicella itala (L.)	-	-	-	-	-	-	+
T. plebeia (Drap.) or *hispida* (L.)	-	-	-	-	+	-	+
Cepaea sp.	-	-	-	1	-	-	-
Pisidium sp.	-	-	-	3	-	-	-
Total				35			

+ present

Some of these plants are annuals, such as *Chenopodium polyspermum* (all-seed) and *Urtica urens* (small nettle), and they will also grow as weeds of cultivation. However, given the composition of the seeds assemblage, it is thought more likely that they were growing on dung-enriched, recently-disturbed ground in the settlement.

Seeds were also present of grassland plants including *Linum catharticum* (dwarf flax), *Potentilla* cf. *reptans* (creeping cinquefoil) and *Prunella vulgaris* (selfheal). In the absence of pollen or insect evidence, however, it is uncertain whether they reflected grassy areas within the settlement or the wider landscape. There was no indication from the waterlogged macroscopic plant remains for such scrub or woodland. Somewhat similar results were given by the waterlogged seeds from 473/A/4, a pit which belonged either to Period A or B (Table 4.36).

There was only a single sample for carbonised remains that could be attributed with certainty to the middle Iron Age (Table 4.35). Cereal remains were absent and the few weed seeds were not necessarily crop processing waste. Cereal remains were also absent from a second sample which belonged either to Period A or Period B.

Late Iron Age (Periods B and C)

Although no samples could be attributed with certainty to Period B, Period C was well-represented in samples for both waterlogged and carbonised remains. The occurrence of waterlogged insect remains enabled a wider picture to be obtained of the landscape, while there were sufficient charred remains to characterise the use of cereals.

Grassland and pasture

The most abundant group of Coleoptera from 706/A were scarabaeoid dung beetles (Species Group 2) which comprised 22% of the terrestrial Coleoptera (Fig. 4.27; Table 4.38). They feed on the dung of large herbivores under pastureland conditions. *Aphodius contaminatus* and *A. granarius* were both well represented. A similar percentage of dung beetles was recorded for the late Iron Age phase of Claydon Pike and *A. granarius* was again very numerous (Robinson forthcoming). Dung beetles were much more abundant than would be expected from ordinary pastureland, suggesting a particular concentration of domestic animals in the vicinity of the settlement.

Chafers and elaterids which feed on roots of grassland plants such as *Agriotes lineatus* (Species Group 11) formed 5% of the terrestrial Coleoptera confirming that there was extensive grassland in the vicinity of the site. Seeds of most species of grassland plants were not particularly abundant in the samples from 706/A and 2530/A (Table 4.36). This was probably a function of the fact that the catchment area from which the seeds derived was smaller than the catchment areas of the Coleoptera, and therefore mostly reflects disturbed ground around the settlement itself. This was in contrast to Claydon Pike, where the settlement area was much smaller, and a larger proportion of the waterlogged seeds were from the surrounding pastureland. However, the same grassland species were present including: *Ranunculus* cf. *repens* (creeping buttercup), *Potentilla anserina* (silverweed), *P.* cf. *reptans* (creeping cinquefoil) and *Prunella vulgaris* (selfheal).

There was also a wet pastureland element including *Carex* spp. (sedges) and *Juncus* spp. (rushes). Seeds of the tussock group of rushes, *Juncus effusus* group, were the most abundant seeds in most of the waterlogged samples (Table 4.36). Rush seeds are very small, prolifically produced and have good dispersive properties. It is probable that the heavily grazed pasture with ill-drained tussocky areas in the floodplain hollows extended on the river gravels from Claydon Pike at least as far as Thornhill Farm and possibly covered several square kilometres in the valley bottom.

Cereal remains were sparse in the samples processed for carbonised plant remains (Tables 4.34–5). Unusually for a site of this date, the great majority of the carbonised seeds were not of arable origin but appear to have been derived from coarse herbage. It seems unlikely that there were any arable plots breaking up this expanse of grassland.

Woodland and scrub

There were no wood or tree dependent beetles in the sample from 70–6/A (Table 4.38). Macroscopic remains of trees or shrubs were exceedingly sparse, with only a single seed of *Rubus fruticosus* agg. (blackberry) in the late Iron Age waterlogged samples (Table 4.36). Scrub seems to have been notably absent from the site, and there was certainly no evidence from which the presence of hedges around any of the enclosures could be inferred. Pollen analysis at Claydon Pike showed the presence of some trees, but macroscopic evidence of trees or shrubs was similarly sparse, and it was suggested that any areas of woodland were probably beyond the river gravels.

Disturbed ground and the environment of the settlement

The wet pasture around Claydon Pike seemed to have been churned in places into dung-enriched mud which supported annual weeds of the *Bidentetea Tripartitae* and the *Juncus bufonius* gp. rushes. There was much less evidence of such communities at Thornhill Farm. This was perhaps a reflection of somewhat better drainage on the gravels at Thornhill Farm, whereas Claydon Pike was surrounded on all sides by floodplain. The

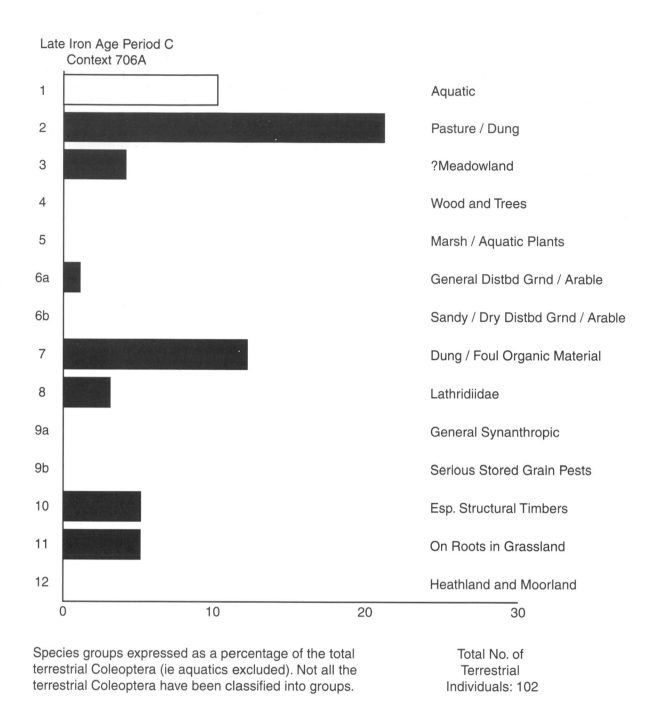

Late Iron Age Period C
Context 706A

1	Aquatic
2	Pasture / Dung
3	?Meadowland
4	Wood and Trees
5	Marsh / Aquatic Plants
6a	General Distbd Grnd / Arable
6b	Sandy / Dry Distbd Grnd / Arable
7	Dung / Foul Organic Material
8	Lathridiidae
9a	General Synanthropic
9b	Serious Stored Grain Pests
10	Esp. Structural Timbers
11	On Roots in Grassland
12	Heathland and Moorland

0   10   20   30

Species groups expressed as a percentage of the total
terrestrial Coleoptera (ie aquatics excluded). Not all the
terrestrial Coleoptera have been classified into groups.

Total No. of
Terrestrial
Individuals: 102

Fig. 4.27   Species Groups of Coleoptera from Thornhill Farm

molluscs from 206/B/3 included the dry-ground terrestrial species *Pupilla muscorum* and *Vallonia costata*, as well as aquatics (Table 4.40). The former species probably reflect conditions on the surface of the gravel terrace.

Various weed communities of somewhat drier habitats predominated throughout most of the settlement. Trampled areas were suggested by seeds of *Plantago major* (great plantain; Table 4.36). There were also seeds of annual plants of Chenopodietalia communities which grow on frequently disturbed, nitrogen-enriched soil around settlements. The most numerous weed seeds in the Iron Age samples were, however, from *Urtica dioica*, the perennial stinging nettle. They represented the next stage of vegetational succession on nutrient-rich neglected ground, and stinging nettle readily invades broken pasture in stock enclosures if grazing pressure is briefly relaxed. The nettle-feeding insects included the weevil *Apion urticarium* and the bug *Heterogaster urticae* (Table 4.38).

The occurrence of the snails *Lymnaea truncatula* and, in some instances *Anisus leucostoma*, in the late Iron Age enclosure ditches suggested that there were pools of stagnant water in the bottom of them (Table 4.40). Seeds of aquatic plants were, however, absent.

Accumulated organic material and structures

The percentage of various Sphaeridiinae and Oxytelinae in 706/A (Fig. 4.27, Species Group 7) which occur in other types of foul vegetable material as well as dung was, at 12% of the terrestrial Coleoptera, what would be expected at a pastoral settlement where there was much dung. Some plant material had been brought to the site and dumped in Pit 706, including *Pteridium aquilinum* (bracken) fronds and cereal debris (Tables 4.34 and 4.37). Members of the Lathridiidae (Species Group 8) which feed on moulds on accumulations of damp plant debris comprised 3% of the terrestrial Coleoptera.

Woodworm beetles (*Anobium punctatum*) were quite well represented for an Iron Age site, comprising 5% of the terrestrial Coleoptera (Fig. 4.27, Species Group 10), and it is likely that they had been derived from a timber structure in the vicinity of 706/A. (The pit itself did not contain any pieces of wood from which the beetles could have emerged.) Other possible indoor, synanthropic beetles were absent.

Site activities and the use of the site

The primary, possibly the sole, purpose of the late Iron Age settlement complex of Thornhill Farm and Claydon Pike appears to have been the management of grazing in the valley bottom. It was suggested in the original assessment of the bone evidence that there could have been an emphasis on the rearing of horses (Levitan 1990), and although the full analysis has since indicated otherwise (see above), the waterlogged plant and invertebrate evidence from the two sites is entirely consistent with this suggestion. Indeed, the selectivity shown by grazing horses tends to result in areas of their pasture becoming overgrazed and other areas very weedy. It has already been noted that the presence of the snail *Lymnaea truncatula*, the intermediate host of the sheep fluke, on the floodplain would have favoured cattle or horses as the main stock rather than sheep (Robinson 1992a). *L. truncatula* also occurred in some of the late Iron Age ditches at Thornhill Farm and Claydon Pike.

As at Claydon Pike, there was no evidence that the settlement at Thornhill Farm experienced flooding in the late Iron Age, and the settlement could have been permanently occupied. The flora of the site suggests that the enclosure ditches were not particularly long-lasting features, and it is uncertain how much of the complex was in use at any one time. It was not possible to determine from the plant and invertebrate remains any certain evidence for the centre of occupation, and it could have shifted with the frequent alterations to the layout of the site.

Carbonised cereal grains and chaff were present but sparse. There were also some waterlogged glumes of spelt wheat in Sample 706/A (Table 4.37). The only crop identified with certainty was *Triticum spelta* (spelt wheat). *Avena* sp. (oats) was also present, but it is uncertain whether it was a cultivated or a wild form (Tables 4.34–5). Spelt wheat along with barley seem to have been the major cereal crops grown in the region in the Iron Age. Only a few of the charred weed seeds, including *Sherardia arvensis* (field madder) and *Galium aparine* (goosegrass), were from species commonly associated with arable agriculture.

The concentration of cereal remains in the late Iron Age features at Thornhill Farm was very much lower than at Claydon Pike, with 0.24 items per litre at Thornhill Farm, compared with 0.82 items per litre at Claydon Pike (V. Straker pers. comm.). There were three times the number of weed seeds as cereal items at Thornhill Farm whereas cereal remains outnumbered weed seeds at Claydon Pike. The reasons for these differences are unclear, although there was probably some relationship between the concentration of cereal remains and the intensity of human occupation. It is thought unlikely that cereals were cultivated at the site. Cereals were probably imported in the ear as spikelets and dehusked prior to their use.

The majority of the charred seeds seem to have been derived from coarse herbage, particularly *Carex* spp. (sedge), unrelated to arable activity (Tables 4.34–5). A waterlogged frond fragment of *Pteridium aquilinum* (bracken) was found in Pit 706. Bracken was imported from the areas of acid soil on higher ground where it would have grown, by many Iron Age sites in the Upper Thames Valley, including Claydon Pike, perhaps for use as bedding. Coarse herbage or sedge hay seems also to have been cut perhaps for a similar purpose, or for use as fodder. As is usual for Iron Age sites in the region, there was evidence neither for the cultivation of horticultural crops nor the collection of wild food plants.

Early Roman (Periods D, E and F)

These early Roman periods were well-represented by samples. The results from samples from settlement features were very similar to those from the late Iron Age samples, so they will not be considered in so much detail. However, contrasting results were obtained from a trackway ditch belonging to Period D or F which was beyond the settlement area.

The environment of the early Roman settlement

Unfortunately the only insect evidence was from a combination of late Iron Age and early Roman samples (Table 4.38). However, they suggested an open landscape of pasture similar to that of the Iron Age. The waterlogged samples likewise contained seeds of the same grassland species (Table 4.36). Seeds from weeds likely to have been growing on nutrient-rich disturbed ground in the settlement were particularly abundant in the ditch 324/B/2. They ranged from *Urtica dioica* (stinging nettle) to *Chenopodium* cf. *rubrum* (red goosefoot), a plant of such habitats as dung-enriched mud. There were several seeds of *Anthriscus caucalis* (bur chervil), a plant which no longer occurs in the region but which is known from other Iron Age and early Roman settlements. This sample also contained water snails of stagnant water, such as *Aplexa hypnorum*, *Lymnaea truncatula* and *Anisus leucostoma*. Unlike the other early Roman ditches, seeds of *Ranunculus* S. *Batrachium* sp. (water crowfoot), *Nasturtium officinale* (water cress) and *Apium nodiflorum* (fool's water cress) suggested that this ditch supported dense aquatic vegetation.

The charred remains from the Period D and E samples were, as was the case with the late Iron Age samples, dominated by remains that were probably of cut coarse herbage rather than remains of cereal processing (Tables 4.34–5). They included seeds of *Rumex* sp. (dock), *Carex* spp. (sedge), a seed capsule of *Juncus effusus* gp. (tussock rush) and stem fragments of *Juncus inflexus* (hard rush). Cereal remains were not entirely absent, *Triticum spelta* (spelt wheat) and *Hordeum* sp. (barley) being identified. The samples from Period F did not contain the seeds from coarse herbage but charred cereal remains were no more abundant than in Periods D and E. *T. spelta* and *Hordeum* sp. were again present.

The results suggested that the primary purpose of the settlement at Thornhill Farm of raising domestic animals continued from the late Iron Age into the early Roman period. Many of the charred remains were perhaps from animal fodder or bedding. Cereals were probably just imported for consumption by the occupants of the settlement.

The environment around the early Roman trackway

The waterlogged seeds from Sample 2620/A/11, from an early Roman trackway ditch south of Trench 8, showed that there was a substantial difference in the flora of the site from that of the late Iron Age and early Roman settlement (Table 4.36). They included species which are characteristic of hay meadows: *Filipendula ulmaria* (meadowsweet), *Rhinanthus* sp. (yellow rattle), *Leucanthemum vulgare* (ox-eye daisy) and *Centaurea* cf. *nigra* (knapweed).

Seeds of the tussock rush (*Juncus effusus* gp.) were greatly reduced without any reduction in the *J. articulatus* group of rushes, which unlike the former, readily grow in wet hay meadows. The ditch belonged to Period D or F. It is possible that this hay meadow was contemporaneous with the early Roman settlement, but it is also possible that there was a general transition from pasture to hay meadow after the abandonment of the settlement.

There was strong evidence that the early Roman settlement at Claydon Pike was surrounded by hay meadows, and these results suggest that the meadowland could have extended as far as Thornhill Farm. This sample also contained a few seeds from annual weeds which perhaps grew along the edge of the ditch.

Middle Roman (Period G)

The evidence from Period G was limited to molluscs (Table 4.40) and charred plant remains from the ditches of the trackway system which replaced the settlement (Table 4.35).

The flots from Feature 110, the Roman roadside ditch which traversed Trench 7, contained rich aquatic mollusc faunas. Whereas the aquatic molluscs of the earlier ditches were all 'slum' species which can tolerate the extremes of stagnation and even temporary drying, the fauna of the Roman roadside ditch included species such as *Gyraulus albus* which require permanent water. There was even a specimen of the flowing water snail *Bithynia tentaculata*. It had perhaps been introduced by floodwater flushing the ditch or a stream diverted along it.

Charred remains were almost absent, with just an unidentifiable cereal grain and a seed of *Galium aparine* (goosegrass). They were perhaps residual from the earlier settlement.

Late Roman (Period H) and Medieval

No samples were available from late Roman (Period H) contexts. The occurrence of ridge and furrow showed that some medieval cultivation took place, but subsequent flooding deposited alluvium in the furrows. A sample of the alluvium was found to contain a molluscan assemblage characteristic of hay meadow (Robinson 1988). A similar fauna was recorded from alluvium overlying the Roman settlement at Claydon Pike, where there was other biological evidence for medieval meadowland. Such alluviation was extensive in the Upper Thames Valley during the early to mid medieval period (Robinson 1992b).

Conclusions

The results from both the late Iron Age and early Roman settlements emphasised their pastoral function. Such an interpretation would be consistent with the layout of the enclosure ditches. Cereals were certainly used but it is thought likely that they were imported rather than grown on the site. The charred plant assemblages were interesting because, unusually for settlements of these periods, they were dominated by remains of coarse herbage rather than cereals. The settlement at Thornhill Farm was likely to have been very similar to the nearby late Iron Age–earliest Roman settlement at Claydon Pike. During the early 2nd century AD, the Roman site at Claydon Pike was reorganised and the surrounding floodplain became hay meadow. It is possible that the hay meadow represented in Sample 2620/A/11, from an early Roman trackway ditch at Thornhill Farm, was a continuation of this meadowland. However, it is also possible that the Period G reorganisation at Thornhill Farm, when the settlement went out of use, was related to the early Roman landscape changes at Claydon Pike. This probably post-dated sample 2620/A/11. The limited details of the subsequent environmental history of Thornhill Farm were consistent with the sequence known from elsewhere in the Upper Thames Valley.

Chapter 5   Discussion and Synthesis

by Alex Smith and Jeff Muir

INTRODUCTION

Thornhill Farm is one of a number of settlements excavated along the gravel terraces of the Upper Thames Valley that have in the past 25 years transformed our understanding of the region in the Iron Age and Romano-British period (Figs 5.1–2). Throughout these periods the area remained intensely settled, as cropmarks on aerial photographs show (Benson and Miles 1974; Leech 1977), although the nature and form of settlements often underwent significant alteration. Of particular importance is the evidence for widespread periodic settlement shift and discontinuity, representing major landscape reorganisation seemingly tied in with changes in site economy. Within Romano-British studies in particular, close analysis of such rural communities has often been neglected in favour of urban and military aspects, and yet it has recently been re-emphasised (Taylor 2001, 46) that the study of rural society and social practice is of vital importance in understanding the history of the province.

INTERPRETATION AS A PASTORAL SETTLEMENT

Extensive excavations between 1979 and 1989 of a cropmark complex near the confluence of the rivers Thames and Coln in Gloucestershire revealed two main areas of occupation, at Claydon Pike to the east and Thornhill Farm to the west. At both sites evidence suggested the practice of specialised pastoral activity, at least within middle to late Iron Age and early Roman contexts. This hypothesis was based upon the following:

The physical organisation of the site. Thornhill Farm in particular was characterised by the intensive redefinition of a series of enclosures, most of which appeared to be nondomestic in function and which were interpreted as paddocks and seasonal pens used in stock management (see Chapter 3 and 'Analysis of site organisation' below).

The plant and invertebrate evidence. Environmental sampling was a crucial part of the archaeological investigation, and it revealed a later prehistoric landscape characterised by grassland and plants supportive of a pastoral interpretation with regard to land usage (see Robinson, Chapter 4).

The faunal evidence. Despite the highly fragmented and very degraded nature of the animal bone assemblage, it appeared at the assessment stage that horse remains were over-represented at

Thornhill Farm, and could therefore be indicative of specialised horse ranching at the site (Levitan 1990). Subsequent full analysis of the faunal assemblage has rendered the specialist horse rearing interpretation more or less obsolete (see Levine, Chapter 4), although pastoralism is still advanced as the primary economic basis of the site, with an emphasis instead upon cattle ranching. Taken together with the other aspects highlighted above, it does therefore seem to be the case that Thornhill Farm – probably along with the later prehistoric phase of Claydon Pike – is likely to have been a specialist stock raising centre, albeit operating largely within a subsistence economy (see below, 'Site economy'). All subsequent analysis and interpretation is based upon this premise.

ANALYSIS OF SITE ORGANISATION

Eight separate structural phases have been identified at Thornhill Farm (see Chapter 2 for summary), ranging from the middle Iron Age (*c* 300–50 BC) to the later Roman period (3rd–4th century AD). Within this broad chronological development, there are three major transformations in settlement character, representing changes in socio-economic strategy tied in with wider developments in the landscape, and particularly with developments at the settlement at Claydon Pike less than 1 km away. To be able to understand in depth the nature of these changes, it would be necessary to look at the social and symbolic aspects of settlement structure and development, which involves detailed spatial analysis of site organisation. Unfortunately, any attempt at such analysis for Thornhill Farm is extremely problematical because, in many cases, the separate structural elements (enclosures, pits, structures etc) have by necessity been assigned to various phases on the bare minimum of evidence, and therefore may not be truly representative of the original spatial layout. Additionally, the positioning of the open area trenches inevitably distorts the true picture. Therefore, although general patterns of settlement shift and organisation can be discerned, more detailed analysis is not possible. This is made all the more difficult by the relative lack of stratified and phased diagnostic artefacts and ecofacts, which ensures that functional interpretation of features is often largely based upon their morphology (see below). The difficulties of interpreting site organisation within settlements of the Upper Thames Valley have been previously highlighted (Hingley and Miles 1984, 59), and open settlements, often with differential levels of stratigraphic integrity such as Claydon Pike and Thornhill Farm, are particularly problematic in this respect.

ANALYSIS OF STRUCTURAL COMPONENTS

Just as there are problems with analysis of site organisation at Thornhill Farm, there are also inherent difficulties with structural analysis of the main component features.

Domestic structures

In total there are 13 features that have been interpreted as possibly representing roundhouses within the Thornhill Farm site, although in most cases the evidence is far from certain (Table 5.1). Virtually all of these are tentatively assigned to Iron Age phases, with the exception of three possible roundhouses that seem to come from a later date (Periods E and F). Different construction methods may well have been used, although there are difficulties in that there is a lack of knowledge of the degree of truncation of the Iron Age ground surface, which could result in postholes and/or gullies remaining in some areas but not others. Nevertheless, it would seem that a number of the middle Iron Age roundhouses (eg S206 and S207; Fig. 3.1) are quite similar in form to other such buildings within the region, in that they are defined by a penannular drip gully, about 13 m in diameter, with an entrance facing east (Allen *et al.* 1984, 91–93). Perhaps the best examples of roundhouses are S200 and S210, which seem to derive from the later Iron Age (see below, 'Site reconstruction'), although they were probably not contemporary (see Chapter 3). Despite being positioned just 1 m from each other, they appear to be of different construction methods, with S200

being defined solely by a ring of postholes, possibly with a porched entrance, and S201 consisting of a penannular gully with an incoherent arrangement of postholes within. S 200 belongs to a class of post-ring houses, and a similar 'porched' example can be found at nearby Claydon Pike (structure XVIII; Allen *et al.* 1984, 91). It is thought that the posts probably represent the inner support ring, with the outline of the walls projecting from the outer 'porch' posts, thus significantly increasing the inner surface area of the building.

Nearly all of the remaining postulated roundhouses have been identified by curvilinear gullies, with their interpretation sometimes strengthened by the presence of domestic material (eg E130; Fig. 3.1). The lack of any coherent internal features within some of these enclosures (eg E11; Fig. 3.19) could suggest that a mass wall technique such as turf was being used, which would not necessarily leave any trace. Such techniques are thought to have become quite widespread in other rural settlement sites in the region during the late Iron Age and Roman periods (Henig and Booth 2000, 95).

Detailed internal spatial analysis of Iron Age domestic roundhouses has been conducted at a number of sites in southern Britain, and this type of approach can provide valuable information on indigenous social practices (Hughes 1995, Oswald 1997). In particular, Hingley (1990, 131) has suggested that there was a conceptual division between a 'public' central space containing the hearth and a 'private' peripheral zone for sleeping, storage and other domestic activities. What studies such as this emphasise is that it is by examining the changing patterns of functional areas – and not just building types – that we may start to understand developments in social organisation. One of the primary ways in which this type of study works is

Table 5.1 Potential domestic structures at Thornhill Farm

Feature no.	Period	Diameter	Entrance orientation	Structural details
S 206	A	*c* 13 m	E	Ring gully
S 207	A	*c* 13 m	E	Part of probable penannular drip(?) gully
S 209	A	*c* 9.6 m	SE	Two gully arcs possibly representing roundhouse. Pits with 'domestic' debris within
E 130	A	*c* 14 m	?	Possible gully around a structure
882	B	?	?	Curvilinear gully with domestic debris in terminals
S 200	C	8.2 m or 11.4 m*	SE	Postring demarcation with porch
S 201	C	*c* 9 m	SE	Recut penannular gully with incoherent arrangement of postholes in interior
(E74)	C	*c* 8 m	?	Ring gully detected as crop mark - roundhouse?
(E 52)	C	8.5 - 10 m	SE?	Cluster of postholes inside rectilinear enclosure. Three possible rings may represent roundhouses
117 & 228	C	*c* 13 m	?	Two curvilinear gullies possibly part of a roundhouse
100 & 104	E	?	?	Two gullies which may have defined site of roundhouse
E 11	F	7 m	W	Penannular gully
E 7	F	6-7 m	?	Annular ditch

* Diameter depends upon whether wall is on circumference of post ring or putative porch.

if we have enough spatial information – specifically from diagnostic finds ('tool kits') – to be able to determine functional areas. Unfortunately at Thornhill Farm we do not have sufficient data to be able to attempt such analysis, as not only did most of the fills from features comprise a mixture of redeposited material, but also many of the structures were obscured by later activity.

Enclosures

Thornhill Farm consisted for the most part of a series of enclosures of varying size and shape. It was felt that enclosure function was likely to prove key in understanding the economic basis of the site, in particular, providing an opportunity for the reconstruction of the stock management system. To this end, attempts were made to classify the enclosures on the basis of morphology and artefact distribution, although results proved to be disappointing, primarily because of the lack of associated functional 'tool kits' as mentioned above. With the scarcity of such diagnostic material, any classification would have to be based upon morphology alone, and although structural comparison with other sites in the Upper Thames Valley (eg Claydon Pike and Farmoor) may provide some indication of function, there are risks with such a strategy (Hingley 1984, 72). It is clear that an integrated contextual approach is needed, concentrating on how and why features were built and used, rather than just abstract structural classification.

Overall, despite the obvious areas of limitation within the data, a general reconstruction of the Thornhill Farm site and economy is possible, and does provide valuable information on socio-economic practice. This is especially important when the site is viewed in a wider perspective, as a component within the Iron Age and Romano–British landscape.

SITE RECONSTRUCTION

Throughout much of its existence, Thornhill Farm would have been characterised by open grassland, punctuated by systems of broad ditched enclosures, smaller enclosures (perhaps for specialist pastoral purposes such as winter corralling, birthing etc), and a number of structural elements, some of which were undoubtedly domestic dwellings (see above). The problems of interpreting settlement organisation have been highlighted above, but it does appear that there were a number of major structural phases reflecting changing socio-economic regimes.

Middle Iron Age (Period A; Fig. 3.1)

The earliest settlement identified at Thornhill Farm belongs to the middle Iron Age, a time of increased diversification and specialisation in the Upper Thames Valley and elsewhere (Allen 2000, 10). This was a period when the first gravel terraces of the Thames floodplain were being colonised by a number of open and enclosed settlements such as Claydon Pike, Glos. (Miles and Palmer 1984) and Mingies Ditch, Oxon. (Allen and Robinson 1993).

At Thornhill Farm, up to three foci of domestic activity were located, although not all may belong to this period, and even if this were the case, they need not all be contemporary, as the location of the settlement may well have shifted. Each of the foci was characterised by at least one probable roundhouse gully – and possibly three in the case of the western salvage area – along with a substantial oval shaped ditched enclosure. In only two cases (S210 and S206) were the definite entrance terminals of the roundhouse gullies found, and in both instances they faced to the east, with that of S206 aligned towards the opening of the large oval enclosure (E149). The function of these large enclosures is unclear, as in no case was there any demonstrable evidence of contemporary internal structures. A possibly comparable enclosure at Claydon Pike (Allen *et al.* 1984, 97, fig. 3.6.1) contained a roundhouse gully, along with large quantities of domestic material, while at least one other at Farmoor, Oxon., seems more likely to have functioned as either an occasional animal pen or for the storage of materials (Area III, enclosure 3; Lambrick and Robinson 1979, 25–26, 70–72). On balance, the latter interpretation seems more likely at Thornhill Farm, at least for enclosure 120, and it could well be that such a combination of one or more roundhouses and a substantial ditched stock enclosure was the basis for a functionally cohesive and largely independent settlement unit. If this was the case, then there may have been three such units surrounding a central open space (Fig. 3.1). Such an arrangement of grouped settlement units is readily paralleled by the Iron Age settlement at Gravelly Guy, Stanton Harcourt (Oxon.), where it was suggested that there were internal divisions between different households within the settlement (Lambrick and Allen, forthcoming).

The only features from the central area at Thornhill Farm were a substantial pit grouping from the Northern Salvage Area and a single pit (3247) containing an almost complete inverted pot in Trench 22. Whilst the single pot deposit may represent a ritual act (although not necessarily contemporary with the period A settlement; see Timby, Chapter 4), it is difficult to interpret the features in this area as representing communal activities. Indeed there may only ever have been a single settlement unit of a family group shifting location over a century or more of occupation, as has been suggested for the middle Iron Age phase at Claydon Pike (Miles *et al.* forthcoming).

Finally, although it does appear to have been an open settlement, it is possible that the substantial ditches from Trench 8 and the western salvage area formed part of an outer boundary, perhaps related to the pastoral function of the site.

Late Iron Age–early Roman (Periods B to F;
Figs 3.5, 3.10, 3.15, 3.18)

The apparent lack of recognisable structural features dating to the latter half of the 1st century BC (Period B) may indicate either a significant lessening of activity, or else continued use of earlier pottery styles at the site. Whatever the case, by the early 1st century AD, there was a radical reorganisation of the settlement, with activity occurring on a much larger scale (Fig. 3.5). The major focus of the site transferred to the east, where a series of subrectilinear enclosures were built alongside domestic roundhouses (Table 5.1). Domestic structures of any type are quite rare in the Upper Thames Valley in the later Iron Age and early Roman period (Allen *et al.* 1984, 100), and therefore their presence here is of particular significance. The clearest examples are probably from Period C (*c* AD 0–50), in particular the post-ring structure 200 and penannular gully S201, although the dating evidence is equivocal (see above, Chapter 3). It is likely that most later buildings were of mass-walled construction which would leave little trace. Both S200 and S201 had entrances facing south-east, with that of S200 being aligned toward the entrance of a large ovoid enclosure (E80) in the same manner as S206 from Period A, suggesting possible continuity in some elements of site structure. The gully of S201 was clearly later than E80, and therefore possibly S200 as well, and its multiple recuts suggest a much longer life span for this structure. Another possible roundhouse from this phase was represented by the posthole cluster within E52, although there is no way of telling if it was contemporary with any of the others, and therefore the total population of the site remains obscure.

The remainder of the eastern side of the site consisted for the most part of subrectangular enclosures, most of which are very difficult to interpret and phase convincingly because of their intensively recut nature and the limited number of sections and recovered finds. These finds did include a small quantity of iron slag and copper alloy waste from enclosure 87 in trench 9, which suggests that at some point, limited metalworking was taking place in this area. There are notable differences between these eastern enclosures and the 'co-axial' enclosure system to the south, although they do both appear to be broadly contemporary. The southern enclosure system was far more clearly organised and coherently aligned, although it does appear to have developed via organic growth rather than as a singular deliberate planning exercise. The function of the co-axial enclosures is hinted at by the possible mini droveways going into E13, E4 and E23, which suggest the corralling and nurturing of livestock. Thus, the number of enclosures needed would have fluctuated with the size of the herd. They were positioned within what appears to have been a network of large outer boundary ditches that physically differentiated the area from that further east, suggesting functional divergence.

In the latter half of the 1st century AD (Period D; *c* AD 50–100; Fig. 3.10), the focus of settlement remained in the east, although the system of enclosures was far more closely knit, and seemingly centred around E58. It is certain that not all were contemporary, although E48, E49 and E58 are thought to have been part of a single working complex. It is likely that many of the enclosures were used as temporary animal pens, possibly during pregnancy or for the nurturing of animals, and the presence of small (*c* 3 m diameter) circular enclosures or stack rings, which could be interpreted as probable fodder stands, strengthens this hypothesis. Similar stack rings have been found in the late Iron Age/early Roman phases at Claydon Pike and Somerford Keynes Neigh Bridge (Miles *et al.* forthcoming) which are also thought to have been involved in pastoral activity. Enclosures E44 and E45 were of a different character to the others, and the small entrance and lack of guide channels in E45 means it is unlikely to have been used for animals. It may well have contained a turf mass-walled structure, as no definite domestic dwellings are known from this period, although no actual traces remain.

One of the more significant features of this period, in terms of understanding site organisation and functionality, is a funnel shaped track or droveway defined by ditches (5006–5008; Fig. 3.10), orientated NE–SW and leading into a central grassland area largely devoid of features. Structural and functional coherence between the droveway and the stock pen/settlement area is provided by two spur ditches orientated towards the latter site. This system was clearly intended to control the movement of livestock within the site. Further to the west, part of the earlier boundary ditch appears to have been recut on a number of occasions, and may well have formed a large enclosure, although sections of double ditching suggest a possible trackway in this area.

In the later 1st–early 2nd century AD (Periods E and F; Figs. 3.15, 3.18) there was the most intensive phase of occupation, according to the quantities of pottery recovered (see Timby, Chapter 4). During Period E, there were two distinct zones of enclosures to the north and south, although this may be more of a reflection of the positioning of the open area trenches than the original spatial pattern. However, it does appear to be the case that the Southern Area (Trench 7) became a renewed focus for activity, with a number of loosely co-axial rectilinear enclosures forming a coherent group, again probably associated with stock-rearing. With this functional hypothesis in mind, it is suggested that the two postholes in the centre of E15 may have represented a fodder rack. The Northern area was dominated by a substantial double-celled enclosure, E62/E75, similar to earlier such features belonging to Period D. This may represent some degree of functional homogeneity between enclosure types, although there is nothing beyond pure morphological similarities to suggest this. E62 contained an irregular group of postholes, which may have formed a possible domestic structure, along with a stack ring or fodder stand, suggesting the enclosure of animals.

The final shift of settlement/stock enclosure organisation (Period F; Fig. 3.18) saw activity concentrate almost entirely in the Southern Area around Trench 7. A possible roundhouse gully (E11) facing west lay in the north-east corner of the trench, and one of the few enclosure groups to have any degree of specific functional interpretation lay in the central area. E30 was screened along its western side, suggesting the segregation of livestock, as would be appropriate during pregnancy and birthing, or possibly to prevent mature calves from reaching their mothers' milk (Lucas 1989). The linear boundaries to the south of the enclosures were probably still in use, although there is a high degree of uncertainty in their phasing, as many were only visible as cropmarks or were subject to very limited excavation.

2nd century–later Roman period (Periods G to H; Figs 3.21, 3.23)

From the early–mid 2nd century AD onwards came the most radical changes in landscape organisation and character at Thornhill Farm. There appears to have been no domestic focus, and the enclosure systems of earlier periods went out of use, representing a complete, large-scale change in land use. The site became characterised by substantial linear trackways that almost certainly linked different settlements in an archaeologically visible way (Fig. 3.21). Trackway 301 entered from the north-east, along a very similar orientation to that of the earlier Period D droveway, and thus providing the only indication of any continuity with the previous settlement. It was traced for almost 600 m across the low gravel terrace and floodplain, and probably linked up with trackway 5036, revealed mostly by cropmarks. This track probably linked the locally important and possibly official site at Claydon Pike, with a small 2nd century AD settlement known at Kempsford Bowmoor (OAU 1989) to the south-west (Fig. 1.2).

It seems that the reorganisation of the landscape involved the creation and/or redevelopment of a certain number of sites (eg Claydon Pike and Kempsford Bowmoor), and the virtual abandonment of others such as Thornhill Farm. There were a few features from the latter site (other than the main trackways) which may indicate some level of activity, although the pottery evidence suggests that this was slight (see Timby, Chapter 4). In particular, there was a ditched trackway in the Northern Salvage Area leading off from trackway 301 into a possible enclosure, while another ditch to the north ran along the same orientation (Fig. 3.21). Some continuing animal traffic is also suggested by the fill of animal trample from the Period F enclosure E30

in Trench 7, although this may have preceded the construction of the main trackways. The evidence overall suggests that the site became part of an outlying field system of an agricultural estate based on the gravel terrace and floodplain, perhaps centred around the complex at Claydon Pike. Communication and transport were clearly important considerations within this landscape, undoubtedly reflecting close connections with supply and trade in the wider region (see below 'The site in its local and regional setting').

In the later Roman period (Period H; Fig. 3.23) the trackways appear to have gone out of use, and the site was characterised by a small number of major linear ditched boundaries. The minimal quantity of pottery from this period suggests a very low level of activity, far from the main domestic centre, which may well have been the small 4th century villa at Claydon Pike.

SITE ECONOMY

The environmental evidence was regarded from the start as a crucial element in understanding the socio-economic nature of the Thornhill Farm site, and as such, significant resources were expended in collecting and analysing the data. Yet the problems that affected other aspects of the site – most notably those concerning the stratigraphic integrity – also had a major impact in the analysis of the floral and faunal remains (see above, Chapter 4). Specifically, it is difficult to reconstruct the chronological development of the agrarian regime in detail, although broad changes can be discerned, which seem to tie in not only with the major intrasite settlement reorganisations, but also with wider developments within the landscape.

During the middle Iron Age the extensive area of uninterrupted gravel terrace at Thornhill Farm became the site of a settlement which appeared to operate a specialised pastoral regime. Whilst the known proportions of animal species present at the site is somewhat arbitrary, it does seem that cattle were most numerous, followed some way behind by sheep and horse. The possible significance of cattle ranching at this time is explored below, although it must be noted that the species proportions given are not chronologically specific, and so the pattern of species representation through time is unknown. More precise indications of the middle Iron Age environment come from the waterlogged macroscopic plant remains, which suggest grassland and dung-enriched disturbed soil, thereby supporting the overall pastoral interpretation.

The increased quantity of environmental samples from the later Iron Age (Period C) provides a clearer indication that the management of grazing on the valley bottom was the primary economic function of the site at this time. This was a period when the physical organisation of the settlement also suggested a marked degree of pastoral intensification (see above). Furthermore, the differential condition of the pastureland may suggest an emphasis on horse rearing, although the general animal bone data in no way corroborates this. It is more likely that cattle were the predominant species nurtured at the site, with possibly a very limited emphasis on horse breeding, perhaps to maintain the population of work animals. It is likely that most horses would have been used as riding, traction or pack animals, although secondary use for bone, hides and possibly meat is indicated on a small scale. Despite the apparent unsuitability of the land for sheep grazing, this species is also well represented (probably more so than is apparent), which reflects the economic importance of this animal.

The overall evidence, at least from the cattle bones, suggests that these animals were reared, butchered and consumed on site, and thus points to a subsistence rather than a commercial economy, although it must still be remembered that the faunal data is not chronologically differentiated. The inhabitants as a whole would have produced food for their own consumption and work animals for their own purposes. Nevertheless, the apparent specialised pastoral nature of the site and lack of evidence for cereal cultivation suggests that some kind of exchange links must have been established with other settlements. It is possible that crops were grown on higher terraces by the Thornhill Farm inhabitants themselves, but on balance, given that the domestic focus lay on the lower gravel terrace, this was probably not the case. Crops such as spelt wheat may have been imported and then processed on site, as indicated by the quernstones, although the quantity of cereal remains was much less than at neighbouring Claydon Pike, suggesting a marked difference in the concentration of domestic habitation. If goods such as cereal crops were being brought into the site, even on a very small scale, then it must undoubtedly have been surplus animals or animal products such as meat or dairy produce that were being exchanged in turn, although in what quantity and how far is uncertain.

The environmental evidence indicates no significant alterations to the patterns of land use after the Roman conquest, with animal husbandry continuing as before, and plant/cereal remains being imported in limited quantities for animal fodder, bedding and consumption by the occupants of the settlement. At the start of the 2nd century AD there are more important indications of a change in site economy, although the evidence is limited to a small number of waterlogged seeds from the trackway ditch to the south of the main settlement. These indicate the presence of hay meadows, which establishes a link with the changing patterns of land use at Claydon Pike where hay meadows also appear at approximately this period (Robinson forthcoming). The changes at Claydon Pike correlate with significant reorganisation in settlement character and the land use developments at Thornhill Farm may be intimately related to this (see below). Although the

seed evidence from Thornhill Farm seems to have come from the final phase of the settlement (Period F), it is quite possible that there was a gradual change from pasture to hay meadow, which was ultimately related to the abandonment of the settlement and the introduction of new trackways. Unfortunately, the chronology of site development is not accurate enough to be sure of any exact correlation.

There is very little evidence to indicate how the land was being used in the later Roman period. It is assumed that the linear boundaries were part of an outlying field system, possibly connected with the modest villa at Claydon Pike, but no suitable samples were recovered from late Roman (Period H) contexts, and so the nature of any agricultural activity remains uncertain.

SOCIAL STATUS AND DIETARY HABITS

Determining the relative social status of archaeological sites is fraught with difficulties, as the measurable indicators such as imported pottery can be quite subjective (eg Brown 1997, 100). The meaning and social value attributed to such objects is likely to have been quite context specific (Faulkner 2000), and we are sometimes guilty of imposing universal interpretative parameters onto specific classes of archaeological finds. Nevertheless, when viewed in their local context, there are aspects of the material culture which may shed light on apparent social and cultural differentiation. Meadows (2001) has examined the social contexts of a number of sites in the Upper Thames Valley – including Claydon Pike – in terms of the consumption of food and drink, and it is useful to briefly compare some of the findings with Thornhill Farm. The late Iron Age–Roman transition phase of Claydon Pike contained relatively large quantities of Roman-style imported goods, including much ceramic material associated with food preparation, storage and to a lesser extent consumption.

At Thornhill Farm the pattern of food preparation and consumption was quite different, with very small amounts of imported Roman-style wares, and an absence of comparable table forms in local coarsewares. Henig and Booth (2000, 173–4, fig. 6.11) have presented the proportion of fine and specialist wares from a selection of 1st and 2nd century AD sites in Oxfordshire and the Upper Thames Valley, and Thornhill Farm contained some of the lowest quantities of such material. Therefore, although the inhabitants of Thornhill Farm did seem to have local and regional trading links, they appear to have either not been able, or to have had no desire, to use new vessels or products such as oil and wine reflective of Roman cooking, eating and drinking habits. The paucity of imported Roman-style goods and lack of wares associated with serving is even more pronounced at Old Shifford Farm (Hey 1996), where it was suggested that the inhabitants were more concerned with the preparation of food to be consumed communally than with the serving of individuals (Meadows 2001, 247). However, in contrast to Old Shifford Farm, an emphasis on individual status is suggested at Thornhill Farm by the quantity of brooches found there, which were the largest single category of small find. Jundi and Hill (1998, 126) have argued that in addition to being tied in with new ways of appearing, such personal items may well be associated with periods of social anxiety, perhaps in this case connected to the eventual abandonment of the settlement in the early 2nd century AD. Such a suggestion may be strengthened by the fact that the highest concentration of brooches did occur in the area of latest settlement activity (Trench 7), dating to the later 1st and early 2nd centuries AD (see Chapter 4).

THE SITE IN ITS LOCAL AND REGIONAL SETTING

Despite the fact that stratigraphic difficulties at Thornhill Farm precluded detailed spatial analysis, the general development, functions and environment of the site are known in some detail (see above). An aspect of particular interest is Thornhill Farm's relationship with other sites in the Upper Thames Valley and southern Cotswolds, specifically Claydon Pike less than 1 km to the east. A wider comparative analysis of the site provides much greater scope for an understanding of its character and place in the local and regional landscape.

Middle Iron Age (*c* 3rd–1st century BC; Fig. 5.1)

It is generally accepted that the population of Britain was rising in the later prehistoric period, and in areas such as the Upper Thames Valley aerial photography has shown settlement density to be high. The wider economy of this and surrounding regions was based upon a broad system of mixed agriculture, which was well suited to exploit the considerable ecological diversity of the landscape.

On the limestone uplands of the Cotswolds faunal remains recovered from a range of Iron Age sites suggest that animal husbandry was carried out on a considerable scale (Darvill 1987, 145–146). Sheep are well represented in the faunal assemblages and were the predominant animal kept on many upland sites. Susceptibility to liver-fluke and foot-rot meant that the animals were less suited to the wetter, lower-lying ground of the river valleys, though they were certainly present in some numbers on the lower gravel terraces, including Thornhill Farm. Although important in the Cotswolds, animal husbandry was not the exclusive mode of production. Hingley and Miles have noted that the many Banjo enclosures which appeared in the region during the middle Iron Age were ideally located to support a mixed economy with easy access to both upland pastures and well-watered valleys (Hingley and Miles 1984, 57). This sugges-

tion is supported by evidence from Wessex, where the excavation of Banjo enclosures at Bramdean (Perry 1986) and Micheldever Wood (Fasham 1987) have revealed grain storage pits and other signs of a mixed economy. The considerable capacity for grain storage demonstrated at sites such as Guiting Power (Saville 1979) confirms that cereal production was practised on the Cotswolds and that it was relatively successful.

Evidence of arable expansion into the gravel terraces of the Upper Thames Valley can be found at sites such as Ashville, Oxon., where cultivation of heavier, wetter soils strongly suggests that increasingly unsuitable land was put under the plough (Jones 1978, 93–110). Inevitably, continued expansion of the arable base could not be sustained indefinitely without fundamental changes to land use. Lambrick has outlined a model, based on the Upper Thames Valley, which views a gradually expanding arable base as a prime source of pressure on traditional pasture (Lambrick 1992). This led to pastoral intensification in the form of enclosed paddocks and artificial water holes, while on the lowest gravel terraces and the floodplain itself, specialist pastoral farms appeared, such as Mingies Ditch, Claydon Pike and Port Meadow, although the latter site appears to have been occupied on a seasonal basis (see below). The initial construction of the Thornhill Farm site would have been part of this intensification.

The socio-economic character of such settlements and the relationships between them and those of the Cotswolds have been the focus of much discussion over the past twenty years (eg Hingley 1984, 1989; Allen and Robinson 1993, 149; Allen 2000, 13; Meadows 2001). Hingley's (1984) social distinction between the communal 'open' settlements of the river valley and independent enclosed settlements of the higher ground has proved in recent years to be blurred (Allen 2000, 14). In particular, the enclosed specialist pastoral sites on the First Gravel Terrace at Mingies Ditch and Watkins Farm are thought more likely to have been established by individual family groups as more or less self-contained units (Allen and Robinson 1993, 149). Quite significantly, an unusually high percentage of horse bones was recovered from both sites, some of which came from immature animals, leading to the suggestion that at least one aspect of their economy was based upon horse rearing, perhaps for the supply of other sites (Wilson and Allison 1990, 61; Wilson 1993, 133).

The specialist nature of these sites implies that they would have been part of a wider agricultural network, and the presence of processed cereal grains suggests relationships with arable sites on the higher and better drained terraces (Allen 1990, 79). A more community-based farming system is better demonstrated by the transhumant pastoral settlement at Farmoor (Lambrick and Robinson 1979) and probably Port Meadow (Atkinson 1942). Such temporary encampments, probably occupied

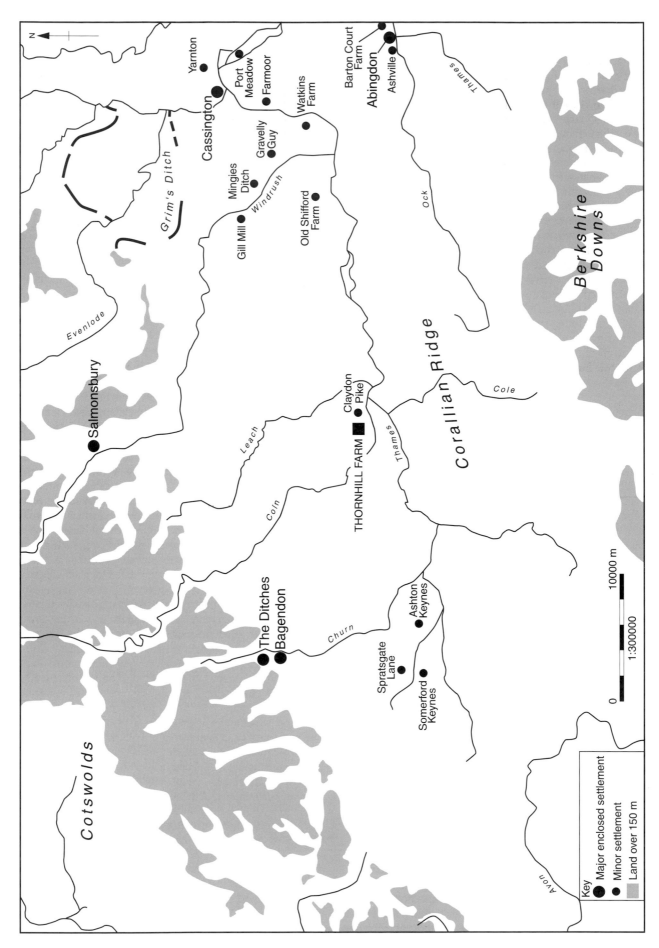

Fig. 5.1   *Thornhill Farm in relation to principal middle-late Iron Age settlements and other sites mentioned in the text*

on a seasonal basis in between episodes of flooding, imply a wider communal aspect to landscape organisation.

At Claydon Pike settlement commenced during the middle Iron Age on gravel islands that provided protection from flooding. Indications are that it operated a pastoral economy, with evidence for roundhouses and associated enclosures that began on the westernmost island and shifted to the east over a period of a century or so (Hingley and Miles 1984, 63). In many ways the site is similar to that at Thornhill Farm, and it is possible that at this stage there was some element of communality between them. Both would have relied upon other sites operating a mixed economy – probably located further to the north on higher, better drained land – to supply them with cereal crop produce. Additionally, both sites contained small quantities of Malvernian pottery and Droitwich Briquetage implying longer distance trade to the north, although the quantities of the latter are minimal at Thornhill Farm.

Late Iron Age (c 1st century BC–mid 1st century AD; Fig. 5.1)

Study of the changing hydrology and sedimentation of the Upper Thames Valley has revealed a marked increase in floodplain alluviation during the late Iron Age and early Roman period (Lambrick 1992). This has been interpreted as evidence of clearance and increased cultivation in the catchment area (Lambrick and Robinson 1979). One of the most logical places to expand cultivation would have been onto the slopes and uplands of the Cotswolds where the soils were relatively dry and light. The net effect would have been increased alluviation in the valley bottom, but more importantly, a considerable increase in pressure on traditional sheep pasture. The demand for more traction animals would have encouraged more intensive methods of cattle production, as would the loss of traditional grazing land. It is suggested that by the late Iron Age this pressure was to lead to significant pastoral intensification.

The radical reorganisation of the Thornhill Farm settlement into a network of paddocks and enclosures suggests close spatial control and intensive care of the livestock, at least at certain critical times of the year. A further indication of intensification was the digging of artificial waterholes, which might also be interpreted as evidence for pressure on pasture. At Claydon Pike the changes occurring during the early 1st century AD were even more pronounced, with a major settlement dislocation transferring activity over 200 metres to another gravel island in the south (Miles et al. forthcoming). The new site at Longdoles Field consisted of a series of pits, gullies, small multiply recut enclosures and linear boundaries, and appears to represent a nucleated settlement associated with livestock farming, with evidence for occupation (although no definite

buildings) and minor industrial activity. The presence of imported Roman tableware, amphorae and mortaria suggests that late Iron Age–early Roman Claydon Pike was possibly of a different (higher?) status than neighbouring Thornhill Farm, with at least some of the inhabitants choosing to express their wealth through Roman style eating habits (Meadows 2001, 235). Interestingly both sites produced around the same number of brooches dating to the 1st–mid 2nd century AD, implying that the wearing of such items had little direct connection with external Roman influences.

Aside from Thornhill Farm and Claydon Pike, very few similar types of settlement are known on the Thames Valley floodplain and lower terraces, perhaps in part because of our relative ignorance of floodplain archaeology. There are a handful of well-known cropmarks, such as those at Port Meadow, which have been plotted, but very few sites have actually been excavated. At Yarnton Worton Rectory Farm excavations revealed a series of enclosures belonging to the late Iron Age and early Roman period, along with domestic material and the probability of domestic buildings (Hey and Timby forthcoming). Despite the detailed analysis of this particular site, the extent to which the floodplain might have been utilised in the later prehistoric period is still difficult to assess. The suitability for settlement would have changed with the shifting hydrology of the valley, and many more sites could be masked by the thick alluvium which covers much of the valley floor. Around Thornhill Farm environmental evidence suggests that these lower lying areas were not used for arable cultivation, but consisted of unbroken grassland, and this is likely to have been the same over much of the Upper Thames Valley area.

Despite the paucity of sites similar to Thornhill Farm and Claydon Pike, there is increasing evidence for late Iron Age settlement in the Thames Valley region. In many cases, such as Barton Court Farm (Miles 1986), these were new settlements built on previously unoccupied sites, while others, like Thornhill Farm, were the subject of radical reorganisation. A number of low-lying middle Iron Age sites, such as Mingies Ditch and Watkins Farm, were abandoned at this time, and two of the principal features of earlier settlements – cylindrical storage pits and circular roundhouse gullies – largely disappeared. Such widespread disruption to intra- and intersite settlement organisation seems to have been at least partly induced by agricultural changes, which may in turn have been linked to wider socio-political changes, in particular the increasing control exerted over the landscape by the native elite.

POLITICS AND TRADE

The emergence of a more hierarchical socio-political system based around increasingly centralised polities was a feature of the later Iron Age in parts of southern and eastern Britain (Haselgrove 1989, 2). The Upper Thames Valley was at the juncture of three such tribal polities, the Dobunni, Atrebates and Catuvellauni, as indicated by coin distributions (Creighton 2000). Thornhill Farm lay within the territory of the Dobunni, whose sphere of influence covered a topographically varied landscape, from the floodplain and valleys of the rivers Thames and Severn, to the exposed limestone uplands of the Cotswolds. At its heart lay the possible tribal capital of Bagendon (Fig. 5.1), although the status and function of this site in late Dobunnic society is still little understood (Clifford 1961; Darvill 1987, 166–168). Whatever its function, Bagendon was clearly a site of special importance to the Dobunni as a great deal of resources were obviously used to raise the extensive dyke system, suggesting a well-developed system of social co-operation or compulsion.

There were a number of other late Iron Age defended sites and linear systems with often quite substantial earthworks, both in the Cotswolds region (eg Salmonsbury, Dunning 1976) and in the Thames Valley itself (eg Abingdon, Allen 1997). The most extensive was that of Grim's Ditch in north Oxfordshire (Fig. 5.1), which eventually at least partially enclosed an area of *c* 80 km², and later contained a notable group of Roman villas, many of which had early origins. Such earthworks may well have been connected with the rise of a socially stratified elite, possibly as trading centres or strongholds along strategically important routes (Lambrick 1998 12). Bagendon and the nearby fort at The Ditches (Trow 1988) possibly formed the centre of an important aristocratic estate (Trow 1990, 111–112). This is suggested not only by their scale, but more importantly by the large quantities of 'luxury' imported goods found there, undoubtedly the result of more intense long distance trade.

The traditional communication routes of the Jurassic Ridge and Thames Valley provided convenient and well established channels for exchange, and artefactual evidence confirms that the Dobunni entered into trade on a regular basis with their neighbours. The study of coinage has proved a useful indicator of Dobunnic trade patterns. Van Arsdell has identified a number of exchange zones, 'gateways' and trade routes, which suggest considerable trade and exchange between the Dobunni and the Catuvellauni to the east, the Corieltauvi to the north-east and the Welsh tribes to the north-west. In addition, coins have been found as far away as Hengistbury Head and Hayling Island on the south coast, perhaps suggesting an extended link with coastal traders (van Arsdell 1994, 26–29).

Classical texts make it clear that British tribes were involved in the export of commodities to the continent. The goods listed by Strabo (Geography IV, 5, 3) are highly unlikely to have all been supplied by the core tribes of the south-east, implying that the tribes of the periphery must have been involved in the supply of some of the raw materials, even if

indirectly. The emergence of Thornhill Farm as a specialised livestock ranch, together with the increasing importance of beef in the late Iron Age diet (King 1991), is therefore of considerable interest, although it must be reiterated that the faunal evidence points to a subsistence level economy, and any trading of commodities is likely to have been quite limited. To what extent Dobunnic beef and hides might have formed part of the British export trade is impossible to quantify. If it existed, exchange is likely to have been indirect, conducted through a series of local transactions and tribute payments. It has been suggested that the accumulated effect of such trading was actually responsible for the emergence of the powerful tribal elite, whose success was based upon the effective control of resources (Haselgrove 1982, 79–88).

Therefore, although it has been suggested that the development and intensification of specialised pastoralism was initiated by the internal stresses of a growing population, it could also have been given significant impetus by increasing demand for raw materials emanating from the continent, and the exploitation of this situation by the native elite.

The coming of Rome (Fig. 5.2)

Although the invasion and advance of the Roman military undoubtedly disrupted the established pattern of trade, it is possible that at least part of the Dobunnic territory continued to be ruled for some time as a client kingdom. By *c* AD 50, a Roman cavalry fort was established at Leaholme (Cirencester), just 4.5 km from Bagendon (Darvill and Holbrook 1994, 53), although whether this was to repress or protect the native population is uncertain. The location of the fort so close to Bagendon has been interpreted as an aggressive move by the Romans, designed to hold down a potentially hostile population, although it has also been suggested that it could have been positioned to support the Dobunni against the marauding tribes of Wales (*op. cit.* 55). On balance, it would seem that the latter is more likely, and the exceptionally early villa at site of The Ditches may have been the residence of one of the pro-Roman native elite. The undesirable location of this villa, in an unusually elevated position away from an ample water source, suggests that the occupant had a personal or political association with the pre-Roman native enclosure (Trow and James 1989, 85). Such continuity of pre-Roman elite power is also suggested by the concentration of 1st century AD villas within the Grim's Ditch earthworks, and the construction of a villa at Woodchester near to the possible Dobunnic oppidum of Minchinhampton (Clarke 1996, 76).

A parallel to The Ditches and Bagendon sites may perhaps be found with the early Roman military occupation at Fishbourne and Chichester in West Sussex, which lay at the heart of Togidubnus's client kingdom, in or near to the old Atrebatic territorial oppidum (Cunliffe 1998). The military presence at

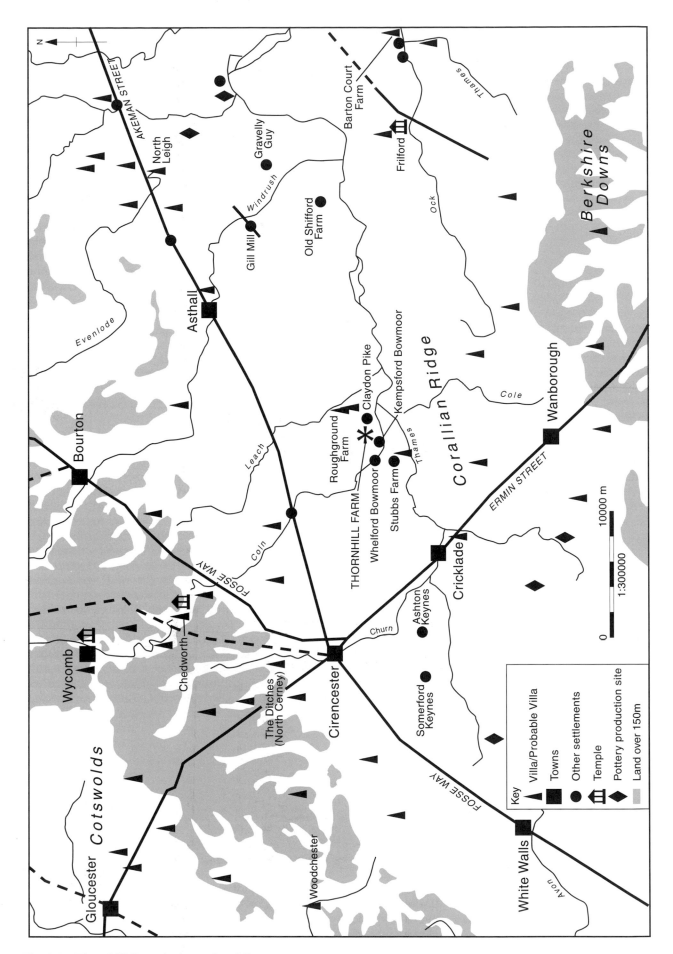

Fig. 5.2   *Thornhill Farm in its regional Roman context*

both sites may been designed both to bolster the power of the local client king, and perhaps also to keep them in check. At the Cotswold site however, it is unlikely that the client kingdom would have lasted long, as occupation at Bagendon soon slid into a terminal decline, suggesting the waning influence of the local leaders, and the eventual incorporation of the territory into the province. The latter event may have coincided with the evacuation of Leaholme and the establishment of the civitas capital of Corinium Dobunnorum (Cirencester) on the site around AD 65–70 (Darvill and Holbrook 1994, 55).

At Thornhill Farm, Claydon Pike and many other settlements in the Upper Thames Valley, the Roman invasion is archaeologically invisible for generations. The excavation and use of animal enclosures at the first two sites went on as before, apparently unaffected by the political upheaval. The only real difference at Thornhill Farm was the creation of a droveway which led away to the northeast of the site. Although droveways are a common feature of the early Roman period of the region, there is no reason to think that the droveway at Thornhill Farm was anything other than an entirely native development. It would appear that neither Thornhill Farm nor Claydon Pike were considered important enough to warrant a military presence at that time.

Reorganisation of the landscape (*c* early 2nd century AD; Fig. 5.2)

At some point in the early 2nd century AD there is evidence for a widespread reorganisation of the landscape in both the Upper Thames Valley and, to a lesser extent, parts of the Cotswolds and the Vale of the White Horse (Henig and Booth 2000, 107). A great variety of sites were affected and in different ways, including the abandonment of the high status 'protovilla' at Barton Court Farm (Miles 1986) and the settlement at Gravelly Guy (Lambrick and Allen forthcoming), and a significant shift of the enclosure site at Old Shifford Farm (Hey 1996). The disruption was such that in the Upper Thames Valley at least, more sites probably terminated in the early 2nd century AD than were occupied throughout the whole Roman period (Henig and Booth 2000, 106). As Lambrick has stated (1992, 84), such widespread and persistent patterns of discontinuity are more likely to have arisen from external political and economic stimuli, rather than purely organic internal developments in economic strategy. They may well be related to the imposition of a more capital intensive system with an emphasis on increased production of resources (*op. cit.*, 105), and it has been suggested that such reorganisation may have been initiated by members of the existing native elite operating from villas founded in the later 1st and early 2nd century AD (Henig and Booth 2000, 110). Whilst this may have been the case in most areas, more direct official involvement

cannot be ruled out in some instances, with a possible example being Claydon Pike (Miles *et al.* forthcoming).

The radical reorganisation at Claydon Pike involved the imposition of a series of rectangular ditched enclosures, one with a large entrance structure and two aisled buildings, and another interpreted as a rectangular religious precinct (temenos), although the evidence for this is slight. At the same time, the associated material culture was also transformed, with a higher incidence of 'Romanized' ceramics (amphorae, mortaria, samian etc.) and a far more diverse range of small finds which indicated very deep-seated lifestyle changes, in terms of personal appearance, building techniques and furnishings (Cool forthcoming). While the presence of Roman material culture alone does not imply the widespread adoption of Roman ideologies (Taylor 2001, 48), when combined with the radical changes in settlement layout and architecture, it does suggest a marked disruption to the previous indigenous socio-economic regime. Both Hingley (1989, 160) and Meadows (2001, 235) have, however, argued for continuity of high status native occupation, while Black (1994, 108–9) has suggested that sites such as this may have been occupied by natives who had served in the Roman army. An alternative put forward by the excavators is that there was a change of land ownership, with the site becoming an official Roman depot or military estate (saltus) associated with the cultivation of hay meadows (Miles and Palmer 1984, 92; Robinson, forthcoming). A recent reappraisal of the site (Miles *et al.* forthcoming) suggests that despite the radical transformation in both settlement layout and material culture, there is no real evidence for direct official involvement, and the only significant assemblage of military finds belongs to the late 2nd–early 3rd centuries AD (Cool forthcoming). This may be connected to the later policing of a site that had some indirect connections with Roman state supply networks. The precise significance of a number of fragments of wooden writing tablets recovered from a nearby well is uncertain, but their existence does indicate writing and record keeping on site.

Crucially, the dating of this phase of the site has recently been re-examined and reassigned to the early 2nd century AD, and is thus more in concordance with the other widespread settlement changes (Miles *et al.* forthcoming). The reorganisation of Claydon Pike may therefore have been broadly contemporary with developments at Thornhill Farm, where the domestic and pastoral elements were replaced by a system of trackways and hay meadows (see above). Thus, this site seems to have become part of an outlying field and trackway system belonging to a centralised agricultural estate specialising in the production of animal fodder, which was based at Claydon Pike. This is of course difficult to substantiate with any certainty, although a radical transformation is also found at nearby Somerford Keynes, Neigh Bridge, where a late Iron Age farmstead was transformed in the early 2nd century AD by the imposition of a regular layout of rectangular ditched enclosures and the construction of a large aisled building interpreted as a tile depot (Miles and Palmer 1990, 23). A substantial curvilinear ditch to the east may well have been part of a religious focus at the site, since it was associated with large numbers of coins, brooches and two sculptural fragments of the Capitoline triad (Henig 1993, 56, 58).

Other known 2nd-century developments in the vicinity of Thornhill Farm include the construction of masonry villas, one lying *c* 3.5 km to the east at Roughground Farm (Allen *et al.* 1993), and another 1.7 km to the north of this at Great Lemhill Farm (RCHME 1976, 77). Low status settlements were also established at Whelford Bowmoor and Kempsford, Stubbs Farm (Miles *et al.* forthcoming), and Kempsford Bowmoor (OAU 1989). The latter site was connected to Thornhill Farm and probably Claydon Pike via a ditched trackway (see above).

The later Roman period (3rd–4th century AD)

In general, the settlement pattern of the Upper Thames Valley established in the 2nd century AD remained fairly stable throughout the later Roman period, although there were many local variations, probably relating to differential social and economic developments. There were some significant changes in the Lechlade–Fairford area, including the apparent dismantling of the aisled building complex, and establishment of a modest masonry-footed villa in the early 4th century AD at Claydon Pike. It operated a mixed agricultural economy, and the late linear ditches at Thornhill may have been a part of its outer field systems. It therefore seems that any official involvement in the area – if such had ever existed – had certainly ceased by this point, and quite possibly much earlier. Developments at this site may well have been connected to other changes in the local settlement pattern during the 3rd century, as the low status sites of Whelford Bowmoor and Stubbs Farm went out of use, and the villa estate at Roughground Farm is interpreted as becoming increasingly centralised (Allen *et al.* 1993). At some point during the later 3rd–early 4th century the area would have been incorporated into

the new province of Britannia Prima, centred on the provincial capital at Cirencester. The province seemingly experienced great prosperity for a time, with a marked increase in villa building and expansion, including the elaborate complexes in the Cotswolds at North Leigh and Woodchester (Fig. 5.2). Both the Cotswolds and the Upper Thames Valley may have seen increasing centralisation in the management of agricultural estates during this later Roman period.

FUTURE RESEARCH

Thornhill Farm has shown how problematic archaeological investigations on the lower gravel terraces can be, but has also illustrated the potential of such sites for understanding large scale landscape developments. The Upper Thames Valley as a whole has become an intensely studied region over the past 25 years, although the lower gravel terraces and floodplain itself have generally not received as much attention as higher areas. Nevertheless, crop mark evidence and limited excavation have proven that this marginal landscape was of increasing economic importance in the later Iron Age and Roman periods, and was undoubtedly related to wider social and agricultural regimes. It is vitally important that sites such as Claydon Pike and Thornhill Farm are not seen as semi-isolated settlements, but as components in the wider changing local, regional and provincial landscape. Furthermore, their importance lies not in abstract classifications of settlement morphology and structural form, but in the analysis of changing functionality, and the reasons behind such developments.

The environmental evidence is a key element in this approach, and its importance was recognised at an early stage by the excavators of Thornhill Farm and Claydon Pike, where it formed a major part of the research programmes. As such there is a great deal of information on the development of land use and to a lesser extent the control of resources during the Iron Age and Roman periods in the Upper Thames Valley, although this has yet to be analysed to its full potential. Detailed landscape studies incorporating environmental and structural and artefactual evidence from a wide range of settlement and non-settlement sites should therefore form a priority for future research in this area.

pottery assemblages were recovered from two of these ditches (2353: sixteen sherds Group 3 and one sherd Group 1; 2354: fourteen sherds Group 3), while no pottery was found in either of the sections cut across the third ditch 2382.

As regards the southern boundary, 2374, it had been recut twice and while its latest recut, which occurred along its northern edge, cut both of the conjoining ditches of E90, it is reasonable to suppose that these ditches were associated with the earlier phase(s) of this ditch. Only nine sherds of pottery were recovered from ditch 2374 (one sherd Group 4, six sherds Group 3 and two sherds Group 2), and they could not be assigned to individual cuts. On this minimal basis the pottery does not provide conclusive dating evidence, although it does not contradict the suggestion that ditch 2374 was initially cut in Period C and continued into Period D. Indeed, given the apparent spatial coherency of ditch 2374 with the later, Period D, E45, it would seem most probable that at least the latest recut was contemporary with that enclosure. However, this relationship cannot be demonstrated as no section was cut through the intersection of ditch 2374 and the eastern boundary of E45.

The intensive recutting and minimal investigation of the eastern boundary of E45 means that any western boundary of E46 on this alignment in Period C cannot be discerned. Indeed, it must remain a matter of speculation whether there even was a western boundary to E46 in Period C or whether a boundary was formed by the eastern side of E82 (Fig. 3.5) and the western side of E90 (Fig. 3.8). This would have left a small entrance between the south-eastern corner of E82 and the north-western corner of E90, with an unknown western terminal of the southern boundary, 2374. In Period D, it is apparent that the eastern side of E45 would have served as the western boundary of E46.

A number of ditches and gullies (2397, 2319, 2293 and 2288) seem to be interpreted most coherently as elements of E46's northern boundary, although their proposed phasing relies on a partially subjective assessment of probabilities.

The curvilinear elements, 2397 and 2319, are stratigraphically the earliest, being cut by all of the other ditches in this area, and are probably Period C features. The only dating evidence consisted of five sherds of Group 3 pottery recovered from 2319. It is noted in the context records that it was thought likely that the curvilinear ditch 2319 continued to the south as ditch 2325. Aside from the fact that both of these ditches were cut by ditch 2293, other evidence is of only partial assistance in our assessment of this possibility. No full section was cut across the southern ditch 2325, and therefore ditch profiles cannot be compared, although on the basis of the plans and partial profiles the ditches are of similar dimensions. In addition, both ditches had a primary and secondary fill. No pottery was recovered from ditch 2325 to assist with dating. Taking these factors into considera-

tion it still seems reasonable, on the balance of probabilities, to interpret ditches 2319 and 2325 as the same feature.

If this reconstruction is accepted, then ditch 2325 would seem to be a precursor to E89. The precise form of this earlier subenclosure (E91) in the north-western corner of E46 is unclear, as ditch 2325 was cut away by the deeper, later ditch 2324, and no section was cut completely across the ditch to the south of the junction of ditch 2324 and 2325. It would seem likely, however, that the increased width of the ditch beyond this junction reflected the continuation of both ditches to the south-west and their termination in approximately the same place.

Returning to the northern boundary, ditch 2293 formed one of its principal east-west elements. Its full extent to the west is unclear, as it had been cut away by the deeper ditches of E48. To the east, it seems very probable from the plan that 2293 turned to the north at its eastern end. This section of ditch was, however, given a different number (2294) during excavation, although dimensions and fill sequence, as far as can be judged on the limited evidence, were very similar. If this reinterpretation is accepted then this ditch 2293/2294 cut a feature 2293/A, which contained 11 sherds of Group 4 pottery. Clearly this places ditch 2293/2294 into the Period D phase of E46 (Fig. A1.2).

The phasing of the other principal east-west ditch, 2288, of the northern boundary is open to interpretation. No pottery was recovered from any of the stack rings (2268, 2269 and 2289) which it cut or from the ditch itself. Its spatial relationship with 2293/2294 strongly suggests that it was contemporary with this ditch, and thus is a Period D feature. However, as ditch 2288 had been recut there is the possibility that it may initially have been dug in Period C, defining a wider entrance in conjunction with the ditches 2319/2325. The ditch 2293/2294 and the feature 2293/A may therefore have been a redefinition of the northern boundary, which restricted this putative earlier entrance. In support of this interpretation, it may be of interest to note that unlike ditch 2288, ditch 2293/2294 did not show any signs of recutting, and therefore seems to be a single phase feature.

The eastern boundary of E46 was beyond the area of the excavations; it can, however, be seen on aerial photographs (Fig. 3.5). It extends from the eastern end of ditch 2288 but does not enclose all of the eastern side. There may have been a genuine gap in the eastern side, but it could also reflect variations in subsoil conditions or ditch fill.

As regards internal features within E46, two subenclosures, E89 and E77, can be placed in Periods D and E respectively (Fig. A1.2). E89 seems to be a replacement of an earlier subenclosure (E91) in the north-western corner of E46. Its western side was formed by the multiply recut eastern side of E45, while its northern side may initially have been formed by a western continuation of 2293. Later within Period D the northern boundary was formed by the southern side of E48 which it seems was obviously laid out with respect to E89, given the common axis of the eastern boundaries of both enclosures. It is apparent that E48 continued in use after E89 whose eastern boundary, 2320/2415, was cut by the most southerly recut of E48's southern boundary, 2320/2317. The eastern boundary of E89 continued to the south beyond ditch 2320/2415 in the form of ditch 2324.

Enclosure 77 was a small rectilinear feature in the south-western corner of E46, with pottery clearly dating to Period E. The precise form of its northern entrance cannot be defined due to inadequate excavation of these features and destruction of potentially contemporary features by a pit complex (2397, 2425, 2426, 2427 and 2485).

Posthole Cluster 2 was located within the subenclosures E89 and E91 (Fig. A1.2). It cannot be phased to either Period C or D as no pottery was recovered from any of the postholes, while the four Group 3 sherds recovered from the two pits to the south (2350 and 2351) of the cluster are insufficient, in terms of context association or quantity, to provide an accurate date.

In terms of forming a coherent building groundplan, while a number of the postholes could be placed on partial arcs, none of these possibilities are particularly convincing and they are not considered further. The most probable building form is a four-poster, consisting of postholes 2341, 2344, 2346 and 2347, which would have delineated a structure approximately 2.5 x 2 m (Fig. A1.2). Three of these features were the deepest in the cluster (2347, 2344 and 2341), which may increase our confidence in the interpretation of these postholes being elements of a four-post structure. As there were only minimal fill descriptions, there is no further evidence to assist in our analysis. Even if this reconstruction is accepted, it does not account for the six other postholes in this area, and given the paucity of postholes on the site as a whole, it might be thought that this cluster is in fact representative of the roundhouse type discussed above (Chapter 3, 'Structure 210') where the posts did not form a coherent pattern.

There is no basis on which we can assess the degrees of likelihood between this latter possibility, a potential four-poster, and the probability that they were not structural elements at all, but may have been related to some other function, as for instance tethering posts or racks.

A1.4 Enclosure group at the northern end of Trench 9 (Fig. A1.3)

Enclosures 70, 71, and 87 have been presented as a group largely on the basis of their spatial coherency and the similarity of their component parts. The conviction that the group continued to evolve from late Period C into Period D is based on analysis of

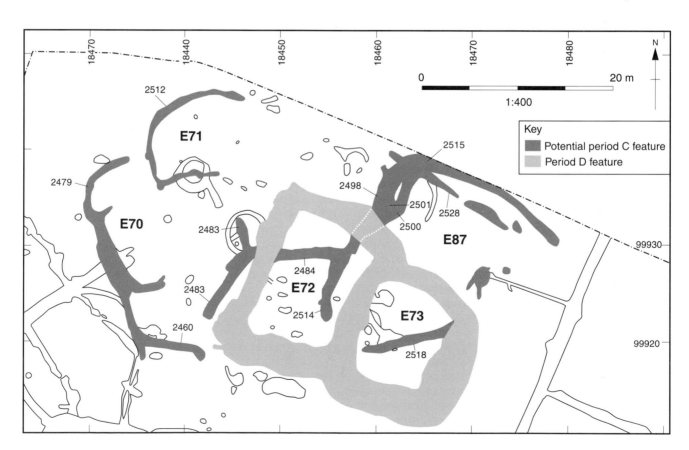

Fig. A1.3   Potential Period C enclosures – Northern Area

the ceramic evidence, first investigated in E87. Ceramics recovered from the main body of the enclosure (2498, 2500, and 2501) were all of Group 3 or earlier giving a reasonably secure Period C date. In marked contrast, ditch 2484 (the western annex), which was recorded as having cut 2514, contained two sherds of Group 5 pottery and a single sherd of Group 4. Since 2484 was itself cut by the Period D enclosure 72, the Group 5 sherds have been dismissed as intrusive and the annex allocated to Period D. The northern enclosure boundary appears to have been remodelled at the same time as ditch 2515, which cut 2528 and contained three sherds of Group 4 pottery.

The E70 ceramic assemblage was dominated by Group 3 material, although a single sherd of Group 5 pottery recovered from ditch 2460 again introduces an element of doubt. No ceramic evidence was recovered from E71 and its inclusion in Period C was based largely on its spatial cohesion with E70.

The dangers of dating the enclosure group on the basis of such a small amount of pottery (especially when some of that pottery has to be dismissed as intrusive) are obvious. The conclusions presented in Chapter 3 are therefore offered merely as a best fit interpretation derived from an inadequate data set. That stated, the fact that E87 was truncated by Period D features (E72 and E73) allows for a degree of confidence in the conclusions.

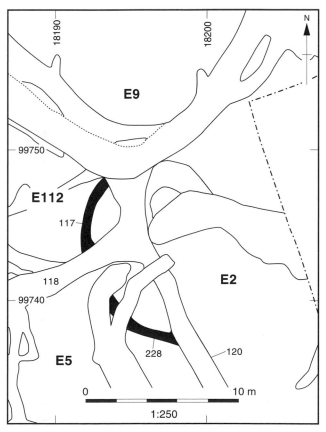

Fig. A1.4   Possible structure – Period C

A1.5 Possible structure – Period C (Fig. A1.4)

In the south-eastern corner of Trench 7 two curvilinear gullies, 117 and 228, were detected which may have formed an incomplete ring-gully of a roundhouse. They were located at the junction of the north-eastern corner of E5, the northern boundary of E2, and the southern end of E9. The high density of features in this area means that the extent of these gullies is only partially reconstructable, the location of only the western terminal of gully 228 being precisely known.

The eastern terminal of gully 228 has been cut away by the north-south ditch 120, while the eastern end of gully 117 disappeared into the large soilmark which marked the conjunction of E5, E2 and E9, and its southern end was cut away by ditch 118. Even though the exact limits of these gullies are unknown it is apparent that a complete ring-gully was not recognised: no continuation of gully 228 was detected to the east of ditch 120, and no comparable gully was recorded beyond the eastern limits of the large soilmark. Given the depth of the gullies (0.22–0.28 m) it is extremely unlikely that their continuations could have been machined away during stripping (see above, Chapter 1), and it is therefore highly probable that the absence is genuine. On this basis, if the features are related then it is apparent that they did not form a continuous ring-gully. This need not preclude these features being structural elements, as buildings of this form have been detected at Claydon Pike and at other sites in the Upper Thames Valley. However, it needs to be accepted that given the minimal character of the evidence any structural interpretation remains speculative.

Other evidence which may be pertinent to a consideration of these features as being related to a structure can be stated quickly. It could be suggested that the gullies defined an entrance which faced to the south-west, and while this is contrary to the often observed trend for roundhouse entrances to face east (eg Parker Pearson 1996, 119), it does broadly parallel the west-facing entrance of the other putative roundhouse in Trench 7 (E11; Fig. 3.19). The density of finds within gullies 117 and 228 is extremely low, with only a small quantity of burnt stone being recovered from a single section of gully 117. This contrasts with the observation of other sites in the Upper Thames Valley where above average finds densities are recorded from the immediate vicinity of roundhouses, and, in particular, in ring-gully terminals.

Given the lack of pottery, the gullies are dated to Period C on the basis of their stratigraphically early position.

A1.6 'Co-axial' enclosure system – Trench 7 (Fig. 3.9)

A series of interlinked enclosures was revealed in the south-eastern corner of Trench 7. The chronological evolution of the enclosures proved difficult to determine due to the complex nature of the archaeology and the relatively low level of ceramics recovered from many of the ditches. In some cases, as with Enclosures 110 and 112, evidence recovered in the form of section drawings was occasionally contradictory and often difficult to interpret. The problem was made worse by the close similarity of ditch deposits and the number of recuts which were sometimes difficult to trace throughout their length. Consequently, it was not always possible to determine which ditch or recut belonged to which enclosure, a problem exacerbated by the number of ditches shared by different enclosures.

Considerable redeposition of pottery was also evident. Where pottery was recovered at all from a feature, there were usually two or more of the Ceramic Groups present. In more than one case, all five pottery groups appeared in the same ditch together. Nevertheless, it was still possible to draw a number of conclusions from the evidence. In most

cases the presence of Group 5 ceramics can be attributed to the disturbance caused by the Roman trackway 301 which cut across the enclosure group, or to the late in-filling of ditches long out of use. The considerable mixing of the other Ceramic Groups in part reflects the intercutting nature of the archaeology. Enclosure 5 is a typical example. Although the E5 ceramic assemblage was dominated by Group 3 pottery, a considerable number of Group 1 sherds were also recovered (Table A1.1). This reflects the generally high density of Group 1 sherds recovered from the south-eastern corner of Trench 7 (see Chapter 3, 'Distribution of redeposited Group 1 pottery') and is probably due to activity predating the enclosure. The E5 pottery assemblage was largely typical of the other enclosures in this group, and on the basis of this and the limited stratigraphical sequences, the enclosure group as a whole was assigned to Period C.

Table A1.1   Ceramic Groups (Enclosure 5)

Group	Number	Weight (g)
1 Total	49	299
2 Total	27	78
3 Total	118	476
4 Total	4	18
5 Total	10	70

Enclosure entrances

Locating enclosure entrances proved problematic. Where entrances were suspected, the frequent cutting and reshaping of later ditches meant that definitive evidence was difficult to obtain. Convincing evidence for ditched entrances was identified in only two cases: E23 and E152. In the case of E23, a pair of parallel gullies (711 and 737), *c* 2 m apart, led directly towards the west facing entrance (Fig. 3.9). Similar arrangements leading to

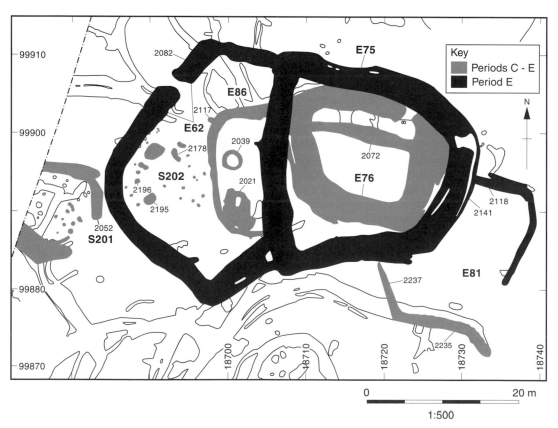

Fig. A1.5   Enclosures 62 and 75 – Trench 9

suspected enclosure entrances were identified in two other cases: E4 and E13. Although later activity ensured that neither entrance could be identified with certainty, the arrangement of parallel gullies was closely comparable with that seen at E23, and could be interpreted as evidence of the former existence of enclosure entrances. The only clear difference between E23 and the other two enclosures was that the entrance to E23 was in the centre of one side, whereas the suggested entrances to E4 and E13 were both located in the corner of their respective enclosures (Fig. 3.9).

The function of parallel gullies at the entrance to an enclosure is open to speculation. The juxtaposition of paddocks and enclosures with drove-ways has become an increasingly recognised feature of late Iron Age sites in the Upper Thames Valley (Lambrick 1992, 103). In this case, the close proximity of the edge of the excavation precluded consideration of the full extent of the gullies. However, if the enclosure group and parallel gullies are accepted as part of the same phase then some form of controlled entry or exit from the enclosures would seem to be a reasonable interpretation.

That said, it should be noted that none of the parallel gullies contained pottery and that the stratigraphy was ambiguous in every case. Although associations between the gullies and their respective enclosures is suggested by their spatial arrangement, phasing is far from certain and should be seen as speculative.

A1.7 Structure 202 – Trench 9 (Fig. A1.5)

The phasing of structure 202 is extremely difficult. It is equally possible to build a case for a Period C or Period E date. Both are outlined below.

Period C

Based purely on ceramic evidence, a Period C date would seem the most plausible. A total of 98 sherds were recovered from the structure. Of these, 37 were Group 3 (Period C) and the rest were earlier, mainly Group 2 (Period B). All of the sherds were recovered from three features: pit 2195 and the postholes 2196 and 2178. Spatially, the structure was less than 5 m to the north-east of two other Period C post-built structures, 200 and 201 (Fig. 3.6), and if it were not for the presence of E62 would certainly have been presented as part of this group.

Period E

It is possible to cast serious doubt on the validity of the Period C argument, however. Much of the Period C ceramic evidence can be discounted by suggesting that postholes 2178 and 2196 did not belong to Structure 202 but were instead part of a linear fenceline together with 2117. The three postholes were equally spaced, 6 m apart, and it might be argued, were aligned on the eastern

terminal of the gully enclosing structure 201 (2052), itself 6 m from 2196. Although structure 202 was close to the Period C post-built structures 200 and 201 in a spatial sense, if the area was a focus for construction during Period C, there is no reason why it should not have continued to be so into Period E. The position of S202 relative to E62 also argues for a Period E date.

A1.8 Enclosures 62 and 75 – Trench 9 (Fig. A1.5)

Enclosures E62 and E75 were tentatively placed in Period E on the basis of their stratigraphic relationships with earlier enclosures and a minimal amount of pottery evidence. The key to the stratigraphic sequence is ditch 2072. This ditch clearly cut enclosure E76 and was cut itself by E75, showing that E75 was later than E76. Although admittedly slim, the pottery evidence supports the stratigraphic sequence. Ditch 2072 contained two sherds of Group 4 (Period D) pottery. If that is accepted as evidence for a Period D date, then E75 would have to be late Period D or later. Given the complete lack of any other features dated to later than Period E in Trench 9, a Period E date for E75 would be a reasonable assumption.

A1.9 Enclosure 2 – Trench 7 (Fig. A1.6)

The entrance to enclosure 2 was complex and poorly understood. The western side of the

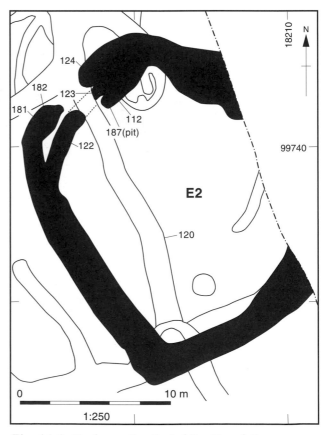

Fig. A1.6 Enclosure 2 – Period E – Trench 7

entrance consisted of two ditches, 181 and 122. Ditch 181 clearly terminated at the entrance, possibly ending in a posthole (182). Ditch 122, however, carried on beyond 181, but whether it terminated or carried on across the entrance is uncertain. The presence of the earlier ditch 120 at this point seems to have confused matters. The excavation records concerning 122 are confused and it is clear that the ditch terminal was never convincingly located on site. The eastern side of the entrance consisted of three separate ditches: 112, 123 and 124. The relationship between the three ditches was not established making interpretation difficult. The inner ditch (112) appears to have terminated at a posthole or small pit (187) *c* 2 m east of 122.

Although it is clear that the entrance to E2 underwent considerable modification during the lifetime of the enclosure it is uncertain whether the various terminals either side of the entrance were straightforward recuts or a deliberate attempt at elaboration. If the former, it is difficult to see why the recuts were so inaccurate. It is unlikely that any of the ditches would have silted up so far as to be invisible, as if they had, their original function would have been negated, making the need for a recut questionable.

A1.10 Enclosure 14 – Trench 7 (Fig. A1.7)

Gullies 481 and 495 were of uncertain phase. The pottery assemblage was relatively early (four sherds Group 1 and one sherd Group 3) but the site records state that gully 495 cut ditch 462 (E14; Period E). The pottery could, however, be redeposited, making a Period E or F date possible for the gullies. A number of pits and postholes were revealed in the south-eastern corner of E14. Although from a spatial perspective the features seemed to be associated with gullies 481 and 495, the ceramic assemblages and stratigraphic relationships proved that they were of various phases. Postholes 522 and 529 were cut by gully 495 and could be as early as Period A, as posthole 529 contained six sherds of Group 1 pottery. Postholes 486 and 557 could have been contemporary with 481 and 495, although 557 might equally have been of any period. Posthole 484 and pit 485 were clearly later than 481 and contained pottery which would be commensurate with a Period E or F date.

A1.11 Enclosures 26, 29 and 30 – Trench 7 (Figs 3.17 and 3.19)

The stratigraphic sequence which linked E26, E29 and E30 was very poorly understood. Enclosure 26

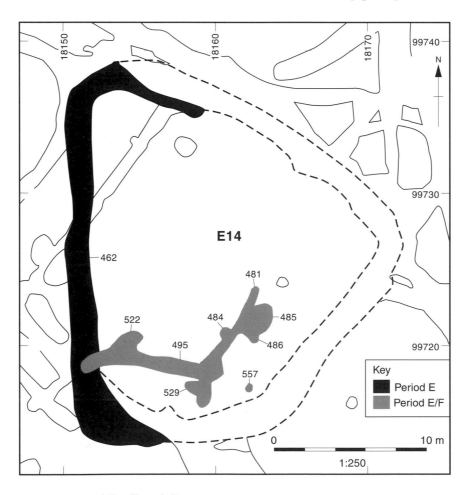

Fig. A1.7 Enclosure 14 – Period E – Trench 7

and E29 were stratigraphically related in very few places, and where they were the sections were not clearly understood. Consequently, the interpretation presented in Chapter 3 is partly based upon the observation of soil marks in the field rather than clear-cut stratigraphic evidence.

Enclosure 30 was of two clear phases. It is possible that the original phase (323; Fig. 3.19) was contemporary with E26 but the evidence is insufficient to be certain. The later phase of E30 (322) was demonstrably later than E26, and presumably was of the same phase as E29. This assumption is based entirely on the spatial coherency of E29 and E30.

It is uncertain whether the postholes (Fig. 3.19) that fringed the western extent of E30 were associated with the original enclosure ditch (323) or its recut (322). A number of postholes (352, 353, 354, 355 and 358) did, however, appear to be cut by 322, and other factors point toward association with the original ditch. The postholes were located so close to the edge of 322 that any structure would have been unstable and their uneven spacing might suggest that some had been cut away by 322. Finally, all of the postholes were relatively shallow (0.10–0.20 m deep), perhaps suggesting that they had been inserted into the upcast of the original enclosure ditch.

A1.12 Enclosure 33 – Trench 7 (Fig. 3.17)

The obvious difficulties encountered in unravelling the stratigraphic sequence of E33 were caused by a number of factors working in concert. The most important of these was the fact that the archaeology

in this corner of Trench 7 was never fully understood on site. The intensive, intercutting nature of the archaeology together with the homogeneous nature of the soils meant that a bewildering mass of detail had effectively merged and was simply beyond reconstruction. The second major factor is that the quality of excavation over this part of the site was compromised by a severe time restriction, which led to a level of trenching (in terms of numbers), which was hopelessly inadequate given the complexity of the archaeology. The result is a very poor understanding of E33 and its possible subenclosures.

A1.13 Western enclosure group – Trench 7 (Fig. 3.19)

The western enclosure group in Trench 7 was very poorly understood. The intensive, intercutting nature of the archaeology meant that the northern subgroup in particular was difficult to reconstruct. This difficulty was compounded by a severe shortage of time, which inevitably led to an inadequate level of trenching.

A1.14 Southern subgroup

Enclosure 22 (Fig. A1.8)

Gully 701, which traversed the centre of this enclosure, was of uncertain phase. This was largely due to contradictory records, which maintained that the gully both cut and was cut by the E22 ditch 698. Since none of the pottery recovered from 701 was later than Group 4 (Period D) it is probably better to assume that it was earlier than E22.

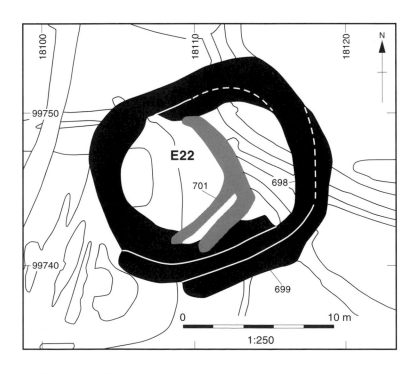

Fig. A1.8   Enclosure 22 – Period F – Trench 7

Enclosure 155

The possible third ditch mentioned in Chapter 3 (749) is more likely to be ditch 723, which has been misidentified (Fig. 3.19).

A1.15 Northern subgroup

Due to the reasons outlined above, the northern subgroup was never fully understood on site. The records relating to the four enclosures were, therefore, inadequate to form a solid interpretation of the archaeology. The reconstruction put forward in Chapter 3 (Fig 3.19) relies heavily on work carried out in post-excavation analysis using field notes and sketches made by the supervisors on site. It is not meant to be a definitive interpretation, but should be considered as a 'best fit' based on the available evidence.

Appendix 2   Pottery: Site Formation Processes, Redeposition and Dating

by David Jennings and Jeff Muir

It is not the intention of this section to present a full discussion of the site formation processes, but to discuss the ways in which the datable finds became incorporated into the archaeological record, and thus to assess the reliability of the dating evidence they provide.

Pottery was the principal datable material which occurred in sufficient quantity to be analysed usefully. The only other finds to which reasonably accurate dates could be given, such as the coins and brooches, occurred in such insignificant quantities that the process of their deposition is not demonstrable.

The pottery from the site has been divided into five chronologically significant groups (see Timby, Chapter 4). The pottery was manually collected, with no dry or wet sieving being undertaken. A total of 10,935 sherds weighing 106.8 kg could be ascribed to the five Ceramic Groups, which gave an overall mean sherd weight of around 9.8 g (Table A2.1). The notable exception to the mean average was the Group 4 material (Fig. A2.1), the average weight of which, at 21.58 g, was notably higher. This higher figure is largely the product of three fabrics: G11 (Savernake ware), G16 (Savernake variant) and G18, which were used predominantly for large storage jars (see Timby, Chapter 4). It is likely that the exceptional average sherd weight of these three Group 4 fabrics derives not from any differential depositional or post-depositional processes, but from the noted hardness of these fabrics and their use for large vessel types. The only other pottery which clearly diverged from the trend occurred in such small quantities that no significance can be ascribed to their average weights: these were two fabrics in Group 5, M11 (a single sherd of a mortarium), and A11 (nine amphora sherds).

Comparative data from other late Iron Age and Roman sites located on the gravels in the Upper Thames Valley demonstrate that the average sherd weight of 9.8 g is exceptionally low (Table A2.2), and while post-depositional deterioration might partially account for the small sherd size, it is unlikely that this is the dominant factor (see Timby, Chapter 4), nor does there seem to be a significant relationship with the types of features in which the pottery was found. Examination of the pottery assemblages from individual enclosures suggests that the complex processes which the pottery underwent prior to its deposition was most significant in the excessive breakage of the pottery.

As with the majority of archaeological sites excavated on the gravels in the Upper Thames Valley, only negative features which cut into the gravel had been preserved. These types of features are obviously liable to have redeposited material incorporated within their fills as they were dug, backfilled or silted-up and recut. At Thornhill Farm it was often difficult to discern discrete fills within

Table A2.1   Average sherd weight of pottery by Ceramic Groups

Group	No. sherds	Total weight (g)	Average weight (g)
1	2113	17255	8.17
2	1434	8433	5.88
3	3642	26957	7.40
4	1734	37424	21.58
5	1949	16111	8.27
Total	10935	106800	9.77

Table A2.2   Comparison of average sherd weights from Upper Thames Valley sites

Site	Period	No. sherds	Total weight (g)	Average weight (g)	Source
Alchester Oxon.	Roman	46500	627750	13.5	P Booth pers. comm.
Claydon Pike, Fairford*	late Iron Age-early Roman	32642	370703	11.3	Green in prep.
Gravelly Guy, Stanton Harcourt	late Iron Age-early Roman	14471	206936	14.3	Green et al. in prep.
Mount Farm, Berinsfield†	early Iron Age-early Roman	686	13079	19.1	Lambrick 1984, 163
Old Shifford, Shifford	late Iron Age-early Roman	4000	58000	14.5	Timby in Hey 1996
Wally Corner, Berinsfield	Roman	2319	37000	15.9	Booth in Boyle et al. 1995
Yarnton	late Iron Age-early Roman	8000	164800	20.6	P Booth pers. comm.

All assemblages retrieved by manual collection

* Only provisional analysis

† Only a limited sample from the site assemblage

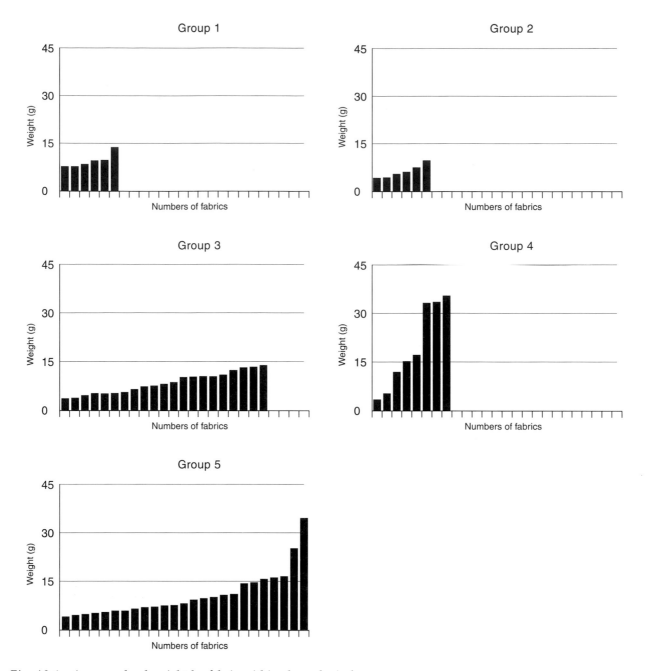

Fig. A2.1   Average sherd weight by fabric within chronological groups

the ditches or the relationships between cutting features, as the fills were derived from the same parent soils. However, the average number of recuts recorded for those enclosures (mean=3; Table A2.3) where data was available, provides a coarse indication of the degree of ditch recutting which occurred on the site. At first it might appear that the action of recutting or digging ditches and enclosures was one

Table A2.3   *The number of ditch recuts per enclosure*

No. recuts	1	2	3	4	5	6	7	8	Mean
No. enclosures	28	19	14	8	6	3	2	1	3

of the principal causes of the excessive breakage of the pottery. However, examination of the average sherd weights from enclosures belonging to different phases suggests that the pottery was principally broken down prior to its incorporation in the fill of the ditches.

Although definitive demonstration of this point is difficult, several lines of argument can be employed to support this interpretation. First, if the main mechanism resulting in the low average sherd weight was the constant reincorporation of material within ditch backfills and its breakage as ditches were recut and cleaned, one would expect the final phase pottery (Group 5) to be less degraded than earlier material,. However, analysis of the Group 5

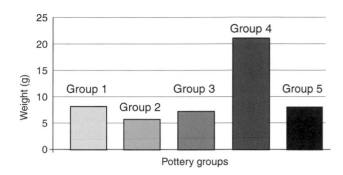

Fig. A2.2   *Average sherd weight by Ceramic Group*

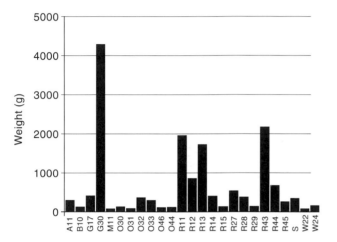

Fig. A2.3   *Group 5 – total sherd weight by fabric*

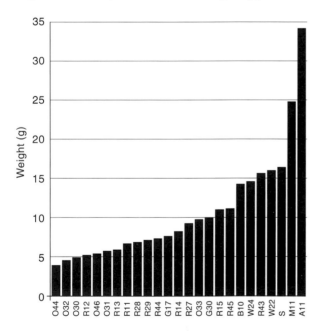

Fig. A2.4   *Group 5 – average sherd weight by fabric*

pottery demonstrates that it is almost as degraded as the pottery from the earlier Ceramic Groups (Table A2.1, Figs A2.1 and A2.2). Figure A2.1 does suggest that a proportion of the Group 5 fabrics (2–5 in number) are less broken down than fabrics in Groups 1–3. However, comparison of Figures A2.3 and A2.4 shows that, with the exception of fabric R43, these fabrics occur in limited quantities, and hence do not constitute the major components of the Group 5 assemblage. Fabric R43 is described as being a hard, buff to dark grey ware and it is therefore possible that it may have been more resilient to breakage than other fabric types. The high degree of breakage in the final phase ceramics suggests that ditch-digging or recutting was not the principal cause of the low average sherd weight.

Analysis of the average sherd size of the Group 3 fabrics also indicates that the breakage of the pottery is not predominantly a consequence of their deposition or redeposition in ditches. Two sets of enclosures were chosen the phasing of which was relatively secure, and which could therefore be taken as providing a real contrast between different phases of the site. The average sherd weight of Group 3 fabrics was relatively constant in both those enclosures dated to Period C by Group 3 pottery, and in enclosures of the later Periods E and F, dated by Group 5 pottery (Table A2.4). If redeposition in the ditches was a significant factor in determining sherd size then one would have expected the Group 3 pottery in those enclosures dated to the later phases to be more degraded. The sample size is 16% of the total Group 3 pottery assemblage, suggesting that the sample is sufficiently large for the results to be reliable.

Both of these observations – the high degree of breakage of the Group 5 pottery and the constant sherd size of the Group 3 material – suggest that the ceramics were broken down in another part of their 'life-cycle', prior to their secondary deposition in the negative features across the site. One would obviously expect there to be exceptions to this statement, given the potential complexity of the intrasite structuring of activities. However, as a general comment it would seem to hold true. The most obvious explanation for the small average sherd size, given the pastoral character of the site, would be that the pottery was being trampled by animals (and humans), after it had been dispersed on the ground surface. This need not preclude the use of middens on the site, the evidence for which would have been subsequently ploughed away, but does suggest that a variety of modes of rubbish disposal may have been in operation. If rubbish was being dispersed on the surface, then one might even tenta-

Table A2.4   *Average sherd weight of Group 3 pottery*

Enclosures	No. sherds	Weight (g)	Average sherd weight (g)
Period C (4, 5, 13, 110, 112)	256	1517	5.9
Periods E and F (6, 7, 11, 22, 29, 30, 33, 35, 36, 37)	333	2412	7.2

tively suggest that material like pottery and burnt stone was intentionally placed in areas which would be exposed to excessive trampling, like the entrances to enclosures, as additional material to metallings laid to provide access across wet ground. This idea is obviously extremely speculative as no evidence of metallings was found at the site (although given the truncation of deposits by later ploughing down to the natural gravel, any remains of metallings would probably have been removed). Metalled surfaces are, however, well-attested at other Iron Age sites such as Mingies Ditch (Allen and Robinson 1993, 65–66) and Danebury (Cunliffe 1984, 128), and the extensive ditch digging at this site would surely have provided adequate material to lay down metalling at places like enclosure entrances, where the ground would doubtlessly have been churned up.

Acceptance of the hypothesis that pottery was being broken down as a consequence of its dispersal on the ground surface, rather than as a result of it being continually broken down by the recutting and digging of ditches, suggests that average sherd size is of limited value in assessing levels of redeposition. One might suggest that substantial assemblages of comparatively large sherds provide reasonably reliable dates for the filling of features, given the obvious caveat that material might be excavated from previously sealed contexts in order to backfill ditches. However, the converse hypothesis, that small sherds are intrinsically indicative of redeposited material, and hence do not provide a date for the filling of the feature, cannot be held to apply.

Other factors also affect our assessment of the levels of redeposition. First, the excavation strategy adopted on the site was explicitly orientated towards the coverage of large areas, with the result that a policy of sampling rather than total excavation was adopted. In addition to sections being excavated along the length of ditches and enclosures, work concentrated on defining the stratigraphic relationships between features where they cut other features. The recording strategy used on the site was not a single context system, but rather a continuous unique numbering system, which had been developed by the OAU from its excavations in the 1970s. In outline, features like a ditch were assigned a unique number, which would be used as a reference for both the fills and the cut (see above, Chapter 1, for a detailed description). A section excavated across the ditch would be assigned a letter, and the individual fills within the cut would then be given a number. Thus, for instance, the third layer within the first section across a ditch given the number 500, would be described as 500/A/3. In theory, the system provided the ability to recognise individual layers within each cut. However, the distinctions between different layers within ditch fills were frequently extremely difficult to distinguish, and the system tends to give primacy to the recognition of the ditch as the fundamental archae-ological entity. The result of these factors is that finds were often collected merely by their feature number and section letter, and were not separated into the discrete layers of the fill.

This fact means that it is not possible to examine the pottery at the detailed level of individual fills within ditches which might enable a closer analysis of the problems of redeposition. While this might seem regrettable, several points indicate that adverse criticism of the recording system and of the retrieval systems might be misplaced. First, it is apparent from the pottery assemblages from ditches where only one fill was distinguishable, that significant quantities of pottery were redeposited. In some cases all five Ceramic Groups are represented in the assemblage. Secondly, the low finds density on the site, and the concerns over redeposition, have meant that assemblages from individual fills are simply too small to provide any form of reliable dating. Indeed, the pottery data from ditches which form parts of an enclosure have had to be amalgamated in order to form an assemblage of sufficient size to provide a relatively reliable date (see Timby, Chapter 4).

This may accentuate the levels of redeposition, as the pottery from earliest fills within a sequence are amalgamated with that from final recuts. However, several observations suggest that this is unlikely to be significant. Enclosures which on the basis of stratigraphy can be dated to a period post-AD 75 (Group 5 pottery), still contain the majority of the five Ceramic Groups (eg Table A2.5, enclosures 29, 30, 36, 37 and Fig. A2.5). Also, excavations at Gravelly Guy, Stanton Harcourt, Oxon. (Lambrick and Allen forthcoming) and Mount Farm, Berinsfield, Oxon. (Lambrick pers. comm.), both Iron Age and Roman gravel sites in the Upper Thames Valley, have shown that there was no consistent chronological distinction or pattern in the finds from the earliest to the latest cuts within complex ditch sequences. Indeed, it was against the background of the different previous and contemporary excavation strategies used on other large gravel sites excavated by the OAU that the methods at Thornhill Farm were adopted. As a consequence, the option of excavating large sections of continuous ditch, as at Gravelly Guy where almost 100% excavation took place to obtain sufficiently large assemblages from individual fills, was not adopted. The experience from previous excavations, the low sherd weight, the homogeneity of the deposits across the site and the demonstrable occurrence of redeposited material in late and single-fill ditches and enclosures would seem to validate this decision.

It can be seen that any assessment of redeposition is at best based on a series of interpretative judgements, and is extremely difficult to quantify in a meaningful way for the site as a whole. Table A2.5 quantifies the percentages of each group of pottery for a sample of the enclosures. The sample was chosen on the bases of the assemblage size and the relatively high degree of confidence of the enclo-

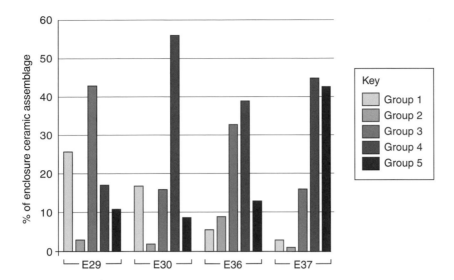

Fig. A2.5   Post AD 75 enclosures containing the majority of Ceramic Groups

sures' dates based on their location in the stratigraphic matrix and their spatial integration with other features. Calculation of the level of redeposition is obviously not straightforward and is prone to circularity of argument. In particular, given that there is a chronological overlap between Group 4 (*c* AD 50–100) and Group 5 (*c* AD 75–120) pottery, it is difficult to decide whether both Ceramic Groups can be considered contemporary with the filling of certain ditches. As a consequence, in the first set of figures in Table A2.5 both Groups 4 and 5 are considered as being contemporary with the filling of the ditch; the second set of figures (shown in brackets) separates the Group 4 and 5 material in those instances where it is thought that a later date is valid, thus tending to produce higher figures of redeposition. The average percentage has been calculated for each set of figures, although the standard deviations indicate that the range of the samples is large and as a result the averages are of limited value in characterising the site-wide levels of redeposition. Indeed, if anything, these statistics indicate what might already be anticipated: that levels of redeposition were highly variable across the site and were dependent on factors like the previous foci of activity and rubbish disposal.

It might be possible to produce 'contour' maps of the density of pottery for each group, revealing the variable intensity of previous activity and rubbish disposal, and this was undertaken for the Group 1 pottery. However, the results were equivocal (see Chapter 3 'Distribution of redeposited Group 1 pottery'), and it was not thought worthwhile to pursue this line of analysis, given the investment of time that would be required to undertake this task adequately.

The discussion within this appendix has focused on defining the central process which structured the form of the pottery assemblage found on the site, in order that the limitations and constraints of the pottery dating can be understood. While it is to be anticipated that there were a variety of rubbish disposal strategies adopted on the site, it has been argued that the major mechanism which resulted in the pottery being deposited in the archaeological features involved the material being exposed to trampling and other processes of disturbance after initial deposition on the ground surface prior to its secondary incorporation in the ditch or pit fills. In terms of dating this means that sherd size cannot be taken as indicative of whether the pottery is redeposited or contemporary with the filling of the feature, as the process of breakage was completed prior to its incorporation in the ditch fill.

Analysis has shown that the levels of redeposition are potentially high but variable across the site. In terms of our use of the pottery for phasing the site, these factors introduce a degree of caution in our appraisal of dates provided by the pottery. It would be difficult to express the variability of our confidence in the dating in rigid terminology, and it is unclear whether this would be useful. The pottery specialist considered that, as a rule of thumb, an assemblage should consist of at least 30 sherds if one is to feel relatively confident that it provides an accurate date (see Timby, Chapter 4). In a number of cases, in order to satisfy this criterion for an enclosure, pottery data had to be amalgamated from all of its constituent contexts. Elsewhere, even though the assemblages are of insufficient size, the dating evidence provided by the pottery is used to phase the site, while its decreased reliability is openly acknowledged. In certain instances our confidence may be increased by the combination of the limited pottery data with evidence for spatial organisation or stratigraphic information. In this way, a best-fit hypothesis, using all of the available evidence, enabled phasing of the site as a whole.

Table A2.5 Quantification of redeposition

Enclosure	Ceramic Groups					Residual secondary refuse %		Secondary refuse %		Intrusive
	Group 1%	Group 2%	Group 3%	Group 4%	Group 5%					
1	23	0	55	22	0	23	(78)	22	(22)	
2	2	4	38	49	7	6	(44)	87	(56)	(7)
6	4	0	10	52	34	66		34		
7	1	2	6	8	83	17		83		
8	13	13	49	25	0	75		25		
9a	0	4	19	71	6	23		77	(71)	(6)
9b	9	0	10	80	1	19		81	(80)	(1)
9c	18	7	24	38	14	48	(86)	52	(14)	
10	1	0	1	90	8	2		98		
11a	2	0	13	50	35	15	(65)	85	(35)	
11b	0	0	5	60	35	5	(65)	95	(35)	
12	9	0	27	63	1	36		64	(63)	(1)
14c	18	0	7	41	34	25	(66)	75	(34)	
15a	1	0	10	78	11	11		89		
15b	2	0	5	30	63	7	(37)	93	(63)	
16	5	0	10	30	55	15	(45)	85	(55)	
26	10	10	3	28	49	23	(51)	77	(49)	
27a	4	0	10	74	12	14		86		
27b	5	0	7	18	70	12	(30)	88	(70)	
29	26	3	43	17	11	72	(89)	28	(11)	
30	17	2	16	56	9	35	(91)	65	(9)	
33c	3	35	18	32	12	56	(88)	44	(12)	
36	6	9	33	39	13	48	(87)	52	(13)	
37	3	1	16	45	35	20	(65)	80	(35)	
104	1	0	2	9	88	3	(12)	97	(88)	
40	62	4	30	0	4	66		30		4
44	10	23	51	14	2	33	(33)	67	(65)	(2)
45	30	3	34	33	0	33	(67)	67	(33)	
46	14	27	23	36	0	41	(64)	59	(36)	
48	3	34	40	22	1	77		23	(22)	(1)
50	10	42	27	18	3	79		21	(18)	(3)
51	5	16	25	54	0	46		54		
57	7	10	37	45	1	54		46	(45)	(1)
58	7	21	65	4	3	28		69		3
60	5	0	71	24	0	5	(76)	95	(24)	
61	26	16	44	5	9	42		44		15
62	1	4	35	59	1	40		60	(59)	(1)
64	3	25	46	26	0	28	(74)	72	(26)	
72	1	6	44	47	2	7	(51)	93	(47)	(2)
73	37	0	63	0	0	37		63		
75	2	5	55	37	1	7	(62)	93	(37)	(1)
76	9	13	62	13	3	22		78	(75)	(3)
81	23	11	34	32	0	68		32		
					Mean	34	54	65	45	
					Standard deviation	23.46	25.75	23.75	25.41	

Appendix 3 Pottery: Description of fabrics and associated forms

by Jane Timby

INTRODUCTION

The fabrics are divided into groups either on the basis of the main tempering agents present (Iron Age material) or by the postulated geographical source of the material (Roman). The following groups are defined for the pre-Roman wares: I calcareous (limestone/fossil-shell tempered); II calcite; III grog; IV rock-tempered; V organic; VI flint and VII sandy. The Roman wares proper are divided into VIII foreign (amphorae, mortaria, finewares); IX regional imports; X local industries and XI source unknown, probably local.

IRON AGE

I. Calcareous

C14: sparse shell-tempered ware.
A black ware with a reddish-brown or grey core. The paste contains a sparse scatter of fossil shell up to 1 mm in size, accompanied by sparse to rare rounded iron compounds, argillaceous pellets and limestone.
Forms: vessels include handmade/wheel-turned necked bowls and jars.

C15: coarse fossil shell-tempered.
A particularly coarse, handmade ware tempered with large fragments of fossil shell, ranging up to 8 mm in size, accompanied by discrete ooliths and limestone rock fragments. The surfaces are generally a reddish-brown with a dark grey inner core.
Forms: handmade slack-sided poorly defined jars/bowls.

C20: other, miscellaneous limestone-tempered wares

C21: Palaeozoic limestone-tempered ware
A moderately soft, generally friable fabric often a reddish-brown in colour with a grey core. The paste contains angular white limestone and calcite up to 1 mm in size. Petrological analyses of similar wares from sites in Gloucestershire have shown the presence of fossil material and indicate a source in the Carboniferous outcrops in the Malvernian area (P Lapuente pers. comm.).
Forms: the fabric almost exclusively occurs as large, handmade storage jars or large diameter hammer-rim bowls (*cf* Spencer 1983, fig. 4). The vessels are undecorated and appear from evidence elsewhere to serve a purely utilitarian function possibly related to heating water (Timby forthcoming). The

ware appears to date from the later 1st century BC and continues to feature in deposits into the 2nd century AD although it is unclear whether the form continued to be manufactured this late.

C22: Palaeozoic limestone-tempered ware
This ware equates with Peacock (1968) fabric B1 and contains a similar mineral suite to fabric C21 above. A source in the Malvern area is likely.
Forms: vessels tend to be black, occasionally brownish in colour and generally occur as handmade jars with thickened rims. Lids are also known. Burnishing is frequently employed both as a surface finish and as a means of decoration.

C23: Palaeozoic limestone-tempered ware with mudstone/shale.
A distinctive variant of fabric C22 with a sparse to moderate frequency of soft argillaceous inclusions, possibly a shale or mudstone.
Forms: similar to C22.

C24: fossil shell and limestone-tempered ware
A reddish-orange, brown or grey ware with a moderate to common frequency of inclusions comprising various fossiliferous fragments: shell, bryozoa, limestone and discrete ooliths. The grade and quantity of inclusions tends to vary from very fine up to 4 mm.
Forms: vessels include various handmade slack-sided jars and bowls, everted rim and beaded rim jars, necked bowls and larger storage vessels. Dates from the middle Iron Age through to the early 1st century AD.

C25
Similar to fabric C14 but with an increased frequency of limestone fragments of Mesozoic origin and some ooliths. Sherds tend to have a black or dark grey surface with a red or grey core.
Forms: include both wheelmade and handmade but wheel-finished vessels, principally necked bowls and beaded rim jars.

C26
A ware superficially identical to fabric C22; a moderately hard black ware with a soapy feel and a limestone temper. The limestone consists of fragments of rock accompanied by fragments of shell and other fossiliferous debris suggesting a Jurassic source. Occasional dark grey rounded argillaceous pellets up to 3 mm across are also present.

Forms: handmade jars.

C27: oolitic limestone-tempered
Hard, black ware with reddish-brown core. Tempered with a common frequency of discrete grains of oolitic limestone up to 1 mm in size.
Forms: handmade and wheel-finished closed forms.

C28: dense sandy ware with sparse limestone
A moderately hard, sandy ware with sparse limestone and fossiliferous inclusions up to 2–3 mm in size. The sand component appears to consist of common to abundant frequency of fairly well-sorted, rounded grains, less than 0.5 mm in size.
Forms: sherds appear to be handmade, probably from jar/bowl forms.

C29: coarse oolitic limestone-tempered ware
A thick-walled dark grey ware with a lighter brown interior and grey core. The paste contains a sparse to common frequency of oolitic limestone rock fragments (ooliths still cemented together) ranging from fine up to 5–6 mm in size.
Forms: poorly formed handmade vessels, probably dating from the mid–late Iron Age or earlier.

II. Calcite-tempered

C31
A moderately hard, grey ware, handmade with a sparse frequency of calcitic inclusions, less than 2 mm in size.

C32
A moderately hard, black ware, similar visually to fabric C22 but tempered with a sparse to moderate frequency of angular calcite fragments. Comparable wares occur on sites around Gloucester (TF30) and at Frocester (TF 7) from perhaps the mid–later 1st century BC and probably into the early 1st century AD.
Forms: handmade jars frequently burnished. Two sherds have curvilinear decoration reminiscent of the Glastonbury style.

III. Grog-tempered (for fabrics E81, E82, E86, E87, E91 see under Wiltshire industries below).

The term 'grog' is used here in a very general sense and is taken to include any material of an argillaceous nature which may be prefired clay, dried clay pellets or naturally occurring compounds.

E80
Miscellaneous grog-tempered wares not classified elsewhere.

E83
A moderately hard, brown or black ware with smooth, soapy surfaces. The paste is tempered with a common frequency of variably sized subangular orange, grey or brown argillaceous fragments, probably 'grog'.
Forms: handmade 'cooking-pot' type jars with internally thickened rims. The exterior is frequently burnished either vertically or horizontally. Comparable wares occur in the Gloucester area in the 1st century AD (Gloucester TF 2A) and around Cirencester (subsumed into Rigby 1982, 156, type fabric 24).

E84
A moderately hard, sometimes softer ware usually in the lighter reddish-brown colour range with a grey or brown core. The paste has an added temper of subangular grog fragments and a natural fine sand temper. Equivalent to Gloucester TF 2C.
Forms: the fabric appears to be used exclusively for large, handmade everted rim storage jars or large diameter hammer-rim bowls comparable to those found in fabric C21 above and discussed by Spencer (1983). The ware appears in the 1st century AD.

E85: grog-tempered native ware
A smooth, soapy ware ranging from a dark reddish-brown through to dark grey or black in colour usually with a darker coloured core. The ware is characterised by a common frequency of argillaceous, rounded to subangular inclusions or variable size. Additional material such as fine organic matter, calcareous fragments and quartz grains is occasionally present.
The fabric is well-known in the Cirencester region (Rigby 1982, 153, fabric 3; Williams 1982, 201, fabric C) and has been noted at Bagendon, The Ditches, North Cerney (Trow 1988, fabric 6) and Lechlade. It does not feature in contemporary deposits on the north side of the Cotswolds in the Gloucester region suggesting that a source for this ware should be sought in the north Wiltshire or south-east Gloucestershire region.
Forms: vessels include handmade, wheel-turned and wheelmade forms and mainly occur as necked bowls. Other forms recorded include various jars, bowls, dishes and rarely beakers.

E88
A very hard ware with a slightly sandy texture and a prominent grog temper. The fabric tends to show a black to dark grey surface colour with a dark red–brown, occasionally light grey, core. The grog temper comprises orange, grey and off-white angular to subangular fragments up to 5 mm in size. Fine rounded grains of quartz sand are visible at x20 magnification.
Forms: used for large handmade storage jars with everted or beaded rims. Probably of 1st century AD date.

E89: flint and grog-tempered ware
A brown, fairly hard ware with a black core and interior surface. The fabric contains a sparse to moderate temper of white, perhaps calcined,

angular flint, up to 1 mm in size, rounded to suban-gular clay pellets, up to 1.5 mm, and rare dark brown iron.
Forms: handmade vessels.

E90: grog and sand-tempered ware
Dark brownish-black ware with a distinctively sandy texture and a sparse to moderate frequency of angular grog up to 2 mm in size. At x20 magnification a common frequency of subangular to rounded, moderately well-sorted quartz sand less than 0.5 mm in size is visible.
Forms: handmade closed forms.

IV. Rock-tempered

E71: coarse Malvernian rock-tempered
A hard, reddish-brown ware with a very coarse rock temper with fragments, mainly angular in shape up to 10 mm in size. The fragments appear to include feldspars, quartzite, biotite mica and sandstones of igneous or metamorphic origin. A source from the pre-Cambrian Malvernian complex would seem likely on macroscopic grounds.
Forms: sherds are very thick-walled (up to 20 mm) and handmade. Possibly Bronze Age urn.

E72: Malvernian rock-tempered ware
A hard, black ware tempered with fragments of Malvernian rock and equating with Peacock (1968) fabric A.
Forms: handmade jars, frequently burnished externally. The ware has a moderately long currency dating from the Iron Age period through to at least the 2nd century AD.

V. Organic-tempered

E10
A moderately hard, dark brown ware with a lighter brown interior and dark grey core. The smooth, soapy fabric is tempered with sparse black organic material and voids, less than 2–3 mm in size, occasional rounded or subangular dark brown clay pellets up to 3 mm and rare calcareous inclusions.
Forms: vessels appear to include wheelmade and handmade/wheel-finished jar and bowl forms.

E11
A moderately hard ware containing finely comminuted organic material, possibly animal dung, and sparse clay pellets, calcareous grains and very fine mica.
Forms: perhaps handmade/wheel-finished closed form.

VI. Flint-tempered

E60: general flint category.

E62: sparse flint-tempered
A hard ware with a sandy texture and occurring in various shades of black, grey and red–brown. The slightly micaceous clay contains sparse white, angular calcined flint (up to 4 mm in size), sparse rounded clay pellets, rare rounded calcareous inclusions (up to 2–3 mm) and fine quartz sand.
Forms: handmade and wheel-finished closed forms.

E63
A moderately hard, occasionally softer, mid greyish-brown ware with a powdery texture. The paste contains a sparse to moderate temper of angular, white, calcined flint (up to 5 mm), sparse rounded dark grey clay pellets (up to 2 mm), and rare organic inclusions.
Forms: wheelmade and handmade/wheel-finished vessels including necked bowls.

VII. Sandy ware

R00: Iron Age sandy ware
A black or brown moderately soft ware with a darker coloured core. Very sandy textured ware with no other visible inclusions.
Forms: thick-walled handmade sherds from cooking jars and bowls probably of mid–later Iron Age date.

ROMAN

VIII. Foreign imports

a) Amphorae

A11: Dressel 20 (*cf* Peacock and Williams 1986, class 25)

A30: Coarse, gritty, unassigned sherds. One unassigned amphora sherd from 1159 is similar to one from Claydon Pike.

A35: A black sand-tempered ware, a Dressel 2–4 from Campania, Italy (Peacock and Williams 1986, class 10).

b) Mortaria

M11: North Gaulish (*cf* Hartley 1977)

c) Finewares

Fabric S: samian
Sherds of both South and Central Gaulish samian are present. Most of the forms appear to date from the Flavian–early Trajanic period, the latest being of Trajanic-early Hadrianic date.
Forms: Drag. 30, Curle 35/36, Drag. 18/31 and Drag. 27.

Two stamped vessels are present:
1. OF.BELLICI. South Gaulish, centrally placed on a Dragendorff 18/31 dish. Late Flavian–early Trajanic.

2. OF.M[ ]. South Gaulish. Dragendorff 18/31. Late Flavian–early Trajanic.

IX. Regional imports

B10: Dorset black-burnished ware (*cf* Gillam 1976)
Forms: jars, straight-sided dish.

X. Local industries

a) Wiltshire industries

E81: Savernake ware (Annable 1962)
A mainly grey ware with a lumpy texture resulting from a common frequency of angular to subangular grog fragments. Other inclusions vary but can include angular flint, calcareous grains, iron and quartz sand. Potential subvariants of this fabric are found below in E82 and E86.
Forms: generally large, handmade storage jars with either beaded, or rounded everted rims. Vessels are usually plain but occasionally show partial surface burnishing or zones of burnished line decoration around the upper body.

E82: Savernake variant
A variant of fabric E81 distinguished by a distinctively sandy texture.
Forms: handmade, wheelmade and handmade/wheel-finished vessels, mainly jars, both everted and beaded rim varieties.

E86: Savernake variant?
A grey, brown, buff or reddish-orange ware with a very soapy feel, tempered with a common frequency of subangular grog. Possibly a variant of Savernake ware or from some closely allied industry.
Forms: large storage jars with beaded or everted rims, necked bowls and lids.

E87
A moderately hard, generally black ware with an orange–brown interior and light grey inner core. Fine sandy temper with a sparse to moderate frequency of subangular to rounded grog/clay pellets, 1 mm and less in size. Probably a product of the Wiltshire industries.
Forms: wheelmade vessels, mainly jars and necked bowls.

E91: Savernake type
A grey, soapy, fabric with a slightly lumpy surface. A slightly finer, more refined version of fabrics E81 and E86.
Forms: mainly wheelmade vessels including necked bowls, beaded rim and everted rim jars. The dating of this ware is not clear but it appears to be in circulation by the later 1st century into the 2nd century.

R13: fine grey sandy ware (Anderson 1978; 1979)
A fine grey sandy ware with no other visible inclusions. Probably a north Wiltshire product.
Forms: wheelmade jars, necked, everted rim and bifid rim types, necked bowls and beakers.

R44: Wiltshire grey sandy ware (Anderson 1979)
Similar to R13 but with a slightly coarser grade of sand.
Forms: wheelmade jars, tankards.

O30: Wiltshire oxidised sandy ware (Anderson 1979)
Oxidized version of R44.

O31
A hard, orange fabric with an orange or a greyish core. The paste contains fine quartz sand and sparse red iron, some of which has caused streaking on the exterior surface.
Forms: a variety of forms were recorded from Roughground Farm, Lechlade, in this fabric (Green and Booth 1993) including flagons, jars, beakers cups, bowls, dishes and lids. It is less common at Thornhill Farm suggesting that production belongs to the latter part of the 1st century and early 2nd century AD. North Wiltshire seems a possible source for this ware.

O32
A fine sandy mid to light orange ware with a distinctive scatter of reddish-brown argillaceous pellets (iron compounds?) throughout. There are no other visible inclusions.
The fabric occurs at Cirencester (TF109) and was recorded at Claydon Pike (fabric 10.7). It does not appear in the Gloucester area suggesting a source somewhere to the south or east of the Cotswolds.
Forms: wheelmade jars.

b) Possible Wiltshire products

R12
A fine grey or black sandy, slightly micaceous ware with rare organic inclusions and rounded argillaceous pellets. A sandier version of fabric R11. A reddish-brown or grey core.
Forms: occurs as necked bowls, jars, tankards and beakers.

R33: wheelmade black-burnished ware
A black sandy ware with a grey or brown core. The matrix contains a common frequency of fine quartz sand and sparse red iron.
Forms: wheelmade wares frequently burnished on the exterior. A wide variety of forms occur in this ware including platters imitating imported 1st century moulded forms, butt beakers, necked jars, bowls, beakers. Later beaker forms carry barbotine dot decoration.
The ware appears to be moderately widespread and is recorded from Cirencester (TF5), Bagendon, Gloucester (TF201) and Frocester (TF32). It first appears during the Neronian period with products

continuing to feature into the early–mid 2nd century AD. The character of the fabric and the distribution pattern suggests a possible source in the Wiltshire/Gloucestershire region.

R34

A black sandy ware with a red–brown core. Similar to fabric R12 but with a slightly coarser, denser grade of sand although still finer than 0.5 mm.
Forms: wheelmade necked bowls, jars, beakers and lids. Probably dating from the later 1st century AD.

R36: well-fired grey ware

A very hard, mid grey ware with an orange or blue–grey core with orange margins. The matrix contains a very sparse scatter of rounded argillaceous pellets and calcareous inclusions or voids with calcareous lining.
Forms: wheelmade closed forms, mainly jars and bowls.

R46

A hard, buff to dark grey ware with a pimply sandy fabric. The paste contains a common to moderate frequency of well-sorted, rounded quartz sand less than 1 mm in size, rare to sparse rounded dark grey clay pellets and rare calcareous inclusions again less than 1 mm in size.
Forms: wheelmade necked jars, beakers and lids.

R47

A grey to off-white sandy ware with dark grey rounded clay pellets. When worn the surfaces of the sherds present a grey speckled appearance. The matrix contains a common frequency of ill-sorted quartz sand (less than 0.5 mm in size), sparse clay pellets (up to 2 mm) and rare angular flint (up to 2 mm).
Forms: jars

O33

A moderately hard, orange sandy ware with macro-scopically visible ill-sorted quartz grains accompanied by rare red iron and clay pellets.
Forms: bowls, jars. Vessels with high relief white painted decoration have been recorded from Claydon Pike. A source in north Wiltshire or south Oxfordshire is likely for this ware.

O35

A moderately hard, dark brownish-orange finely micaceous ware with sparse red iron and rare ferruginous sandstone.
Forms: at Roughground Farm, Lechlade, this fabric featured as jars, bowls, cups and lids (Green and Booth 1993, fabric 13.6).

c) Oxfordshire industries

R11: fine grey sandy ware (Young 1977, 202)
A fine grey sandy ware with a sparse frequency of dark grey or brown rounded clay pellets and rare iron.

Forms: wheelmade necked jars and bowls, squat flanged bowls and beakers.

W22: Oxfordshire whiteware (Young 1977, 93)
No featured sherds.

d) Severn Valley and allied wares

R48: charcoal-tempered Severn Valley ware
A generally grey ware with a very similar clay type to fabric O41 but distinguished by moderate to common frequency of black organic material, possibly charcoal. A similar fabric is well-known in the Gloucester area (TF17).
Forms: Vessels are both handmade and wheelmade. The former generally occur as large storage jars; the latter as necked jars and bowls, carinated bowls and dishes.

R49: reduced Severn Valley ware
A grey fired version of the more common oxidised (orange) Severn Valley ware (fabric O43).
Forms: as O43.

O40: general Severn Valley ware types not classified elsewhere.

O41: Severn Valley ware charcoal-tempered oxid-ised version of R48.

O42: handmade Severn Valley ware variant of O43 used exclusively for large storage jars (Glos TF 23).

O43: Severn Valley ware proper (Glos TF 11B; Webster 1976).
Forms: necked bowls, wide-mouthed and narrow necked jars, tankards, carinated cups and beakers.

O47: Severn Valley ware variant. A very finely micaceous, orange ware with few visible inclusions. Forms as above.

O49: Severn Valley ware variant with a marked grog component. The orange ware has a grey core and a soapy feel. The paste contains a moderate temper of subangular grog up to 1.5 mm in size.
Forms: wheelmade vessels.

XI. Source unknown, probably local

O12

A moderately soft ware with a brownish-orange exterior and core and pale orange interior. The paste has a fine sandy texture and contains very fine white mica, sparse red iron and rare white possibly calcareous inclusions.
Forms: wheelmade closed forms.

O28

A sandy micaceous ware with a brownish-red to dark grey exterior and dark grey core. The paste contains a moderate frequency of ill-sorted,

rounded, polished quartz grains (up to 1 mm in size), sparse fine white mica and rare red iron.
Forms: an uncommon ware, the only recorded form being a bowl or dish with post-firing perforations.

O44

A very fine, well-levigated, smooth orange ware with no added temper. No visible inclusions.
Forms: a wheelmade ware, rare at Thornhill Farm but better represented at Roughground Farm, Lechlade (Green and Booth 1993, fabric 13.2), where it featured as flagons, jars, beakers, bowls, dishes and lids.

O45

A very fine, moderately hard, orange ware with a smooth, soapy feel. The only visible inclusions in the matrix are sparse rounded iron grains ranging up to 2 mm in size.
The fabric has been recorded from Cirencester (Rigby 1982, fabric 19) and Claydon Pike (Booth forthcoming, fabric 10.5).
Forms: the ware occurs in deposits post-dating AD 55 at Cirencester, and features as flagons and honeypots.

O46

A very fine, smooth orange ware with a dark grey core. The finely micaceous clay matrix is characterized by a scatter of white calcareous specks less than 0.5 mm in size.
Forms: the only form recorded in this fabric is a ring-necked flagon. A small number of sherds were also recorded from Roughground Farm, Lechlade (Green and Booth 1993, fabric 13.3).

O83

A hard, sandy reddish-orange ware with a light brown interior. The matrix is characterised by a moderate frequency of highly visible well-sorted rounded quartz sand, 1 mm in size.
Forms: no featured sherds.

R22: black sandy ware

A hard, dark grey–black ware with a grey core with red–brown margins. The fabric contains a common frequency of ill-sorted round quartz sand ranging in size from very fine to 0.5 mm in size and sparse fine red iron.
Forms: wheelmade necked bowls and jars.

R23: sand-tempered ware with quartzite

A medium grade sandy ware with rare but prominent grains of subangular quartzite up to 5 mm in size and rare rounded calcareous inclusions. Generally brown or black in colour.
Forms: thick-walled, handmade closed forms.

R24: sand-tempered ware with iron

A medium grade sand-tempered ware with rare but prominent rounded red–brown iron inclusions up to 2 mm in size. The surfaces are generally a reddish-brown with a dark grey core.
Forms: beaded rim bowl and necked everted rim jar/bowl.

R26

A hard, black sandy ware tempered with a sparse to common frequency of moderately well-sorted, rounded polished quartz sand up to 1 mm in size.
Forms: wheelmade jars, bowls, lids, and platters.

R27

A hard, black sandy ware with a dark grey core. The fabric contains a sparse to moderate frequency of ill-sorted, rounded, quartz sand ranging from fine to 2 mm in size
Forms: bowls, jars.

W20: general whiteware sandy category

W24: white sandy ware

A greyish or yellowish white, moderately hard, medium grade sandy ware. The only visible inclusions are those of a moderate to common frequency of ill-sorted rounded quartz sand ranging up to 1 mm in size. A similar fabric has been recorded from Roughground Farm Lechlade (Green and Booth 1993, fabric 10.2) and Claydon Pike (fabric 8.4).
Forms: no featured sherds but noted as jars and bowls elsewhere.

Appendix 4   Palaeopathology

by Marsha Levine, L B Jeffcott and K E Whitwell

INTRODUCTION

Nineteen abnormal anatomical elements were recovered from Thornhill Farm. Some were pathological, while others are better described as abnormal or even merely unusual. Because none of these elements come from complete skeletons – indeed, most were solitary – detailed diagnoses are not possible. Moreover, because animal palaeopathology, as a field of study, is relatively new, we hardly know what we can learn from such assemblages. Nevertheless, it is important to start building up a body of data which will in the future help us to better understand human–animal relationships. Unfortunately, resources are available here for only a relatively superficial investigation of the data.

EQUID

454/C/1 (Record no. 3689)

Lower P3/4, right. There is a growth at the base of the crown on the lingual surface. The aetiology for this condition is unknown

151/A (Group 17, Record no. 702–4)

Left metatarsal, central, 3rd and 4th (fragment) tarsals fused together. This is a case of spavin. There is a proliferation of periarticular new bone around the proximal end of the metatarsal and on the tarsals, the joint surfaces of which have fused together and have collapsed proximo-distally. The damage could have been caused initially by a trauma or sprain and developed over a relatively long period of time. There are no fracture lines, so it does not appear to have developed in response to a fracture. This horse would have been lame and must have gone through a period of total disuse when the damage first occurred.

2530/A/2 (Group 15, Record no. 674)

Right metatarsal fused to 3rd tarsal. This horse had a very serious, chronic osteoarthropathy, possibly of an infective nature. There is an extensive development of new bone around and throughout the whole joint. The inflammation would have extended into the substance of the bone. This condition would have been very painful and would have incapacitated the animal. It could have resulted from an injury that went septic. The animal would have been very lame.

The question arises of why such an animal would have been kept alive for such a long time. One possibility is that it could have been suckling a foal. If the injury had occurred when the horse was six months pregnant, by the time it had suckled its foal for another six months, the condition would have had time to develop. A second possibility is that the horse could have survived out of sheer neglect.

CATTLE

2040/A (Record no. 4673)

Left, upper 3rd molar, with V-shaped wear on its occlusal surface. This rather old cow was not masticating properly.

601/A (Record no. 4674)

Left, upper 3rd molar, with V-shaped wear on its occlusal surface. This rather old cow was not masticating properly.

727/B/3 (Group 312, Record no. 4395–4407)

Left mandible. The P2 has apparently not developed. There is a gap between the P3 and the P4. The M3 has only two segments. The P4 and the M1 are crowded. This type of variability in the dentition should be described as a developmental variant rather than an abnormality. It is relatively common at Thornhill Farm and at other sites.

250/H (Group 334, Record no. 4522–6)

Right mandible. This is another good example of an individual with a variant dentition. The P2 apparently did not develop. The M3 has only two segments.

197/A/3 (Record no. 2260)

Left scapula. The glenoid cavity is irregular, roughened and not as round as it should be. There is some osteophyte formation, but the surface of the bone is not seriously eroded. This condition could be described as a rather minor arthropathy, perhaps caused by early osteoarthritis or joint disease, resulting from wear to the joint capsule. The damage could perhaps have been caused either by an injury to the right foot, or possibly by the use of the animal for traction.

4028/A/1 (Record no. 2007)

Left pelvis, acetabulum. This bone is slightly abnormal. The antero-medial notch is partly overgrown with bone, but the acetabular fossa is still relatively deep. Such a condition is not incompatible with use of the animal for work, but there are many other causes for abnormalities of the acetabulum.

803/B/2 (Record no. 2003)

Left pelvis, acetabulum. The antero-medial notch is bridged-over by bone leaving a foramen. The acetabular fossa is relatively shallow, and there is some evidence of eburnation. This kind of osteoarthropathy can develop because a shallow hip joint is relatively easy to disarticulate. It is compatible with use of the animal for work. However, again it is important to remember that there are many other causes for abnormalities of the acetabulum.

456/C/2 (Record no. 2106)

Left pelvis, acetabulum. Because of the high level of post-mortem damage sustained by this bone, its identification as cattle is uncertain but probable. Even in its incomplete state it is possible to say that there was a minor arthropathy on the acetabulum.

2396/E/1 (Record no. 268)

Right central metacarpal, fused to the fully ossified 5th metacarpal. It is unusual for the 5th metacarpal to fuse to the central metacarpal but normal.

2396/E/1 (Group 24, Record no. 797)

Left navicular cuboid (central + 4th tarsal) fused to 2nd + 3rd tarsal. This individual's tarsal bones were ankylosed and the 3rd and central tarsals had collapsed. The condition might possibly be developmental or related to breed. It does not seem to be the result of an infection.

1122/G (Record no. 382)

Right metatarsal. There is proliferative bone development on the lateral surface of the distal shaft. The new bone is located where metatarsal 4 would have articulated with the central metatarsal. It might have resulted from some kind of insult to the bone.

SHEEP

164/A (Group 145, Record no. 2899)

Left maxillary cheekteeth. The crowding of the M1 and the M2 has caused abnormal wear to the occlusal surface of these teeth. The unusually heavy accumulation of cementum and the flaring out of the roots could have resulted from a root infection.

202/A/4 (Record no. 6074)

Right mandible. Unilateral periodontal disease resulted from a gingival pocket full of food becoming septic. The resulting infection of the 2nd molar root has resulted in an abscess, with local inflammation, and osteomyelitis.

590/A/2 (Record no. 909)

Left calcaneum. New bone has developed on the groove for the deep flexor tendon. This may have been the result of damage to the superficial flexor tendon. Alternatively, the new bone could be a pressure facet, caused by the tendon putting heavier than usual pressure on the bone, thus causing a false joint to form.

This damage might have been caused by the animal's posture, if, for example, the animal held its leg in an unusual position for a long period of time, because of damage to the tendon or because of some other site of pain. This lesion was probably not a serious problem for the sheep.

DOG

323/I/1 (Record no. 978)

Dog tibia. The diaphysis of this bone is curved, but it is not pathological since its growth plates are normal. The bone probably belongs to a small chondrodystrophoid , that is, bandy-legged, terrier breed, intermediate in shape between a Pekinese (chondrodystrophoid) and a Pomeranian (non-chondrodystrophoid; John Grandage, pers. comm.).

113/I1 (Group 106, Record no. 2559)

Dog mandible. Because of its very poor preservation, it is very difficult to make sense of this specimen. The M1 was shed and its alveolus almost filled in with bone. The P2, 3 and 4 are present. Inflammation resulted in new bone growth on the mandibular ramus. There are no gingival pockets or loosening of the teeth around the premolars.

Abnormal bone growth may result when there is insufficient calcium or too much phosphorus in the diet. Dogs that are fed too much meat may develop new bone. Alternatively, the swelling might have resulted from osteomyelitis, that is, a septic tooth.

Appendix 5
Hypothetical Adjustment Curve for Cattle

by Marsha Levine

Using 3 years as the age when the permanent dentition is complete in cattle, the formula for the hypothetical cattle adjustment curve can be written as follows:

$y=(2x+1)/6$ (or $y=.33x+0.167$) where:

The slope of the curve is 0.33
The y intercept is 0.167
x is the average age for each year (ie 0.5, 1.5, 2.5).

Curve C is the number of cheekteeth in an adult dentition divided by the average number of cheekteeth in each age class up to 3 years of age (that is, at 0.5, 1.5 and 2.5 years; Table A5.1 and Fig. A5.1). Curve A, the adjustment factor, is a line plotted between two points on C: at the insection of 1.00 on the y axis and at 2.5 years on the x axis when the dentition is complete; and at the intersection of 0.67 (6/9) on the y axis and 1.5 on the x axis when the maximum number of teeth are in the jaw (Table A5.1).

Because no teeth are known to be definitely fetal, teeth which might possibly be fetal teeth are added

Table A5.1   Data for Cattle Adjustment Curve (Figure A5.1)

Age in years	No. of well developed mandibular cheekteeth	Curve C	Curve A
0.0	3	2.00	0.17
0.5	5	1.20	0.33
1.0	6	1.00	0.50
1.5	9	0.67	0.67
2.0	8	0.75	0.83
2.5	6	1.00	1.00
3.0	6	1.00	1.00

to those 0–1 year old. Then, in order to determine the average adjusted frequency of the teeth in each age class from birth to 3 years of age, the original frequency of the teeth in each age class (from 0 to 3 years) is multiplied by 1/0.167+0.33 (average age). The 'average age', for example, of teeth 0–1 year old is 0.5 years.

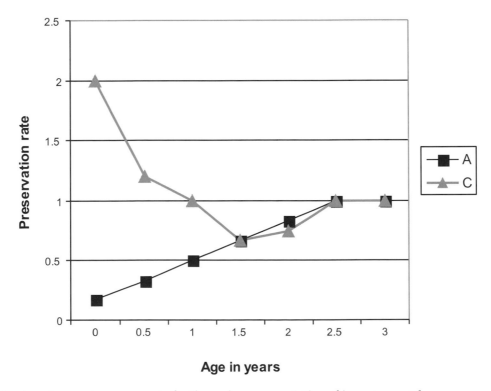

Fig. A5.1   Adjustment curve to compensate for the under–representation of immature cattle

Appendix 6
Context and Feature Table for Small Finds

Context	Feature	Trench	Structure/enclosure	Phase	Context	Feature	Trench	Structure/enclosure	Phase
3	Layer	-	-	-	689	Ditch	7	-	-
101	Ditch	7	E9	E	722	Ditch	7	E155	F
110	Ditch	7	Trackway 301	G	761	Pit	7	-	-
113	Gully	7	-	-	776	Pit	7	-	-
116	Gully	7	E9	E	795	Ditch	7	-	-
121	Finds ref	7	-	-	801	Gully	8	-	-
133	Ditch	7	E8	-	802	Gully	8	-	-
145	Gully	7	-	-	803	Ditch	8	E120	A
146	Ditch	7	-	-	840	Ditch	8	E300	-
166	Pit	7	-	-	847	Gully	8	-	-
176	Pit	7	E9	E	855	Ditch	8	-	-
179	Pit	7	-	-	859	Ditch	-	-	-
192	Ditch	7	E11	F	872	Pit	8	-	A
197	Ditch	7	-	-	877	Ditch	8	E125	D
214	Finds Ref	7	-	-	897	Ditch	-	-	-
221	Ditch	7	E11	F	899	Ditch	8	E127	D
235	Ditch	7	E5	C	913	Ditch	8	-	-
311	Layer	0	-	-	927	Gully	8	-	-
313	Ditch	7	-	-	937	Ditch	8	-	-
322	Ditch	7	E30	F	942	Gully	8	-	-
323	Ditch	7	E30	F	1021	Ditch	7	-	-
334	Ditch	7	E29	F	1037	Ditch	7	-	-
344	Ditch	7	-	-	1039	Ditch	7	-	-
365	Ditch	7	E29	F	1046	Ditch	7	E36	F
372	Layer	7	-	-	1051	Ditch	7	E37	F
389	Ditch	7	E27	E	1073	Ditch	7	E33	E
397	Gully	7	E152	C	1080	Ditch	7	E37	F
402	Ditch	7	-	-	1088	Ditch	7	-	-
431	Ditch	7	-	E	1091	Ditch	7	E37	F
456	Gully	7	-	-	1123	Ditch	7	E35	F
458	Gully	7	E26	E	1158	Finds ref	7	-	-
459	Ditch	7	E29	F	2011	Ditch	9	E61	C
462	Ditch	7	E14	E	2016	Ditch	9	E58	D
465	Ditch	7	E15	E	2020	Ditch	9	E86	D
468	Gully	7	E54	F	2042	Ditch	9	E68	-
470	Ditch	7	-	-	2052	Ditch	9	S201	C
489	Ditch	7	E154	F	2064	Ditch	9	E62	E
524	Pit	7	-	-	2071	Ditch	9	E76	D
526	Gully	7	E15	E	2085	Natural	9	-	-
528	Ditch	7	E16	F	2090	Ditch	9	E62	E
536	Ditch	7	E27	E	2214	Ditch	9	E47	-
537	Ditch	7	E27	E	2239	Ditch	9	E49	D
537	Ditch	7	E27	E	2268	Ditch	9	-	-
569	Gully	7	-	-	2274	Gully	9	E74	C
612	Pit	7	E25	-	2284	Ditch	9	E48	D
620	Ditch	7	E34	-	2292	Ditch	9	E57	D
630	Ditch	7	-	-	2295	Ditch	9	-	-
643	Pit	7	-	-	2314	Pit/ditch	9	-	-
653	Ditch	7	E33	E	2325	Gully	9	-	-
670	Ditch	7	-	-	2352	Post hole	9	-	-

Context	Feature	Trench	Structure/ enclosure	Phase
2371	Ditch	9	E49	D
2374	Ditch	9	E46	C
2379	Post hole	9	E 45	D
2396	Ditch	9	-	-
2426	Pit	9	-	-
2471	Pit	9	-	-
2515	Ditch	9	E87	C/D
2516	Ditch	9	-	-
2522	Gully	9	E44	D
3004	Layer	22	-	-
3006	Layer	22	-	-
3046	Ditch	22	E50	E
3077	Ditch	22	E150	C
3106	Grave	22	-	-
3173	Post hole	22	-	-
3195	Ditch	22	E57	D
3197	Post hole	22	-	-
3200	Ditch	22	E54	D
3213	Ditch	22	-	-
3215	Ditch	22	E64	E
3235	Ditch	22	E98	D
3253	Ditch	22	-	-
3286	Pit	22	-	-
3316	Pit	22	-	-
3375	Pit	22	-	-

Bibliography

Amour-Chelu, M and Clutton-Brock, J, 1985 Notes on the evidence for the use of cattle as draught animals at Etton, *Antiq J* **65/2**, 297–302

Allen, T G, 1990 *An Iron Age and Romano-British enclosed settlement at Watkins Farm, Northmoor, Oxon*, Thames Valley Landscapes: the Windrush Valley 1, Oxford Archaeology

Allen, T G, 1991 An 'oppidum' at Abingdon, Oxfordshire, *South Midlands Archaeol* **21**, 97–9

Allen, T G, 1997 Abingdon: West Central Redevelopment Area, *South Midlands Archaeol* **27**, 47–54

Allen, T G, 2000 The Iron Age background, in *Roman Oxfordshire* (M Henig and P Booth), 1–33, Gloucestershire

Allen, T G, and Robinson, M A, 1993 *The prehistoric landscape and Iron Age enclosed settlement at Mingies Ditch, Hardwick-with-Yelford, Oxon*, Thames Valley Landscapes: the Windrush Valley 2, Oxford Archaeology

Allen, T, Miles, D and Palmer, S, 1984 Iron Age buildings in the Upper Thames region, in *Aspects of the Iron Age in central southern Britain* (eds B Cunliffe and D Miles), 89–101, Oxford

Allen, T G, Darvill, T C, Green, L S and Jones, M U, 1993 *Excavations at Roughground Farm, Lechlade, Gloucestershire: a prehistoric and Roman landscape*, Thames Valley Landscapes: the Cotswold Water Park 1, Oxford Archaeology

Anderson, A S, 1978 Wiltshire fine wares, in *Early fine wares in Roman Britain* (eds P Arthur and G Marsh) BAR Brit. Ser. **57**, 373–92, Oxford

Anderson, A S, 1979 *The Roman pottery industry of north Wiltshire*, Swindon Archaeol Soc Rep 2

Annable, F K, 1962 A Romano-British pottery in Savernake Forest, kilns 1–2, *Wiltshire Archaeol Nat Hist Mag* 58, 142–55

Atkinson, D, 1942 *Report on excavations at Wroxeter (the Roman city of Viroconium) in the county of Salop, 1923–1927*, Oxford

Atkinson, R J C, 1941 A Romano-British potters' field at Cowley, Oxon., *Oxoniensia* 6, 9–21

Atkinson, R J C, 1942 Archaeological sites on Port Meadow, Oxford, *Oxoniensia* 7, 24–35

Barrett, J and Bradley, R J, 1980 The later Bronze Age in the Thames Valley, in *Settlement and society in the British later Bronze Age* (eds J Barrett and R Bradley), BAR Brit. Ser. **83/1**, 247–269, Oxford

Bartosiewicz, L and van Neer, V, 1997 *Draught cattle: their osteological identification and history*, Annales, Musée Royal de l'Afrique Centrale, Sciences Zoologiques **281**, Tervuren

Benson, D and Miles, D, 1974 *The Upper Thames Valley: an archaeological survey of the river gravels*, OAU Survey **2**, Oxford

Black, E W, 1994 Villa owners: Romano-British gentlemen and officers, *Britannia* **25**, 99–110

Boessneck, J, 1969 Osteological differences between sheep (*Ovis aries* linne) and goats (*Capra hircus* linne), in *Science in Archaeology* (2nd edn, eds D Brothwell and E Higgs), 331–358, London

Boon, G C, 1969 Belgic and Roman Silchester: the excavations of 1954–8, with an excursus on the early history of Calleva, *Archaeolog* **102**, 1–81

Boon, G C and Savory, H N, 1975 A silver trumpet-brooch with relief decoration, parcel gilt, from Carmarthen, and a note on the development of the type, *Antiq J* **55**, 41–61

Booth, P, forthcoming, The Roman pottery from Claydon Pike, in Miles *et al.* forthcoming

Boyle, A, Dodd, A, Miles, D, and Mudd, A, 1995 *Two Oxfordshire Anglo-Saxon Cemeteries: Berinsfield and Didcot*, Thames Valley Landscapes Monograph No. **8**, Oxford Archaeology

Boyle, A, Jennings, D, Miles, D and Palmer, S, 1998 *The Anglo-Saxon cemetery at Butler's Field, Lechlade, Gloucestershire*, Thames Valley Landscapes **10**, Oxford Archaeology

Brailsford, J W, 1962 *Hod Hill, 1, Antiquities from Hod Hill in the Durden collection*, London

Brain, C K, 1967 Hottentot food remains and their bearing on the interpretation of fossil bone assemblages, *Scientific Papers of the Namib Desert Research Station* **32**, 1–7

Brain, C K, 1969 The contribution of Namib Desert Hottentots to an understanding of Australopithecine bone accumulations, *Scientific Papers of the Namib Desert Research Station* **39**, 13–22

Brain, C K, 1976 Some principles in the interpretation of bone accumulations associated with man, in *Human origins: Louis Leakey and the East African evidence* (eds G L Isaac and E McCown), Perspectives in Human Evolution **3**, Menlo Park, California

Brain, C K, 1981 *The hunters or the hunted?*, Chicago

Brodribb A C C, Hands, A R, and Walker, D R, 1972 *Excavations at Shakenoak Farm, near Wilcote, Oxfordshire*, Part III, *site F*, privately printed

Brothwell, D R, 1981 *Digging up bones* (3rd edn), London and Oxford

Brown, L, 1984 Objects of stone, in *Danebury, an Iron Age Hillfort in Hampshire 2, the excavations of 1969–1978: the finds* (ed. B Cunliffe), CBA Res Rep **52**, London

Brown, W A B and Christofferson, P V, 1960 Postnatal tooth development in cattle, *American Journal of Veterinary Research* XXI/80, 7–34

Brown, D H, 1997 The social significance of imported medieval pottery, in *Not so much a pot, more a way of life* (eds C Cumberpatch and P Blinkhorn), Oxbow Monograph **83**, Oxford, 95–112

Bull, G and Payne, S, 1982 Tooth eruption and epiphysial fusion in pigs and wild boar, in Wilson *et al.* 1982, 55–71, Oxford

Bushe-Fox, J P, 1916 *Third report on the excavations on the site of the Roman town at Wroxeter, Shropshire, in 1914*, Reports of the Research Committee of the Society of Antiquaries of London **4**, Oxford

Bushe-Fox, J P, 1932 *Third report on the excavations of the Roman fort at Richborough, Kent*, Reports of the Research Committee of the Society of Antiquaries of London **10**, Oxford

Campion, G F, 1938 Roman relics found at Broxtowe, *The Thoroton Society of Nottinghamshire, Excavation Section*, Third Annual Report for the year 1938, 6–18

Caughley, G, 1966 Mortality patterns in mammals, *Ecology* **58**, 906–18

Clapham, A R, Tutin, T G and Moore, D M, 1987 *Flora of the British Isles* (3rd edn), Cambridge

Clarke, S, 1996 Acculteration and continuity: re-assessing the significance of Romanization in the hinterlands of Gloucester and Cirencester, in *Roman imperialism: post-colonial perspectives* (eds J Webster and N Cooper), Leicester Archaeological Monograph **3**, 71–84

Clifford, E M, 1961 *Bagendon: a Belgic oppidum: a record of the excavations 1954–56*, Cambridge

Coe, D, Jenkins, V and Richards, J, 1991 Cleveland Farm, Ashton Keynes: Second Interim Report: Investigations May–August 1989, *Wiltshire Archaeological and Natural History Magazine* **84**, 40–50

Connor, A and Buckley, R, 1999 *Roman and medieval occupation in Causeway Lane, Leicester: excavations 1980 and 1991*, Leicester

Cool, H E M, (forthcoming) The small finds from Claydon Pike in Miles *et al.* forthcoming

Cracknell, S and Mahany, C (eds), 1994 *Roman Alcester: southern extramural area, 1964–1966 excavations*, Part 2, *finds and discussion*, Roman Alcester Series **1**; CBA Res Rep **96**, London

Creighton, J, 2000 *Coins and power in late Iron Age Britain*, Cambridge

Cromarty, A M, Foreman, S and Murray, P, 1999 The excavation of a later Iron Age enclosed settlement at Bicester Fields Farm, Bicester, Oxon., *Oxoniensia* **LXIV**, 153–234

Crummy, N, 1983 *The Roman small finds from excavations in Colchester, 1971–9*, Colchester Archaeological Report **2**, Colchester

Cunliffe, B, 1971 *Excavations at Fishbourne, 1961–1969*, Volume II, *the finds*, Reports of the Research Committee of the Society of Antiquaries of London **27**, Leeds

Cunliffe, B, 1984 *Danebury: an Iron Age hillfort in Hampshire* **2**, *the excavations 1969–78: the finds*, CBA Res Rep **52**, London

Cunliffe, B W, 1991 *Iron Age communities in Britain* (3rd edn), London

Cunliffe, B W, 1998 *Fishbourne Roman palace*, Stroud

Curle, J, 1911 *A Roman frontier post and its people: the fort of Newstead in the parish of Melrose*, Glasgow

Dahl, G and Hjort, A, 1976 *Having herds: pastoral herd growth and household economy*, Stockholm

Dannell, G B and Wild, J P, 1987 *Longthorpe II, the military works-depot: an episode in landscape history*, Britannia Monograph Series **8**, London

Darlington, J and Evans, J, 1992 *Roman Sidbury, Worcester: excavations 1959–1989*, Transactions of the Worcestershire Archaeological Society **13**, 5–104

Darvill, T C, 1987 *Prehistoric Gloucestershire*, County Library Series, Gloucester

Darvill, T C, Hingley, R C, Jones, M U and Timby, J R, 1986 A Neolithic and Iron Age site at The Loders, Lechlade, Gloucestershire, *Trans Bristol Gloucestershire Archaeol Soc* **104**, 23–44

Darvill, T C and Holbrook, N, 1994 The Cirencester area in the prehistoric and early Roman periods, in *Cirencester: town and landscape. An urban archaeological assessment* (eds T C Darvill, and C Gerrard), Cirencester, 47–56

Debard, E, 1979 Le gisement Pléistocène Supérieur de la grotte de Jaurens, à Nespouls, Corrèze, France: étude sédimentologique du remplissage, *Nouvelles Archives du Muséum d'Histoire Naturelle de Lyon* **17**, 17–24

De Roche C D, 1977 An analysis of selected groups of Early Iron Age pottery from the Oxford Region, Unpubl. B. Litt thesis, Univ. Oxford

Dickinson, T M, 1976 The Anglo-Saxon burial sites of the Upper Thames region, and their bearing on the history of Wessex *c* AD 400–700, unpubl. DPhil thesis, Univ. Oxford

Dobney, K M, Jaques, S D, and Irving, B. 1996 *Of butchers and breeds: report on vertebrate remains from various sites in the City of Lincoln*, Lincoln

Down, A, 1979 *Chichester excavations IV, the Roman villas at Chilgrove and Upmarden*, Chichester

Down, A, 1981 *Chichester excavations V*, Chichester

Dunning, G C, 1976 Salmonsbury, Bourton-on-the-Water, Gloucestershire, in *Hillforts: later prehistoric earthworks in Britain and Ireland* (ed. D W Harding), 76–118, London

Eisenmann, V, 1986 Comparative osteology of modern and fossil horses, half-asses, and asses, in *Equids in the ancient world* (eds R H Meadow and H-P Uerpmann), Beihefte zum Tübinger Atlas des Vorderen Orients, Reihe A, Naturwissenschaften **19**, 67–116, Wiesbaden

Eisenmann, V and Baylac, M, 2000 Extant and

fossil Equus (Mammalia, Perissodactyla) skulls: a morphometric definition of the subgenus Equus, *Zoologica Scripta* **29/2**, 89–100

Eisenmann, V and Beckouche, S, 1986 Identification and discrimination of meta-podials from Pleistocene and modern Equus, wild and domestic, in *Equids in the ancient world* (eds R H Meadow and H-P Uerpmann), 117–163

Elsdon, S, 1994 The Iron Age pottery, in *Crickley Hill: the hillfort defences* (ed. P Dixon), 203–41, Nottingham

Ewbank, J M, Phillipson, D W, Whitehouse, R D and Higgs, E S, 1964 Sheep in the Iron Age: a method of study, *Proc Prehist Soc* **30**, 423–36

Fasham, P J, 1987 *A Banjo enclosure at Micheldever Wood, Hampshire*, Hampshire Field Club Monograph **5**, Winchester

Faulkner, N, 2000 *The decline and fall of Roman Britain*, Stroud

Fell, C I, 1961a, The Shenberrow Hill Camp, Stanton, Gloucestershire, *Trans Bristol Gloucestershire Archaeol Soc* **80**, 16–24

Fell, C I, 1961b, The coarse pottery, in *Bagendon, a Belgic oppidum: a record of the excavations, 1954–56*, (E M Clifford), 212–67, Cambridge

Fell, C I, 1964 The pottery, in Early Iron Age pottery from Rodborough Common and Duntisbourne Abbots (E M Clifford), *Trans Bristol Gloucestershire Archaeol Soc* **83**, 145–6

Finberg, H P R, 1955 *Gloucestershire: The history of a landscape*, London

Finberg, H P R, 1975 *The Gloucestershire landscape*, London

Fitzpatrick, A P, 1997 *Archaeological excavations on the route of the A27 Westhampnett bypass, west Sussex, 1992, 2, the late Iron Age, Romano-British, and Anglo-Saxon cemeteries*, Wessex Archaeology Report **12**, Salisbury

Fox, A, 1952 *Roman Exeter (Isca Dumnoniorum): excavations in the war damaged areas, 1945–47*, Manchester

France, N E and Gobel, B, 1985 *The Romano-British temple at Harlow*, Gloucester

French, C A I, 1994 *The Haddon farmstead and a prehistoric landscape at Elton: the archaeology along the A605 Elton-Haddon Bypass, Cambridgeshire*, Cambridge

Frere, S S, 1972 *Verulamium excavations* I, Reports of the Research Committee of the Society of Antiquaries of London **28**, Oxford

Frere, S S, 1984 *Verulamium excavations* III, Oxford University Committee for Archaeology Monograph **1**, Oxford

Frere, S S and St. Joseph, J K, 1974 The Roman fortress at Longthorpe, *Britannia* **5**, 1–129

Friendship-Taylor, R M, 1974 Excavation of the Belgic and Romano-British site at Quinton, *Journal of the Northampton Borough Council Museums and Art Gallery* **11**, 2–59

Garrod, A P and Heighway, C M, 1984 *Garrod's Gloucester: archaeological observations, 1974–81*, Gloucester

Gillam, J P, 1976 Coarse fumed ware in north Britain and beyond, *Glasgow Archaeological Journal* **4**, 57–80

Grant, A, 1982 The use of tooth wear as a guide to the age of domestic ungulates, in Wilson *et al.* 1982, 91–108, Oxford

Grant, A, 1991 Animal husbandry, in *Danebury: an Iron Age hillfort in Hampshire 5, the excavations, 1979–1988* (eds B Cunliffe and C Poole), CBA Research Report **73**, 447–82, London

Green S, and Booth, P, 1993 The Roman pottery, in Allen *et al.* 1993, 113–42

Greenough, P R and Weaver, A D (eds), 1997 *Lameness in cattle*, Philadelphia

Gregory, T, 1992 *Excavations in Thetford, 1980–1982, Fison Way*, East Anglian Archaeology Report **53**, Gressenhall

Guerin, C, Philippe, M *et al.* 1979 Le gisement Pléistocène Supérieur de la Grotte de Jaurens, à Nespouls, Corrèze, France: historique et généralités, *Nouvelles Archives du Muséum d'Histoire Naturelle de Lyon* 17, 11–16

Halstead, P, 1985 A study of mandibular teeth from Romano-British contexts at Maxey, in *The Fenland Project* 1, *Archaeology and environment in the lower Welland Valley* (ed. F Pryor), East Anglian Archaeology **27**, Cambridge

Halstead, P, Hodder, I and Jones, G, 1978 Behavioural archaeology and refuse patterns: a case study, *Norwegian Archaeological Review* **11/2**, 118–31

Hambleton, E, 1999 *Animal husbandry regimes in iron age Britain: a comparative study of faunal assemblages from British iron age sites*, Oxford

Hands, A R, 1993 *The Romano-British roadside settlement at Wilcote, Oxfordshire, I, excavations, 1990–92*, BAR Brit. Ser. **232**, Oxford

Hands, A R, 1998 *The Romano-British roadside settlement at Wilcote, Oxfordshire, II, excavations, 1993–96*, BAR Brit. Ser. **265**, Oxford

Hannan, A, 1993 Excavations at Tewkesbury, 1972–74, *Trans Bristol Gloucestershire Archaeol Soc* **111**, 21–75

Harcourt, R, 1979 The animal bones, in *Gussage All Saints: an Iron Age settlement in Dorset* (ed. G J Wainwright), 150–160, London

Hartley, K F, 1977 Two major potteries in the first century AD, in *Roman pottery studies in Britain and beyond* (eds J Dore and K Greene), BAR Int. Ser. **30**, 5–17, Oxford

Haselgrove, C, 1982 Wealth, prestige and power: the dynamics of late iron age political centralisation in south-east England, in *Ranking, resource and exchange: aspects of the archaeology of early European society* (eds C Renfrew and S Shennan), 79–88, Cambridge

Haselgrove, C, 1989 The later Iron Age in southern Britain and beyond in *Research on Roman Britain*

1960–89 (ed. M Todd), Britannia Monograph Series **11**, 1–18, London

Hearne, C M, and Adam, N, 1999 Excavation of an extensive late Bronze Age settlement at Shorncote Quarry, near Cirencester, 1995–96, *Trans Bristol & Gloucestershire Archaeol Soc* 117, 35–73

Hattatt, R, 1985 *Iron Age and Roman brooches*, Oxford

Hawkes, C F C and Hull, M R, 1947 *Camulodunum: first report on the excavations at Colchester, 1930–39*, Report of the Research Committee of the Society of Antiquaries of London **XIV**, Oxford

Henig, M, 1993 *Roman sculpture from the Cotswold region with Devon and Cornwall*, Corpus Signorum Imperii Romani, Great Britain, **1/7**, Oxford

Henig, M and Booth, P, 2000 *Roman Oxfordshire*, Stroud

Hey, G, 1996 Iron Age and Roman settlement at Old Shifford Farm, Standlake, *Oxoniensia* **60**, 94–175

Hey, G and Timby, J, forthcoming, 'Yarnton: Iron Age and Romano-British Settlement and Landscape: results of excavations 1990–8', Thames Valley Landscapes monograph, Oxford Archaeology (http://www.oxfordarch.co.uk/yarnton/index.htm)

Hingley, R, 1984 Towards social analysis in archaeology: Celtic society in the Iron Age of the Upper Thames Valley, in *Aspects of the Iron Age in central southern Britain* (eds B Cunliffe and D Miles), 77–88, Oxford

Hingley, R, 1989 *Rural settlement in Roman Britain*, London

Hingley, R, 1990 Public and private space: domestic organisation and gender relations among Iron Age and Romano-British households, in *The social archaeology of houses* (ed. R Samson), 125–148, Edinburgh

Hingley, R and Miles, D, 1984 Aspects of Iron Age settlement in the Upper Thames Valley, in *Aspects of the Iron Age in central southern Britain* (eds B Cunliffe and D Miles), 52–71, Oxford

Hughes, G, 1995 *Excavation of a late prehistoric and Romano-British settlement at Thornhill Farm, Chepstow, Gwent*, BAR Brit. Ser. **244**, Oxford

Hyland, A, 1990 *Equus: the horse in the Roman world*, London

Ireland, C, 1983 The pottery, in *The East and North Gates of Gloucester* (ed. C Heighway), Western Archaeological Trust Monograph **4**, 96–124

Jackson, D and Dix, B, 1987 Late Iron Age and Roman settlement at Weekley, Northants, *Northamptonshire Archaeol* **21**, 41–93

Jarrett, M J and Wrathmell, S, 1981 *Whitton: an Iron Age and Roman farmstead in South Glamorgan*, Cardiff

Jones, M K, 1978 The plant remains, in Parrington 1978, 93–110

Jones, A, 1998 Excavations at Wall (Staffordshire) by E Greenfield in 1962 and 1964 (Wall Excavation Report no. 15), *Transactions of the Staffordshire Archaeological and Historical Society* **37**, Stafford, 1–57

Jundi, S and Hill, J D, 1998 Brooches and identities in first century AD Britain: more than meets the eye? In *Proceedings of the seventh annual theoretical Roman archaeology conference, Nottingham, 1997* (eds C Forcey, J Hawthorne and R Wicher), 125–137, Oxford

Kerney, M P, 1976 A list of fresh and brackish-water Mollusca of the British Isles, *Journal of Conchology, London* **29**, 26–8

King, A, 1991 Food production and consumption – Meat, in *Roman Britain: recent trends* (ed. R F J Jones), 15–20, Sheffield

King, R, 1998 Excavations at Gassons Road Lechlade 1993 in Boyle *et al.* 1998, 269–281

Kloet, G S and Hincks, W D, 1977 *A check list of British insects, 2nd edition (revised): Coleoptera and Strepsiptera*, Royal Entomological Society of London Handbook for the Identification of British Insects **11/3**, London

Kratochvil, Z, 1969 Species criterior on the distal section of the tibia in *Ovis ammon f. aries* L. and *Capra aegagrus f. hircus* L., Acta Veterinaria (Brno) 38, 483–90

Lambrick, G, 1980 Excavations in Park Street, Towcester, *Northamptonshire Archaeol* **15**, 35–118

Lambrick, G, 1992 The development of late prehistoric and Roman farming on the Thames gravels in *Developing landscapes of lowland Britain: the archaeology of the British gravels: a review* (eds M Fulford and E Nichols), 78–105, London

Lambrick, G, 1998 Frontier territory along the Thames, *British Archaeology* 30, 12–13

Lambrick, G and Allen, T, forthcoming 'Gravelly Guy, Stanton Harcourt: the development of a prehistoric and Romano-British landscape', Thames Valley Landscapes, Oxford Archaeology

Lambrick, G and Robinson, M A, 1979 *Iron Age and Roman riverside settlements at Farmoor, Oxfordshire*, CBA Res Rep **32**, London

Langdon, J, 1986 *Horses, oxen and technological innovation: the use of draught animals in English farming from 1066 to 1500*, Cambridge

Lauwerier, R C G M and Hessing, W A M, 1992 Men, horses and the Miss Blanche effect: Roman horse burials in a cemetery at Kesteren, the Netherlands, *Helinium* **1/2**, 78–109

Lauwerier, R C G M and Robeerst, A J M M, 2001 Horses in Roman times in the Netherlands, in *Animals and man in the past* (eds H Buitenhuis and W Prummel), 275–90, Groningen

Laws, K, 1991 The worked bone objects, in *Maiden Castle, excavations and field survey, 1985–6* (N M Sharples), Historic Buildings and Monuments Commission for England, Archaeological Report **19**, 236–238, London

Leach, P, 1982 *Ilchester, 1, excavations, 1974–1975,* Western Archaeological Trust Excavation Monograph **3**, Bristol

Leach, P, 1993 The pottery, in *The Uley shrines: excavation of a ritual complex on West Hill, Uley, Gloucestershire, 1977–9* (A Woodward and P Leach), English Heritage Archaeological Report **17**, 219–49, London

Leech, R, 1977 *The Upper Thames Valley in Gloucester and Wiltshire: an archaeological survey of the river gravels,* Committee for Rescue Archaology in Avon, Gloucestershire and Somerset Survey **4**, Gloucester

Legge, A J, 1992 *Excavations at Grimes Graves, Norfolk, 1972–1976: animals, environment and the Bronze Age economy,* **4**, London

Levine, M A, 1982 The use of crown height measurements and eruption-wear sequences to age horse teeth, in Wilson *et al.* 1982, 223–250, Oxford

Levine, M A, 1983 Mortality models and the interpretation of horse population structure, in *Hunter-gatherer economy in prehistory* (ed. G N Bailey), 23–46, Cambridge

Levine, M A, 1986 The vertebrate fauna from Meare East 1982, in *Somerset Levels Papers* 12 (ed. J M Coles), 61–71, Thorverton

Levine, M A, 1995 Animal bone, in *Excavations at North Shoebury: settlement and economy in south-east Essex, 1500 BC–AD 1500* (eds J J Wymer and N R Brown), East Anglian Archaeology Report **75**, 130–141, Chelmsford

Levine, M A, 1999a Botai and the origins of horse domestication, *Journal of Anthropological Archaeology* **18**, 29–78

Levine, M A, 1999b The origins of horse husbandry on the Eurasian Steppe, in *Late prehistoric exploitation of the Eurasian steppe* (eds M A Levine, Y Y Rassamakin, A M Kislenko and N S Tatarintseva), 5–58, Cambridge

Levitan, B, 1990 Assessment of the vertebrate assemblage (Appendix C), in OAU, Fairford Thornhill Farm post-excavation assessment, Unpubl. MSS, 40–3, OAU, Oxford

Lowther, A W G, 1937 Report on excavations at Verulamium in 1934, *Antiq J* **17**, 28–55

Lucas, A T, 1989 *Cattle in ancient Ireland,* Irish Studies **1**, Studies in Irish Archaeology and History, Kilkenny

Lyman, R L, 1994 *Vertebrate taphonomy,* Cambridge

Mack, R P, 1964 *The coinage of ancient Britain,* London

Mackreth, D F, 1996 *Orton Hall Farm: a Roman and early Anglo-Saxon farmstead,* E Anglian Archaeol **76**

Maltby, M, 1996 The exploitation of animals in the Iron Age: the archaeozoological evidence, in *The Iron Age in Britain and Ireland* (eds T C Champion and J R Collis), 17–27, Sheffield

Manning, W H, 1985 *Catalogue of the Romano-British iron tools, fittings and weapons in the British Museum,* London

Marean, C W and Frey, C J, 1997 Animal bones from caves to cities: reverse utility curves as metholodogical artifacts, *American Antiquity* **62/4**, 698–711

Matschke, G, 1967 Aging European wild hogs by dentition, *Journal of Wildlife Management* **31/1**, 109–113

McWhirr, A D, 1976 Cirencester (Corinium): A civitas capital in the West Country in *The Roman West Country: classical culture and Celtic society* (eds K Branigan and P J Fowler), London

Meadows, K I, 2001 The social context of eating and drinking at native settlements in early Roman Britain, unpublished PhD Thesis, University of Sheffield

Miles, D, 1986 *Archaeology at Barton Court Farm, Abingdon, Oxon: an investigation into the late Neolithic, Iron Age, Romano-British and Saxon settlements,* Oxford Archaeological Unit Report **3**, CBA Res Rep **50**, Oxford and London

Miles, D, 1989 The Romano-British countryside, in *Research on Roman Britain 1960–89* (M Todd), Britannia Monograph Series **11**, 115–126, London

Miles, D and Palmer, S, 1984 Fairford/Lechlade: Claydon Pike, *South Midlands Archaeol* **14**, 93–8

Miles, D and Palmer, S, 1990 Claydon Pike and Thornhill Farm, *Current Archaeology* **121**, XI/1, 19–23

Miles, D, Palmer, S, Smith, A and Edgeley Long G, forthcoming, 'Iron Age and Roman settlement in the Upper Thames Valley: Excavations at Claydon Pike and other sites within the Cotswold Water Park', Thames Valley Landscapes Monograph, Oxford Archaeology (http://www.oxfordarch.co.uk/cotswoldweb/index.htm)

Mourer-Chauviré, C, 1980 Le gisement Pléistocène Supérieur de la Grotte de Jaurens, à Nespouls, Corrèze, France: les équidés (*Mammalia, Perissodactyla*), *Nouvelles Archives du Muséum d'Histoire Naturelle de Lyon* 18, 17–60

Mudd, A, Williams, R J, and Lupton, A, 1999 *Excavations alongside Roman Ermine Street, Gloucestershire and Wiltshire: the archaeology of the A419/A417 Swindon to Gloucester road scheme* 2, Oxford

Mulville, J and Levitan, B, forthcoming, The animal bones, in Lambrick and Allen forthcoming

Munson, P J, 2000 Age-correlated differential destruction of bones and its effect on archaeological mortality profiles of domestic sheep and goats, *Journal of Archaeological Science* **27**, 391–407

Niblett, R, 1985 *Sheepen: an early Roman industrial site at Camulodunum,* CBA Res Rep **57**, London

OAU, 1988 Whelford Bowmoor: archaeological assessment, October 1988, unpubl. MSS, Oxford Archaeology

OAU, 1989 Bowmoor, Kempsford, Gloucestershire: archaeological assessment, September 1989, unpubl. MSS, Oxford Archaeology

OAU, 1993 Stubbs Farm, Kempsford, Gloucestershire: archaeological evaluation, unpubl. MSS, Oxford Archaeology

OAU, 1998 Multi-Agg Quarry Extension, Kempsford, Gloucestershire: Archaeological evaluation report, unpubl., Oxford Archaeology

OAU, 2001 Cotswold Water Park Project, Gloucestershire: revised archive assessment and updated post-excavation research design, unpubl., Oxford Archaeology (http://www.oxfordarch.co.uk/cotswoldweb/index.htm)

OA 2003 Cotswold Community, Wiltshire and Gloucestershire 2002. Archaeological Excavation Interim Report. unpubl. MSS, Oxford Archaeology

O'Neil, H, 1952 Whittington Court Roman Villa, Whittington, Gloucestershire, *Trans Bristol Gloucestershire Archaeol Soc* 71, 13–87

Oswald, A 1997 A doorway on the past: practical and mystic concerns in the orientation of roundhouse doorways, in *Reconstructing Iron Age societies* (eds A Gwilt and C Haselgrove), Oxbow Monograph **71**, 87–95, Oxford

Owles, E and Smedley, N, 1967 Two Belgic cemeteries at Boxford, *Proc Suffolk Inst Archaeol* **31/1**, 88–107

Parker-Pearson, M, 1996 Food, fertility, and front doors in the first millennium BC, in *The Iron Age in Britain and Ireland: recent trends* (eds T C Champion and J R Collis), 117–172, Sheffield

Parrington, M, 1978 *The excavation of an Iron Age settlement, Bronze Age ring ditches, and Roman features at Ashville trading estate, Abingdon (Oxfordshire), 1974–76*, CBA Res Rep **28**, London

Parry, C, 1998, Excavations near Birdlip, Cowley, Gloucestershire, 1987–8, *Trans Bristol Gloucestershire Archaeol Soc* 116, 25–92

Partridge, C, 1981 *Skeleton Green, a late Iron Age and Romano-British site*, Britannia Monograph Series No. **2**, London

Partridge, C, 1989 *Foxholes Farm: a multi-period gravel site*, Hertfordshire Archaeological Trust Monograph, Hertford

Payne, S, 1969 A metrical distinction between sheep and goat metacarpals, in *The domestication and exploitation of plants and animals* (eds P J Ucko and G W Dimbleby), 295–306, London

Payne, S, 1972 Partial recovery and sample bias: the results of some sieving experiments, in *Papers in economic prehistory* (ed. E S Higgs), 49–64, Cambridge

Payne, S, 1973 Kill-off patterns in sheep and goats: the mandibles from Asvan Kale, *Anatolian Studies* 23, 281–303

Payne, S, 1985 Morphological distinctions between the mandibular teeth of young sheep, *Ovis*, and goats, *Capra, Journal of Archaeological Science* **12**, 139–47

Payne, S and Bull, G, 1988 Components of variation in measurements of pig bones and teeth, and the use of measurements to distinguish wild from domestic pig remains, *Archaeozoologia* **II** 1/2, 27–66

Payne, S and Munson, P, 1985 Ruby and how many squirrels? The destruction of bones by dogs, in *Palaeobiological investigations: research design, methods and data analysis* (eds N R J Fieller, D D Gilbertson and N G A Ralph), BAR Int. Ser. **266**, 31–39, Oxford

Peacock, D P S, 1968 A petrological study of certain Iron Age pottery from western England, *Proc Prehist Soc* **34**, 414–27

Peacock D P S, and Williams, D F, 1986, *Amphorae and the Roman economy: an introductory guide*, London

Perry, B T, 1986 Excavations at Bramdean, Hampshire, 1983 and 1984, with some further discussion of the 'Banjo' syndrome, *Proc Hampshire Fld Club* **42**, 35–42

Price, E, 2000 *Frocester: A Romano-British settlement, its antecedents and successors* 2, Gloucester

Rackham, O, 1980 *Ancient woodland: its history, vegetation and uses in England*, London

Rawes, B, 1981 The Romano-British site at Brockworth, Glos., *Britannia* **12**, 45–77

RCHME, 1976 *Iron Age and Romano-British monuments in the Gloucestershire Cotswolds*, London

Richmond, I, 1968 *Hod Hill*, 2, *excavations carried out between 1951 and 1958 for the trustees of the British Museum*, London

Rigby, V, 1982 The pottery, in *Early Roman occupation at Cirencester* (eds J Wacher and A McWhirr), Cirencester Excavations **1**, 153–200, Cirencester

Robinson, M A, 1988 Molluscan evidence for pasture and meadowland on the floodplain of the Upper Thames basin, in *The exploitation of wetlands* (eds P Murphy and C French), BAR Brit. Ser. **186**, 101–12, Oxford

Robinson, M A, 1992a Environmental archaeology of the river gravels : past achievements and future directions, in *Developing landscapes of lowland Britain: the archaeology of the British gravels: a review* (eds M Fulford and E Nichols), Society of Antiquaries Occasional Papers **14**, 47–62, London

Robinson, M A, 1992b Environment, archaeology and alluvium on the river gravels of the south Midlands, in *Alluvial archaeology in Britain* (eds S P Needham and M G Macklin), Oxbow Monograph **27**, 197–208, Oxford

Robinson, M, forthcoming, Environmental evidence from Claydon Pike, Gloucestershire, in in Miles *et al.* forthcoming

Roe, F, forthcoming, The worked stone from Claydon Pike, Gloucestershire, in Miles *et al.* forthcoming

Saunders, R L, 1998 The use of Old Red Sandstone in Roman Britain: a petrographical and archaeological study, unpubl. PhD Thesis, University of Reading

Saville, A, 1979 *Excavations at Guiting Power Iron Age site, Gloucestershire, 1974*, Committee for Rescue Archaeology in Avon, Gloucestershire and Somerset Occasional Paper **7**, Bristol

Saville, A, and Ellison, A, 1983 Excavations at Uley Bury hillfort, Gloucestershire, 1976, in *Uley Bury and Norbury hillforts* (ed. A Saville), Western Archaeological Trust Monograph **5**, 1–24, Bristol

Serjeantson, D, 1991 The bird bones, in *Danebury: an Iron Age hillfort in Hampshire* **5**, *the excavations, 1979–1988: the finds* (ed. B Cunliffe), CBA Res Rep **73**, 479–48, London

Sisson, S, and Getty, R, 1975 *Sisson and Grossman's the anatomy of the domestic animals*, Philadelphia

Sisson, S and Grossman, J D, 1953 *The anatomy of the domestic animals*, Philadelphia

Smith, C R, 1852 Notes on Saxon sepulchral remains found at Fairford, Gloucestershire, *Archaeologia* **37**, 77–82

Smith, D J, Hird, L and Dix, B, 1989 The Roman villa at Great Weldon, Northamptonshire, *Northamptonshire Archaeol* **22**, 23–67

Spencer, B, 1983 Limestone-tempered pottery from south Wales in the late Iron Age and early Roman periods, *Bulletin of Celtic Studies* **30**, 405–19

Stead, I M, 1976 The earliest burials of the Aylesford Culture, in *Problems in economic and social archaeology* (eds G de G Sieveking, I H Longworth and K E Wilson), 401–416, London

Stead, I M, 1986 The brooches, in *Baldock: the excavation of a Roman and pre-Roman settlement, 1968–72* (eds I M Stead and V Rigby), Britannia Monograph Series **7**, 109–124, London

Stead, I M and Rigby, V, 1989 *Verulamium: the King Harry Lane site*, English Heritage and British Museum Publications, Archaeological Report **12**, London

Stokes, J, 1853 *The ox as a beast of draught in place of the horse, recommended after a satisfactory experience of thirty years' employment of ox labor*, London

Swan, V G, 1975 Oare reconsidered and the origins of Savernake ware in Wiltshire, *Britannia* **6**, 36–61

Taylor, J, 2001 Rural society in Roman Britain, in *Britons and Romans: advancing an archaeological agenda* (eds S James and M Millett), CBA Rep **125**, 46–59, York

Timby, J R, 1990 Severn Valley wares: a reassessment, *Britannia* **21**, 243–52

Timby, J R, 1998 *Excavations at Kingscote and Wycomb, Gloucestershire*, Cotswold Archaeological Trust Monograph, Cirencester

Timby, J R, 1999 Later prehistoric and Roman pottery, in Mudd *et al.* 1999, 320–365

Timby, J R, 2000a, Pottery, in *Frocester: a Romano-British settlement, its antecedents and successors* 2 (E Price), Gloucester and District Archaeology Group, 125–168, Gloucester

Timby, J R, 2000b, The Pottery, in *Late Iron Age and Roman Silchester: excavations on the site of the Forum-Basilica 1977, 1980–86* (M Fulford and J Timby), Britannia monog **15**, 180–312

Timby, J, 2001 The pottery, in A Bronze Age burnt mound at Sandy Lane, Charlton Kings, Gloucestershire: excavations in 1971 (M Leah and C Young), *Trans Bristol Gloucestershire Archaeol Soc* **119**, 59 – 82

Timby, J R, unpubl. a The pottery from Abbeydale, Glos suburbs, unpubl. MSS, Gloucester Excavation Unit, Gloucester

Timby, J R, unpubl. b The pottery from Coppice Corner, Kingsholm, Glos, unpubl. MSS, Gloucester Excavation Unit, Gloucester

Timby, J R, unpubl. c The pottery from Saintbridge, Glos suburbs, unpubl. MSS, Gloucester Excavation Unit, Gloucester

Timby, J R, forthcoming The pottery from Huntsman Quarry, Naunton, Glos. *Trans Bristol Gloucestershire Archaeol Soc*

Timby, J R, in prep. The pottery, in Report on the Eastern Relief Road scheme, Tewkesbury

Todd, M, 1981 *The Iron Age and Roman settlement at Whitwell, Leicestershire*, Leicestershire Museums, Art Gallery and Record Services Archaeological Reports Series **1**, Leicester

Trow, S D, 1988 Excavations at Ditches hillfort, North Cerney, Gloucestershire, 1982–3, *Trans Bristol Gloucestershire Archaeol Soc* **106**, 19–85

Trow, S D, 1990 By the northern shores of Ocean: some observations on acculturation process at the edge of the Roman world, in *The early Roman empire in the west* (eds T Blagg, M Millet), 103–119, Oxford

Trow, S D, and James, S, 1989 Ditches villa, North Cerney: an example of locational conservatism in the early Roman Cotswolds, in *The economies of Romano-British villas* (eds K Branigan and D Miles), 83–87, Sheffield

van Beek, G C, 1983 Dental morphology: an illustrated guide (2nd ed.), Bristol

van Arsdell, R D, 1989 *Celtic coinage of Britain*, London

van Arsdell, R D, 1994 *The coinage of the Dobunni: money supply and coin circulation in Dobunnic territory*, Studies in Celtic Coinage **1**, Oxford University Committee for Archaeology Monograph **38**, Oxford

von den Driesch, A, 1976 *A guide to the measurement of animal bones from archaeological sites as developed by the Institut fur Palaeoanatomie, Domestikationsforschung und Geschichte der Tiermedizin of the University of Munich*, Peabody Museum Bulletin **1**, Cambridge, Massachusetts

Waldén, H W, 1976 A nomenclatural list of land Mollusca of the British Isles, *Journal of Conchology, London* **29**, 21–5

Ward-Perkins, J B, 1938 The Roman villa at Lockleys, Welwyn, *Antiq J* **18**, 339–376

Webster, G, 1965 Further investigations on the site of the Roman fort at Waddon Hill, Stoke Abbott, 1960–62, *Proc Dorset Natur Hist Archaeol Soc* **86**, 135–149

Webster, G, 2002 *The Legionary Fortress at Wroxeter, Excavations by Graham Webster, 1955–85*, English Heritage Archaeological Report **19**, London

Webster, P V, 1976 Severn Valley ware, *Trans Bristol Gloucestershire Archaeol Soc* **94**, 18–46

Wedlake, W J, 1958 *Excavations at Camerton, Somerset*, privately printed

Wedlake, W J, 1982 *The excavation of the shrine of Apollo at Nettleton, Wiltshire, 1956–1971*, Reports of the Research Committee of the Society of Antiquaries of London **40**, Dorking

Wenham, G and Fowler, V R, 1973 A radiographic study of age changes in the skull, mandible and teeth of pigs, *Journal of Agricultural Science, Cambridge* **80/3**, 451–61

Wheeler, R E M and Wheeler, T V, 1936 *Verulamium, a Belgic and two Roman cities*, Reports of the Research Committee of the Society of Antiquaries of London **11**, Oxford

Williams, D F, 1982 Iron Age and Roman pottery from Cirencester and Bagendon, in *Early Roman occupation at Cirencester* (eds J Wacher and A McWhirr), Cirencester Excavations **1**, 201–2, Cirencester

Wilson, B, 1978 The animal bones, in Parrington 1978, 110–138

Wilson, B, 1979 The vertebrates, in Lambrick and Robinson 1993, 128–33

Wilson, B, Grigson, C and Payne, S, 1982 *Ageing and sexing animal bones from archaeological sites*, BAR Brit. Ser. **109**, Oxford

Wilson, R, 1993 Reports on the bone and oyster shell, in Allen and Robinson 1993, 123–134

Wilson, R and Allison, E, 1990 The animal and fish bones, in Allen 1990, 57–61

Woodward, P J, Davies, S M and Graham, A H, 1993 *Excavations at the Old Methodist Chapel and Greyhound Yard, Dorchester, 1981–1984*, Dorset Natural History and Archaeological Society Monograph **12**, Dorchester

Woods, P J, and Hastings, B C, 1984 *Rushden: the early fine wares*, Northampton

Workshop of European Anthropologists, 1980 Recommendations for age and sex diagnoses of skeletons, *J of Human Evolution* **9**, 517–49

Young, C J, 1977 *Oxfordshire Roman pottery*, BAR Brit. Ser. **43**, Oxford

Zeder, M A, 1986 The Equid remains from Tal-e Malyan, southern Iran, in *Equids in the ancient world* (eds R H Meadow and H-P Uerpmann), Beihefte zum Tübinger Atlas des Vorderen Orients, Reihe A, Naturwissenschaften **19**, 366–412, Wiesbaden

Index

Where period subentries are grouped together, they are given in chronological not alphabetical order.